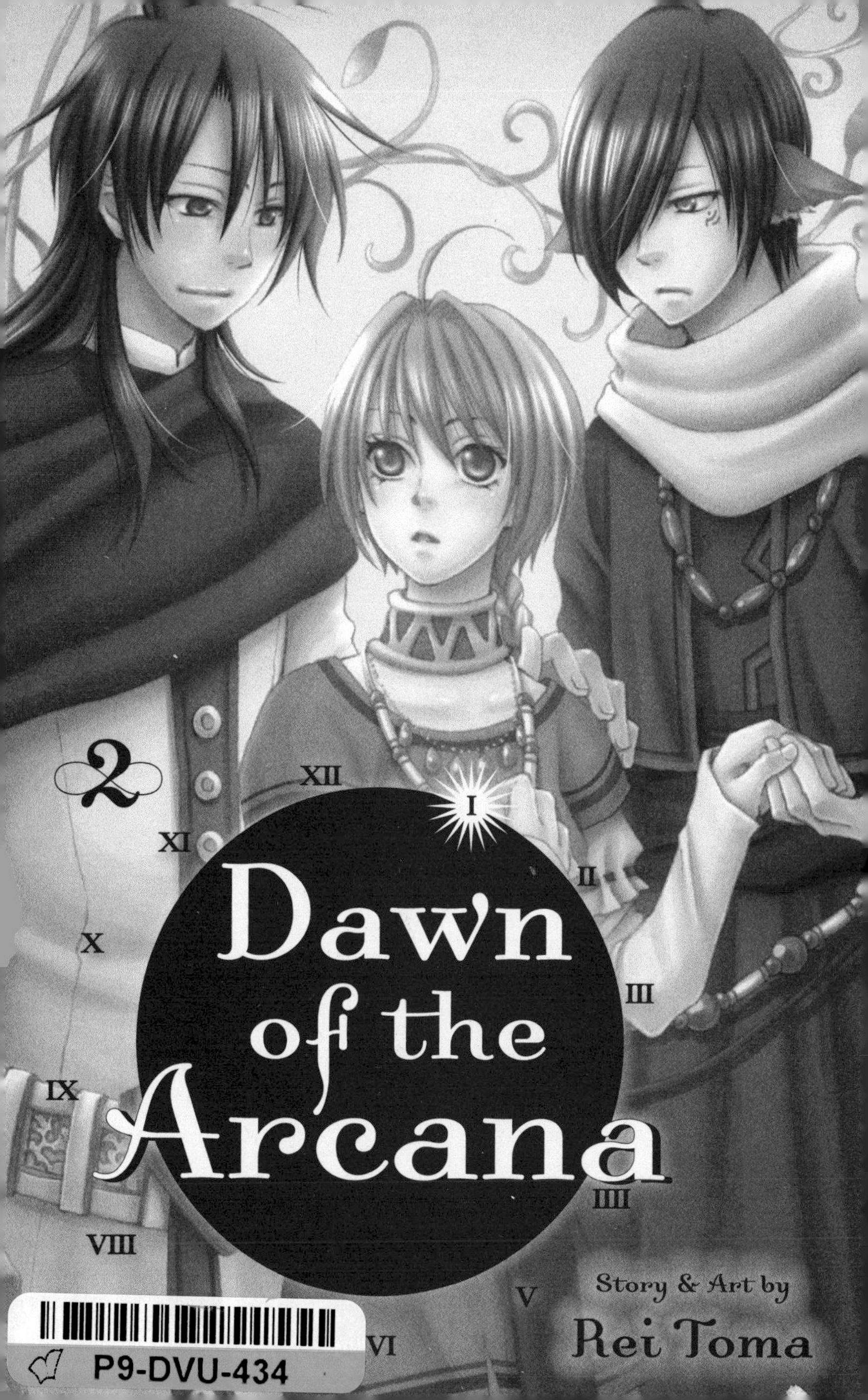
XII
I
II
III
IIII
V
VI
VIII
IX
X
XI

2

Dawn of the Arcana

Story & Art by
Rei Toma

Dawn of the Arcana

Volume 2

XII

XI

X

CONTENTS

IX

VIII

VII

VI

characters

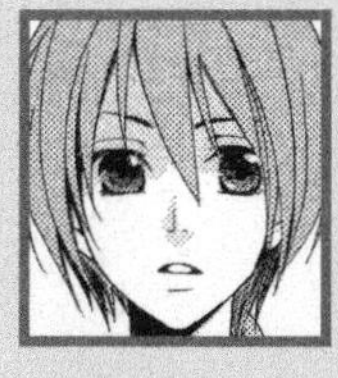

Nakaba
The princess royal of Senan. Strong of will and noble of spirit, she possesses a strange power.

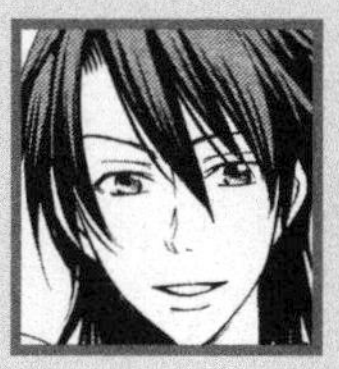

Caesar
The second-born prince of Belquat. Nakaba's husband through a marriage of political convenience. Headstrong and selfish.

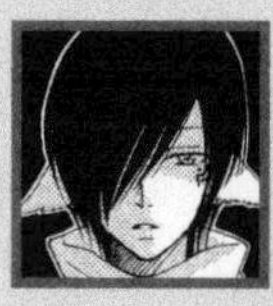

Loki
Nakaba's attendant. His senses of perception are unmatched.

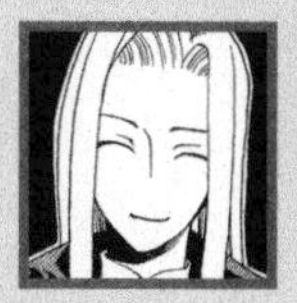

Bellinus
Caesar's attendant. Always cool and collected.

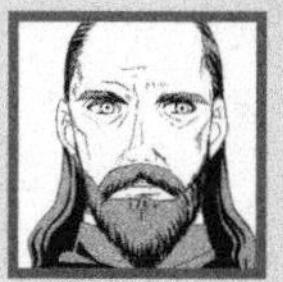

Guran
King of Belquat.

story

• Wed to Prince Caesar as a symbol of peace between their two countries, Nakaba is actually little more than a hostage. Unbeknownst to King Guran, she is a survivor of the race he tried to destroy for fear of their power.

• Caesar rode valiantly in the joust held to celebrate their wedding, but he was defeated by Loki, who fought to clear the charges of treason brought against him. Caesar was crestfallen, but what feelings did Nakaba's heartfelt words of encouragement stir within him?

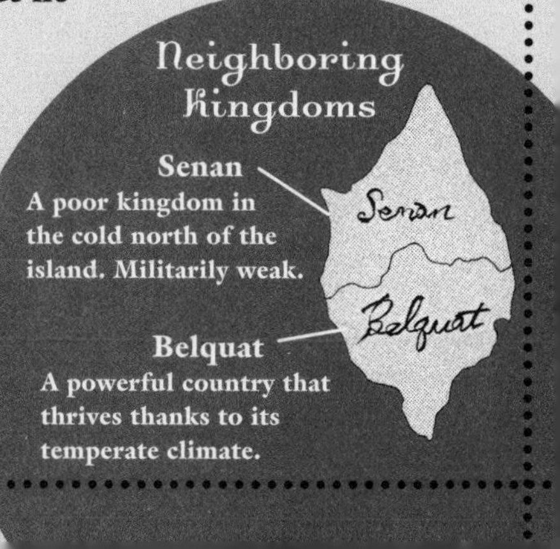
Neighboring Kingdoms
Senan
A poor kingdom in the cold north of the island. Militarily weak.
Senan
Belquat
Belquat
A powerful country that thrives thanks to its temperate climate.

Hello! Rei Toma here.
Thanks for picking up the second volume of *Dawn of the Arcana*! I put everything I've got into each and every volume, so nothing makes me happier than to know you're enjoying the series.

…Which brings me to today's **surprise!!**

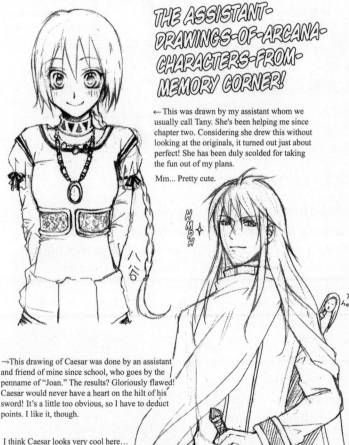

THE ASSISTANT-DRAWINGS-OF-ARCANA-CHARACTERS-FROM-MEMORY CORNER!

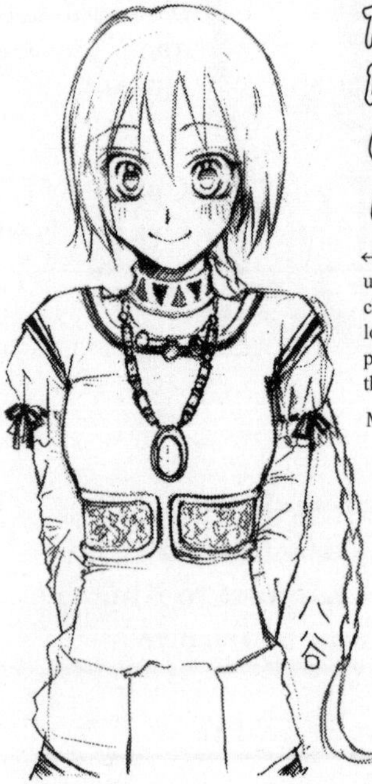
八谷

← This was drawn by my assistant whom we usually call Tany. She's been helping me since chapter two. Considering she drew this without looking at the originals, it turned out just about perfect! She has been duly scolded for taking the fun out of my plans.

Mm... Pretty cute.

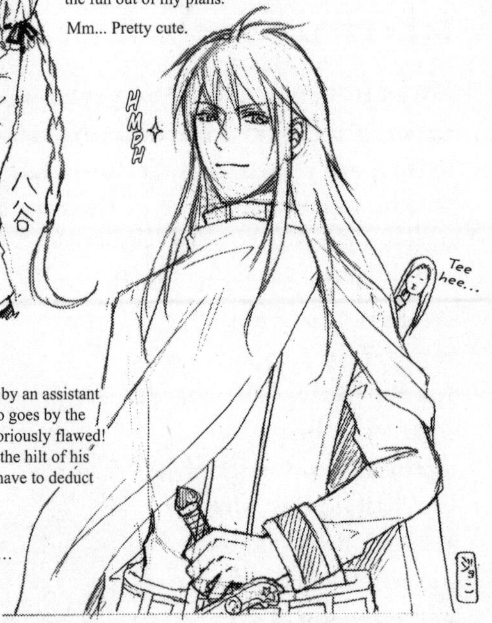
HMPH
Tee hee...

→This drawing of Caesar was done by an assistant and friend of mine since school, who goes by the penname of "Joan." The results? Gloriously flawed! Caesar would never have a heart on the hilt of his sword! It's a little too obvious, so I have to deduct points. I like it, though.

I think Caesar looks very cool here… Very princely. Bellinus over his shoulder is a nice touch, too.

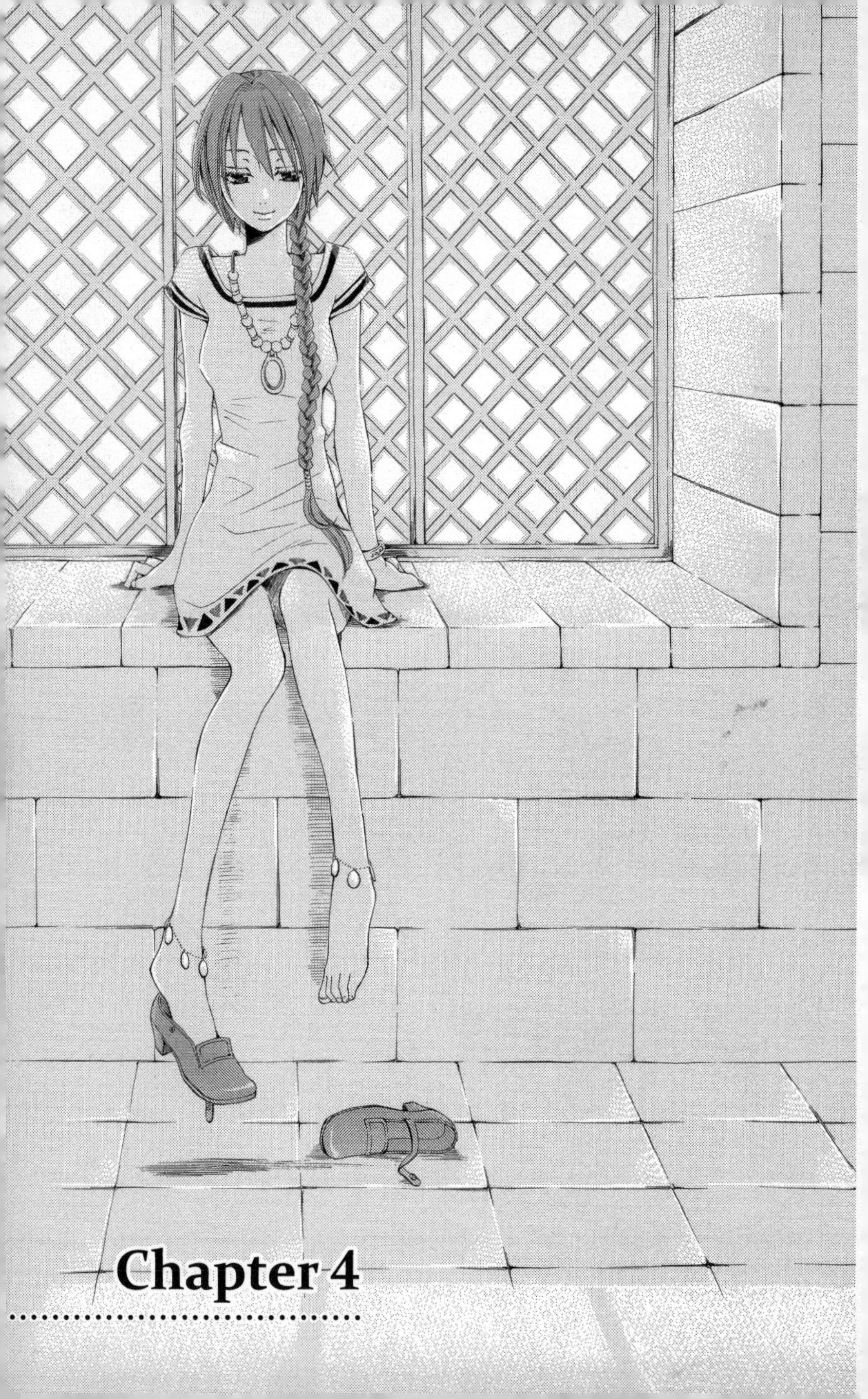

Chapter 4

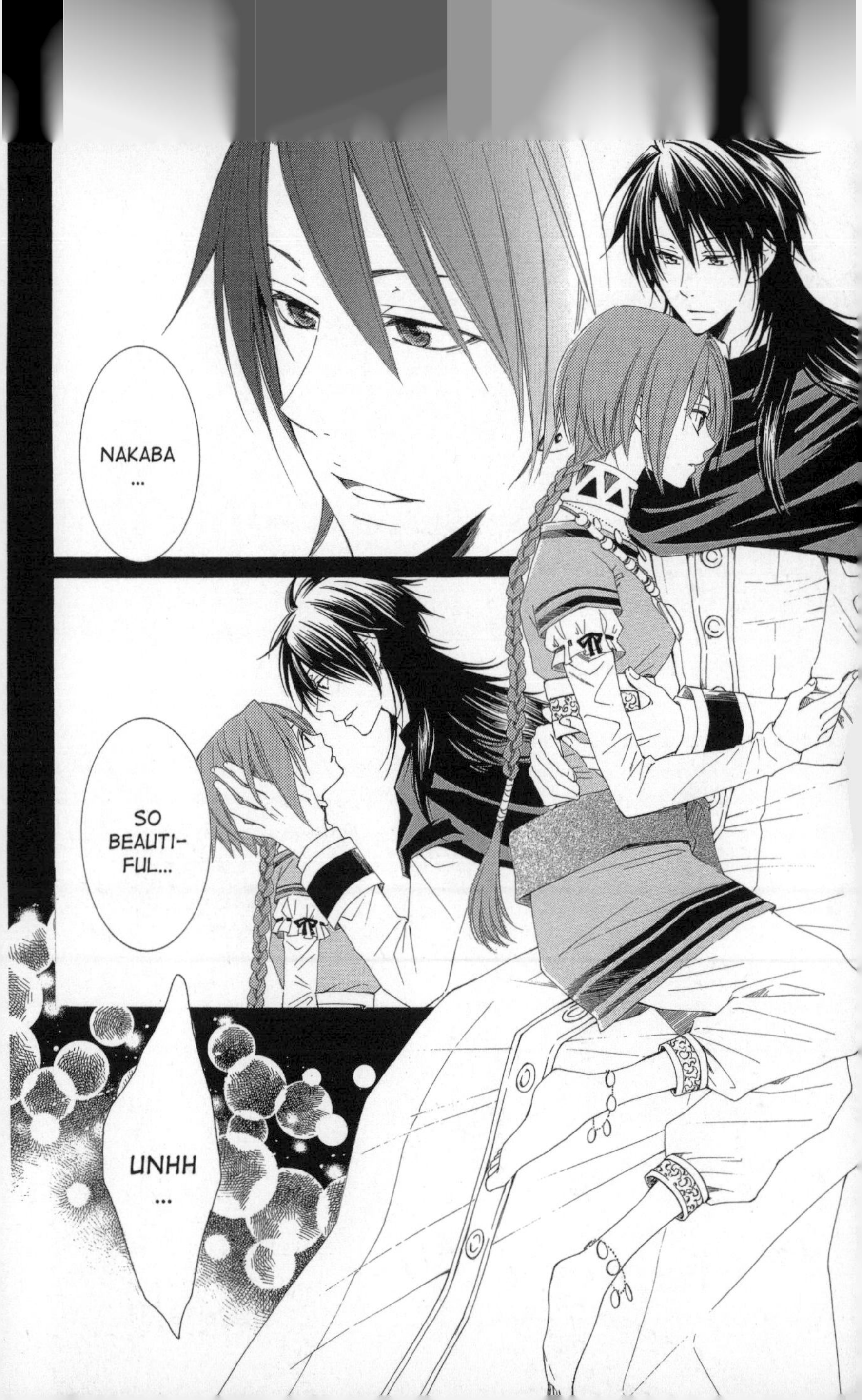
NAKABA ...
SO BEAUTI-FUL...
UNHH ...

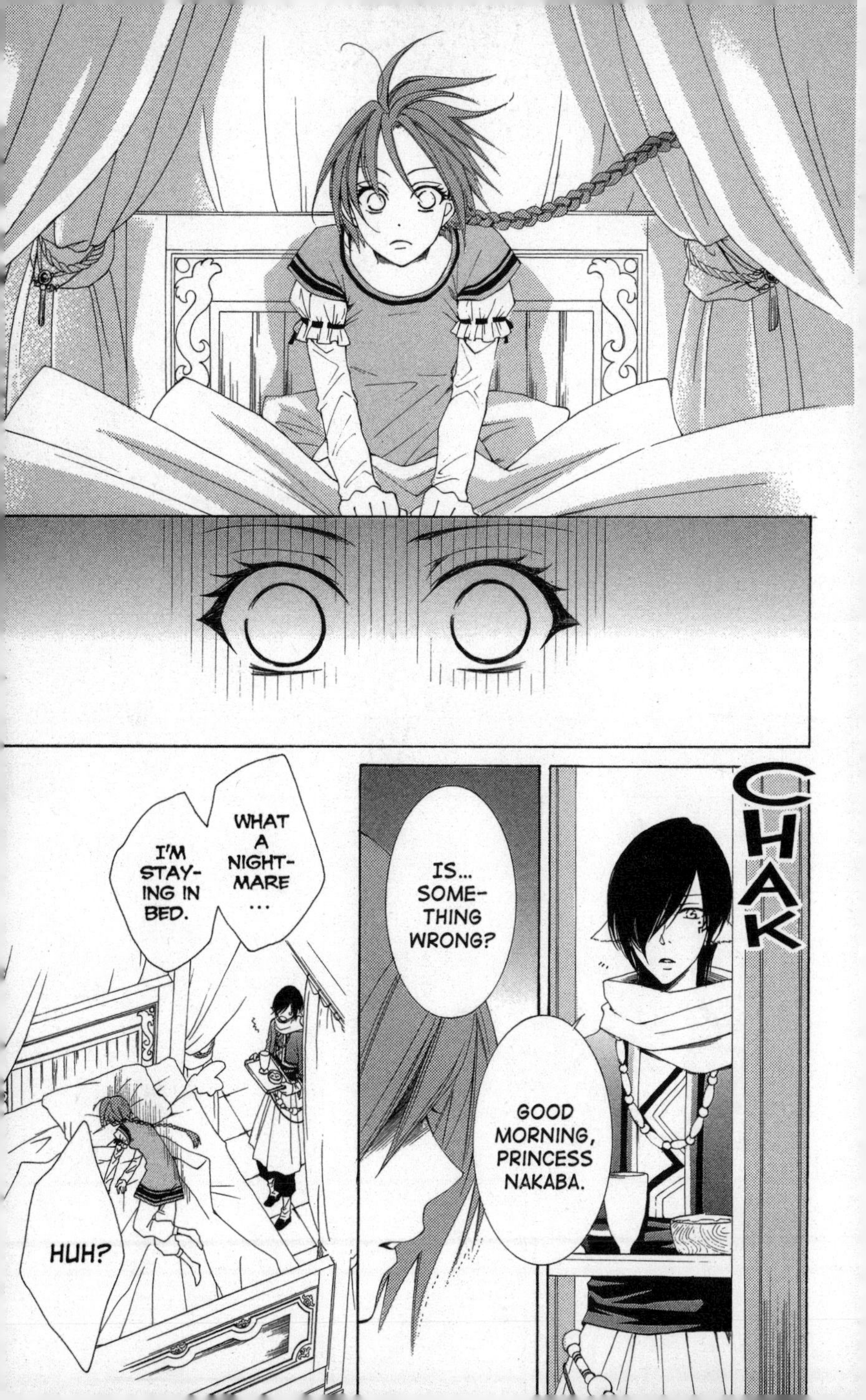
CHAK
GOOD MORNING, PRINCESS NAKABA.
IS... SOMETHING WRONG?
WHAT A NIGHTMARE...
I'M STAYING IN BED.
HUH?

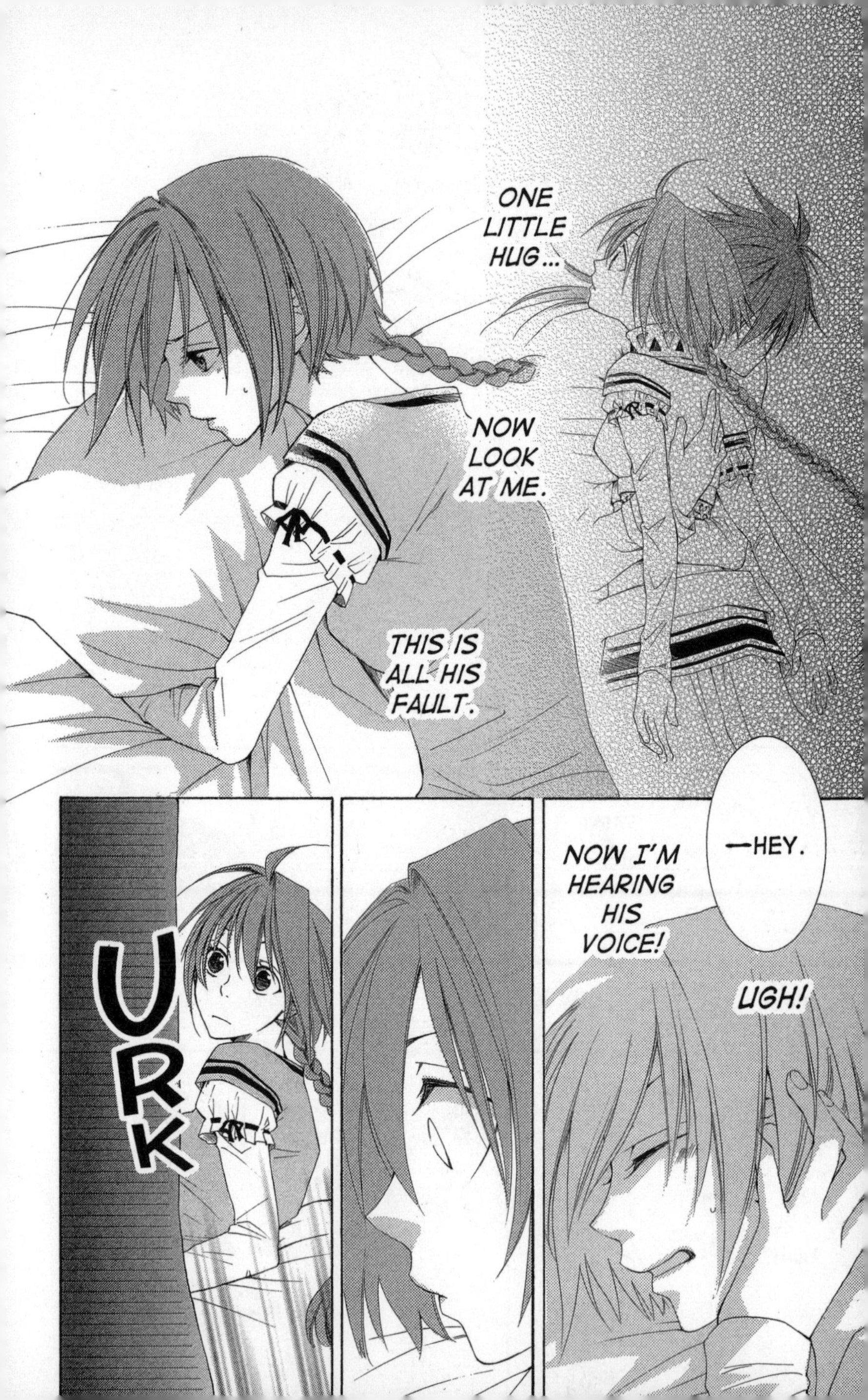
ONE LITTLE HUG...
NOW LOOK AT ME.
THIS IS ALL HIS FAULT.
—HEY.
NOW I'M HEARING HIS VOICE!
UGH!
URK

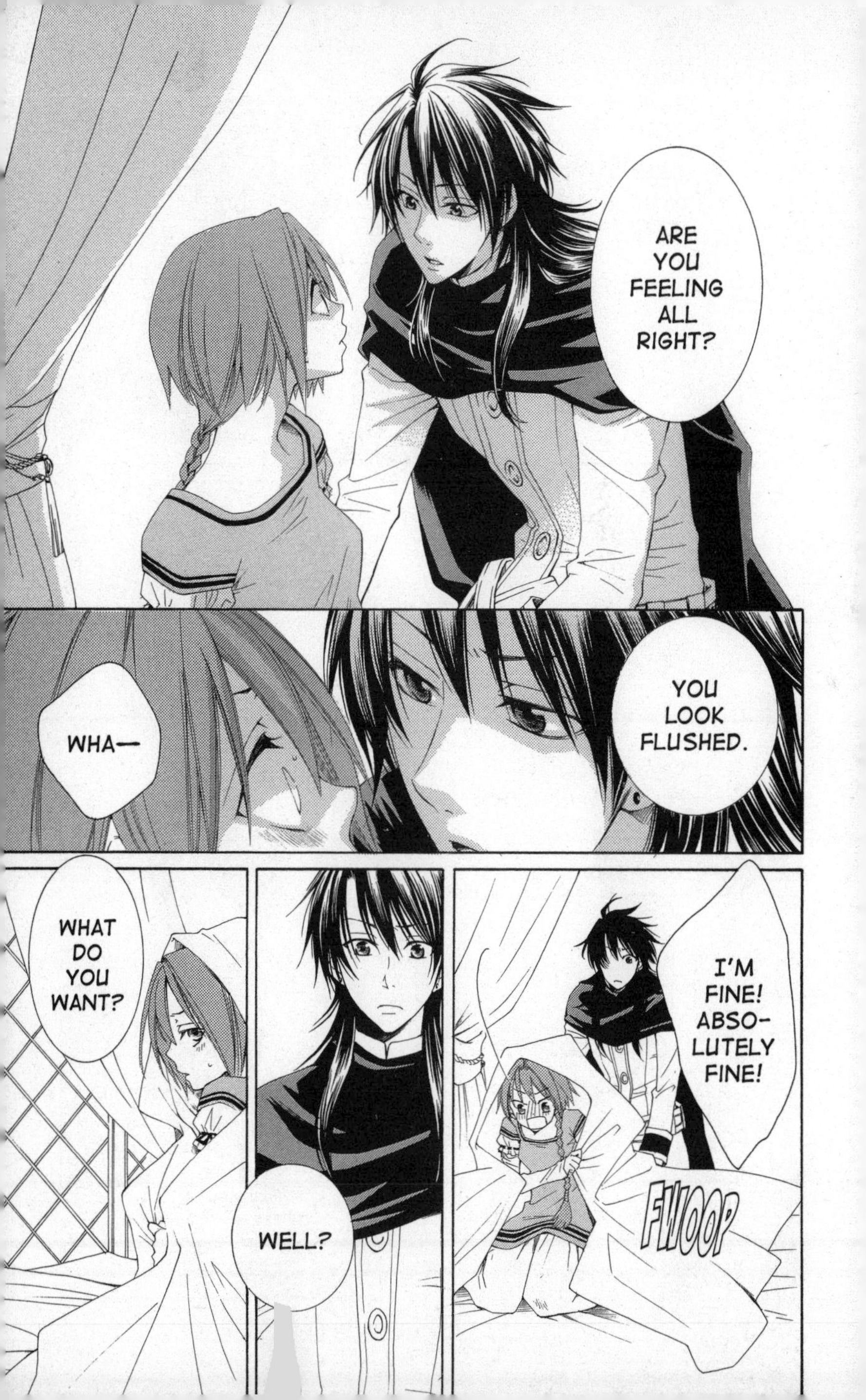
ARE YOU FEELING ALL RIGHT?
YOU LOOK FLUSHED.
WHA—
I'M FINE! ABSO-LUTELY FINE!
FWOOP
WELL?
WHAT DO YOU WANT?

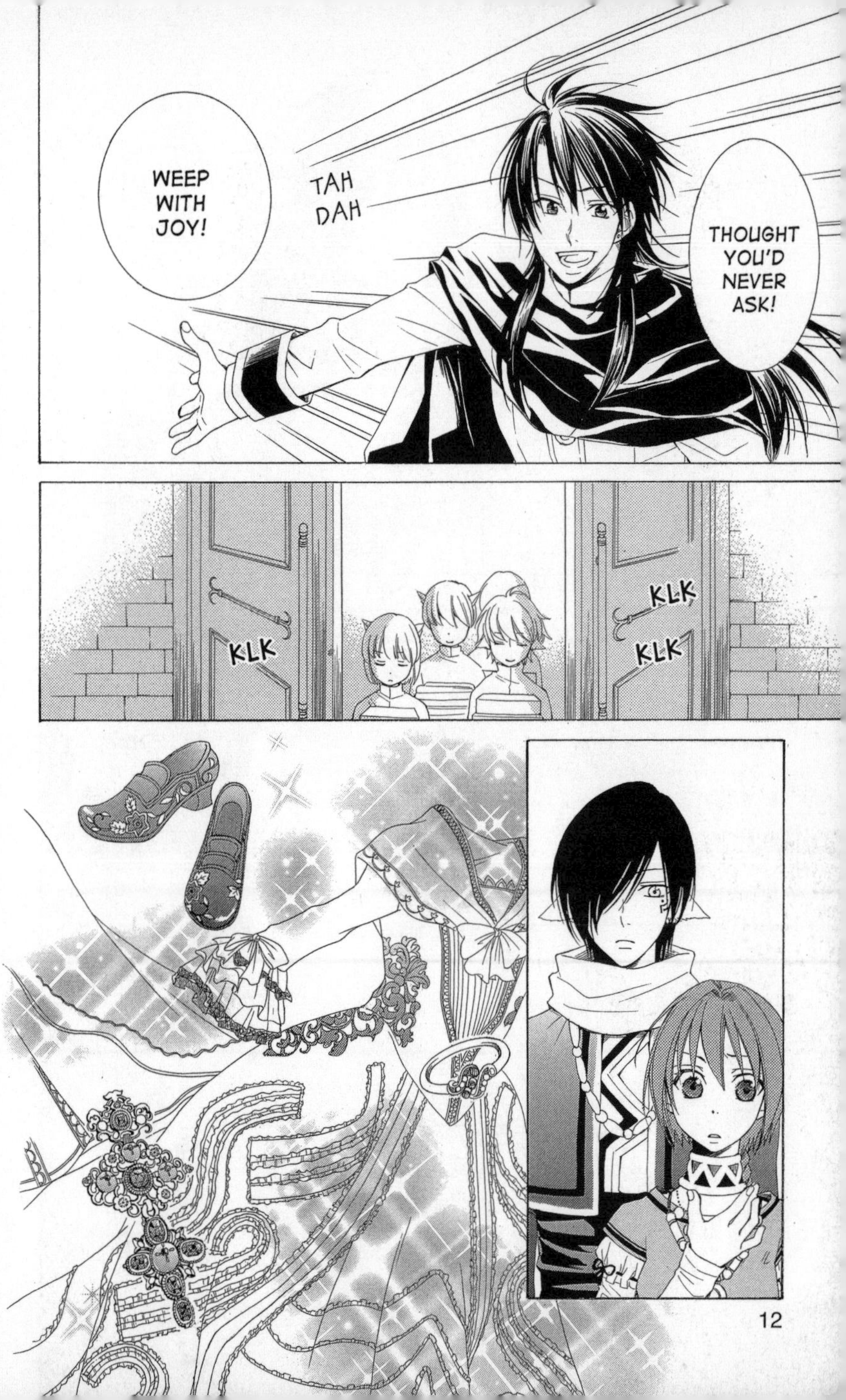
THOUGHT YOU'D NEVER ASK!
TAH DAH
WEEP WITH JOY!
KLK
KLK
KLK

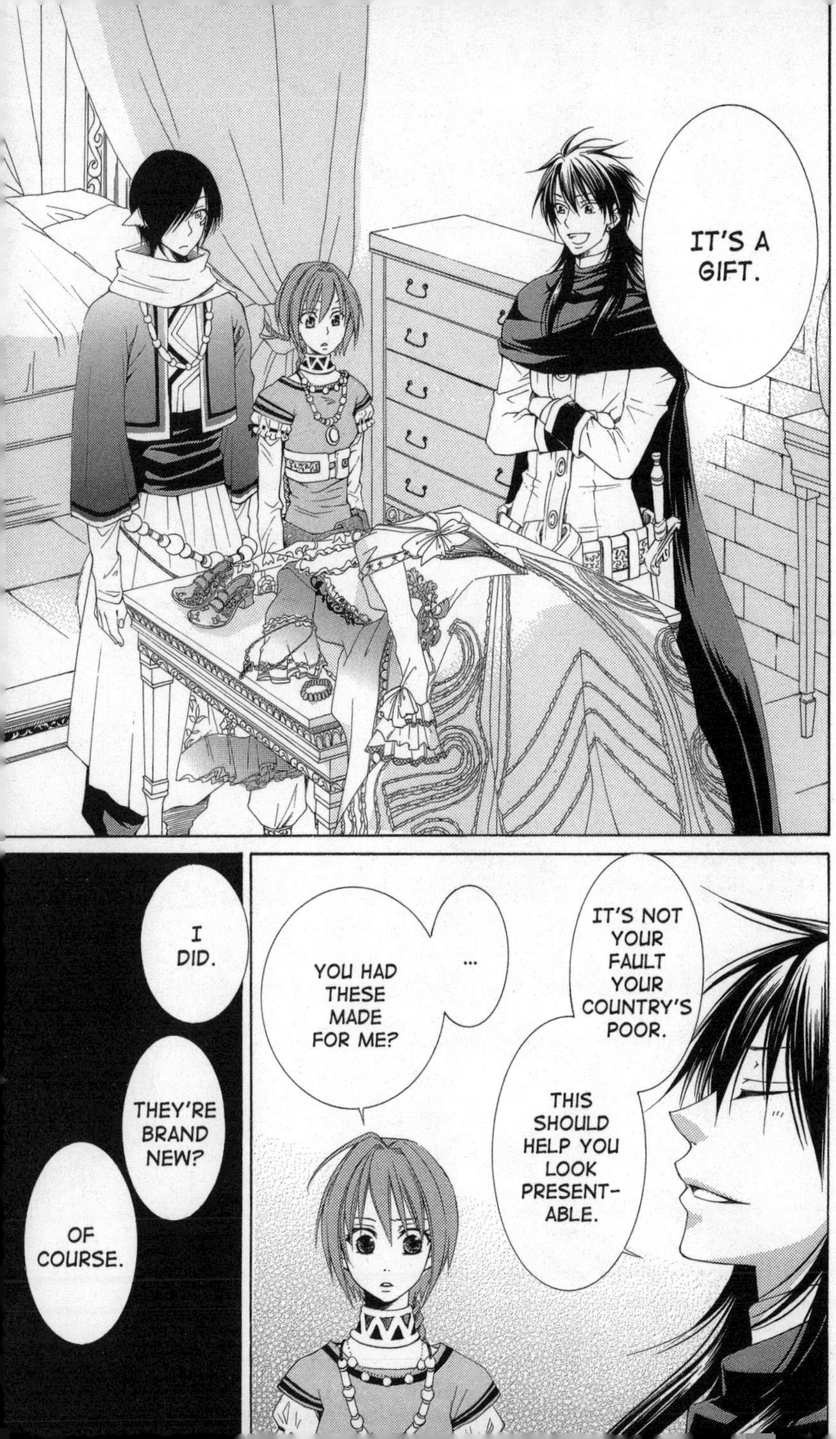
IT'S A GIFT.
IT'S NOT YOUR FAULT YOUR COUNTRY'S POOR.
THIS SHOULD HELP YOU LOOK PRESENT-ABLE.
...
YOU HAD THESE MADE FOR ME?
I DID.
THEY'RE BRAND NEW?
OF COURSE.

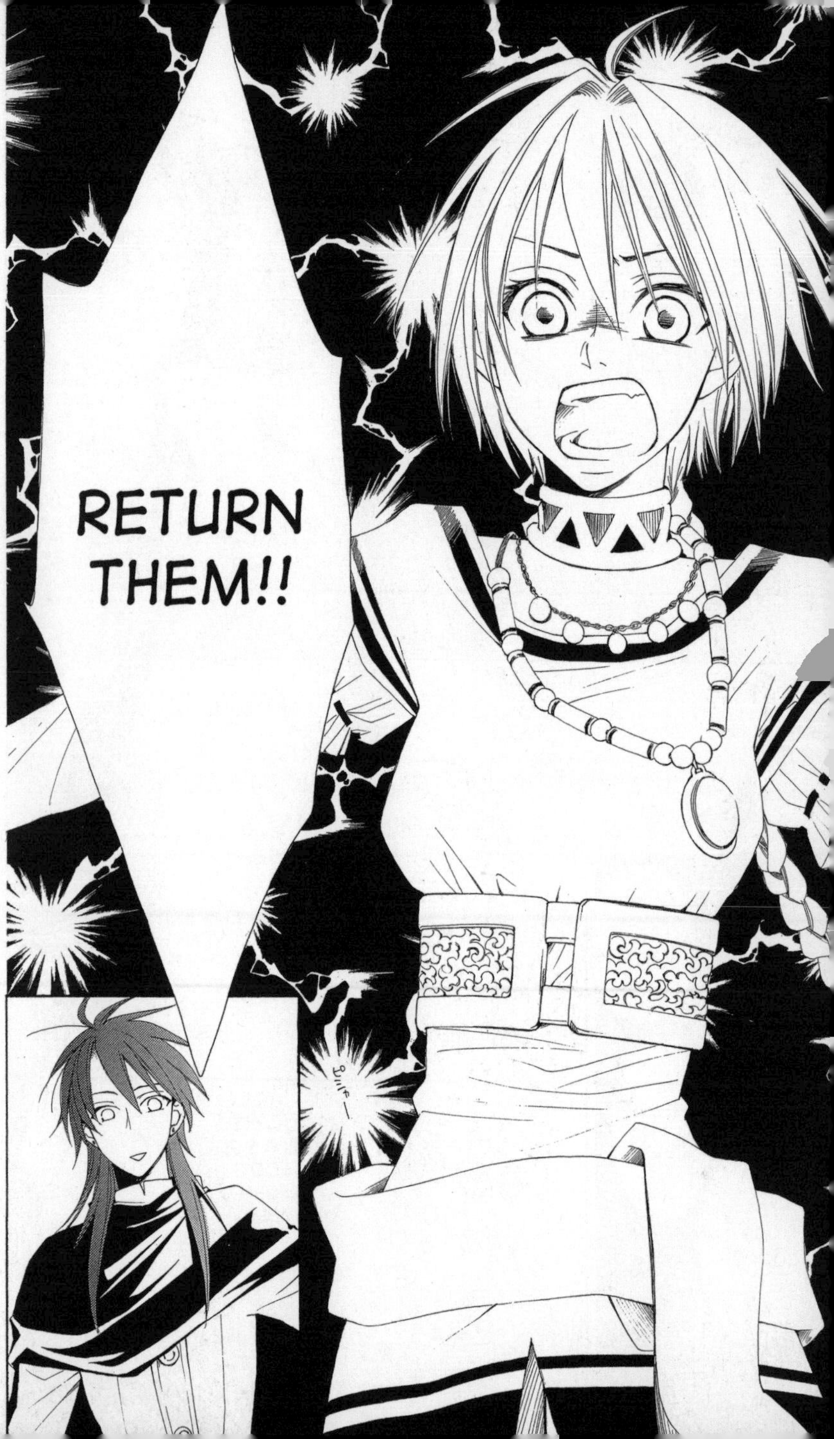
RETURN THEM!!

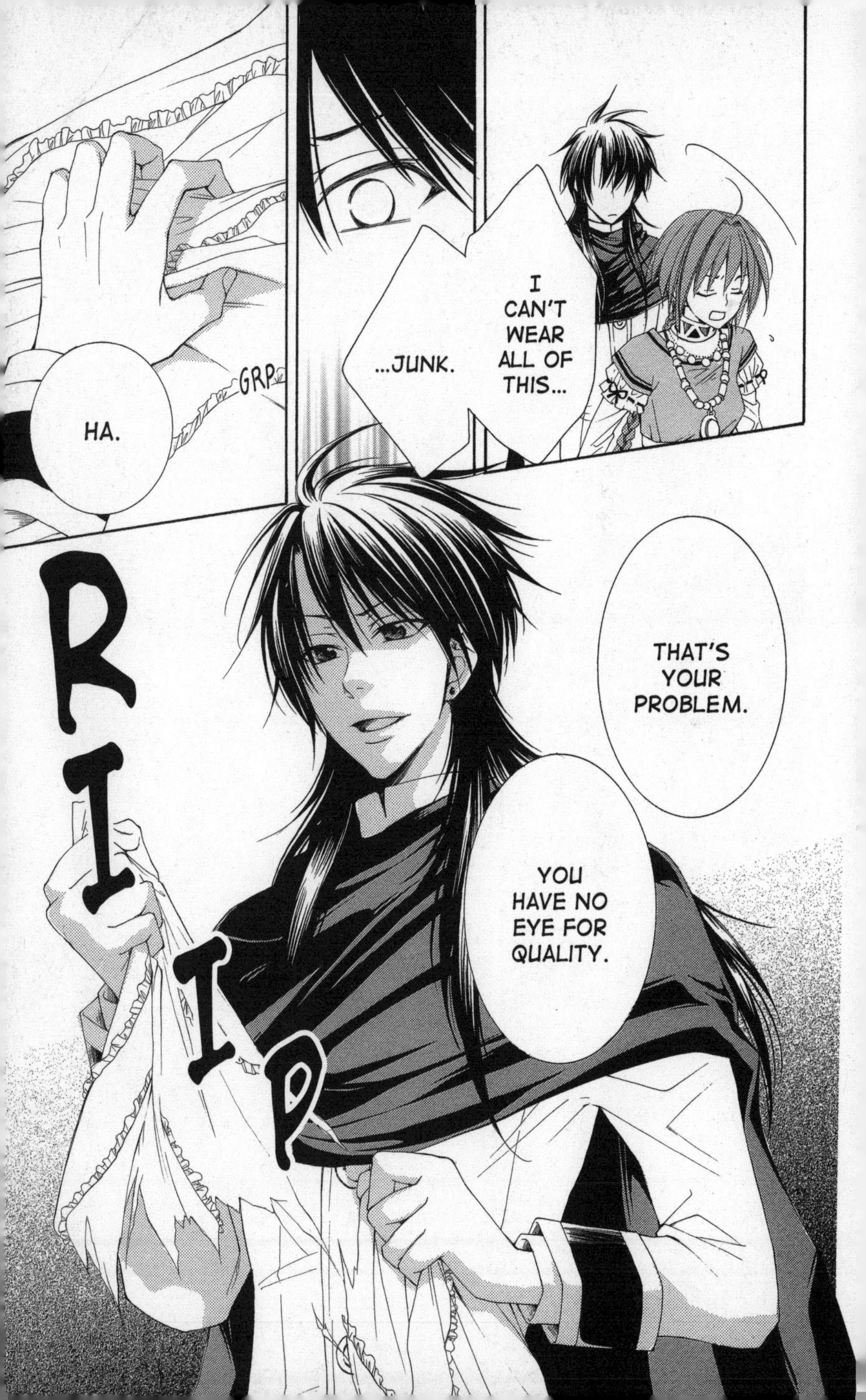
I CAN'T WEAR ALL OF THIS...
...JUNK.
GRP
HA.
THAT'S YOUR PROBLEM.
YOU HAVE NO EYE FOR QUALITY.
RIP

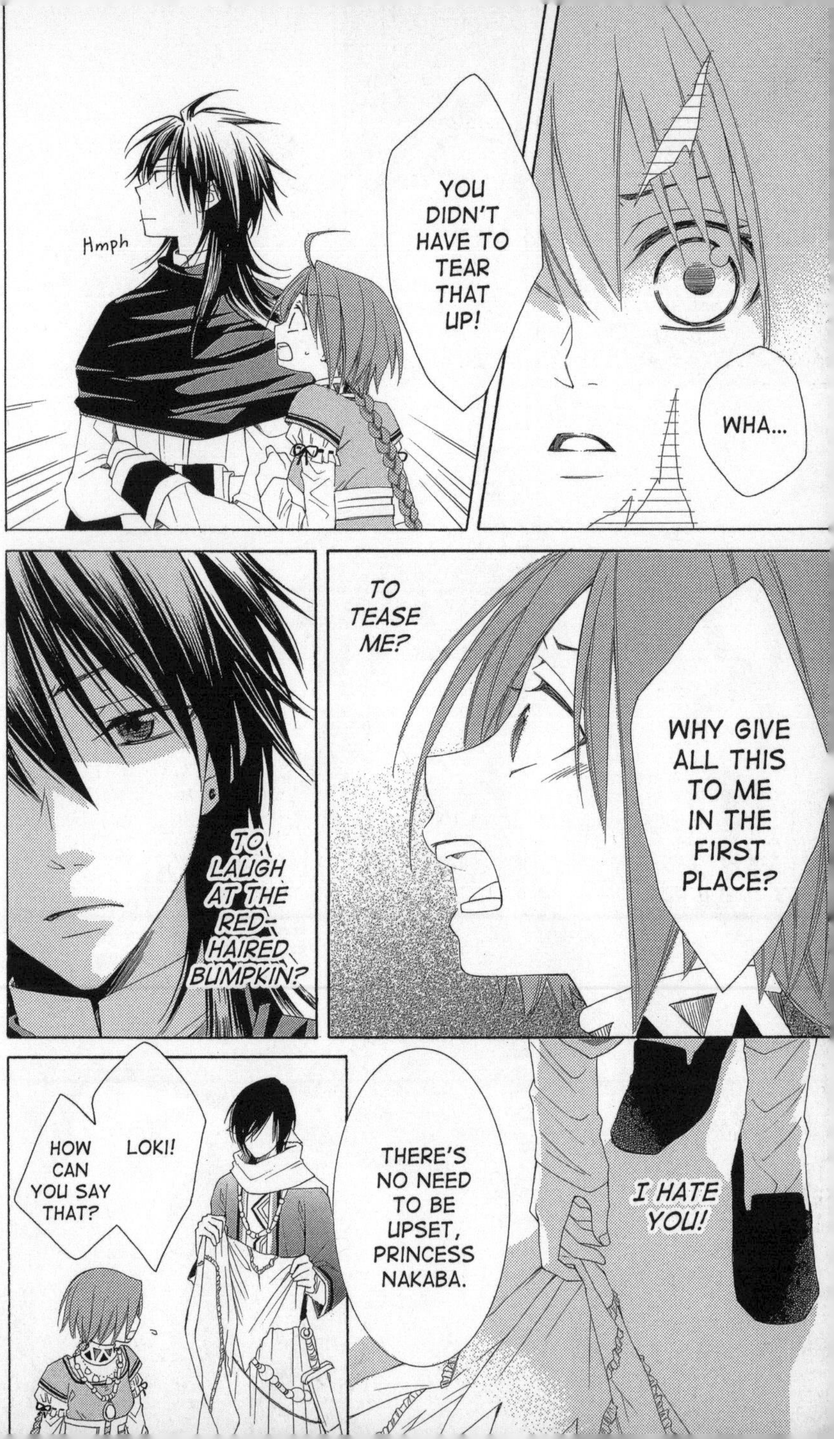
WHA...
YOU DIDN'T HAVE TO TEAR THAT UP!
Hmph
WHY GIVE ALL THIS TO ME IN THE FIRST PLACE?
TO TEASE ME?
TO LAUGH AT THE RED-HAIRED BUMPKIN?
I HATE YOU!
THERE'S NO NEED TO BE UPSET, PRINCESS NAKABA.
LOKI!
HOW CAN YOU SAY THAT?

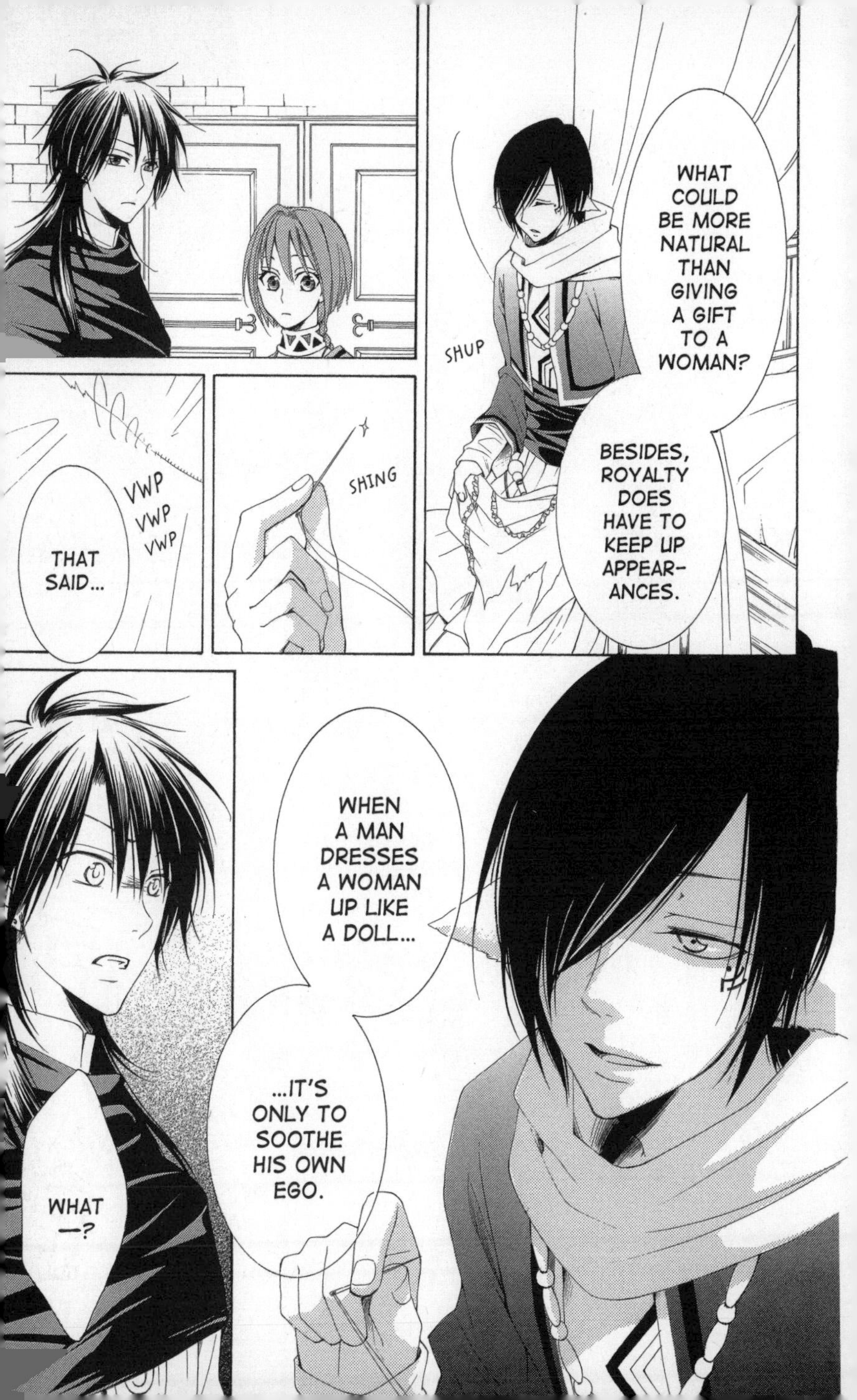
WHAT COULD BE MORE NATURAL THAN GIVING A GIFT TO A WOMAN?
SHUP
BESIDES, ROYALTY DOES HAVE TO KEEP UP APPEAR-ANCES.
SHING
VWP VWP VWP
THAT SAID...
WHEN A MAN DRESSES A WOMAN UP LIKE A DOLL...
...IT'S ONLY TO SOOTHE HIS OWN EGO.
WHAT—?

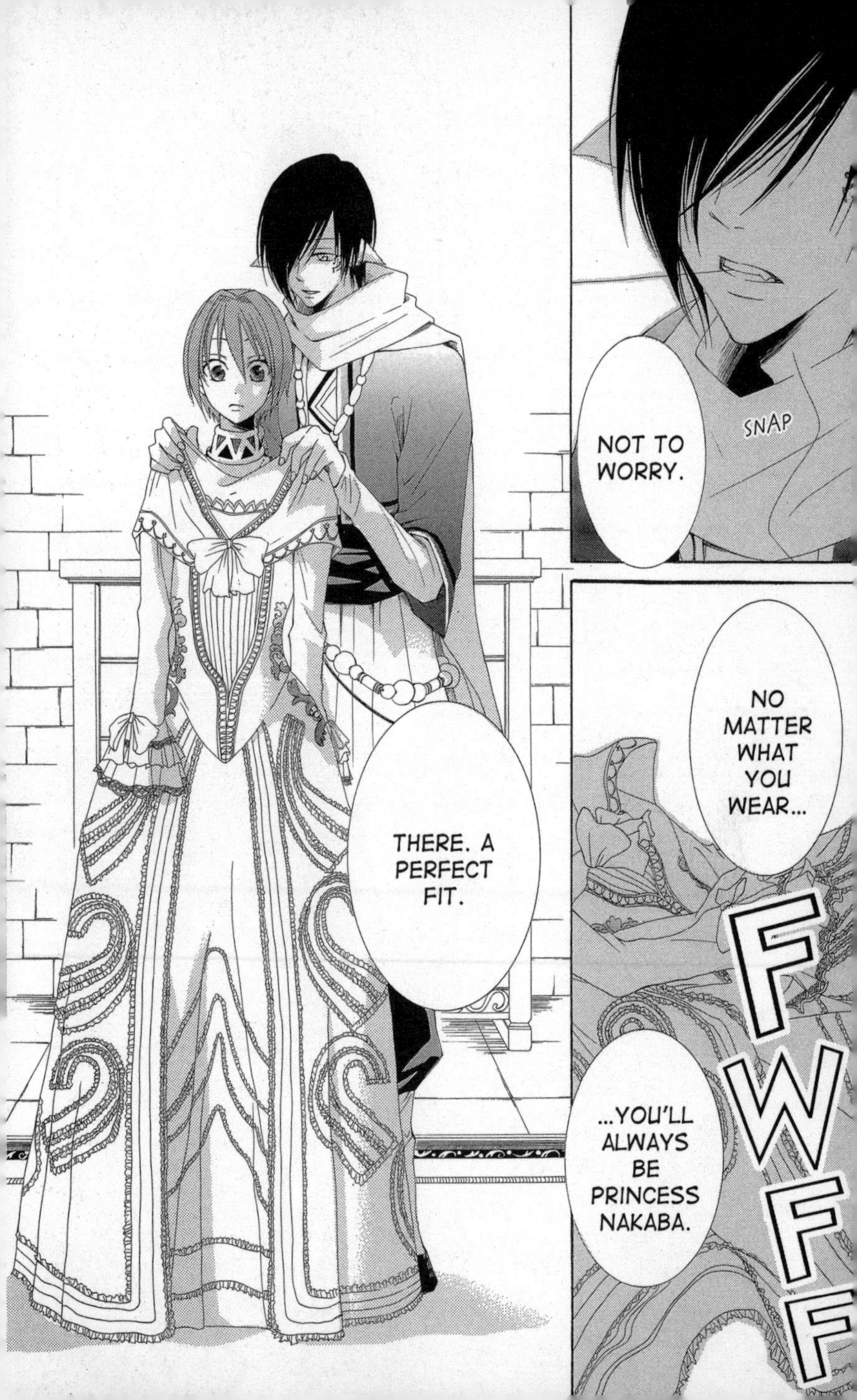
NOT TO WORRY.
SNAP
NO MATTER WHAT YOU WEAR...
FWFF
...YOU'LL ALWAYS BE PRINCESS NAKABA.
THERE. A PERFECT FIT.

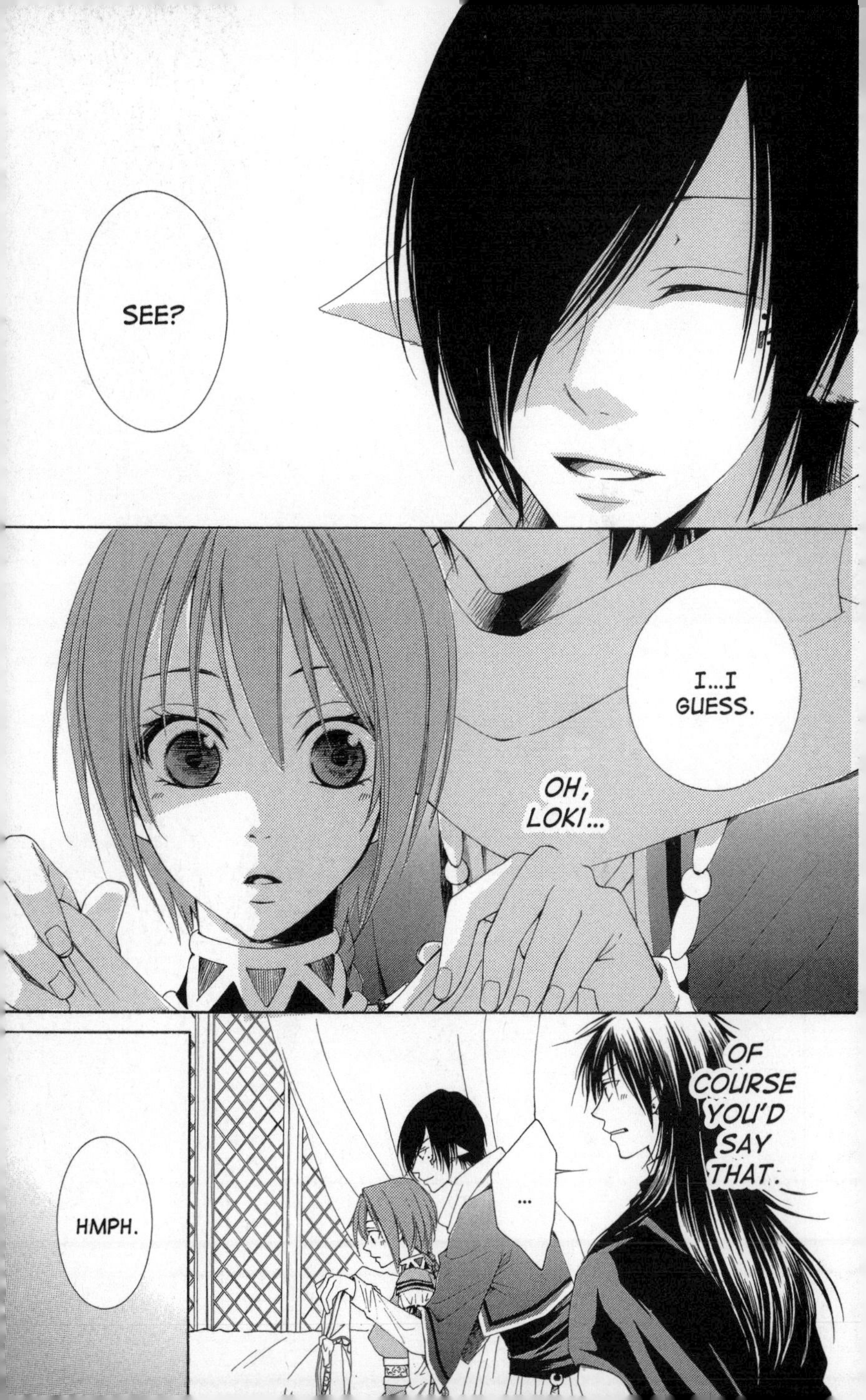
SEE?
I...I GUESS.
OH, LOKI...
OF COURSE YOU'D SAY THAT.
...
HMPH.

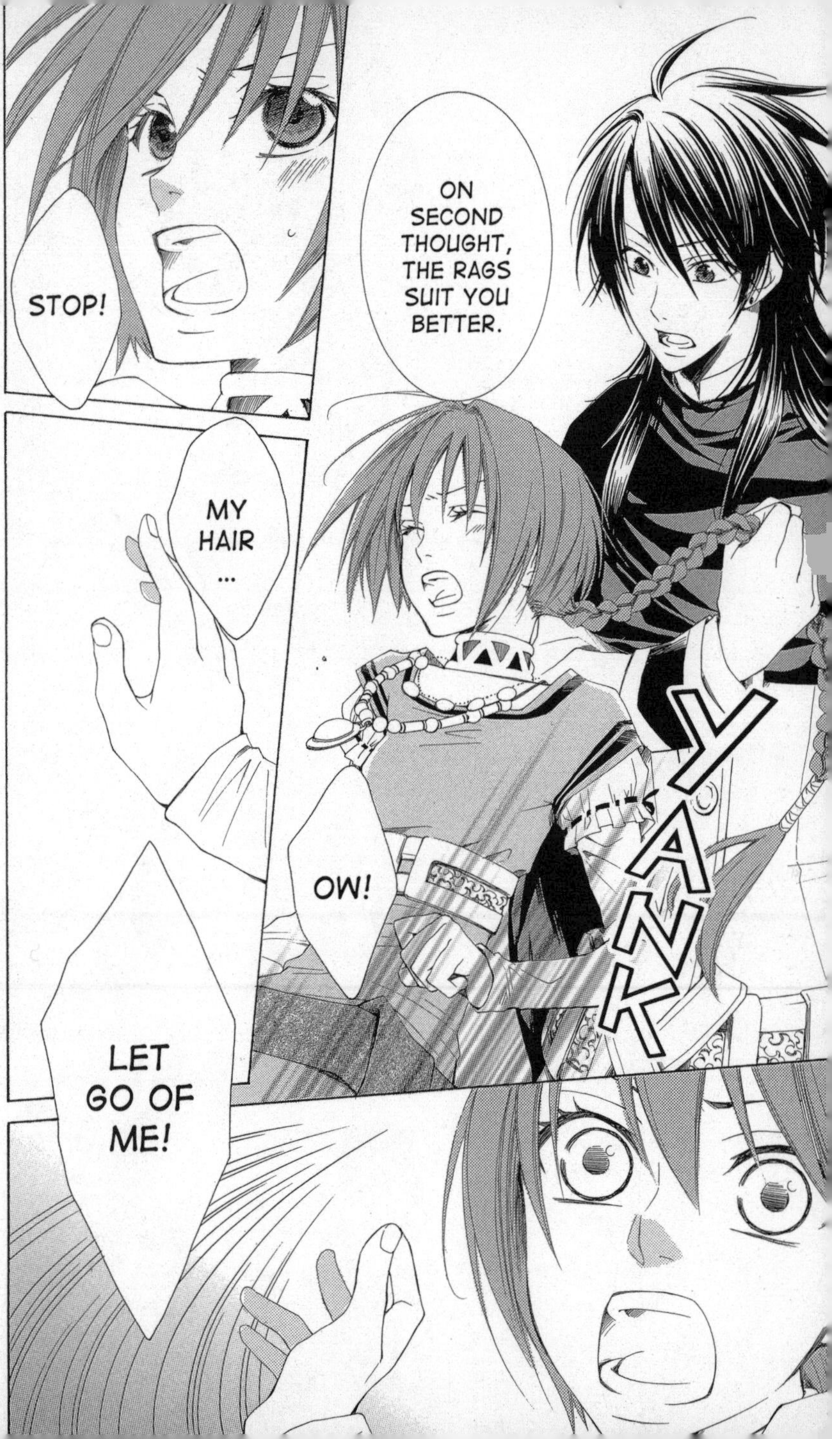
ON SECOND THOUGHT, THE RAGS SUIT YOU BETTER.
YANK
OW!
STOP!
MY HAIR ...
LET GO OF ME!

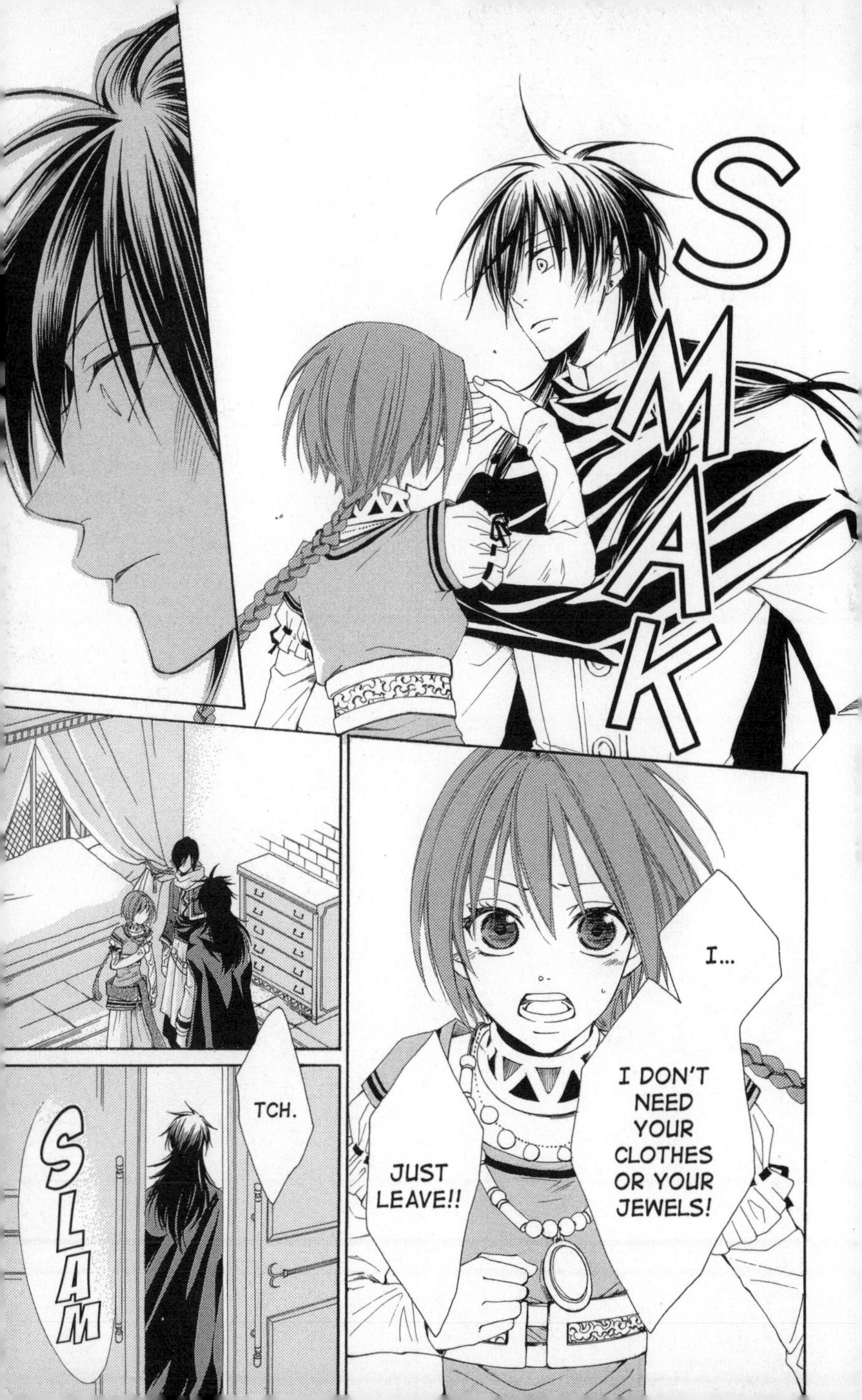
SMAK
I...
I DON'T NEED YOUR CLOTHES OR YOUR JEWELS!
JUST LEAVE!!
TCH.
SLAM

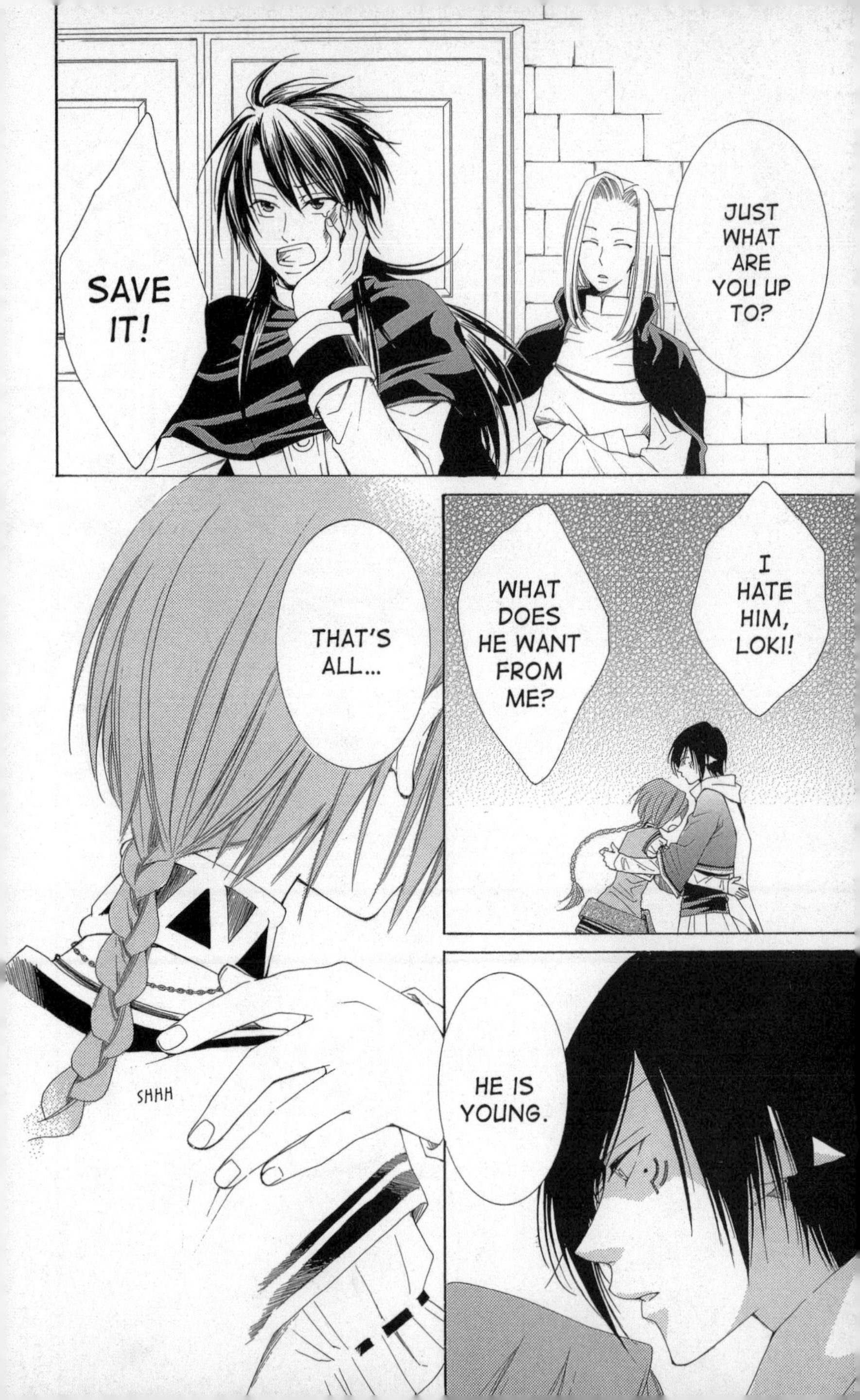
JUST WHAT ARE YOU UP TO?
SAVE IT!
I HATE HIM, LOKI!
WHAT DOES HE WANT FROM ME?
HE IS YOUNG.
THAT'S ALL...
SHHH

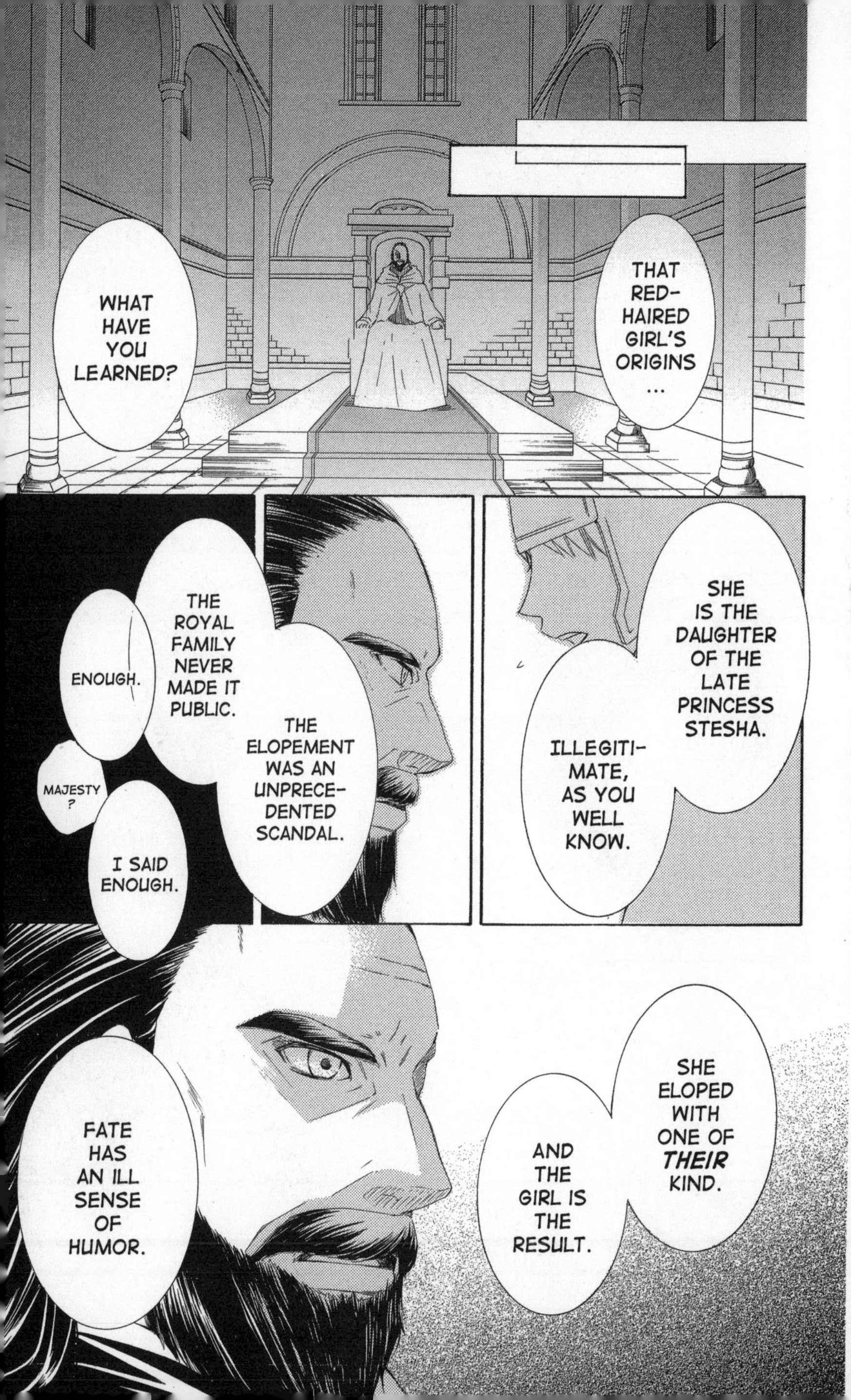
THAT RED-HAIRED GIRL'S ORIGINS ...
WHAT HAVE YOU LEARNED?
SHE IS THE DAUGHTER OF THE LATE PRINCESS STESHA.
ILLEGITI-MATE, AS YOU WELL KNOW.
THE ELOPEMENT WAS AN UNPRECE-DENTED SCANDAL.
THE ROYAL FAMILY NEVER MADE IT PUBLIC.
ENOUGH.
MAJESTY?
I SAID ENOUGH.
SHE ELOPED WITH ONE OF *THEIR* KIND.
AND THE GIRL IS THE RESULT.
FATE HAS AN ILL SENSE OF HUMOR.

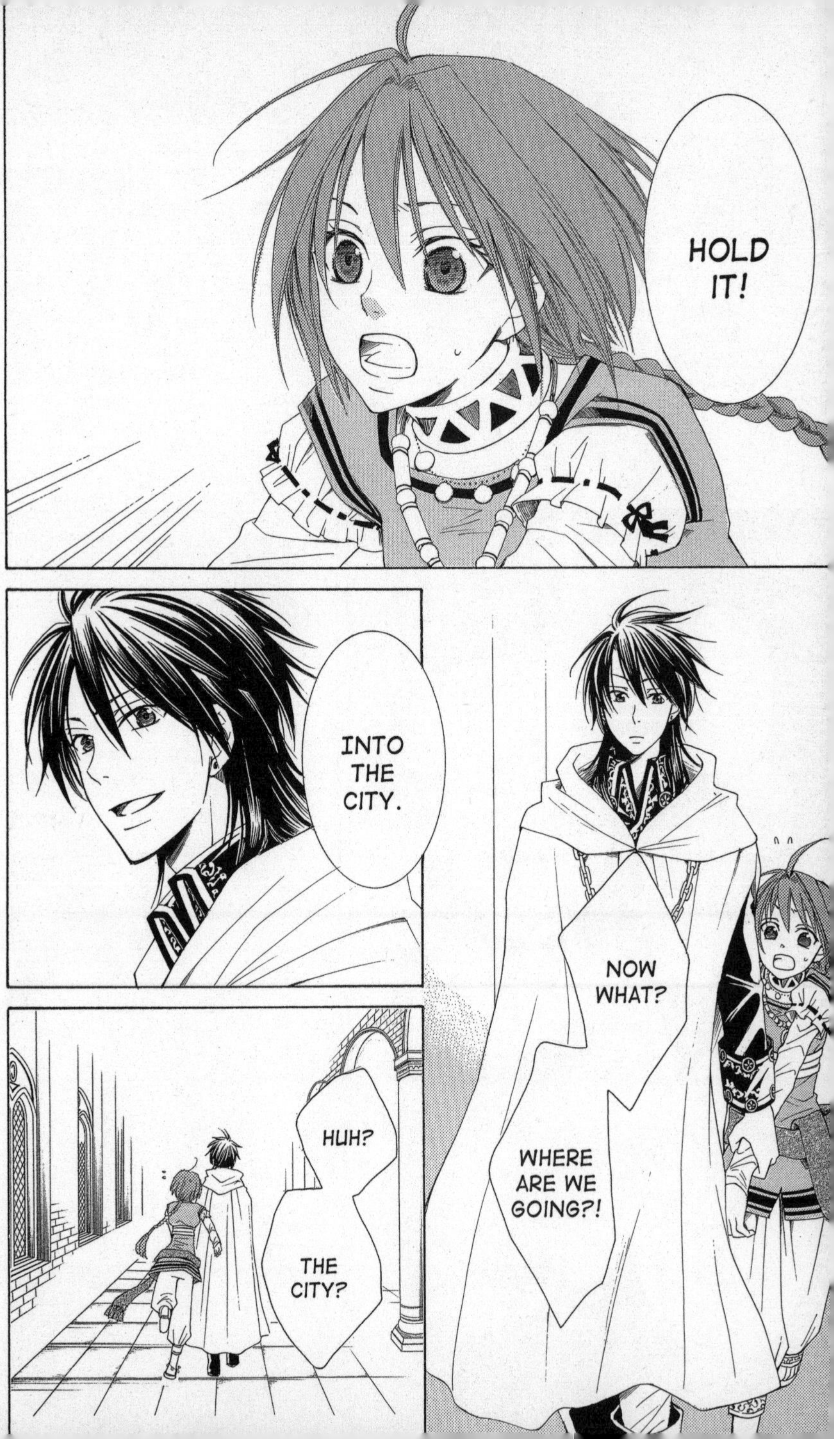
HOLD IT!
NOW WHAT?
WHERE ARE WE GOING?!
INTO THE CITY.
HUH?
THE CITY?

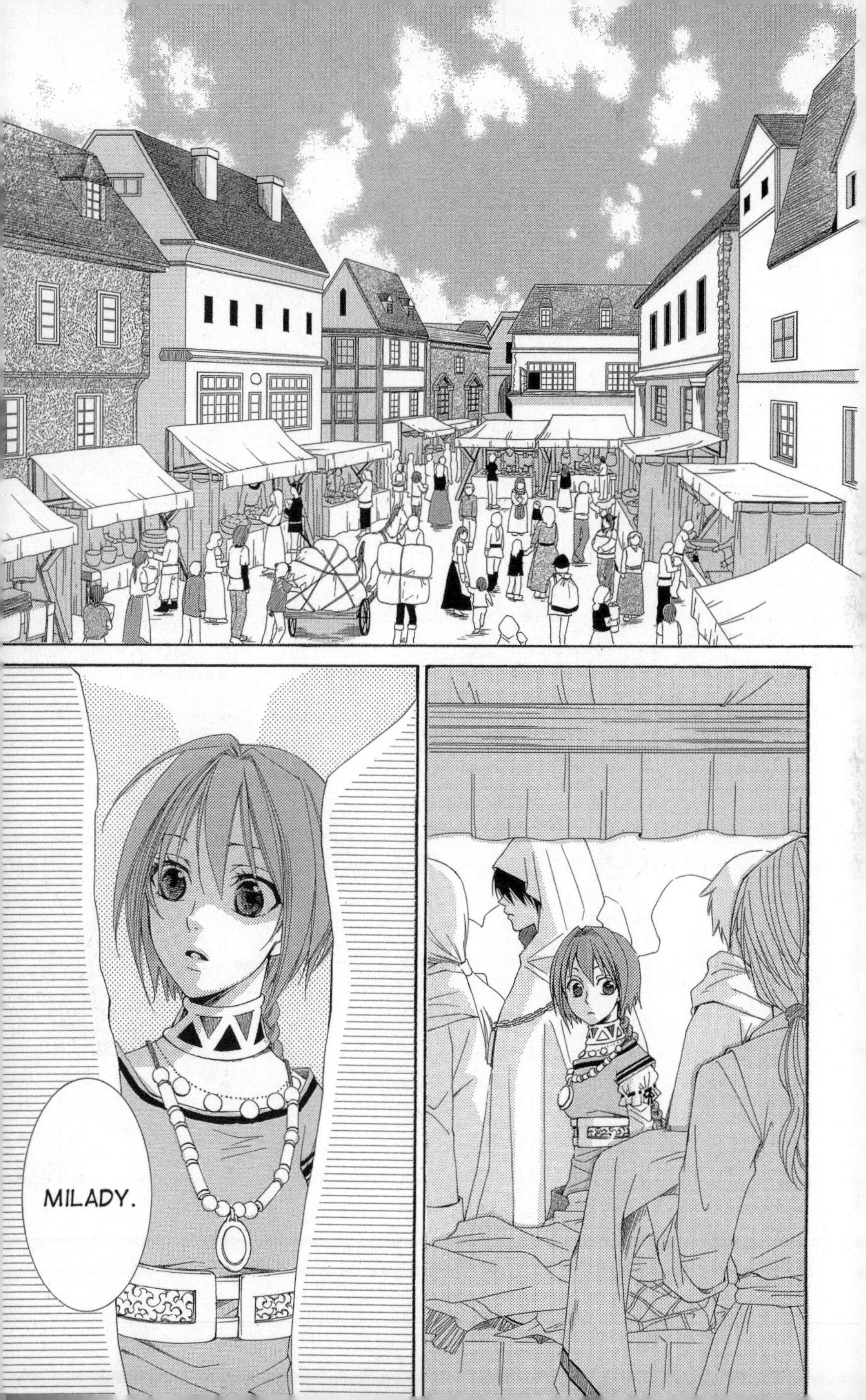
MILADY.

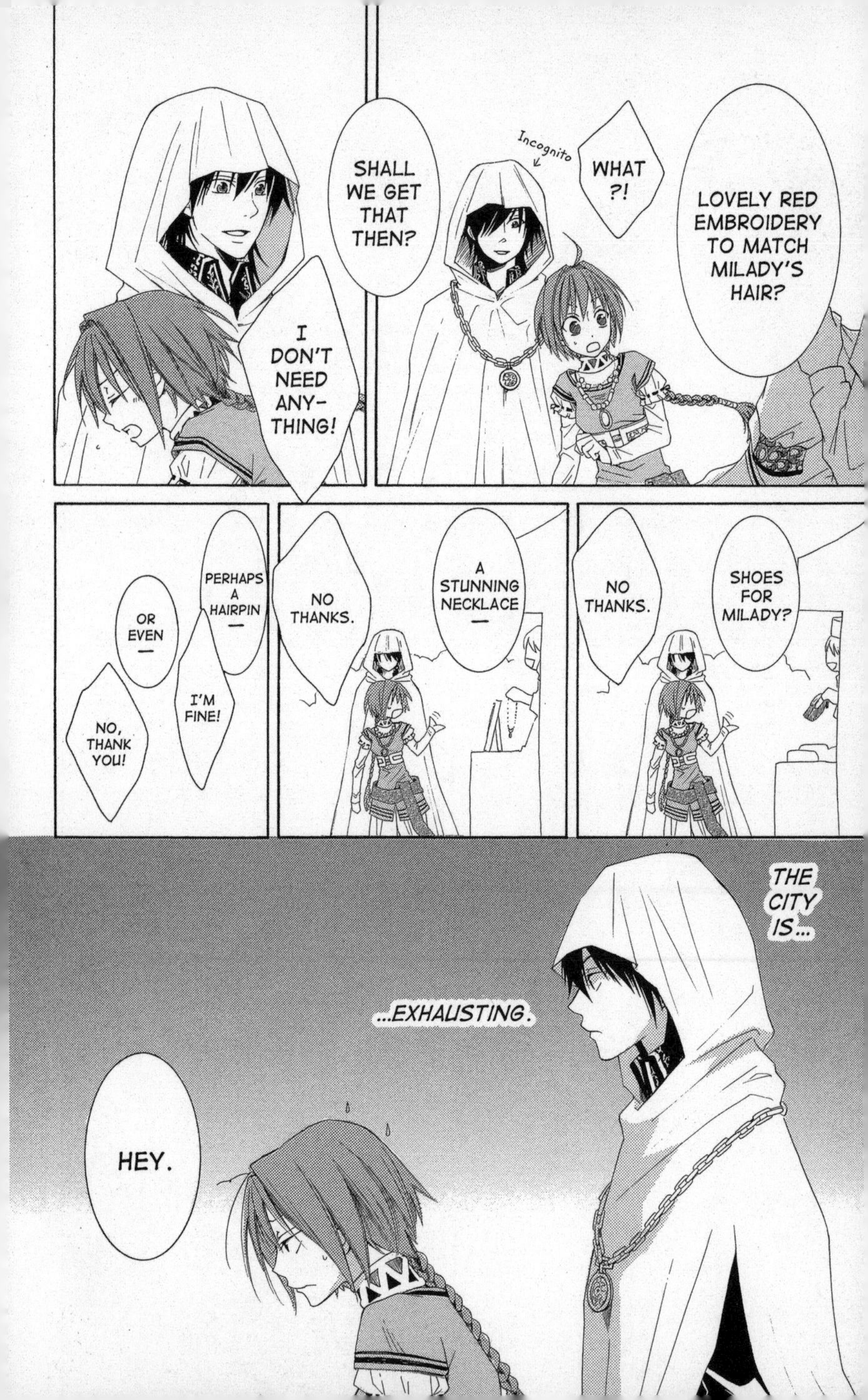
LOVELY RED EMBROIDERY TO MATCH MILADY'S HAIR?
WHAT?!
Incognito
SHALL WE GET THAT THEN?
I DON'T NEED ANY-THING!
SHOES FOR MILADY?
NO THANKS.
A STUNNING NECKLACE —
NO THANKS.
PERHAPS A HAIRPIN —
I'M FINE!
OR EVEN —
NO, THANK YOU!
THE CITY IS...
...EXHAUSTING.
HEY.

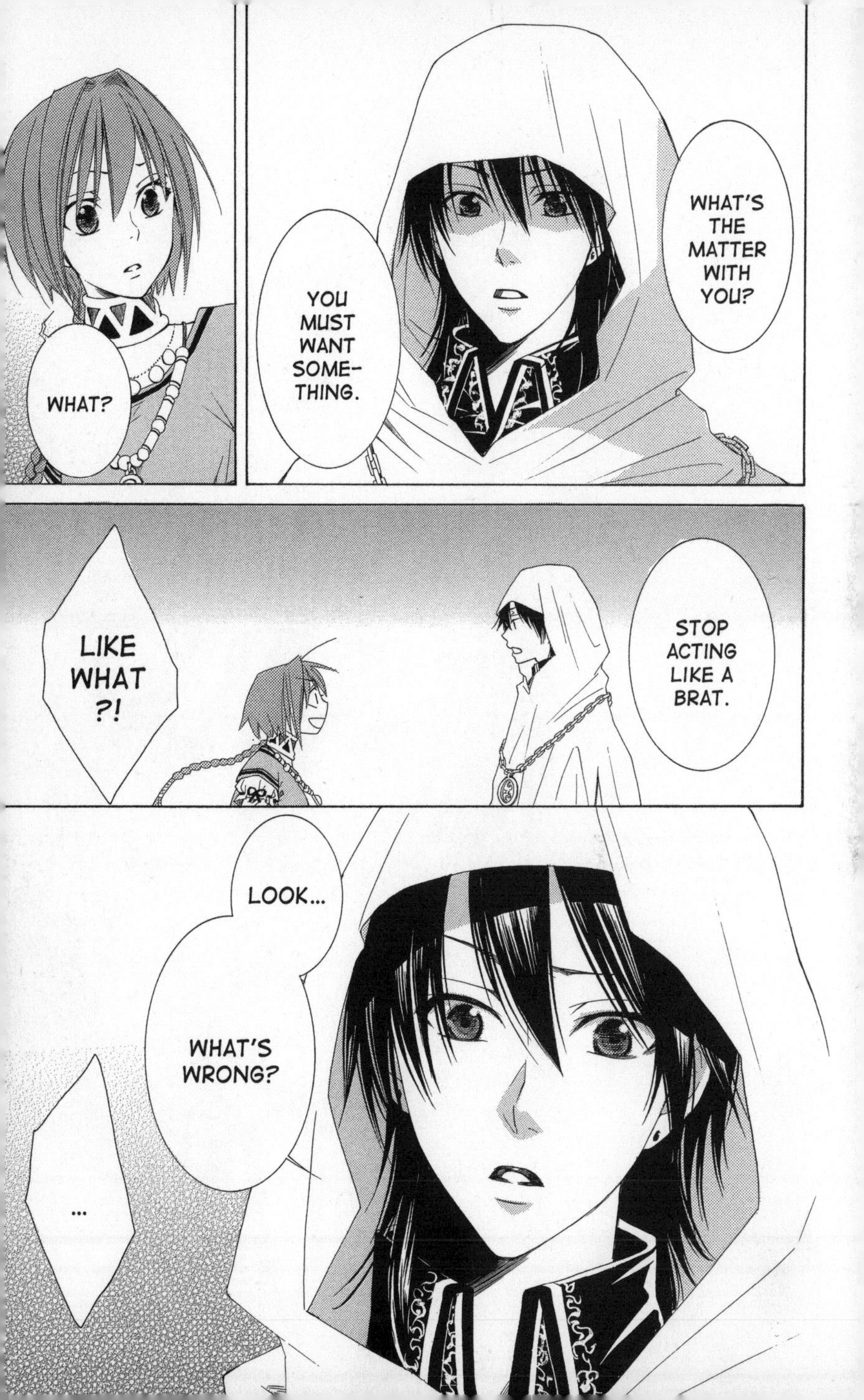
WHAT'S THE MATTER WITH YOU?
YOU MUST WANT SOME-THING.
WHAT?
STOP ACTING LIKE A BRAT.
LIKE WHAT?!
LOOK...
WHAT'S WRONG?
...

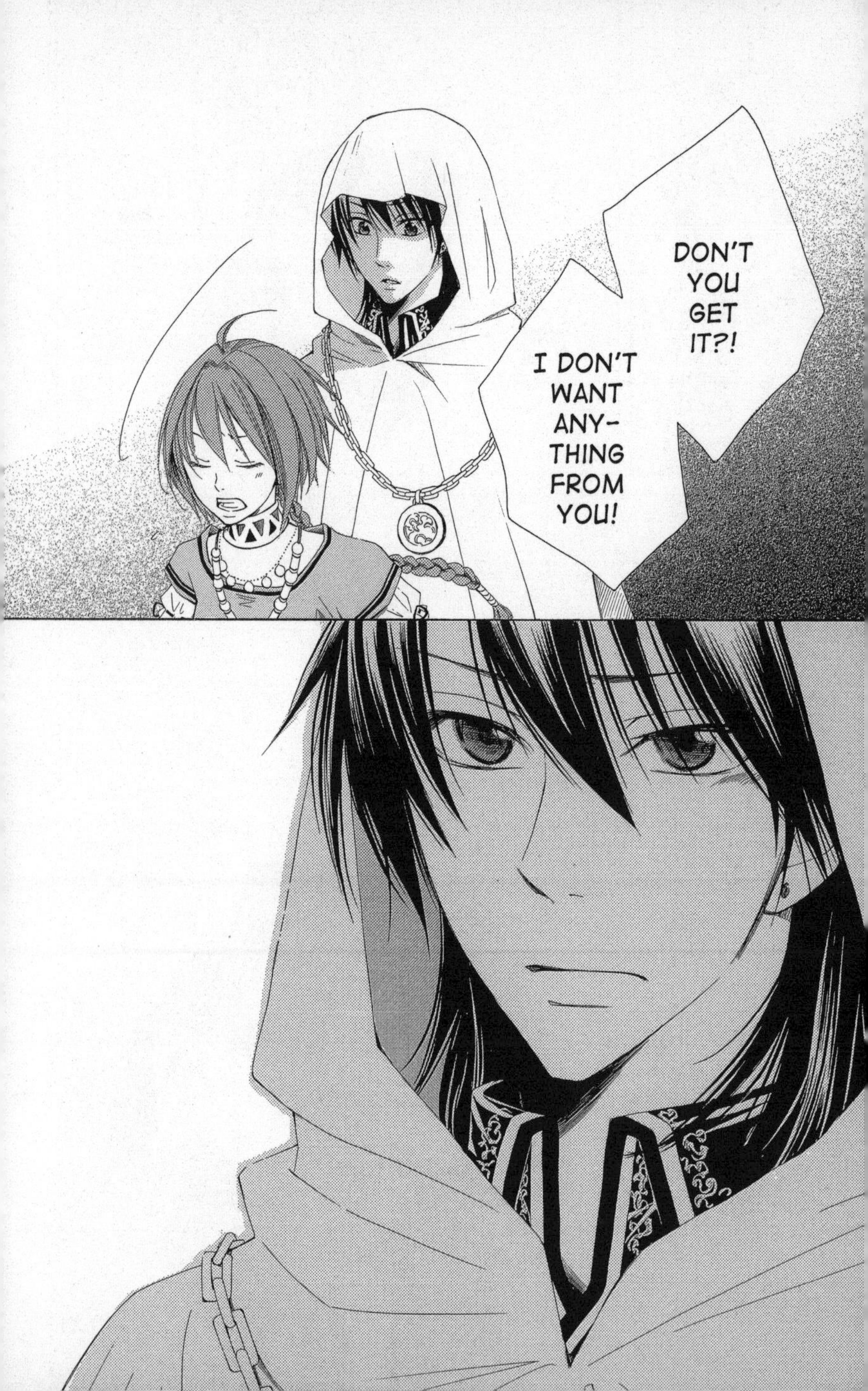
DON'T YOU GET IT?!
I DON'T WANT ANY-THING FROM YOU!

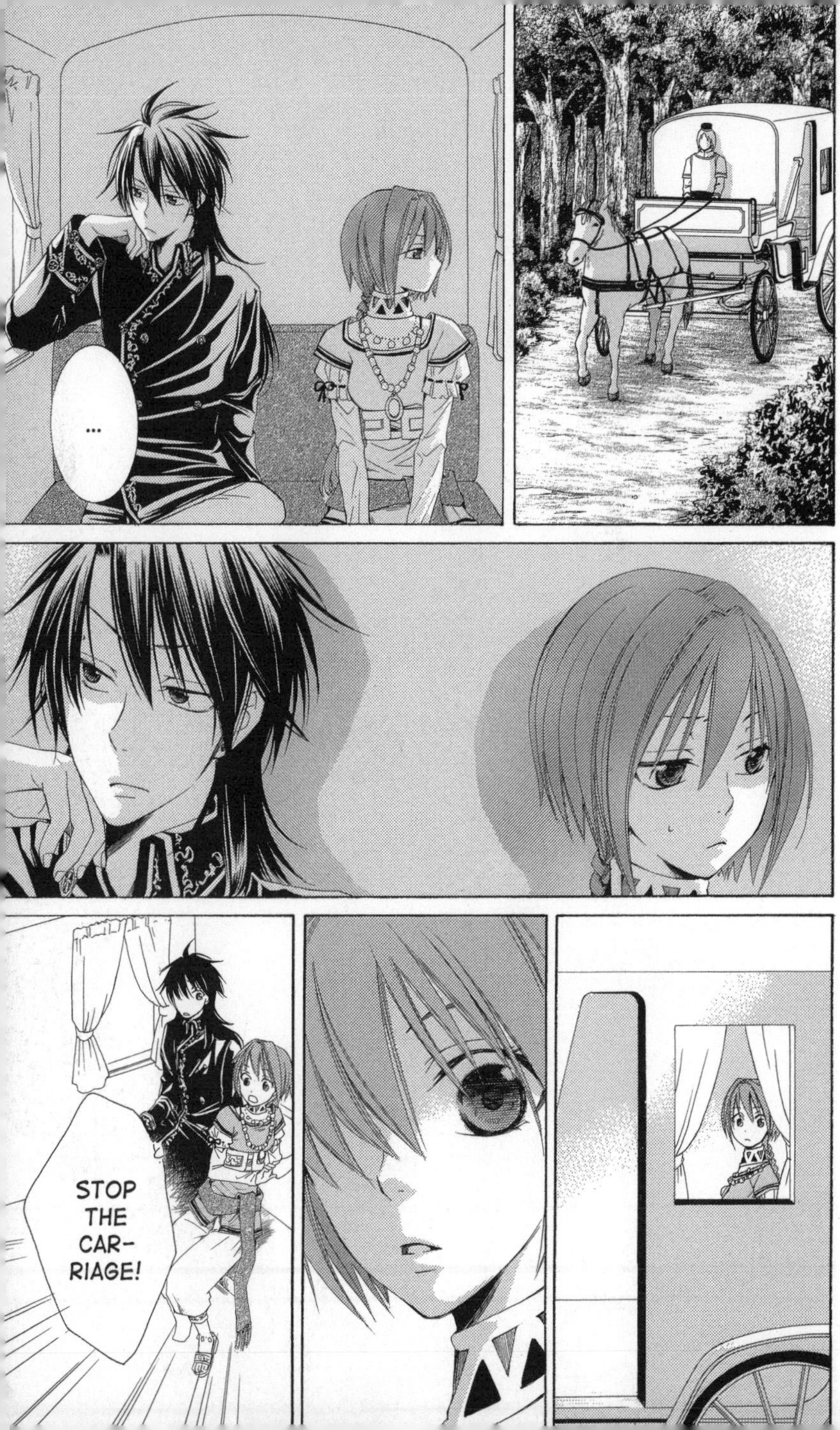
...
STOP THE CAR-RIAGE!

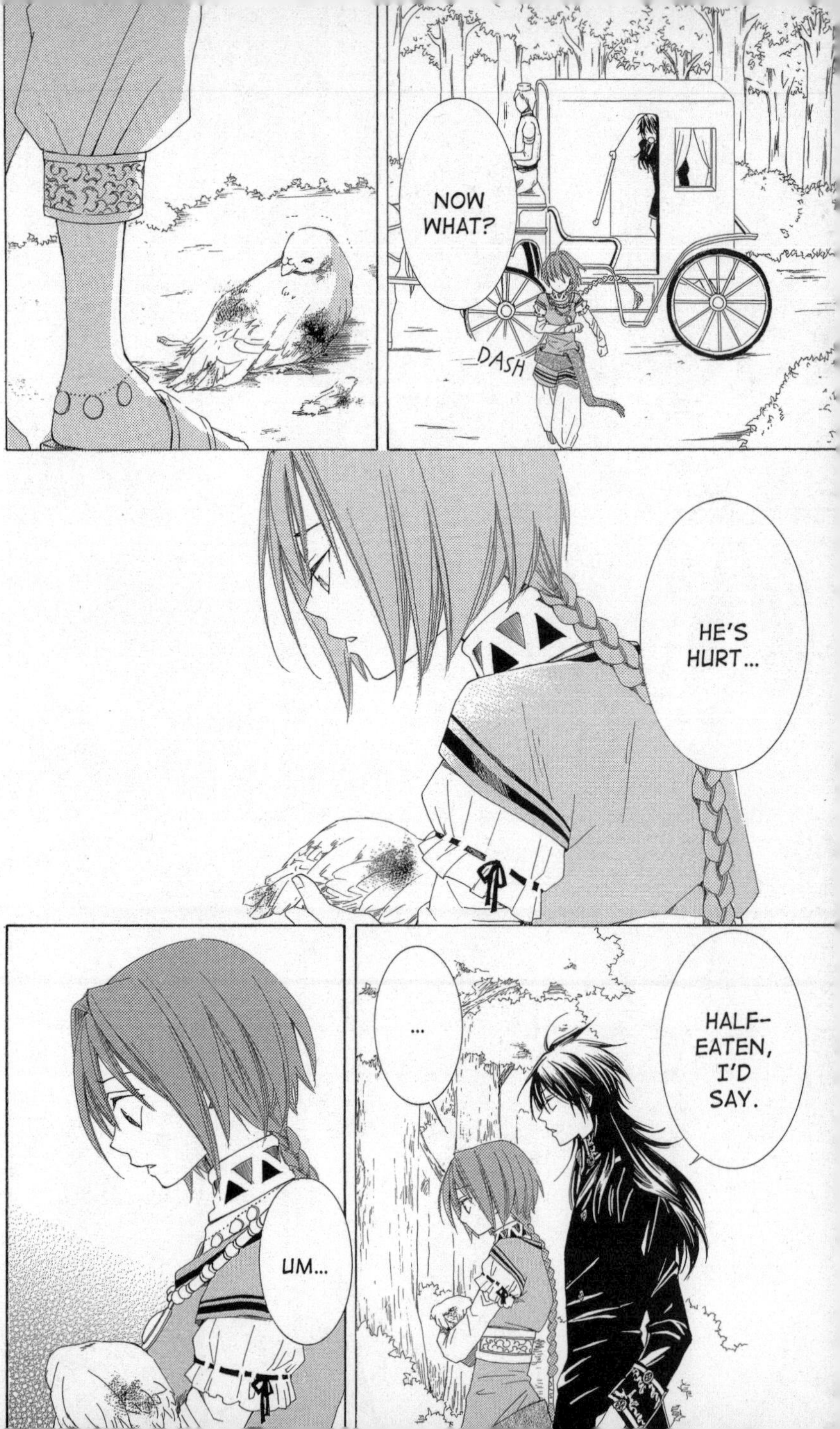
NOW WHAT?
DASH
HE'S HURT...
HALF-EATEN, I'D SAY.
...
UM...

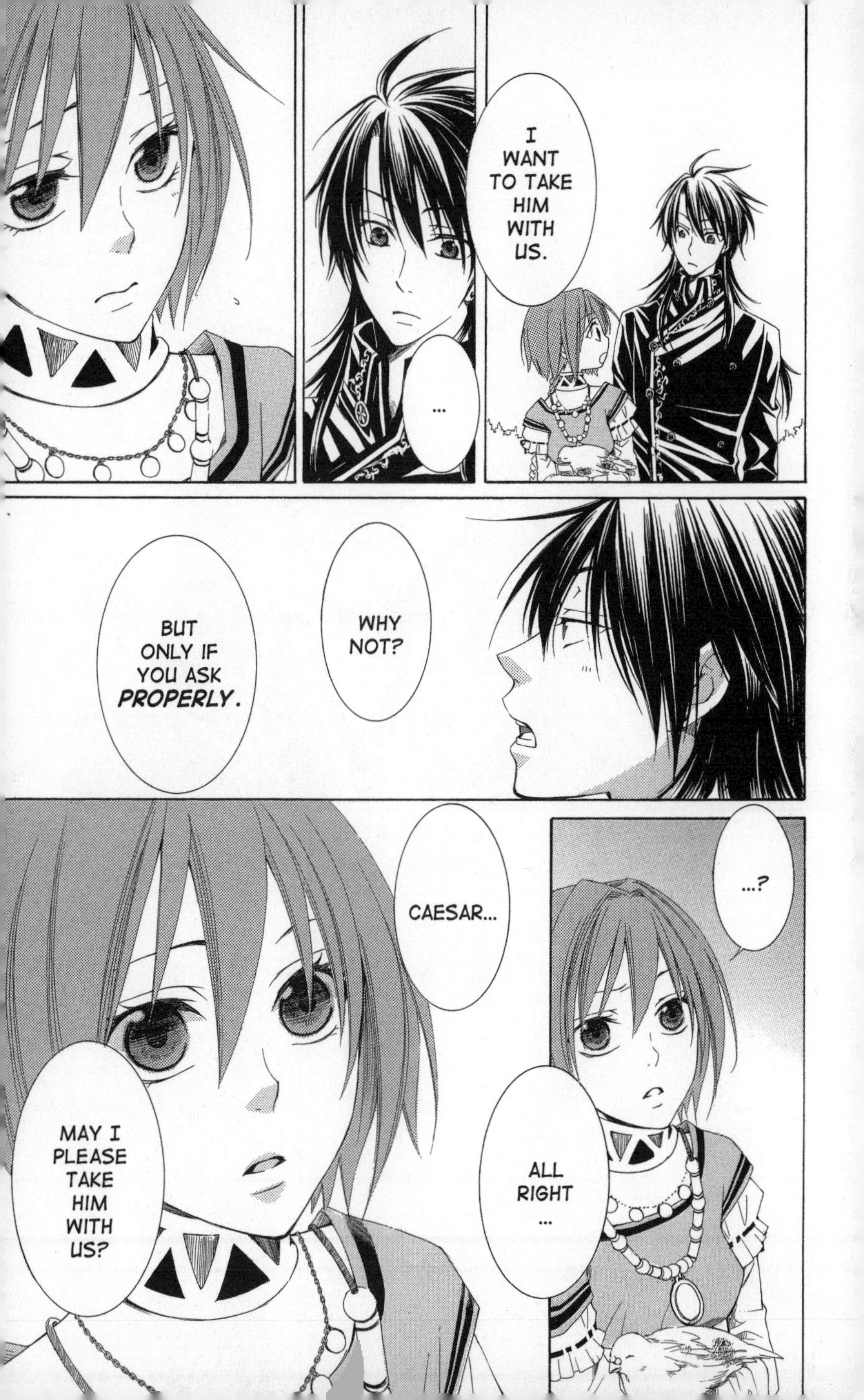
I WANT TO TAKE HIM WITH US.
...
WHY NOT?
BUT ONLY IF YOU ASK *PROPERLY*.
...?
ALL RIGHT ...
CAESAR...
MAY I PLEASE TAKE HIM WITH US?

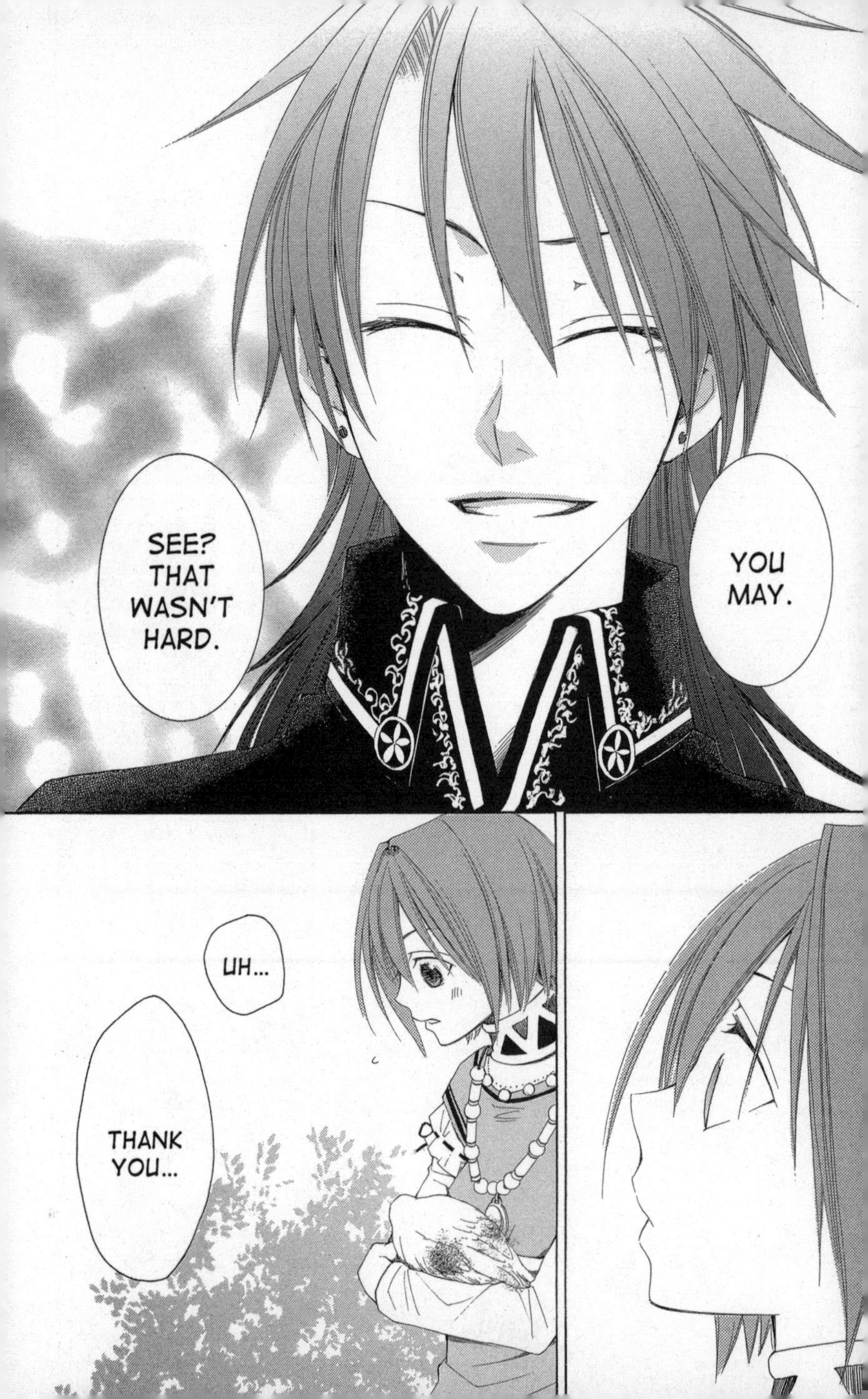
YOU MAY.
SEE? THAT WASN'T HARD.
UH...
THANK YOU...

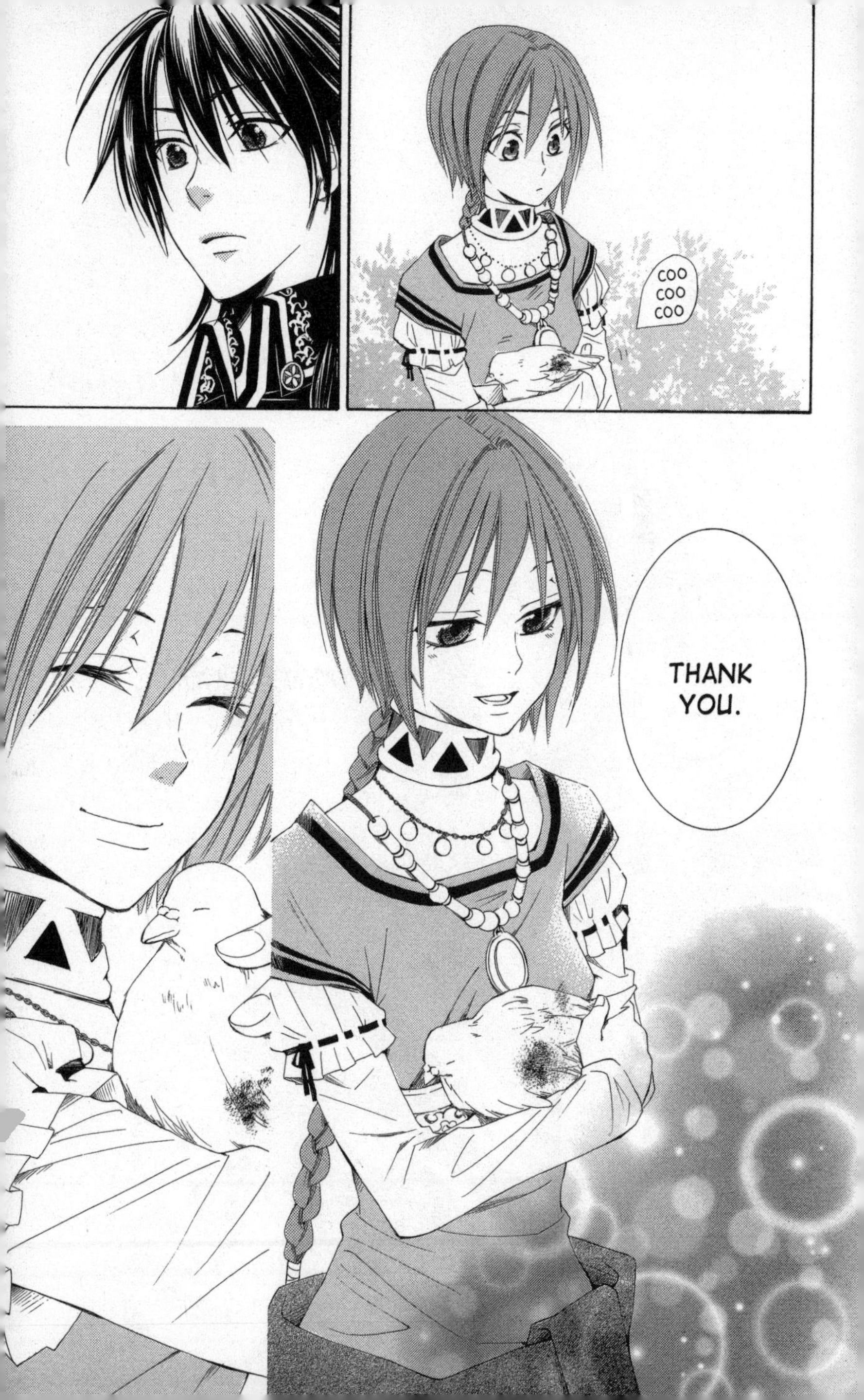
COO COO COO
THANK YOU.

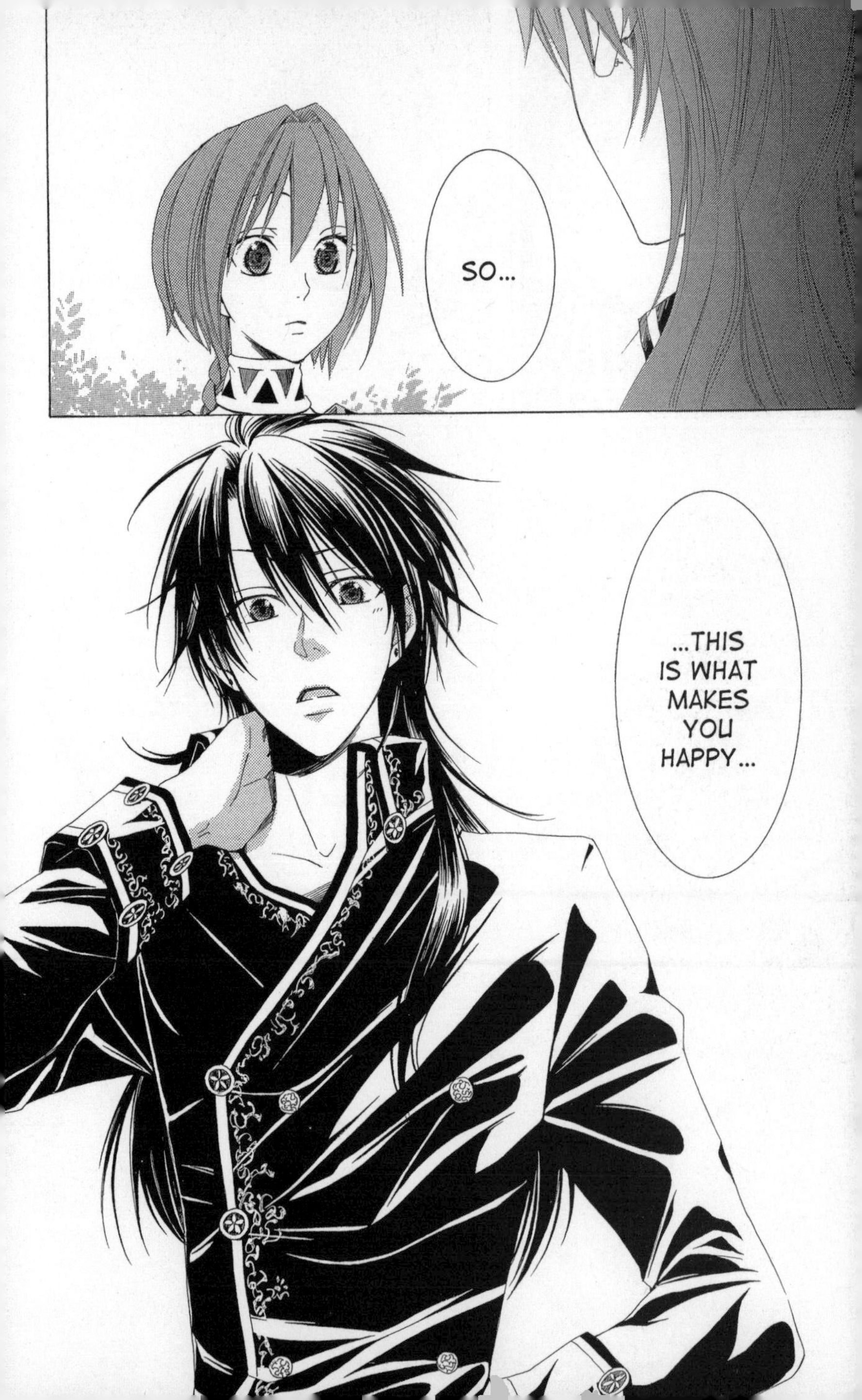
SO...
...THIS IS WHAT MAKES YOU HAPPY...

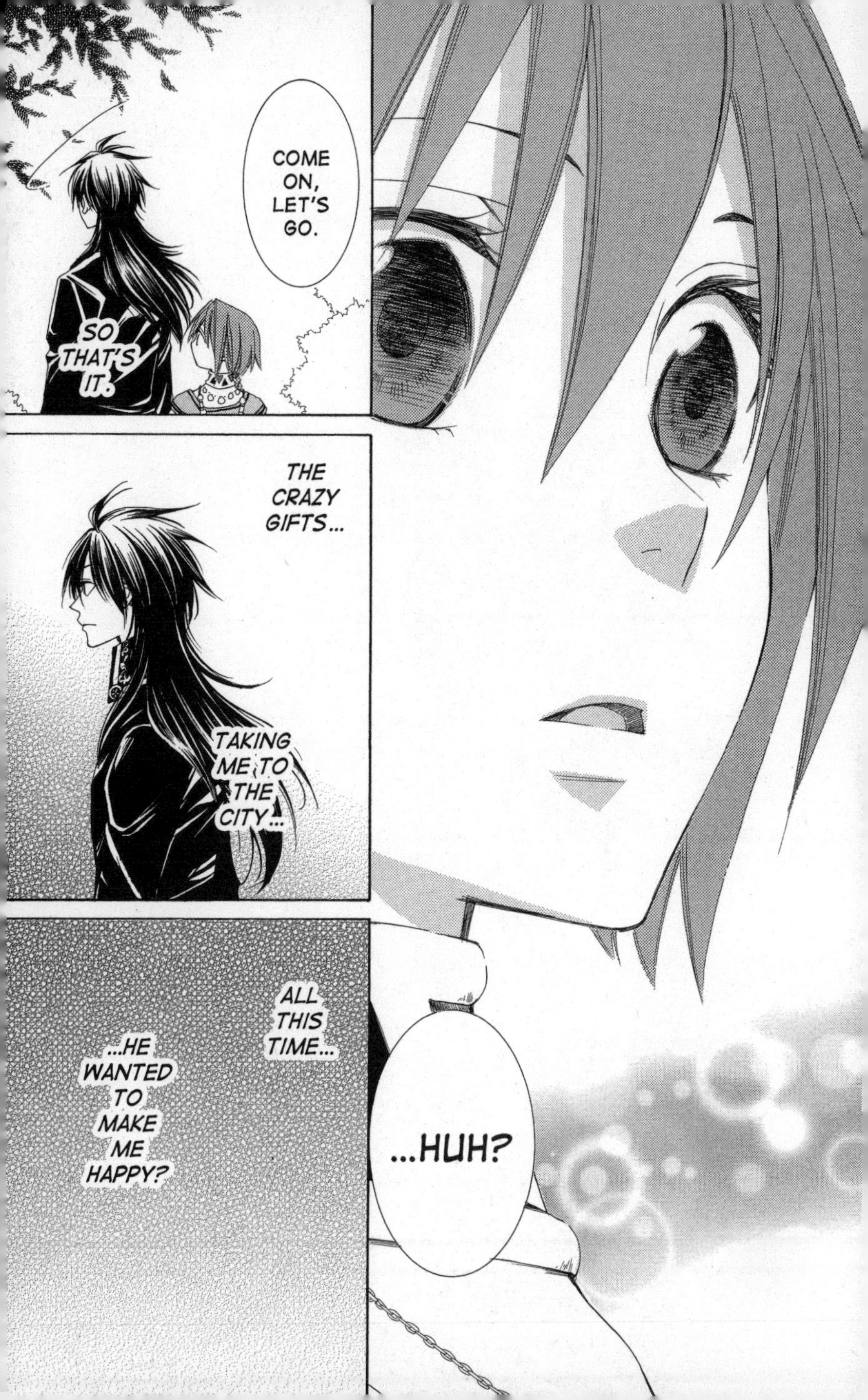
...HUH?
COME ON, LET'S GO.
SO THAT'S IT.
THE CRAZY GIFTS...
TAKING ME TO THE CITY...
ALL THIS TIME...
...HE WANTED TO MAKE ME HAPPY?

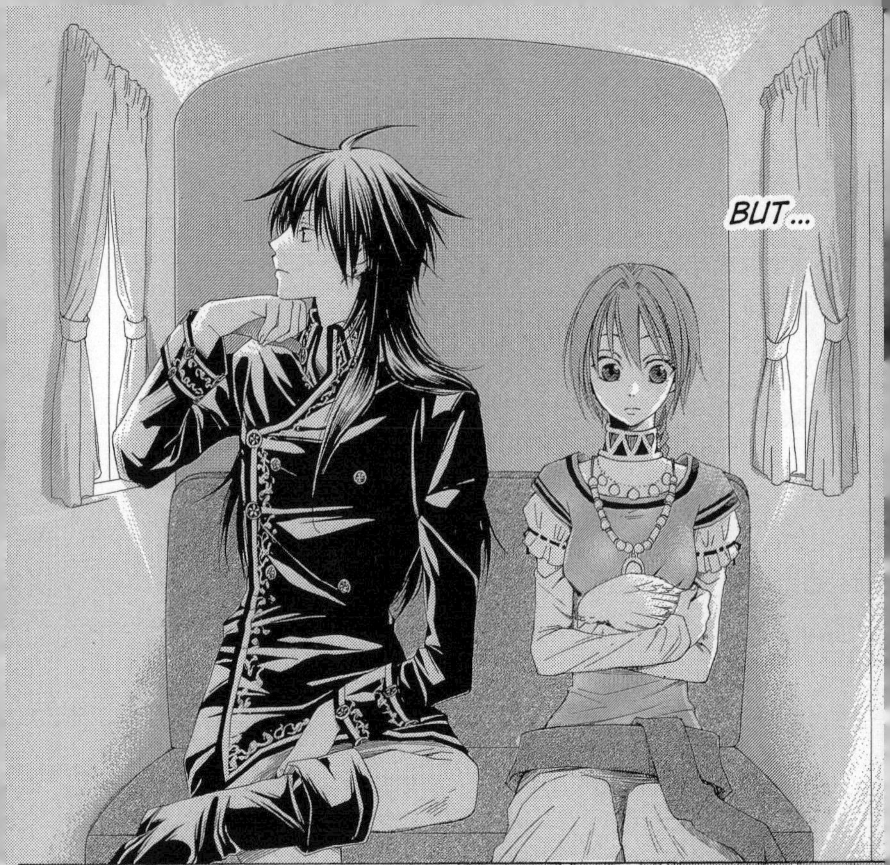
BUT...
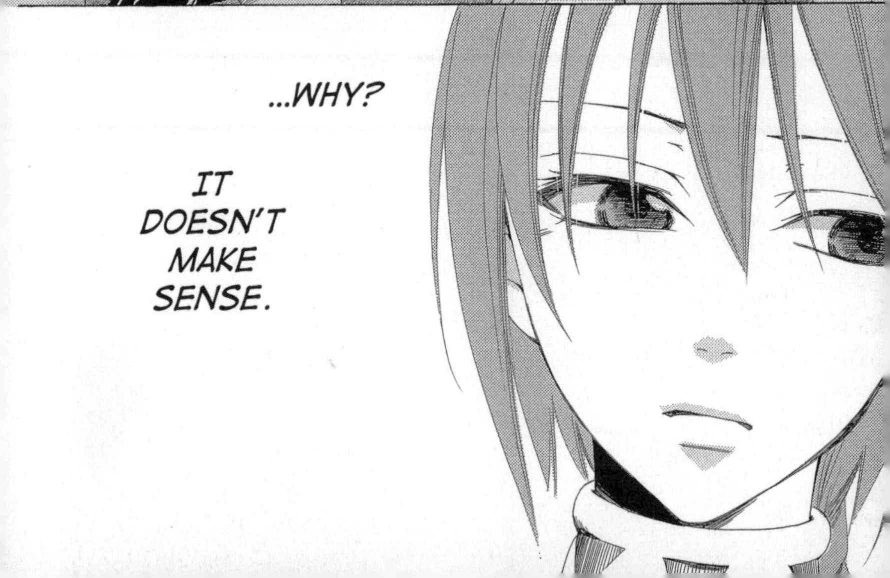
...WHY?
IT DOESN'T MAKE SENSE.

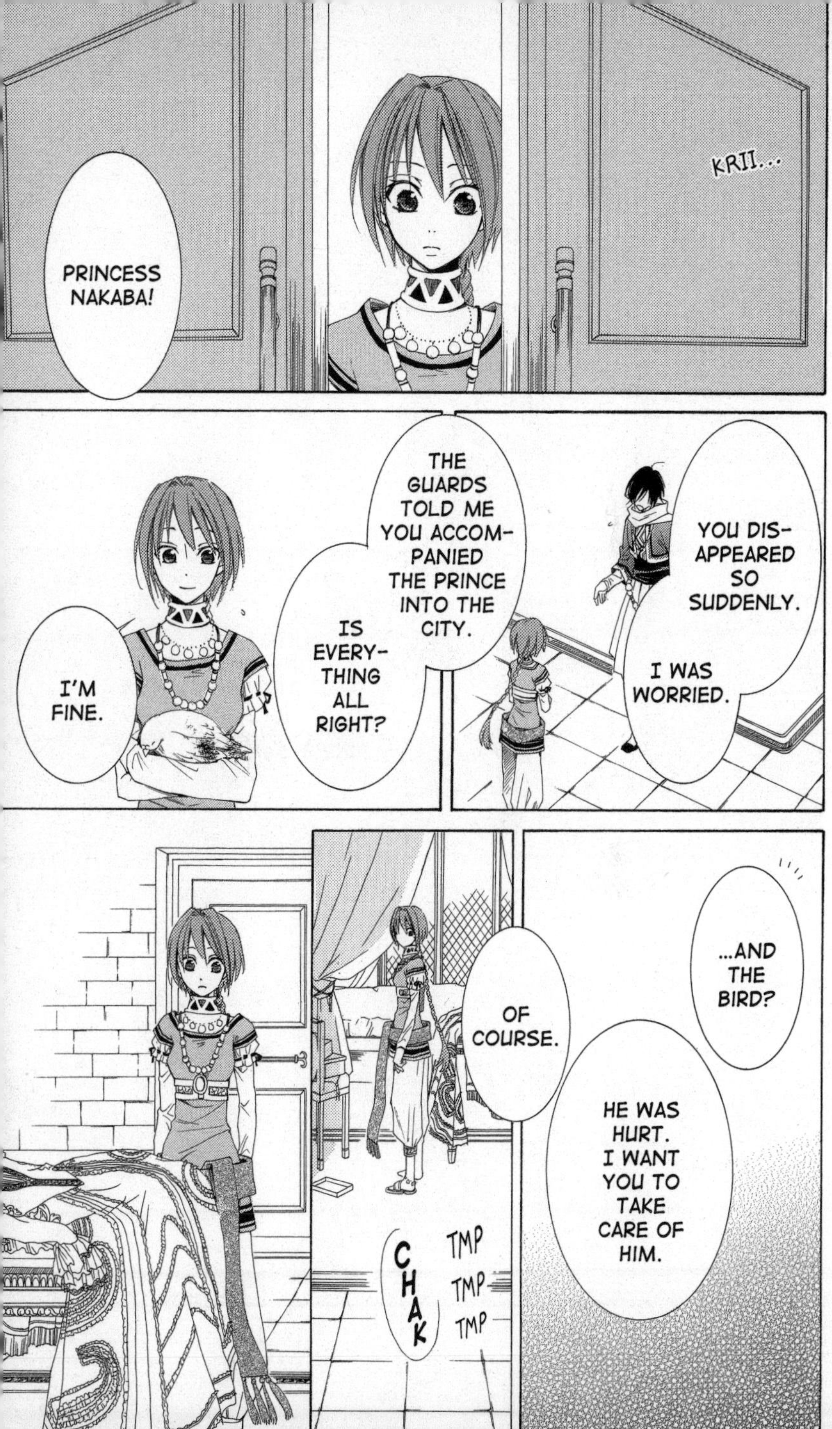
KRII...
PRINCESS NAKABA!
YOU DIS-APPEARED SO SUDDENLY.
I WAS WORRIED.
THE GUARDS TOLD ME YOU ACCOM-PANIED THE PRINCE INTO THE CITY.
IS EVERY-THING ALL RIGHT?
I'M FINE.
...AND THE BIRD?
HE WAS HURT. I WANT YOU TO TAKE CARE OF HIM.
OF COURSE.
TMP TMP TMP
CHAK

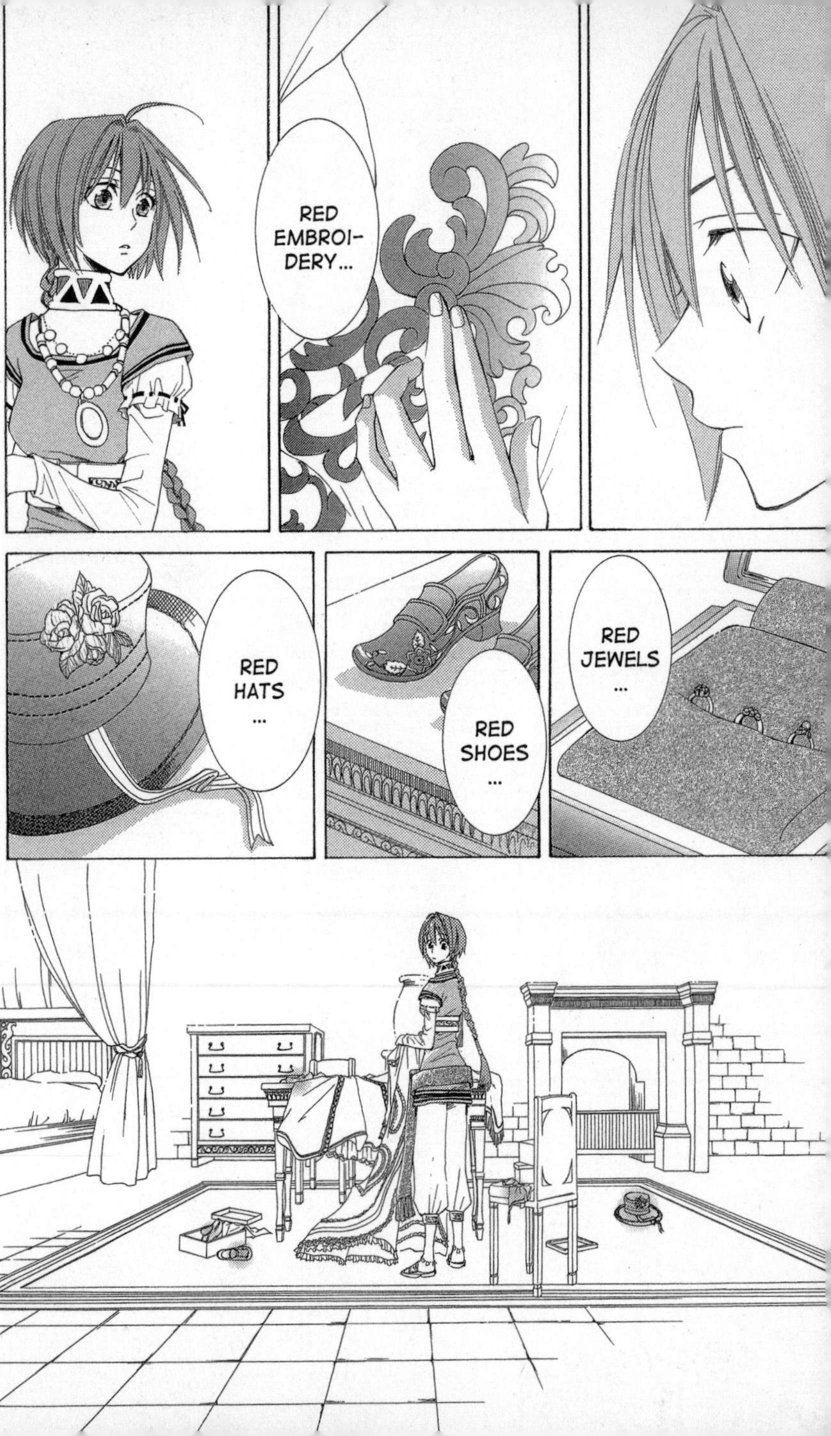
RED EMBROI-DERY...
RED JEWELS ...
RED SHOES ...
RED HATS ...

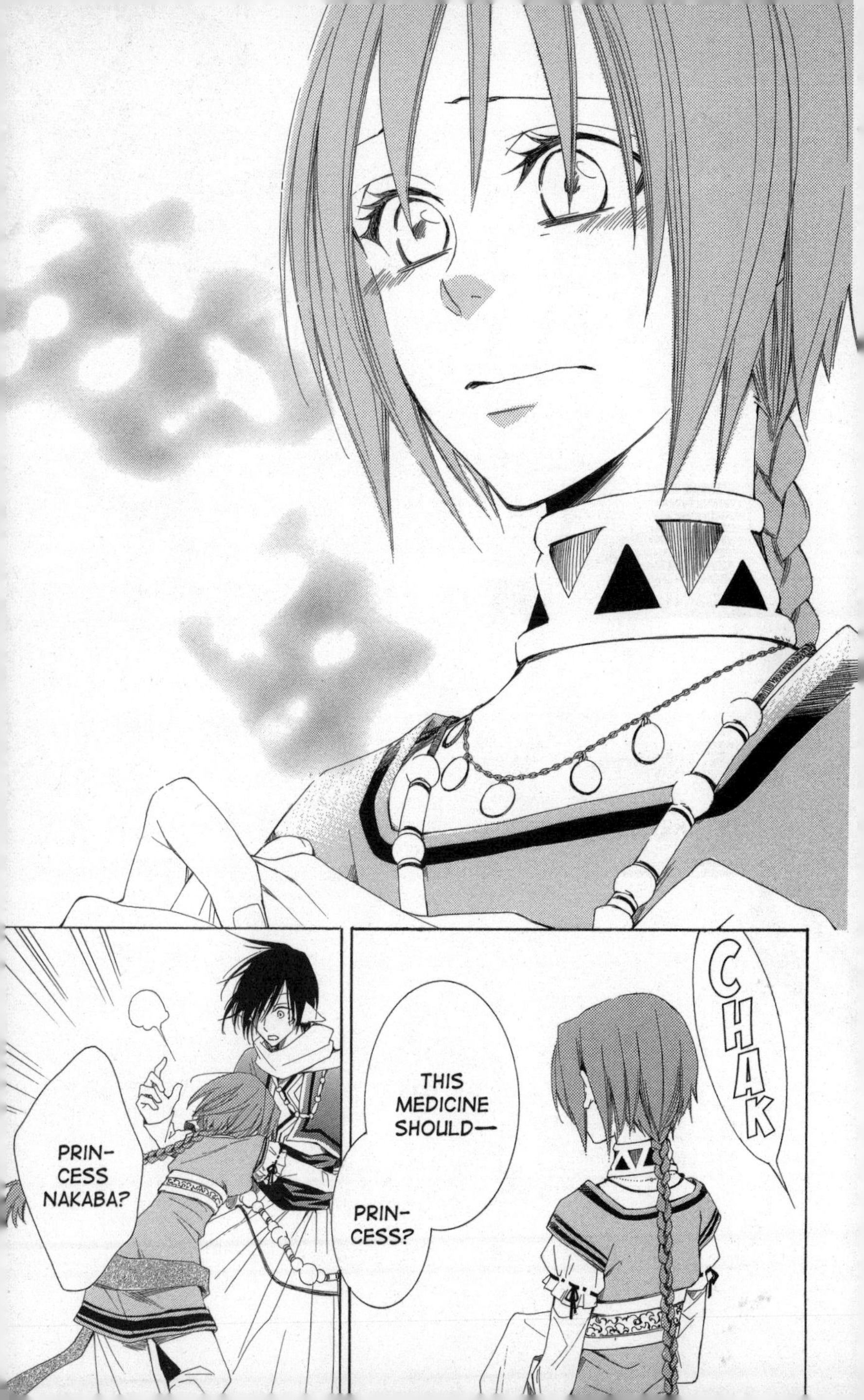
CHAK
THIS MEDICINE SHOULD—
PRIN-CESS?
PRIN-CESS NAKABA?

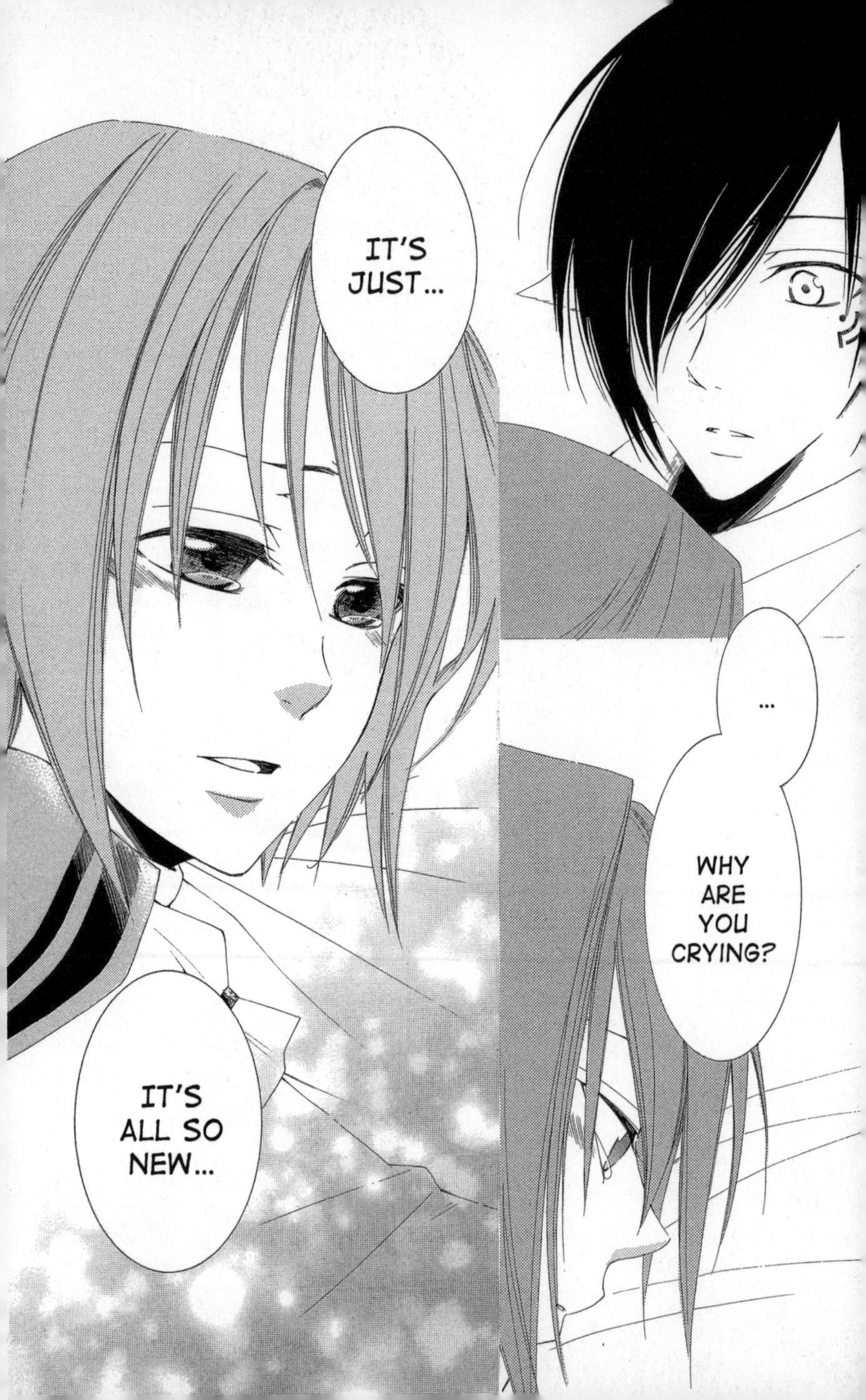
...
WHY ARE YOU CRYING?
IT'S JUST...
IT'S ALL SO NEW...

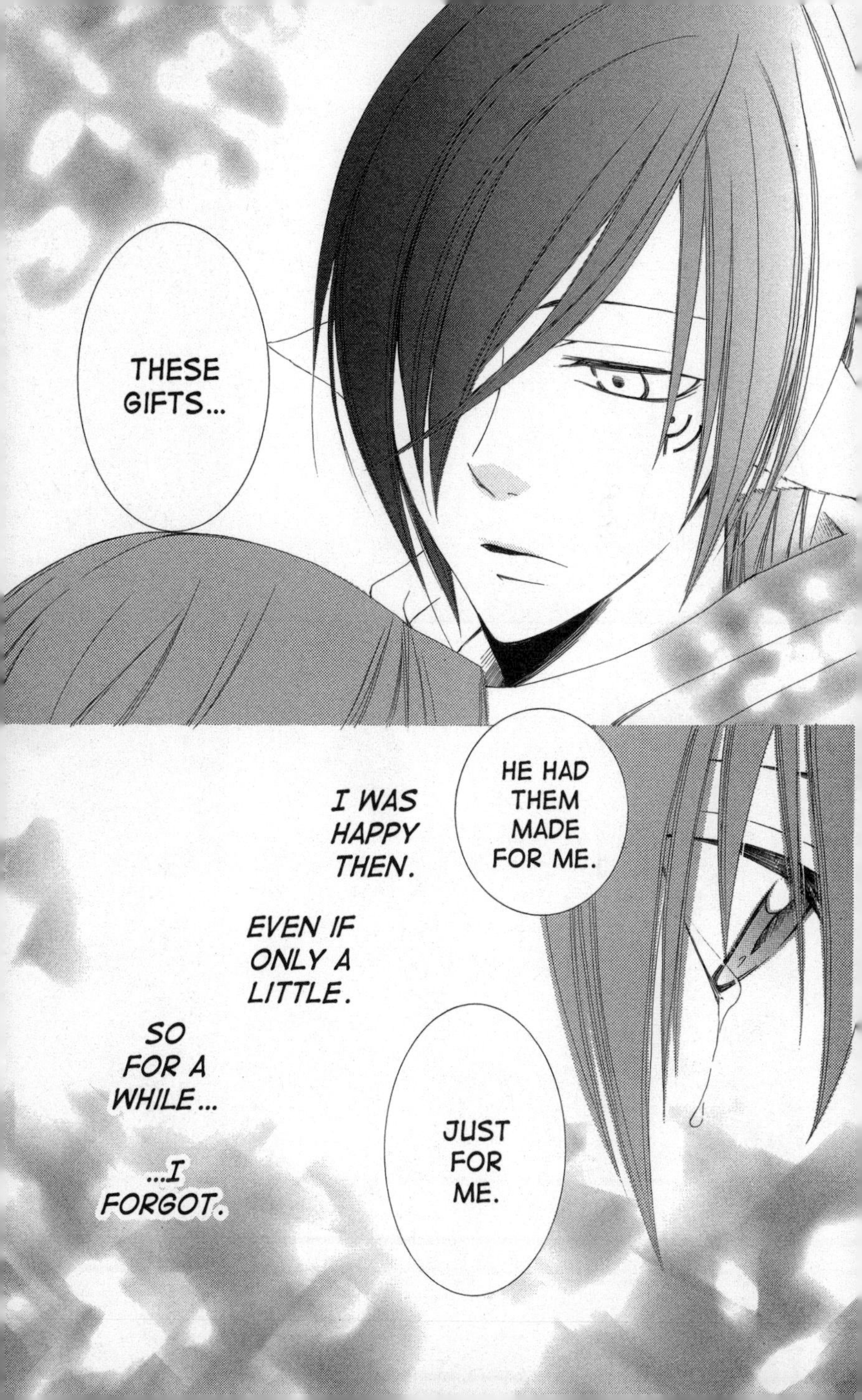
THESE GIFTS...
HE HAD THEM MADE FOR ME.
I WAS HAPPY THEN.
EVEN IF ONLY A LITTLE.
SO FOR A WHILE...
JUST FOR ME.
...I FORGOT.

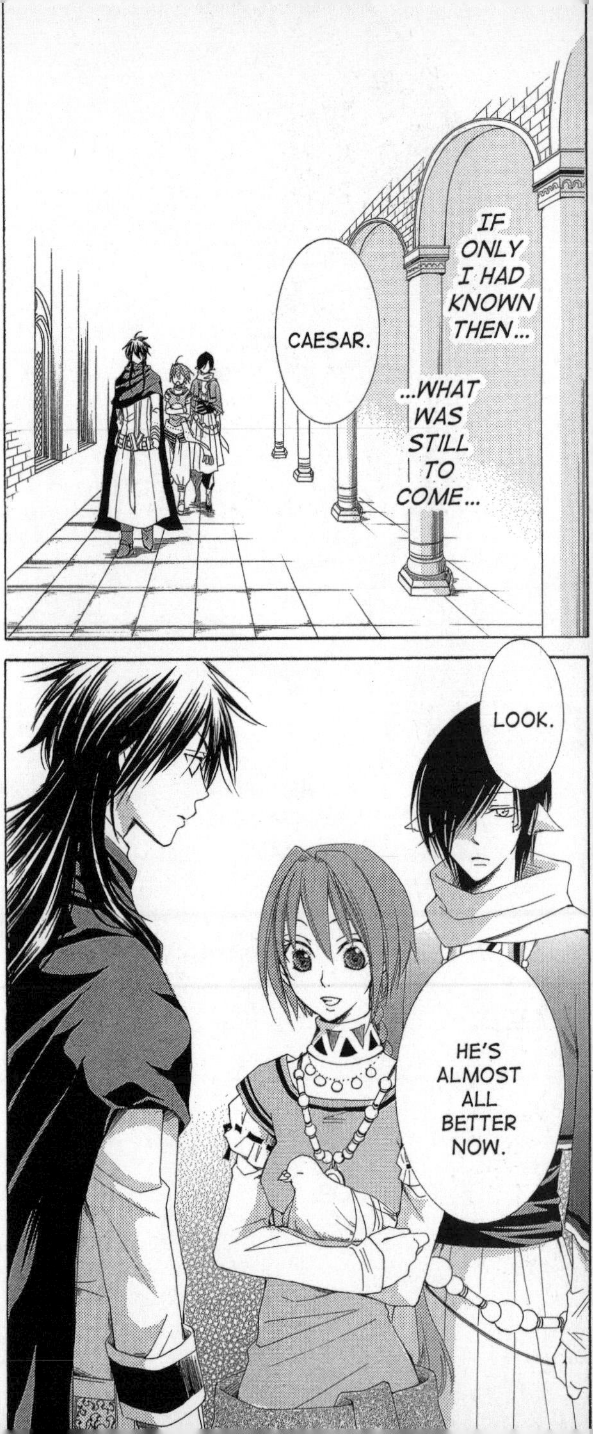
IF ONLY I HAD KNOWN THEN...
...WHAT WAS STILL TO COME...
CAESAR.
LOOK.
HE'S ALMOST ALL BETTER NOW.

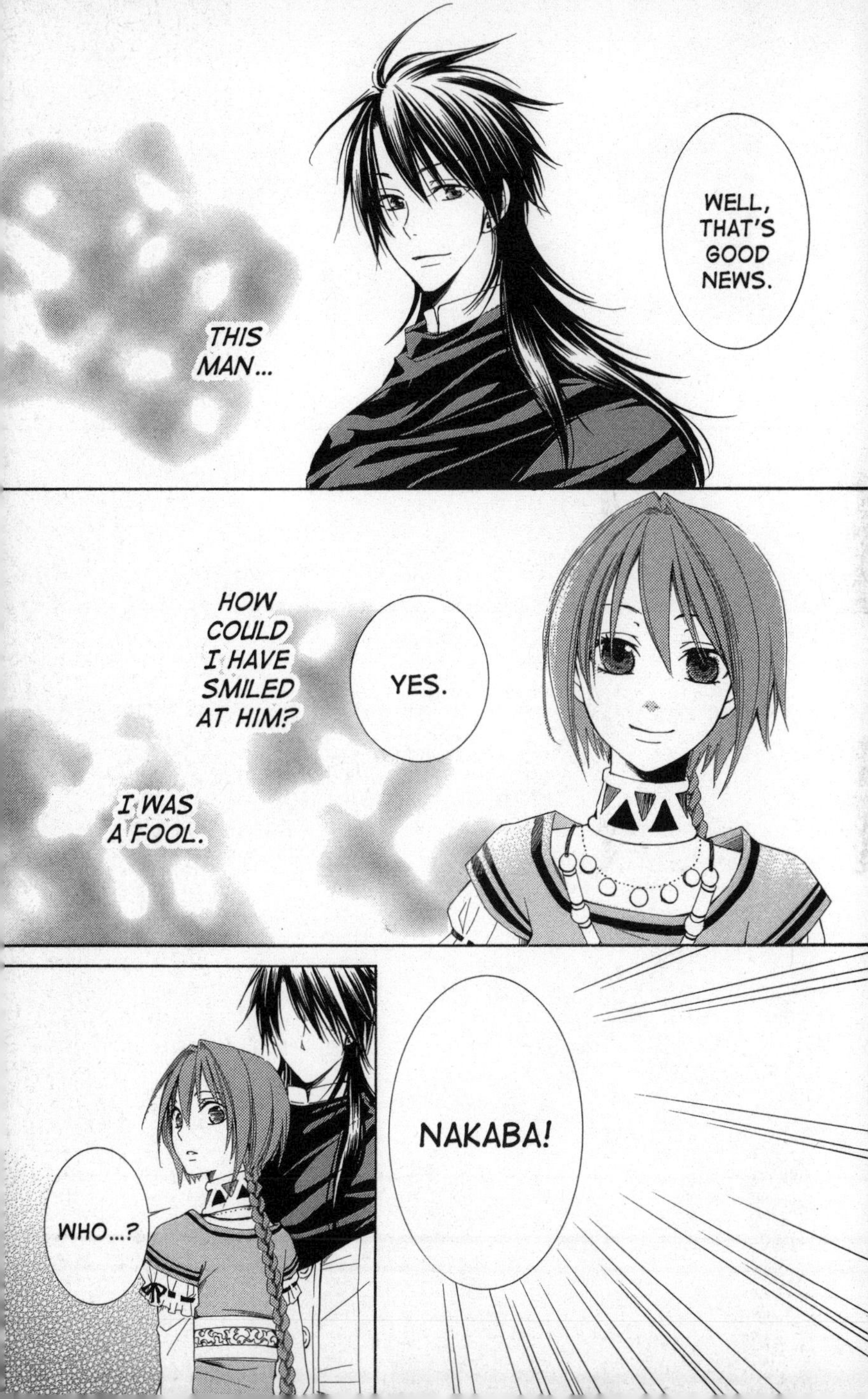

WELL, THAT'S GOOD NEWS.
THIS MAN...
YES.
HOW COULD I HAVE SMILED AT HIM?
I WAS A FOOL.
NAKABA!
WHO...?

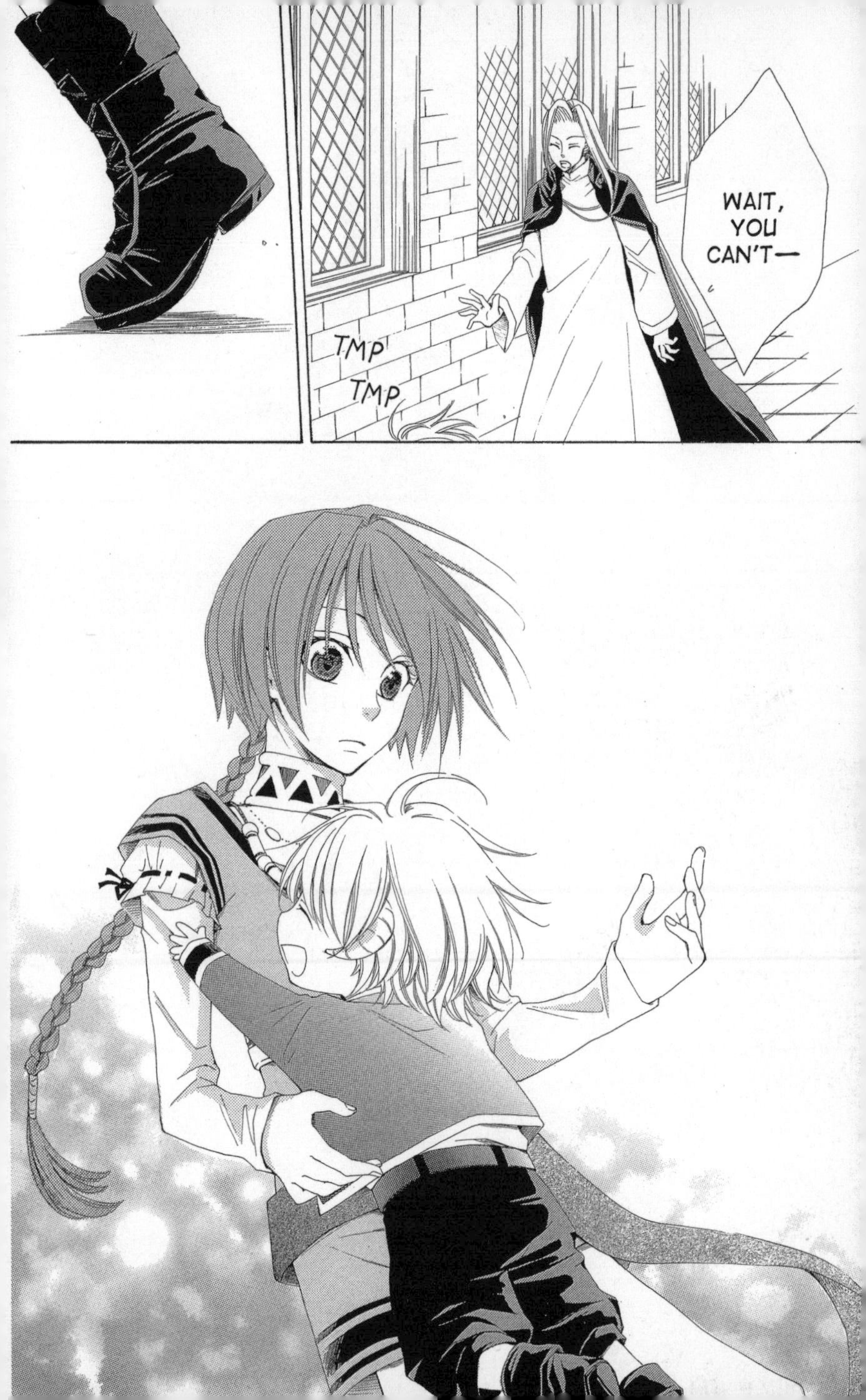
WAIT, YOU CAN'T—
TMP
TMP

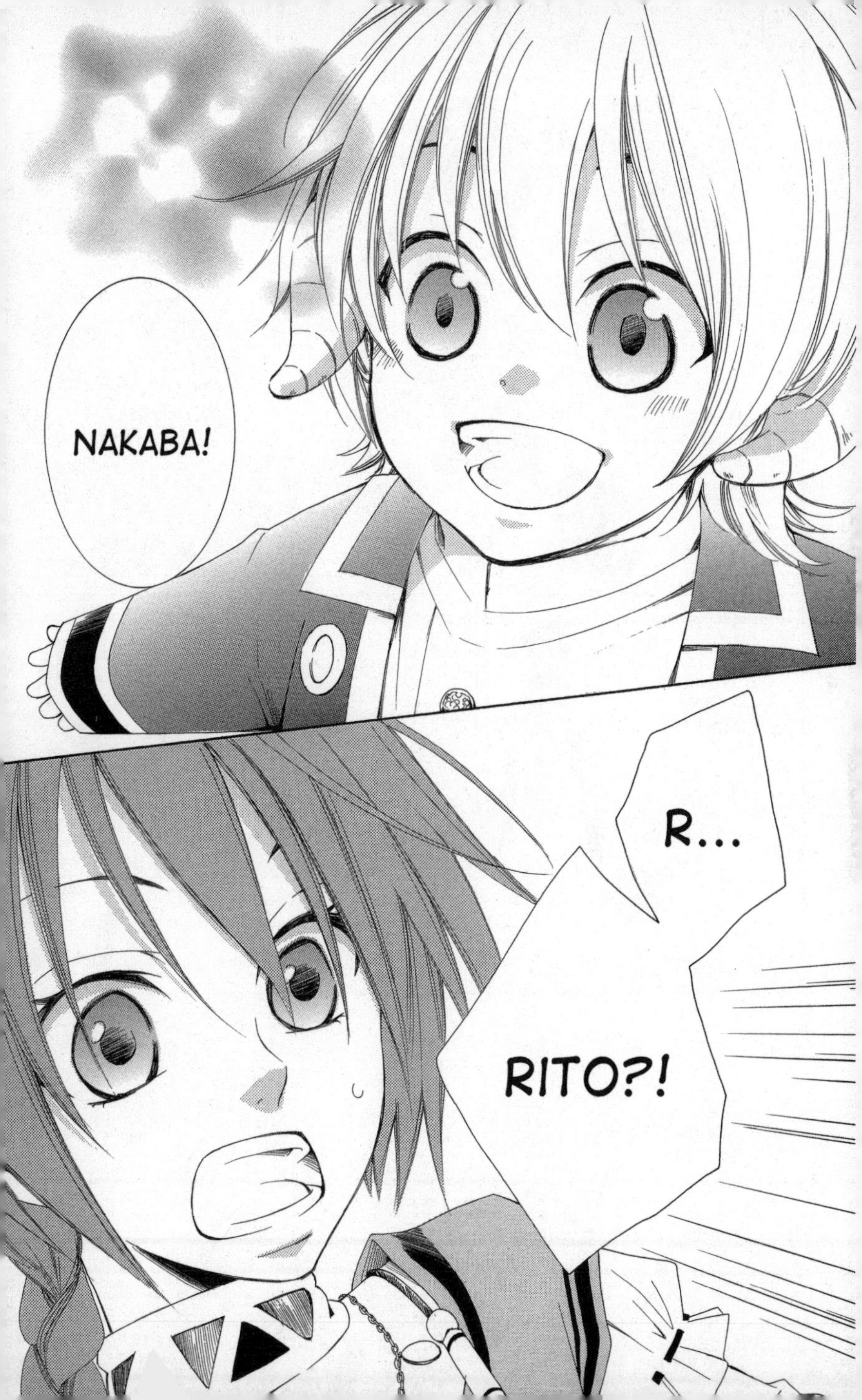
NAKABA!
R...
RITO?!

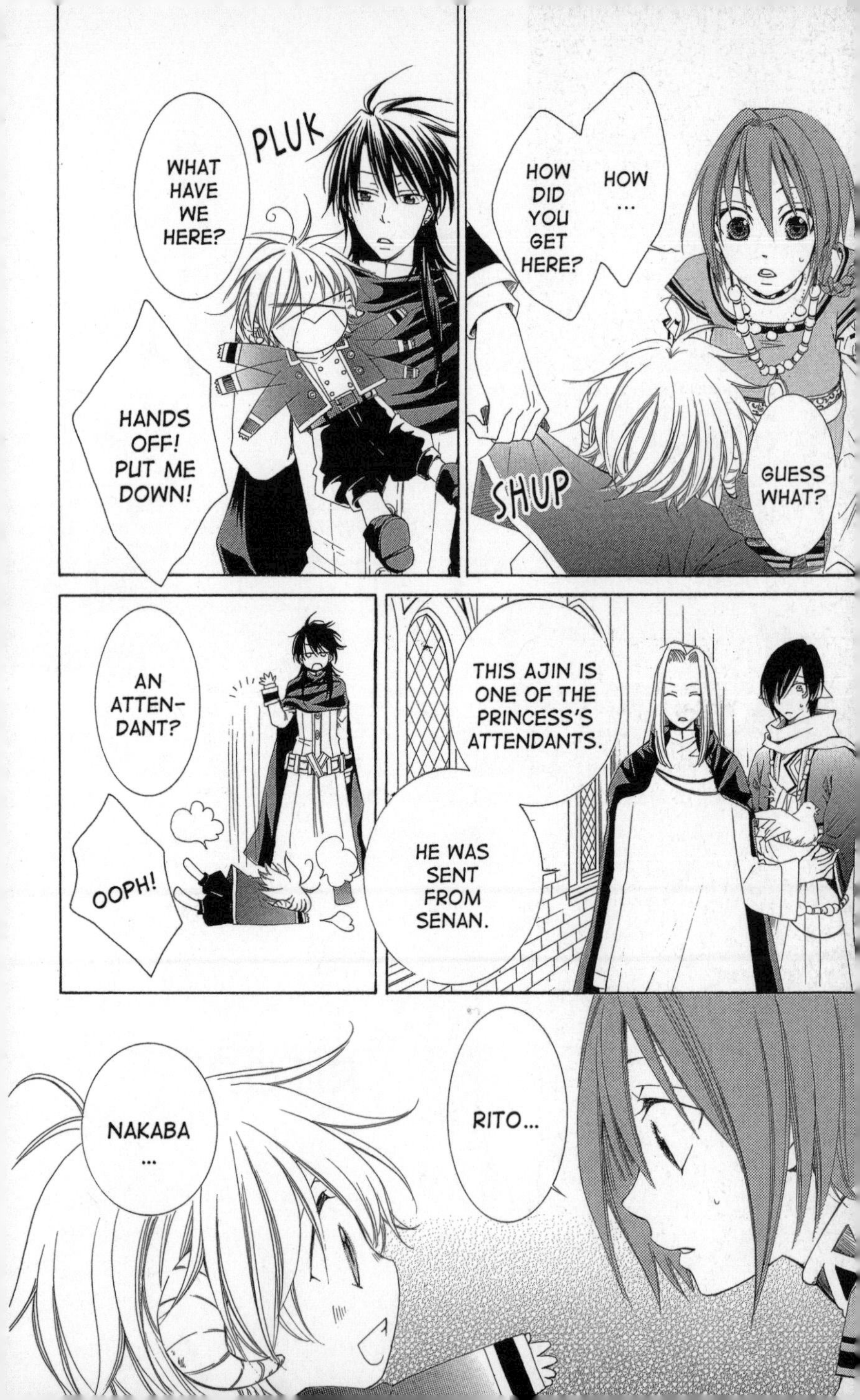
HOW...
HOW DID YOU GET HERE?
GUESS WHAT?
SHUP
PLUK
WHAT HAVE WE HERE?
HANDS OFF! PUT ME DOWN!
THIS AJIN IS ONE OF THE PRINCESS'S ATTENDANTS.
HE WAS SENT FROM SENAN.
AN ATTENDANT?
OOPH!
RITO...
NAKABA...

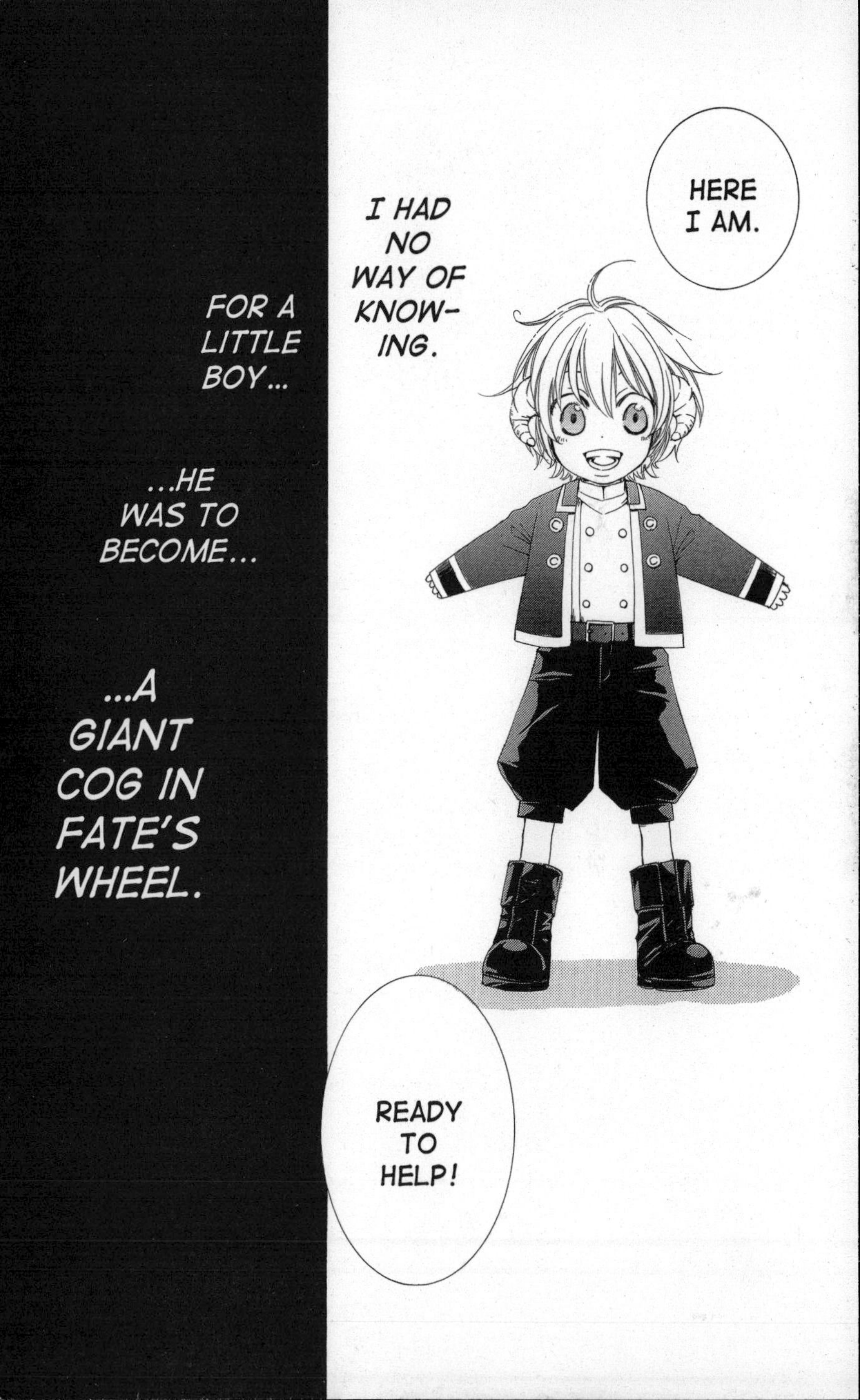
HERE I AM.
I HAD NO WAY OF KNOWING.
READY TO HELP!
FOR A LITTLE BOY...
...HE WAS TO BECOME...
...A GIANT COG IN FATE'S WHEEL.

Chapter 5

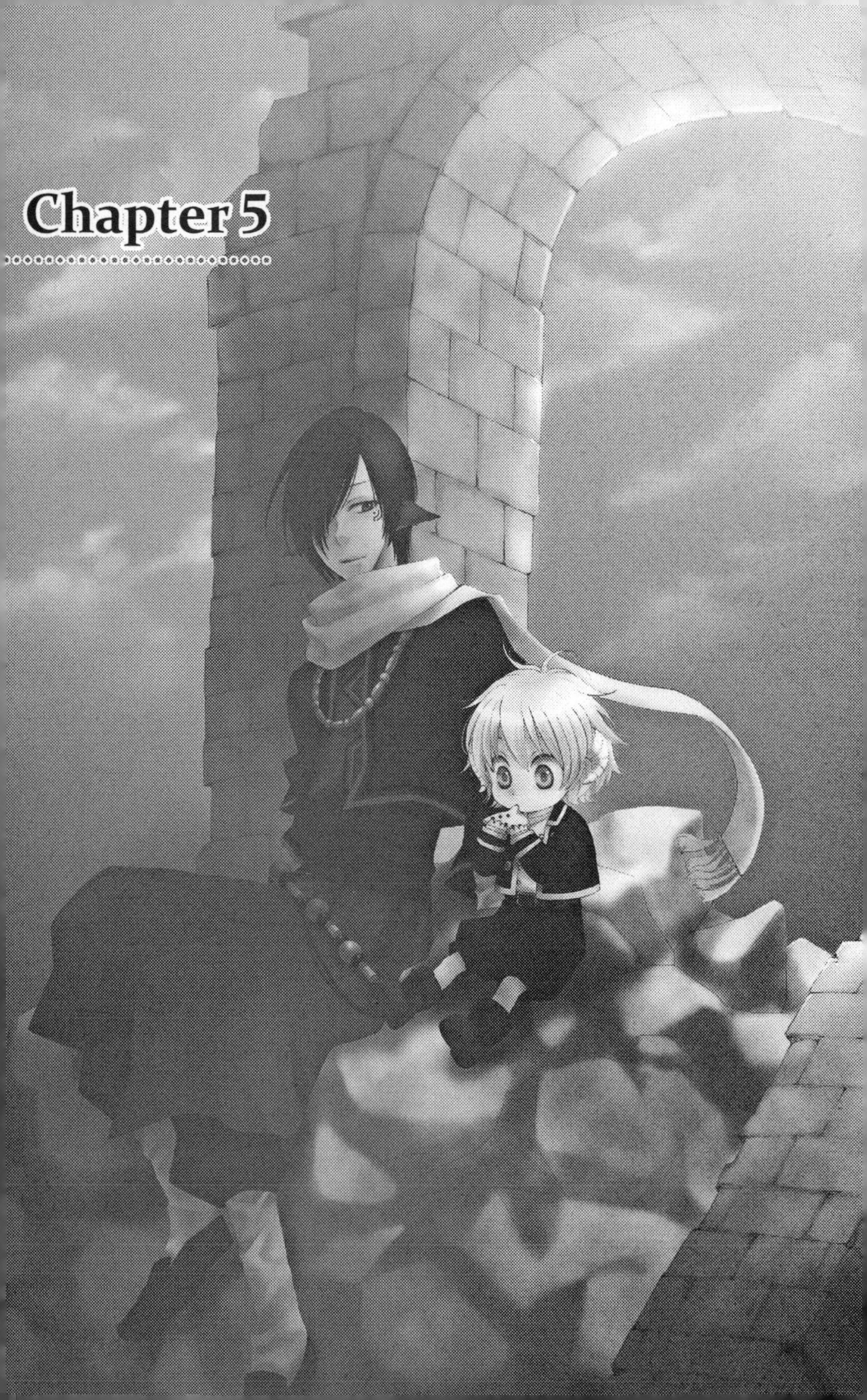

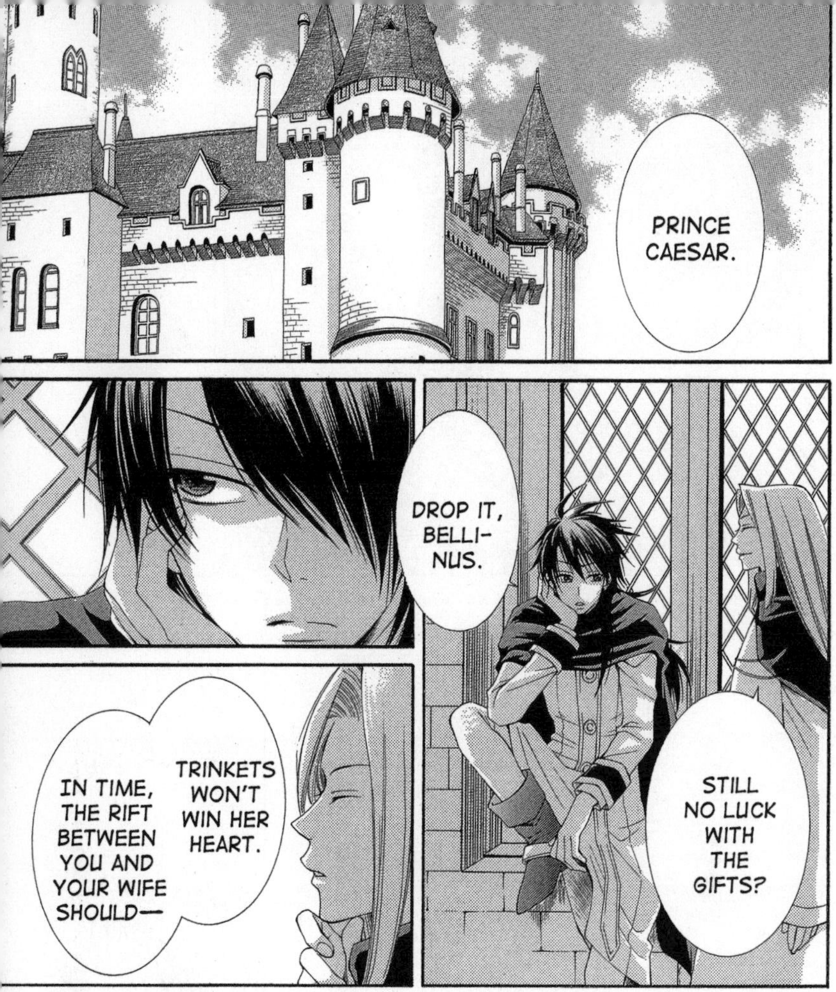
PRINCE CAESAR.
STILL NO LUCK WITH THE GIFTS?
DROP IT, BELLI-NUS.
TRINKETS WON'T WIN HER HEART.
IN TIME, THE RIFT BETWEEN YOU AND YOUR WIFE SHOULD—

Dawn of the Arcana

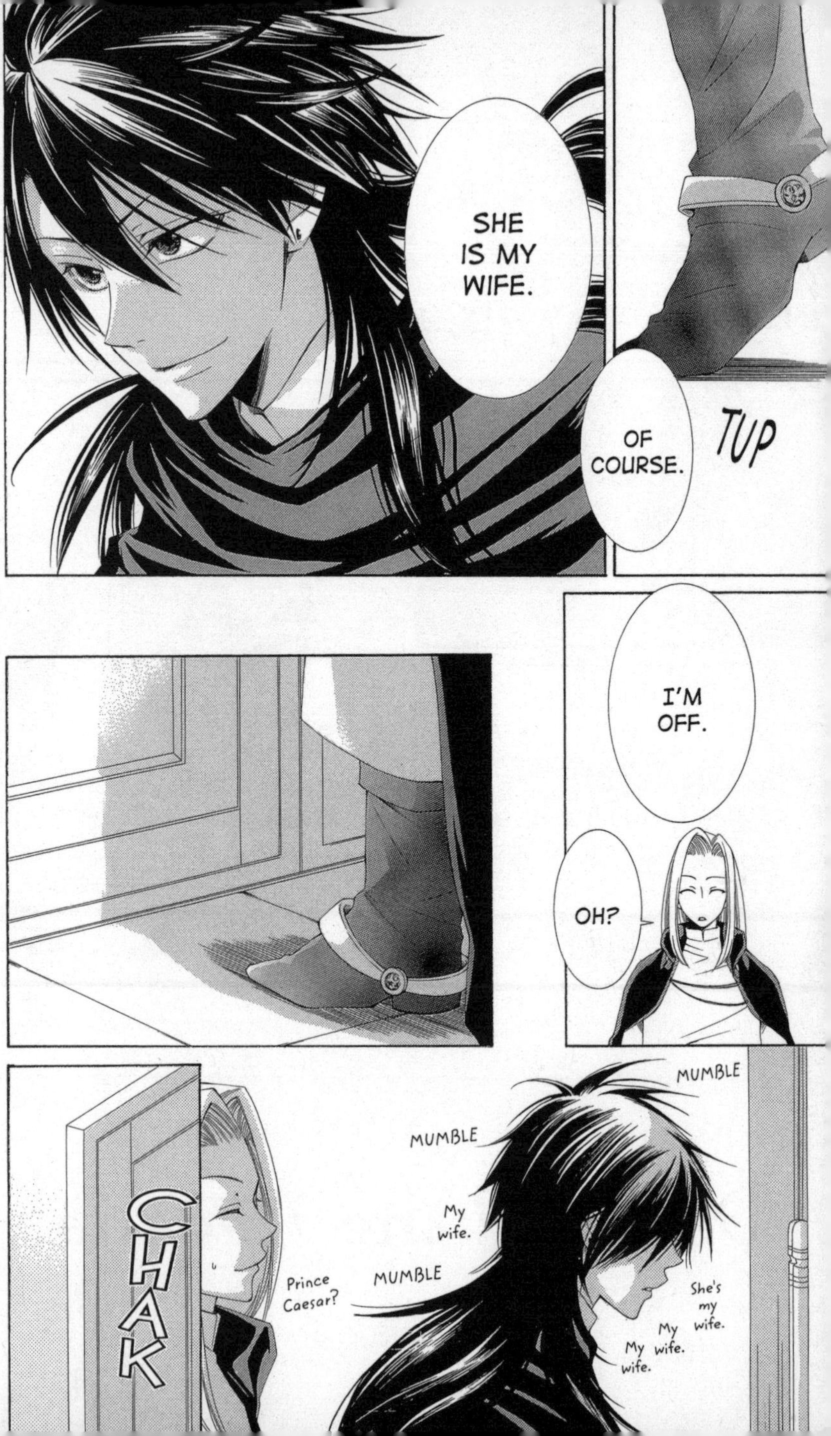
SHE IS MY WIFE.
OF COURSE.
TUP
I'M OFF.
OH?
MUMBLE
MUMBLE
My wife.
She's my wife.
My wife.
My wife.
MUMBLE
Prince Caesar?
CHAK

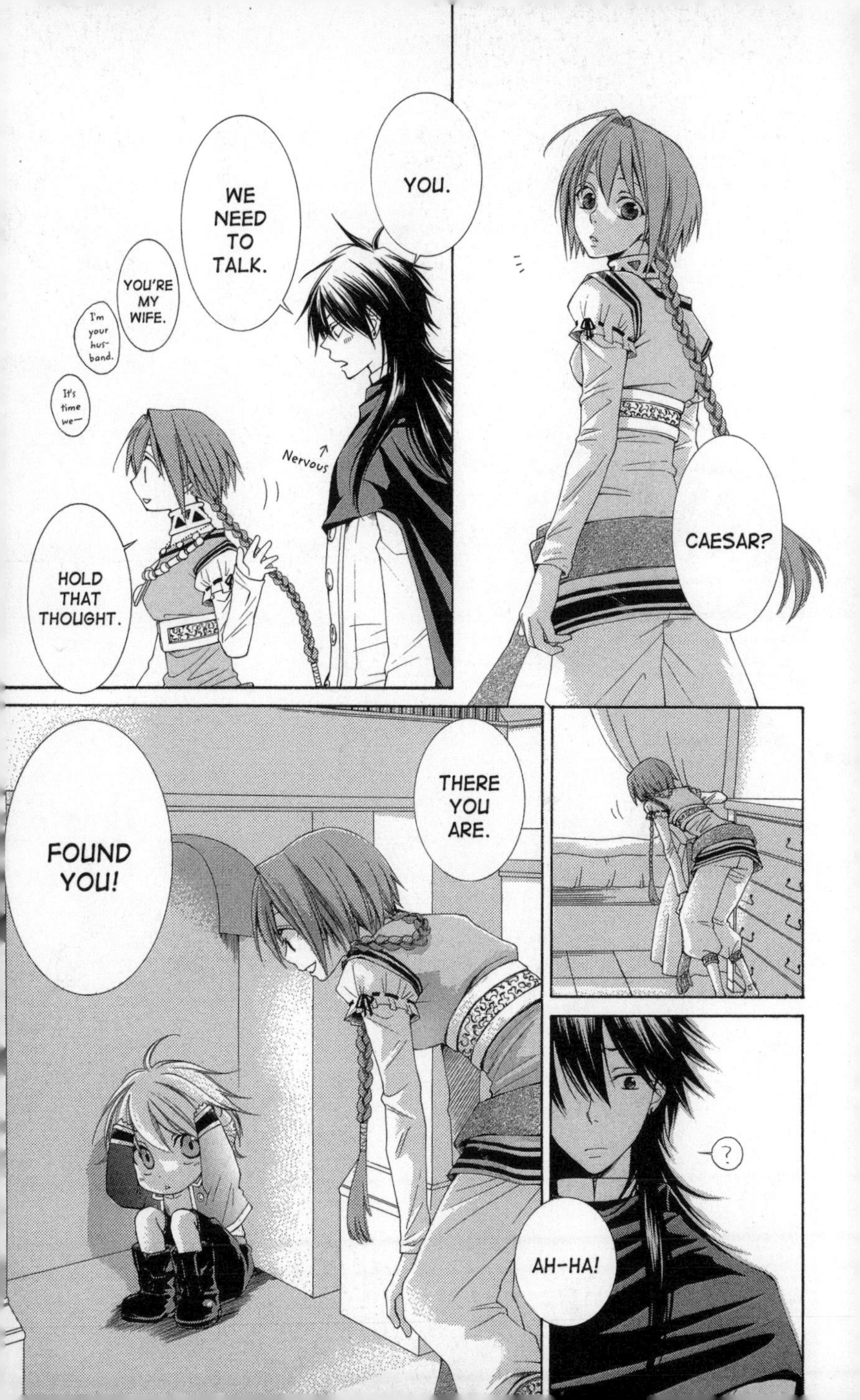
CAESAR?
YOU.
WE NEED TO TALK.
YOU'RE MY WIFE.
I'm your hus-band.
It's time we—
Nervous
HOLD THAT THOUGHT.
?
AH-HA!
THERE YOU ARE.
FOUND YOU!

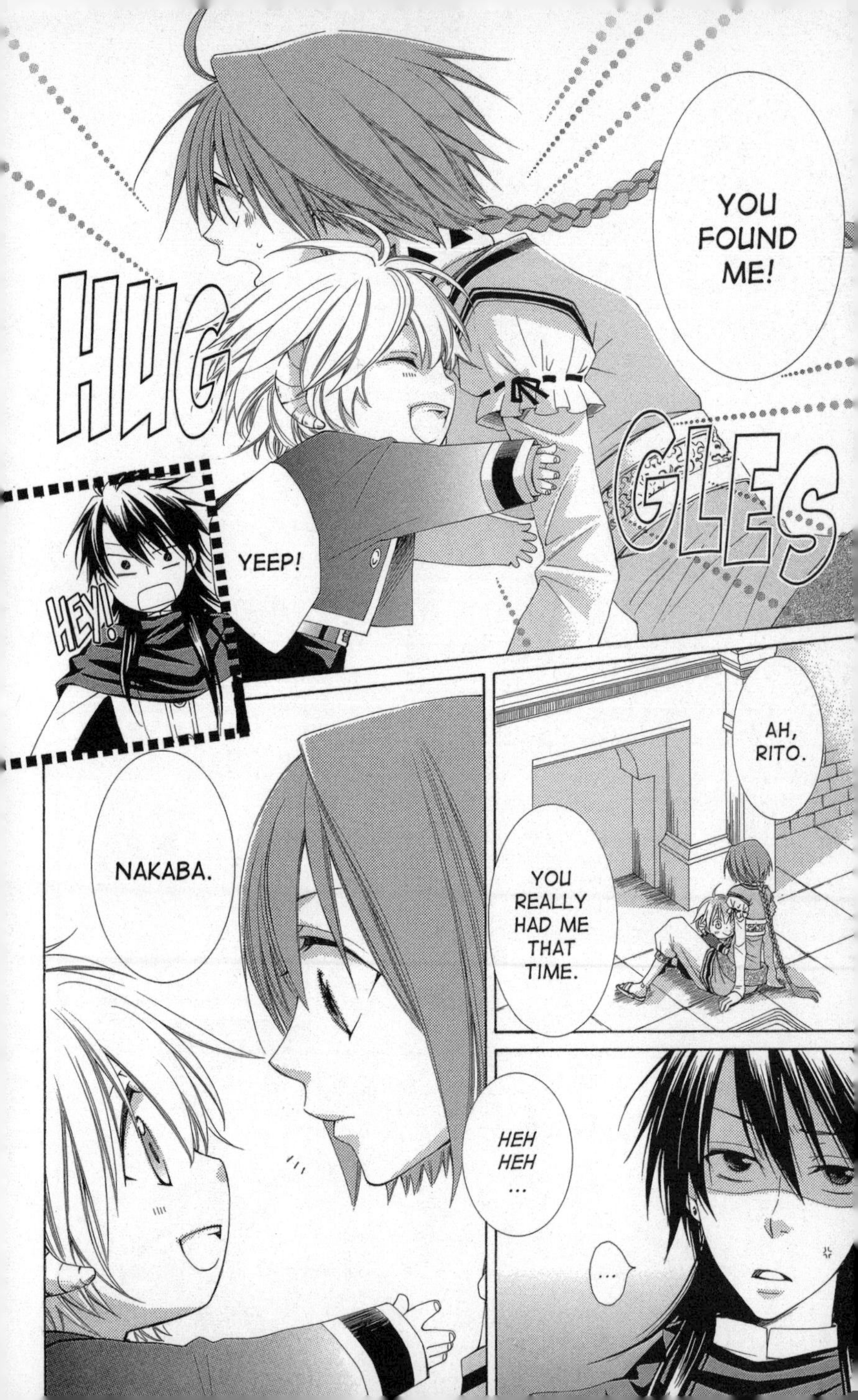
YOU FOUND ME!
HUG GLES
YEEP!
HEY!
AH, RITO.
YOU REALLY HAD ME THAT TIME.
HEH HEH ...
...
NAKABA.

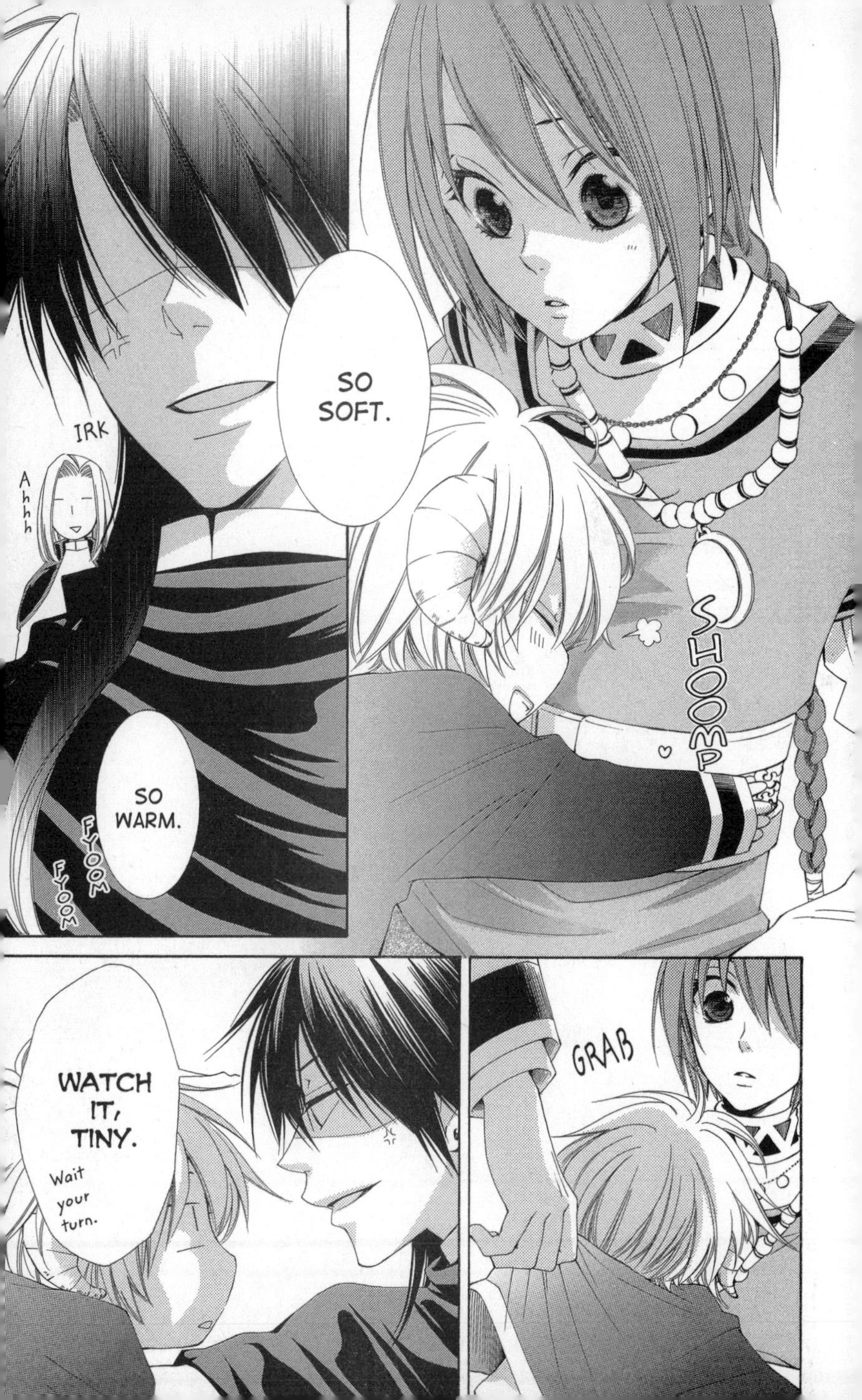
SHOOMP
SO SOFT.
IRK
Ahhh
SO WARM.
FYOOM FYOOM
GRAB
WATCH IT, TINY.
Wait your turn.

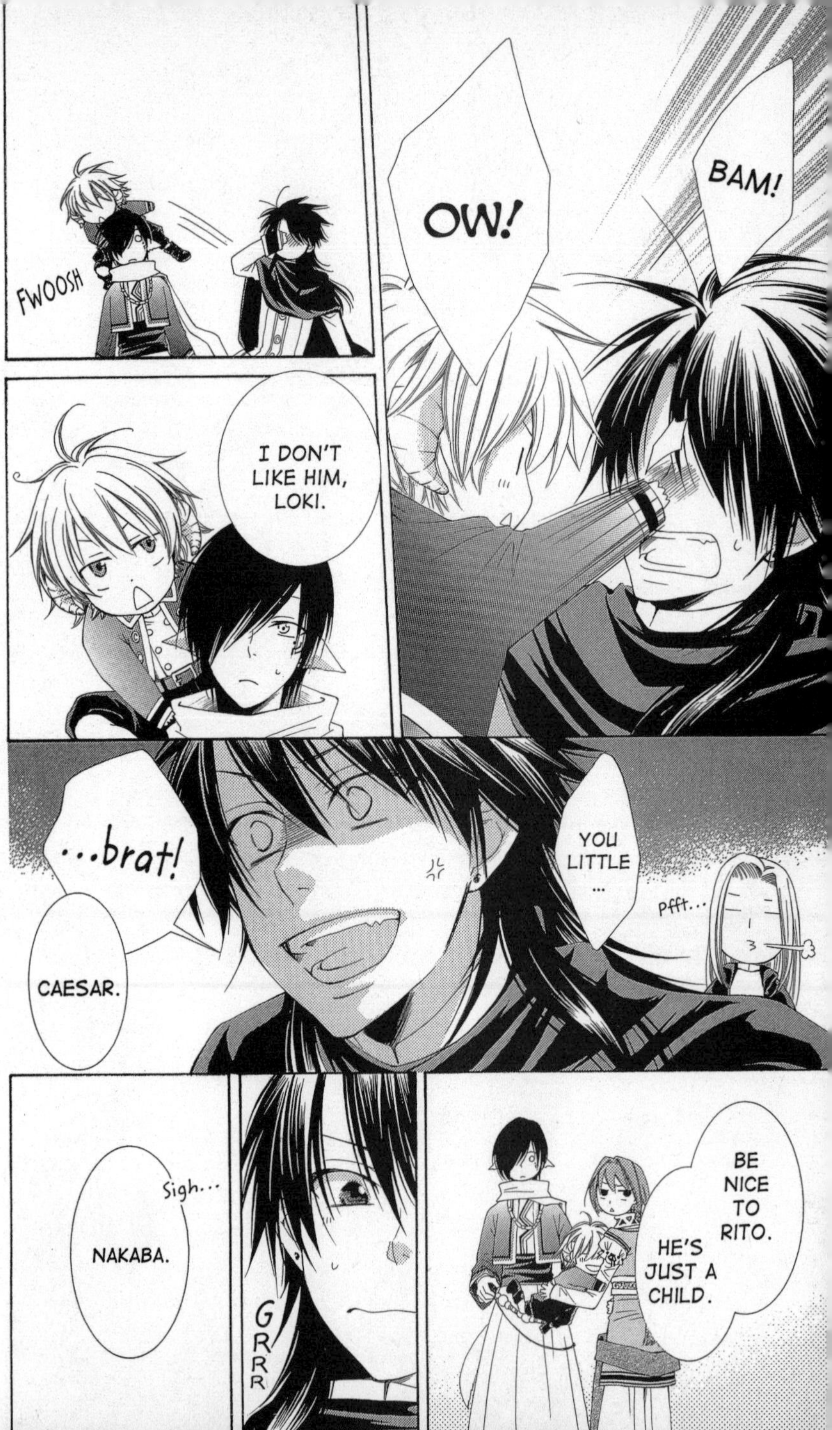
BAM!
OW!
FWOOSH
I DON'T LIKE HIM, LOKI.
YOU LITTLE ...
pfft...
...brat!
CAESAR.
BE NICE TO RITO.
HE'S JUST A CHILD.
GRRR
Sigh...
NAKABA.

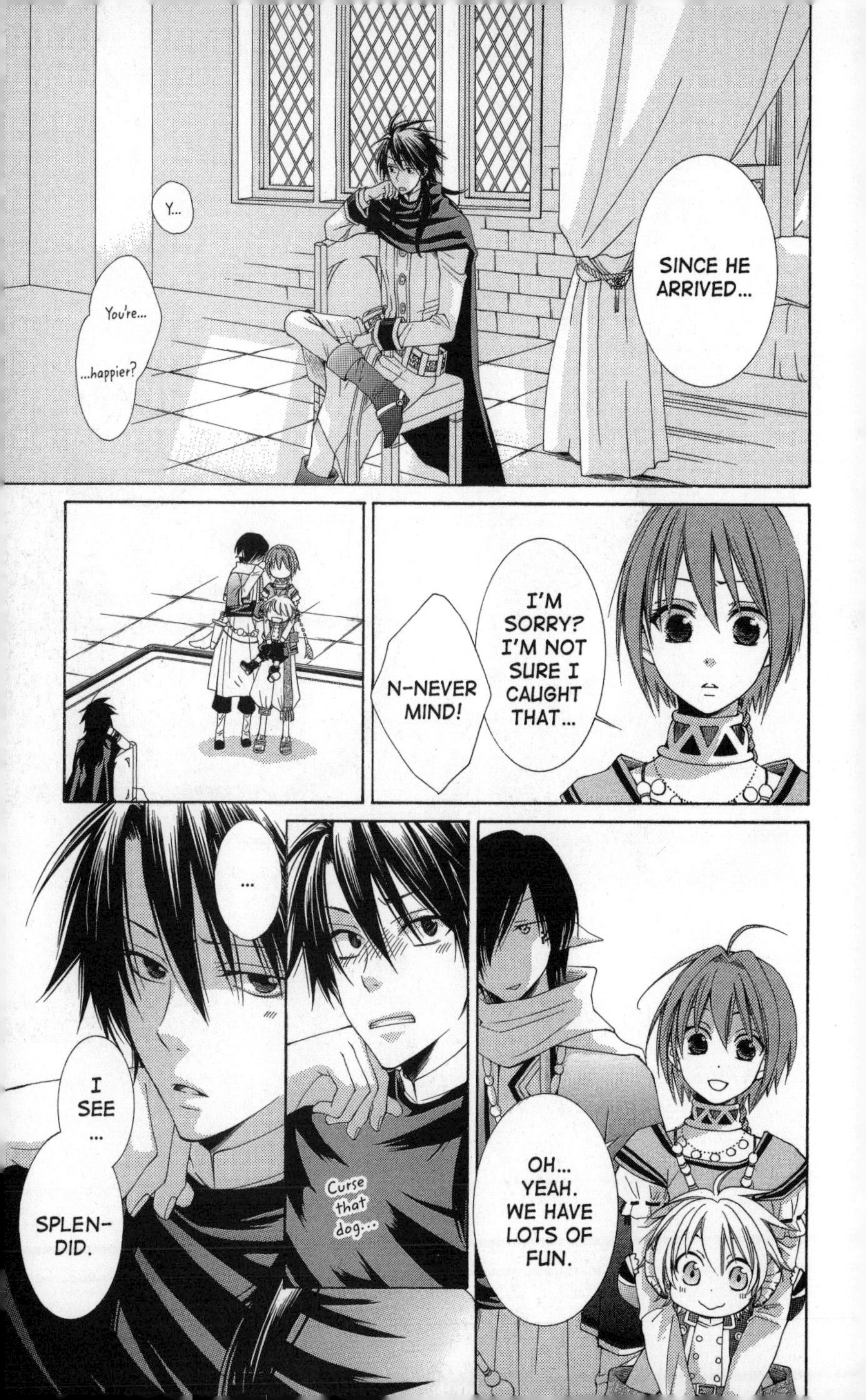
SINCE HE ARRIVED...
Y...
You're... ...happier?
I'M SORRY? I'M NOT SURE I CAUGHT THAT...
N-NEVER MIND!
OH... YEAH. WE HAVE LOTS OF FUN.
Curse that dog...
...
I SEE ...
SPLEN-DID.

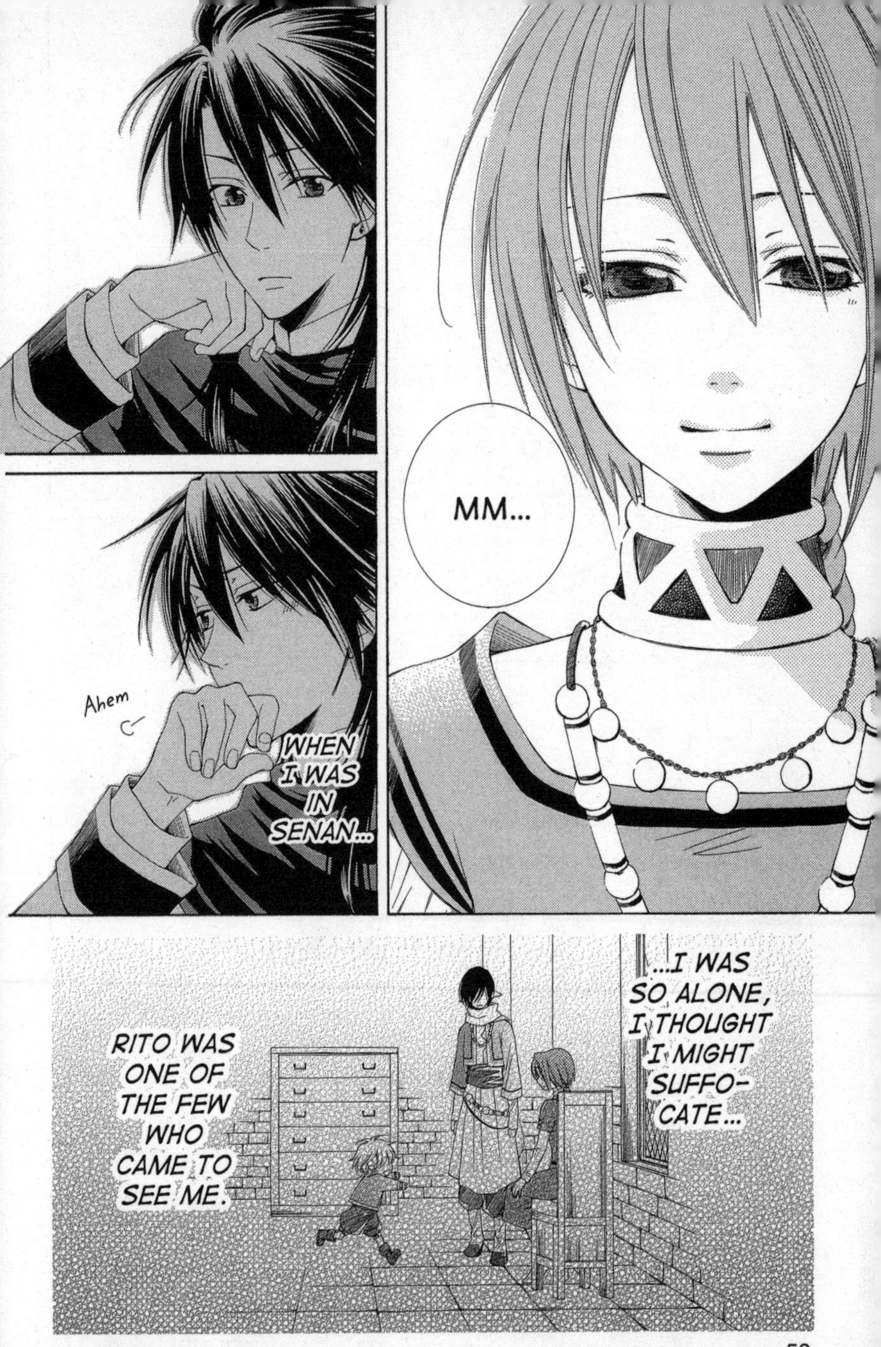
MM...
Ahem
WHEN I WAS IN SENAN...
...I WAS SO ALONE, I THOUGHT I MIGHT SUFFO-CATE...
RITO WAS ONE OF THE FEW WHO CAME TO SEE ME.

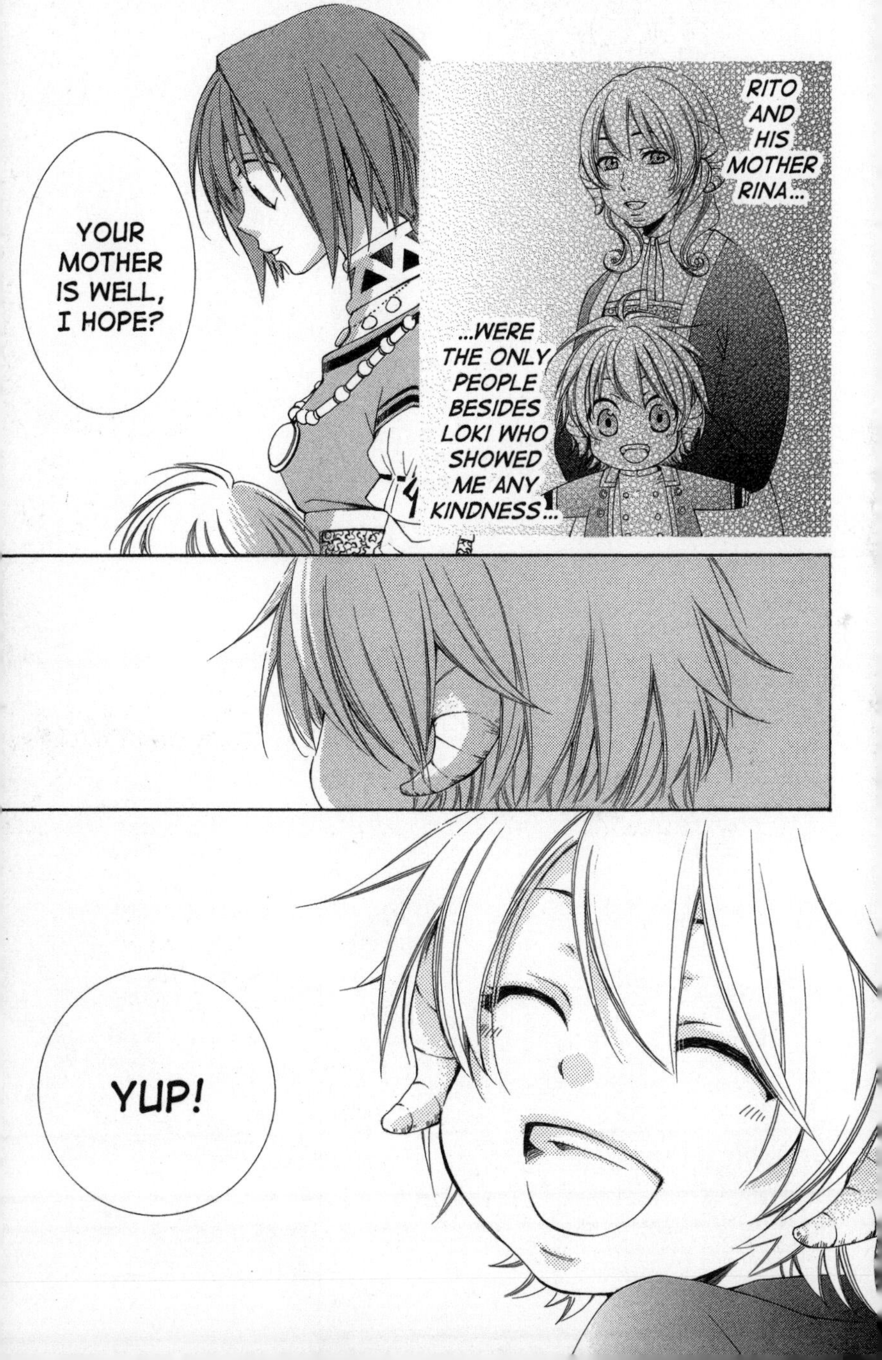
RITO AND HIS MOTHER RINA...
...WERE THE ONLY PEOPLE BESIDES LOKI WHO SHOWED ME ANY KINDNESS...
YOUR MOTHER IS WELL, I HOPE?
YUP!

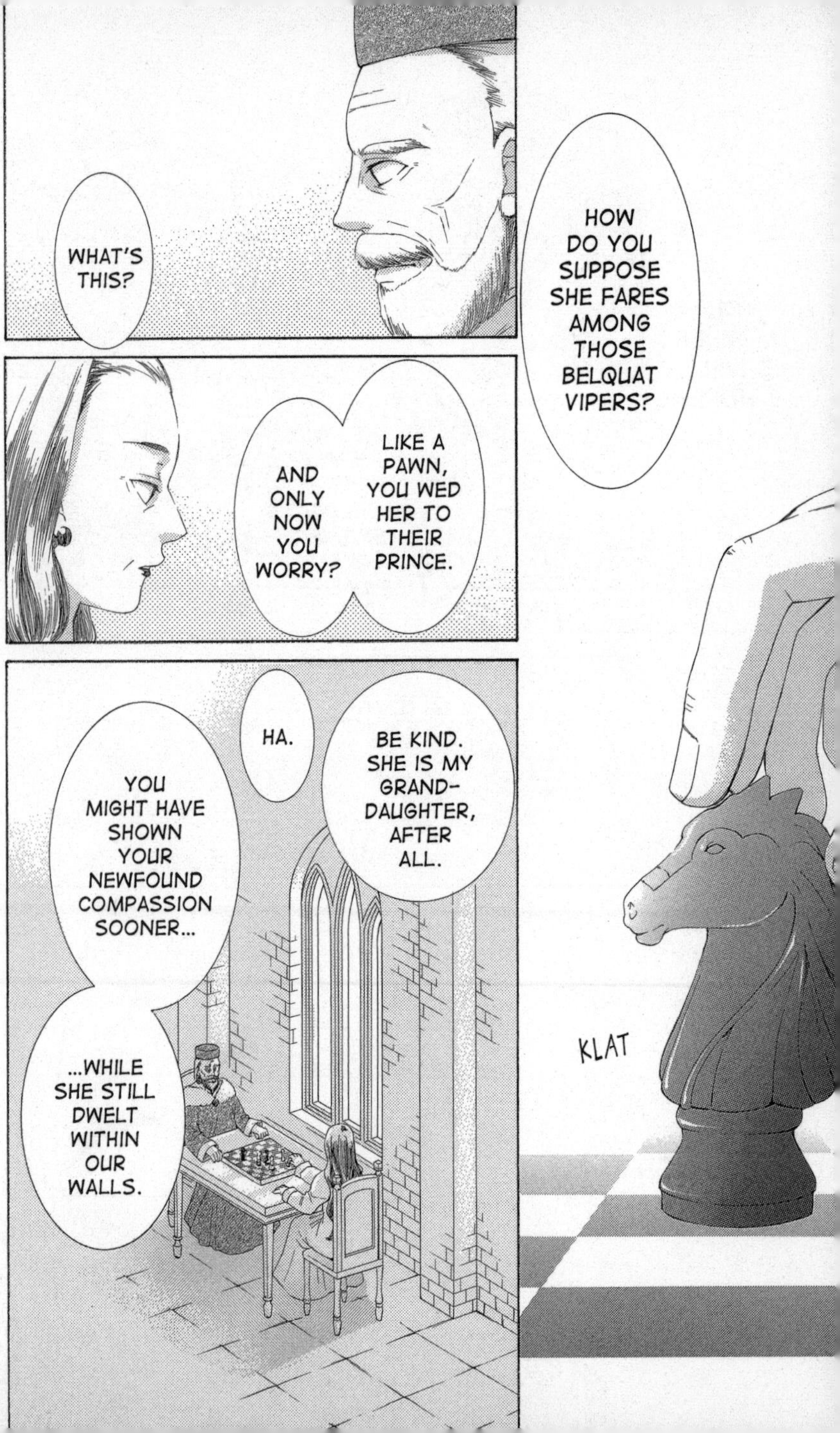
HOW DO YOU SUPPOSE SHE FARES AMONG THOSE BELQUAT VIPERS?
KLAT
WHAT'S THIS?
LIKE A PAWN, YOU WED HER TO THEIR PRINCE.
AND ONLY NOW YOU WORRY?
BE KIND. SHE IS MY GRAND-DAUGHTER, AFTER ALL.
HA.
YOU MIGHT HAVE SHOWN YOUR NEWFOUND COMPASSION SOONER...
...WHILE SHE STILL DWELT WITHIN OUR WALLS.

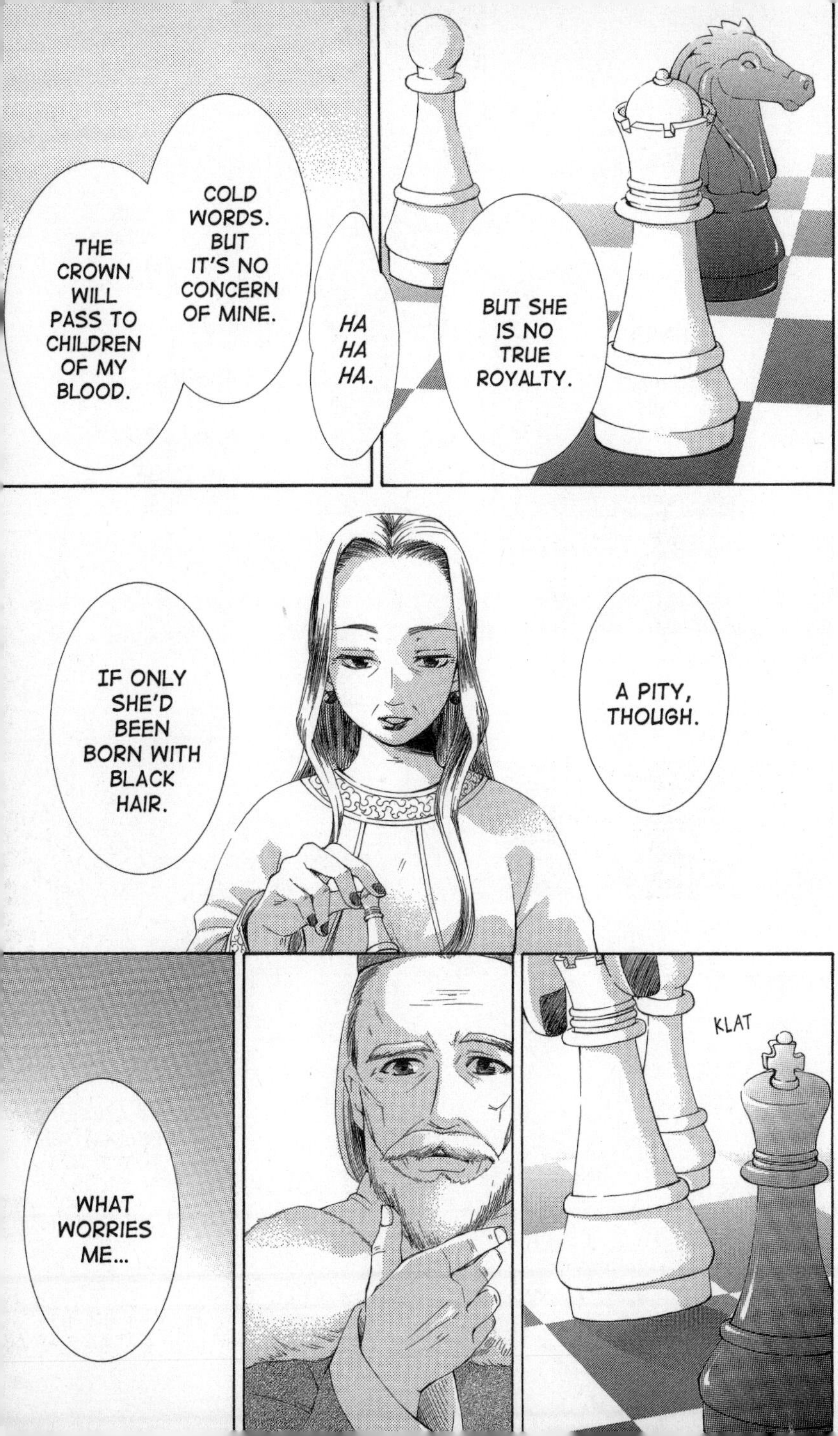
BUT SHE IS NO TRUE ROYALTY.
HA HA HA.
COLD WORDS. BUT IT'S NO CONCERN OF MINE.
THE CROWN WILL PASS TO CHILDREN OF MY BLOOD.
A PITY, THOUGH.
IF ONLY SHE'D BEEN BORN WITH BLACK HAIR.
KLAT
WHAT WORRIES ME...

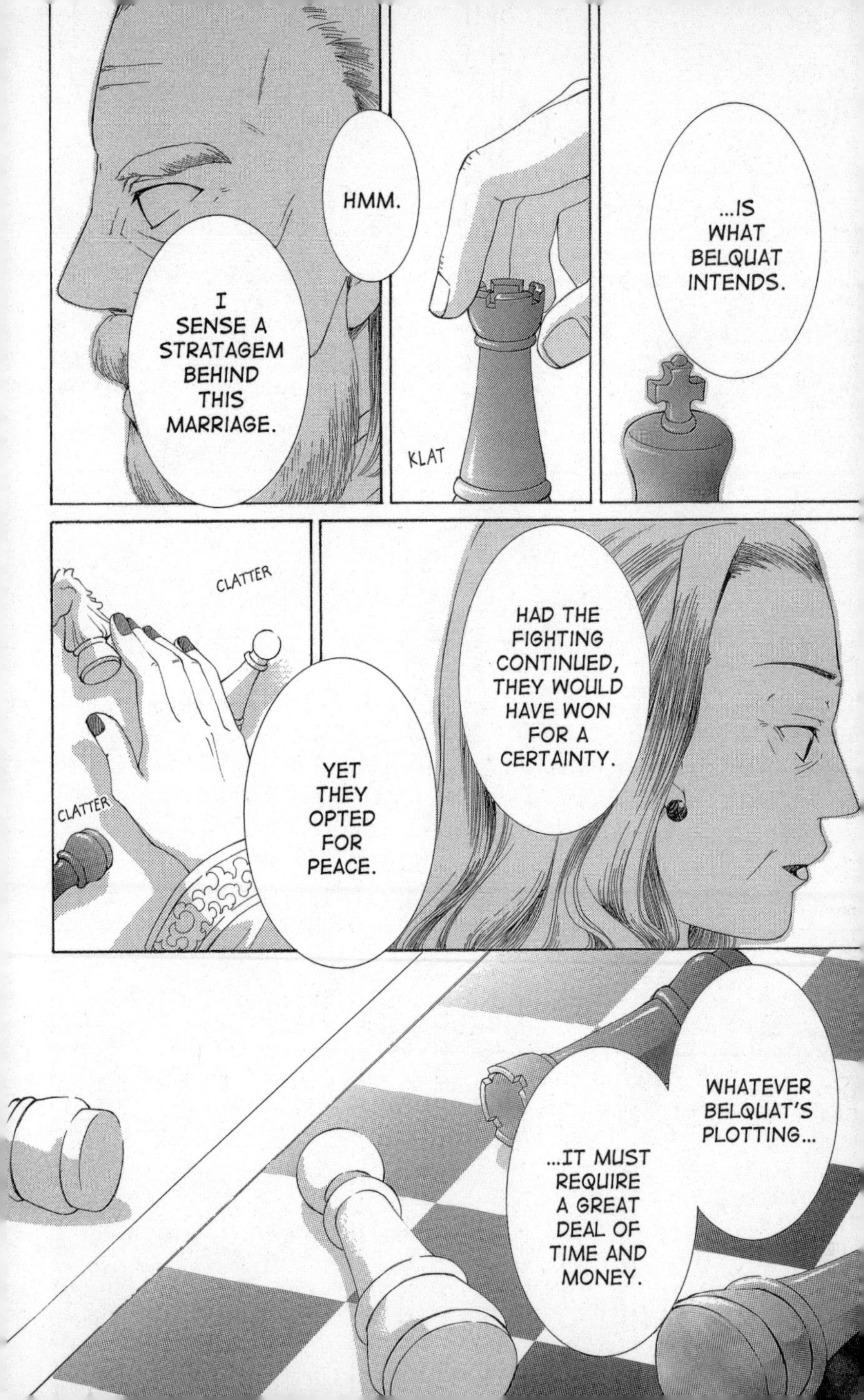
...IS WHAT BELQUAT INTENDS.
HMM.
KLAT
I SENSE A STRATAGEM BEHIND THIS MARRIAGE.
HAD THE FIGHTING CONTINUED, THEY WOULD HAVE WON FOR A CERTAINTY.
YET THEY OPTED FOR PEACE.
CLATTER
CLATTER
WHATEVER BELQUAT'S PLOTTING...
...IT MUST REQUIRE A GREAT DEAL OF TIME AND MONEY.

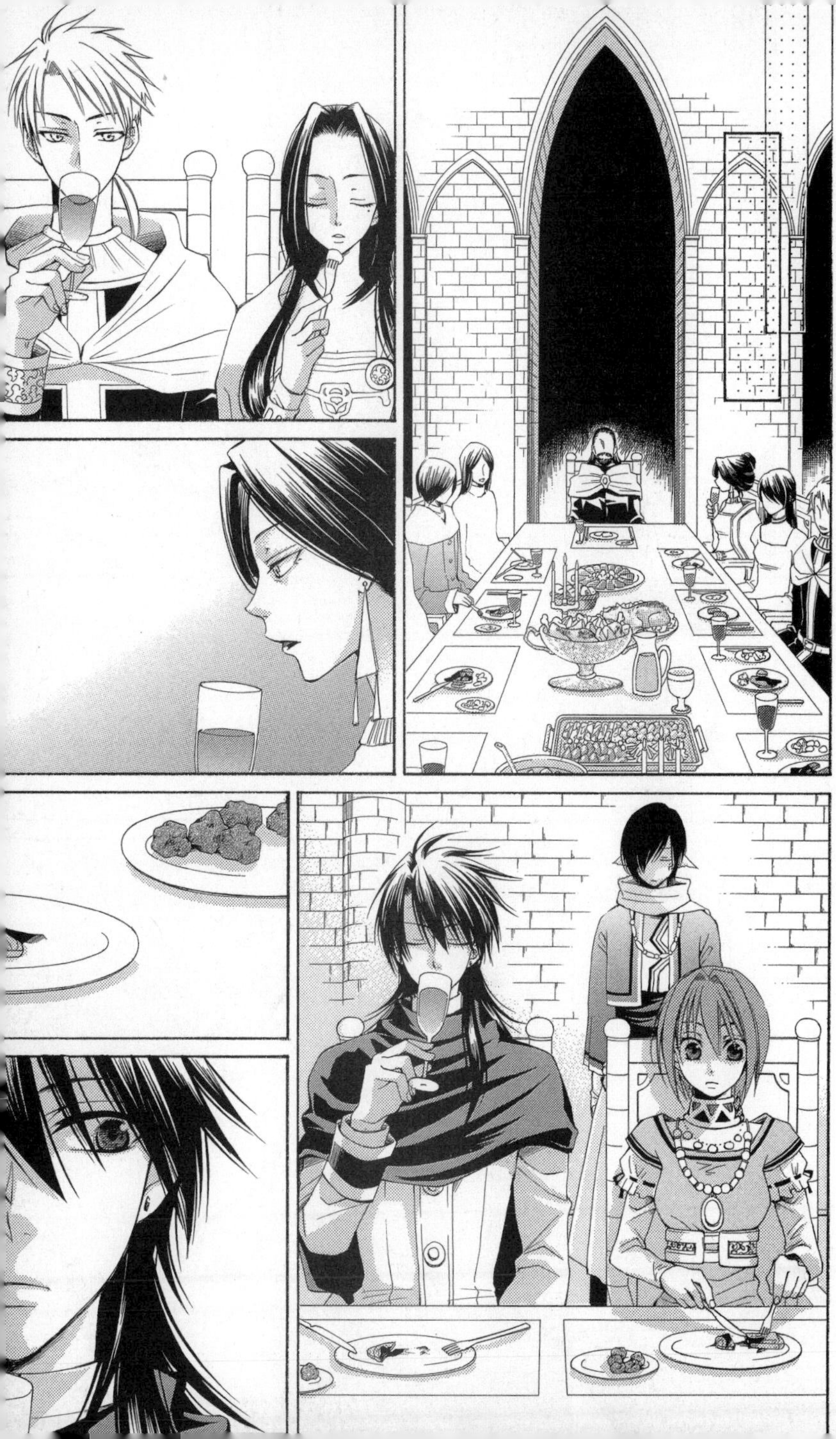

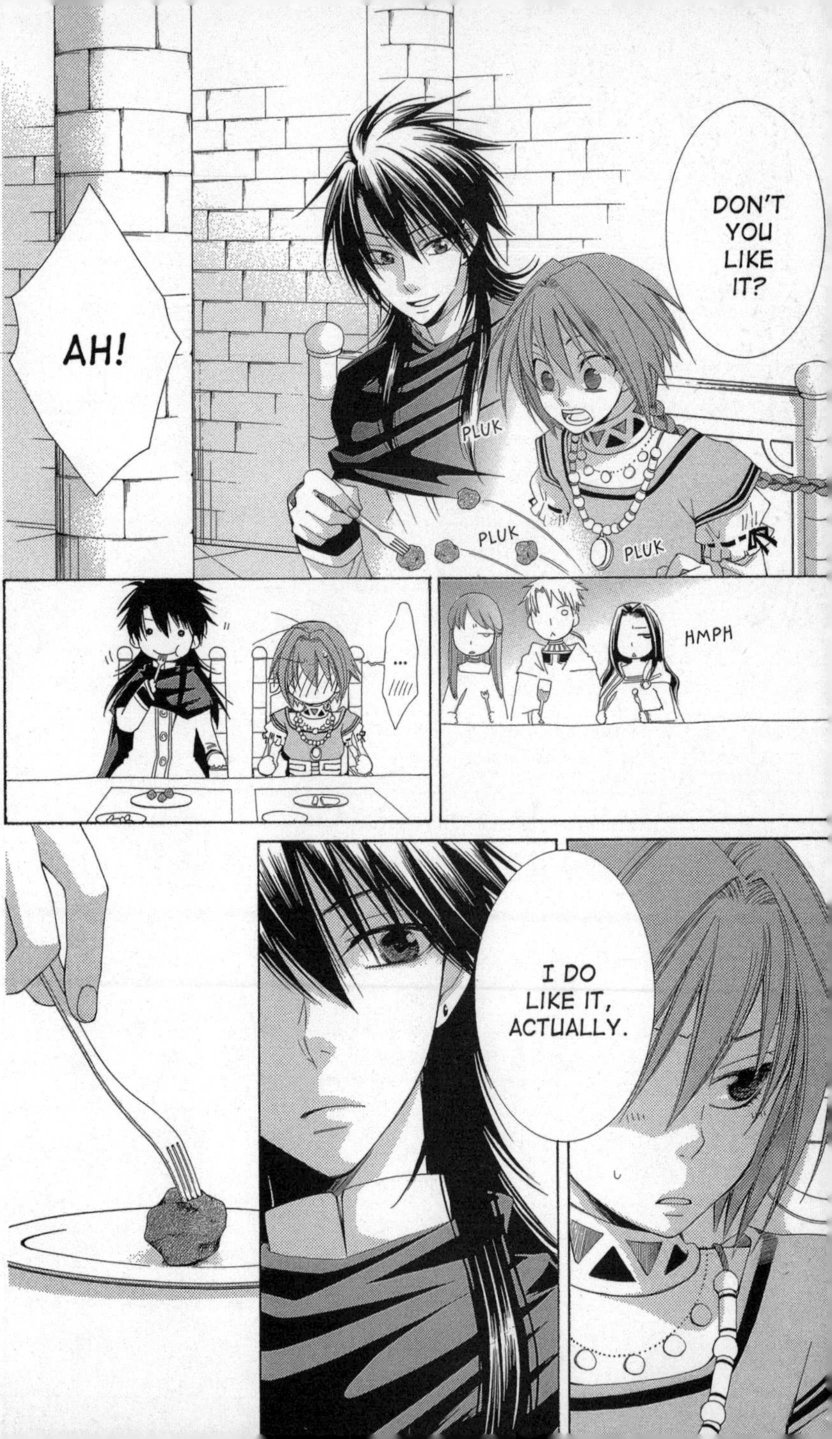
DON'T YOU LIKE IT?
AH!
PLUK
PLUK
PLUK
HMPH
...
I DO LIKE IT, ACTUALLY.

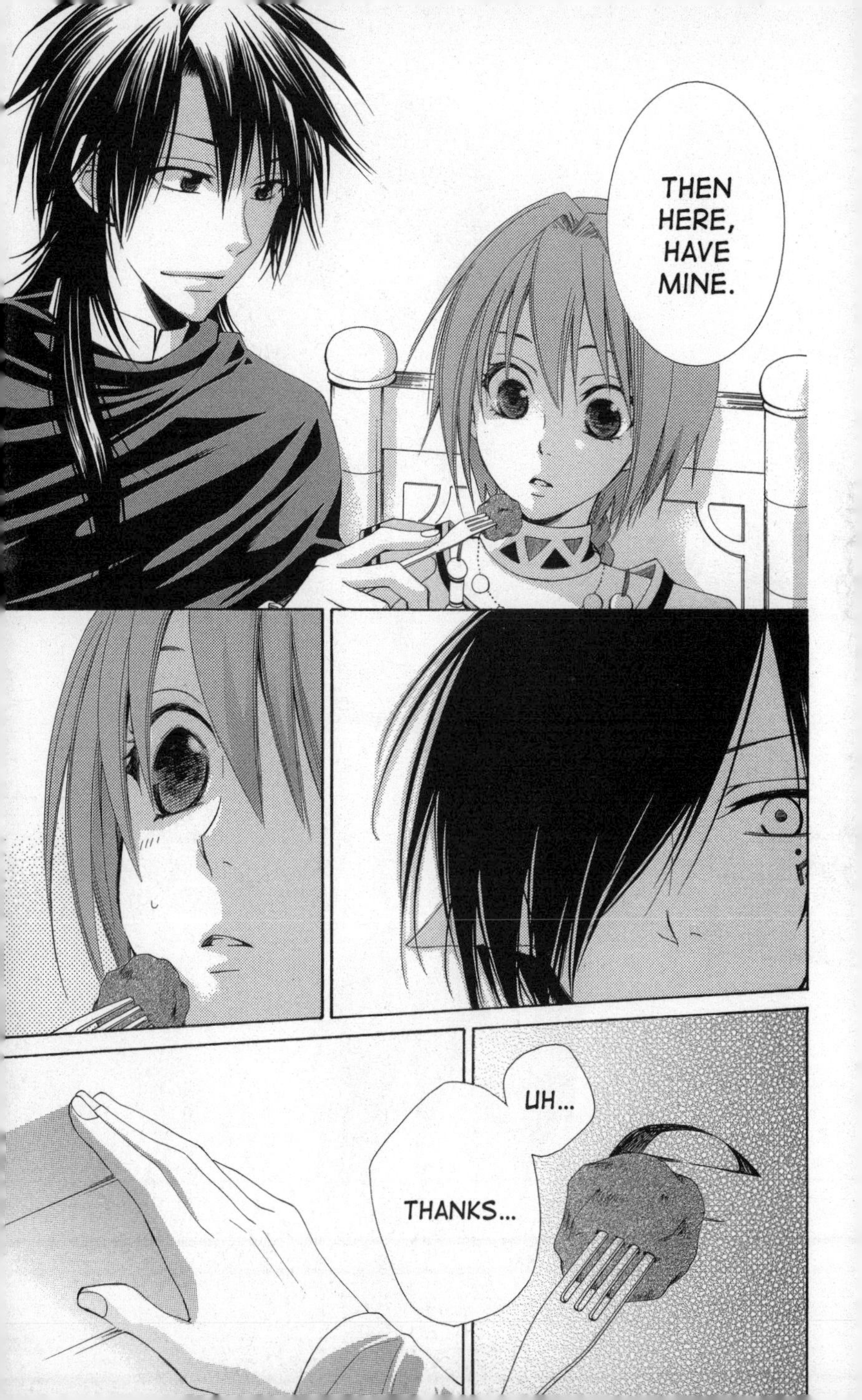
THEN HERE, HAVE MINE.
UH...
THANKS...

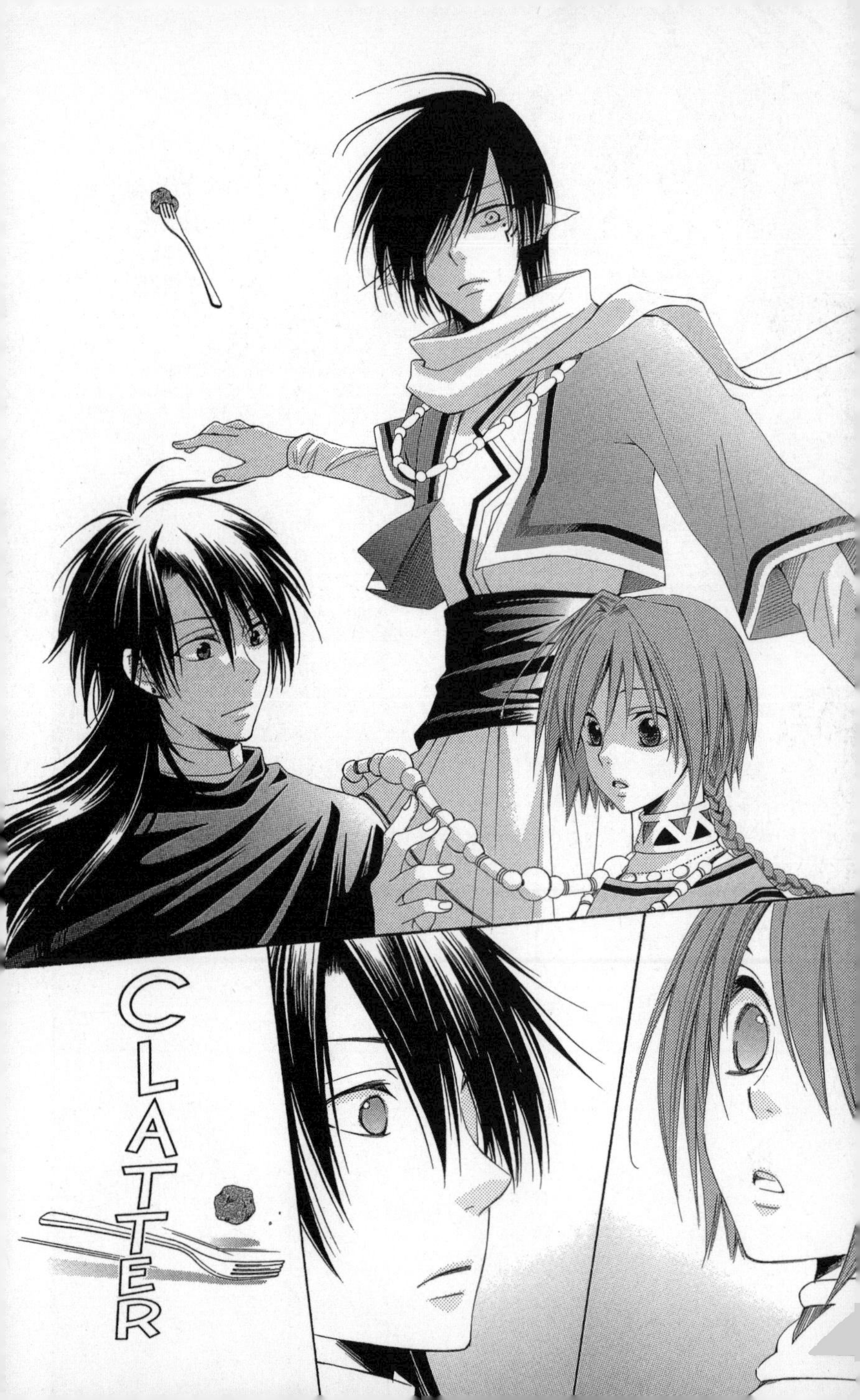
CLATTER

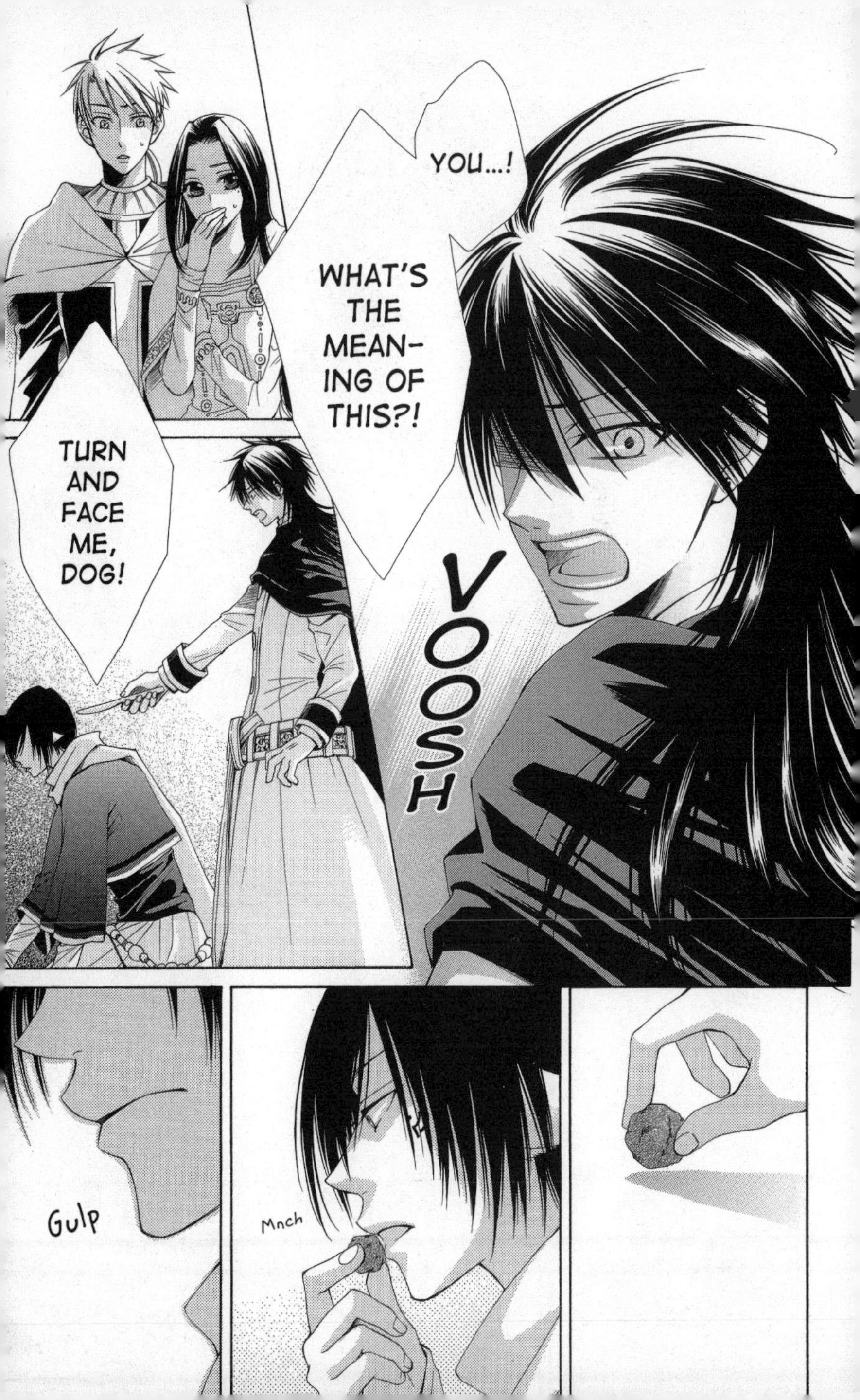
YOU...!
WHAT'S THE MEANING OF THIS?!
VOOSH
TURN AND FACE ME, DOG!
Mnch
Gulp

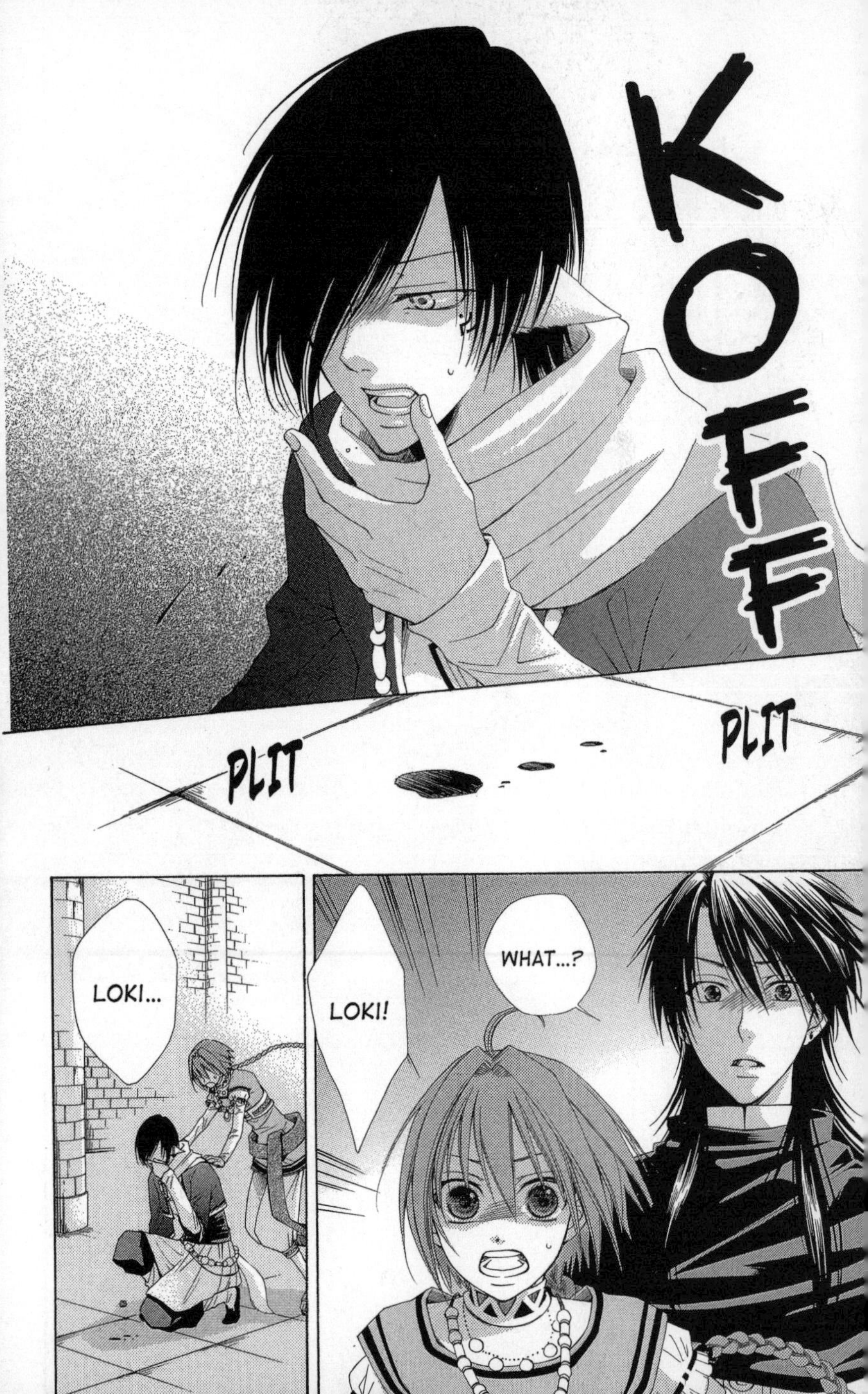
KOFF
PLIT
PLIT
WHAT...?
LOKI!
LOKI...

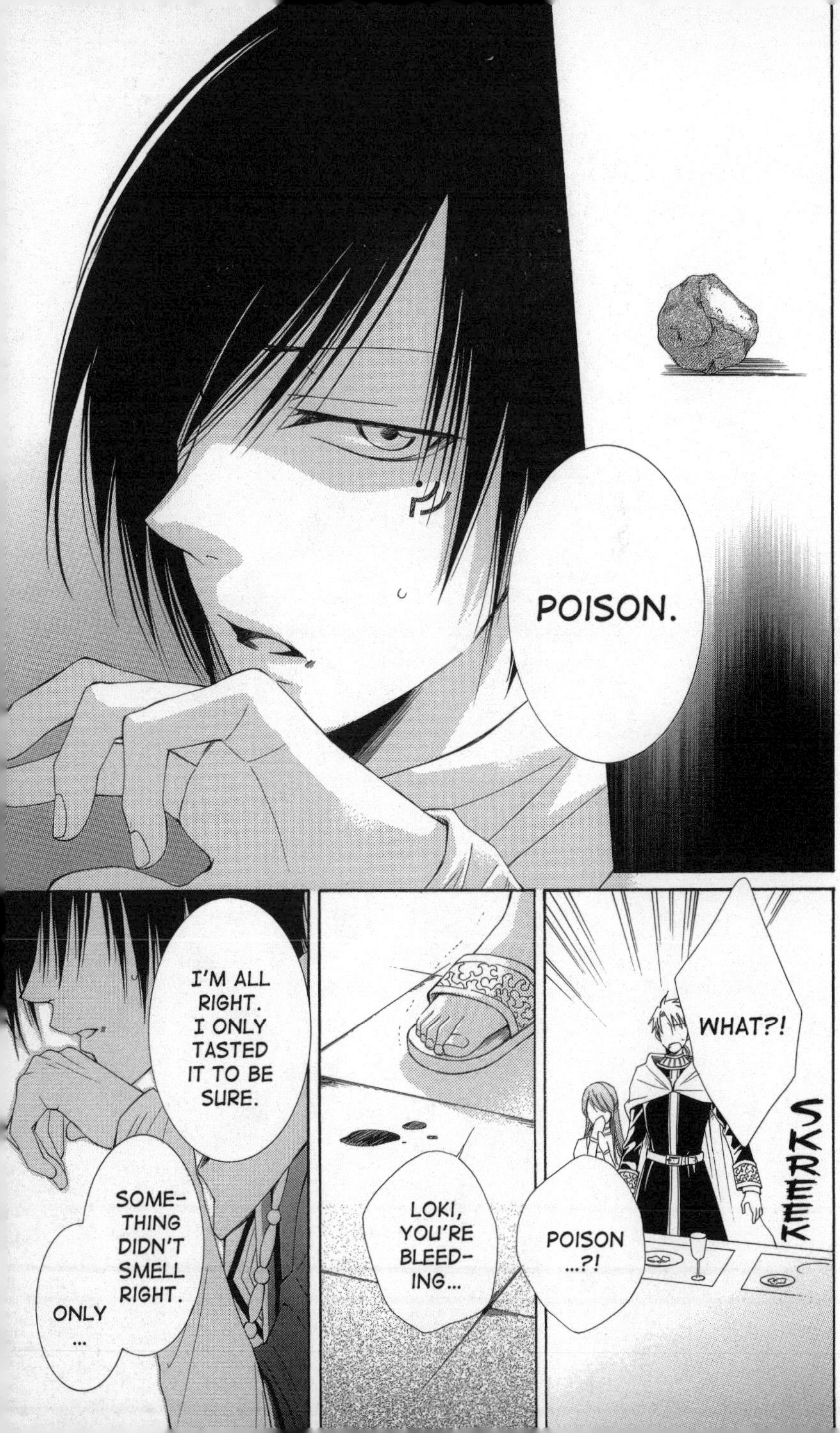
POISON.
WHAT?!
SKREEK
POISON ...?!
LOKI, YOU'RE BLEEDING...
I'M ALL RIGHT. I ONLY TASTED IT TO BE SURE.
SOMETHING DIDN'T SMELL RIGHT.
ONLY ...

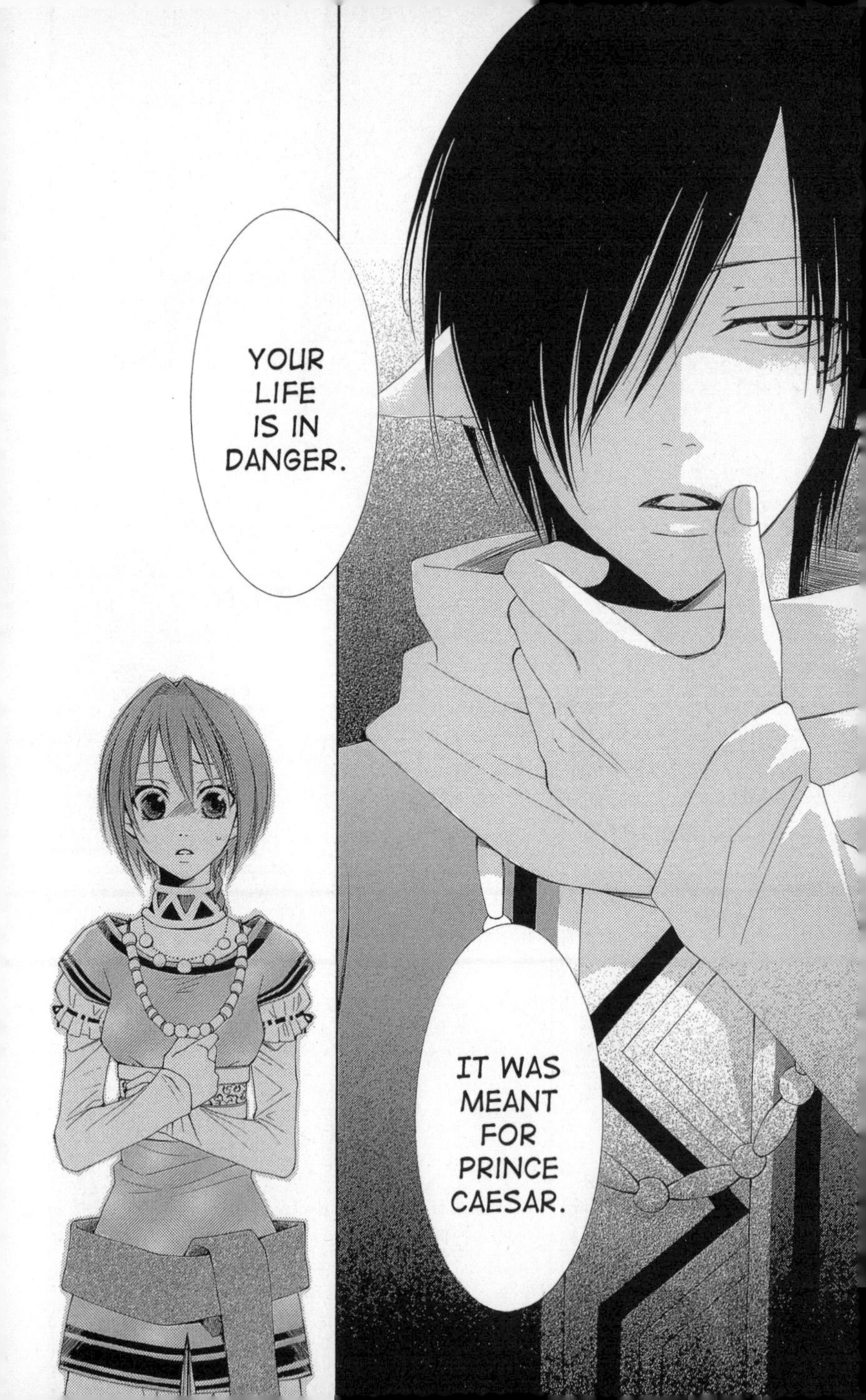
YOUR LIFE IS IN DANGER.
IT WAS MEANT FOR PRINCE CAESAR.

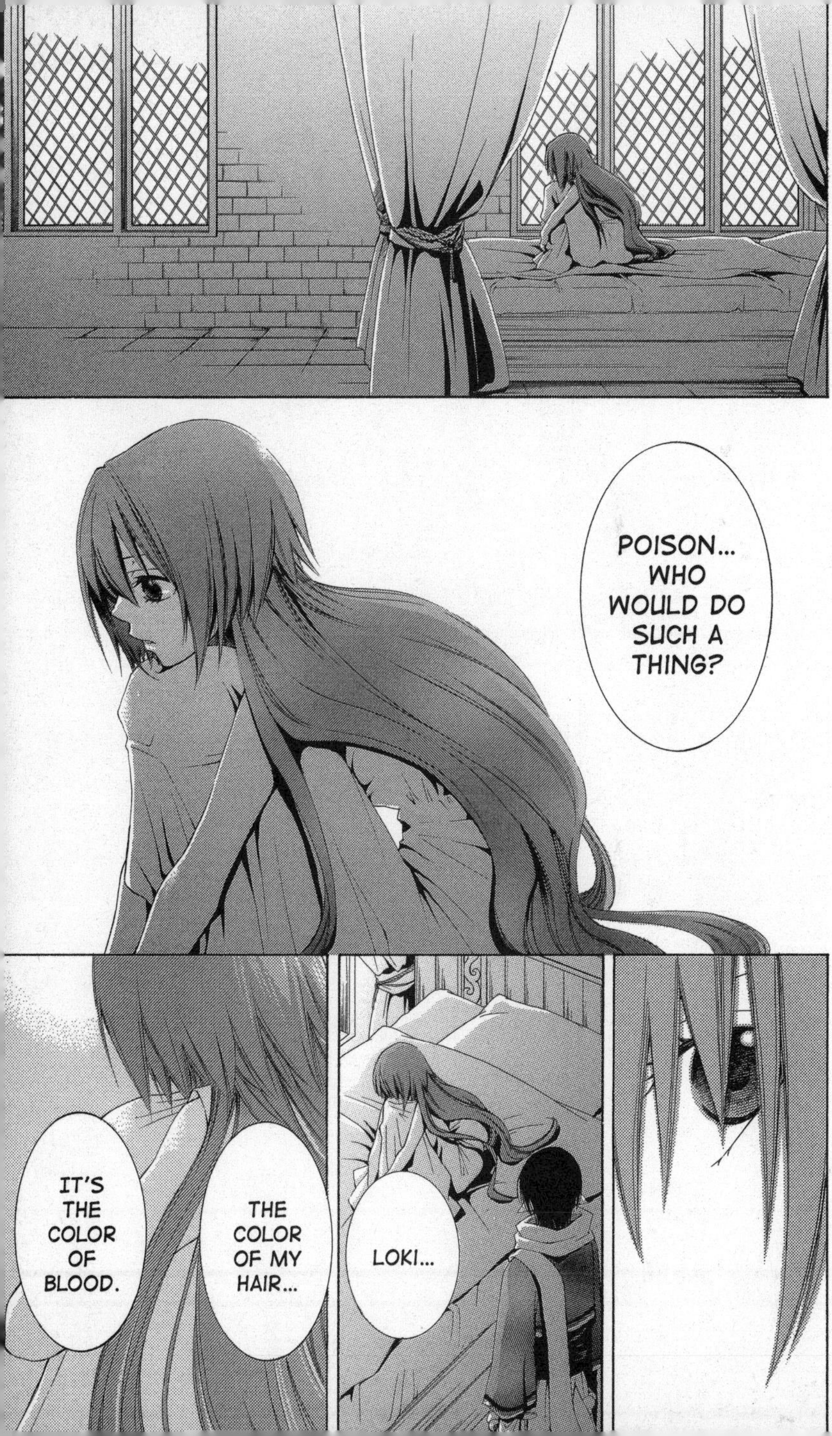
POISON... WHO WOULD DO SUCH A THING?
LOKI...
THE COLOR OF MY HAIR...
IT'S THE COLOR OF BLOOD.

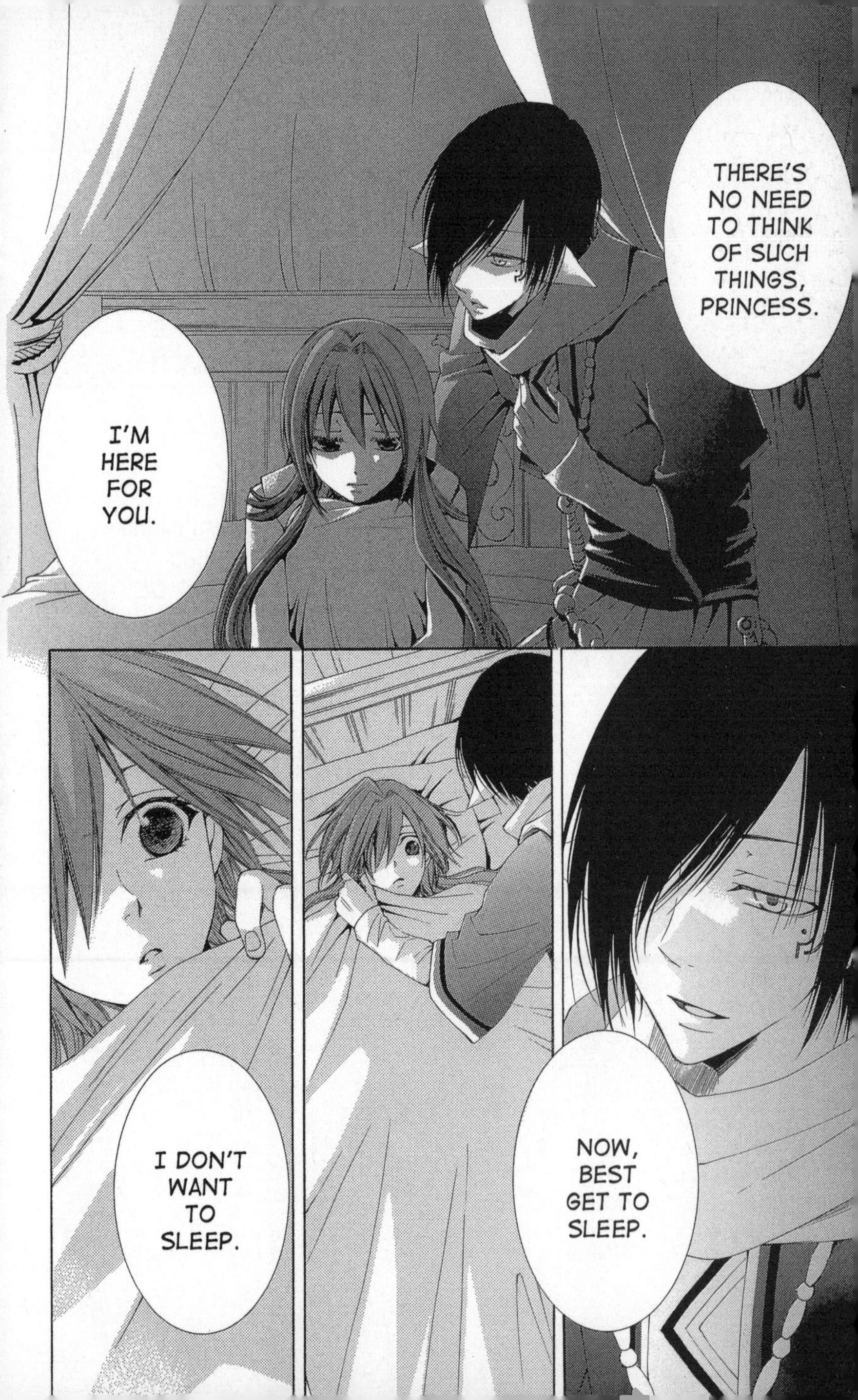
THERE'S NO NEED TO THINK OF SUCH THINGS, PRINCESS.
I'M HERE FOR YOU.
NOW, BEST GET TO SLEEP.
I DON'T WANT TO SLEEP.

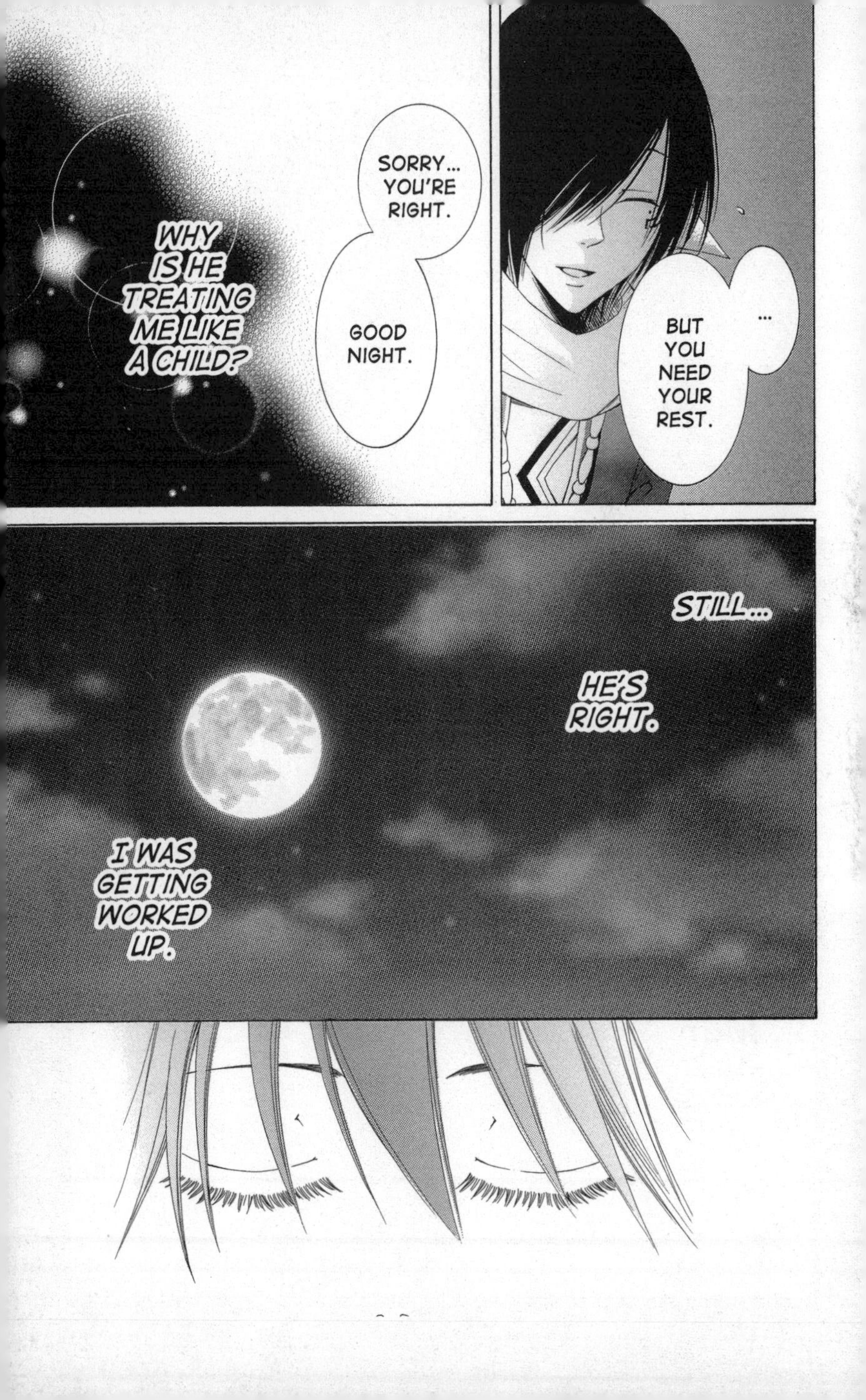
...
BUT YOU NEED YOUR REST.
SORRY... YOU'RE RIGHT.
GOOD NIGHT.
WHY IS HE TREATING ME LIKE A CHILD?
STILL...
HE'S RIGHT.
I WAS GETTING WORKED UP.

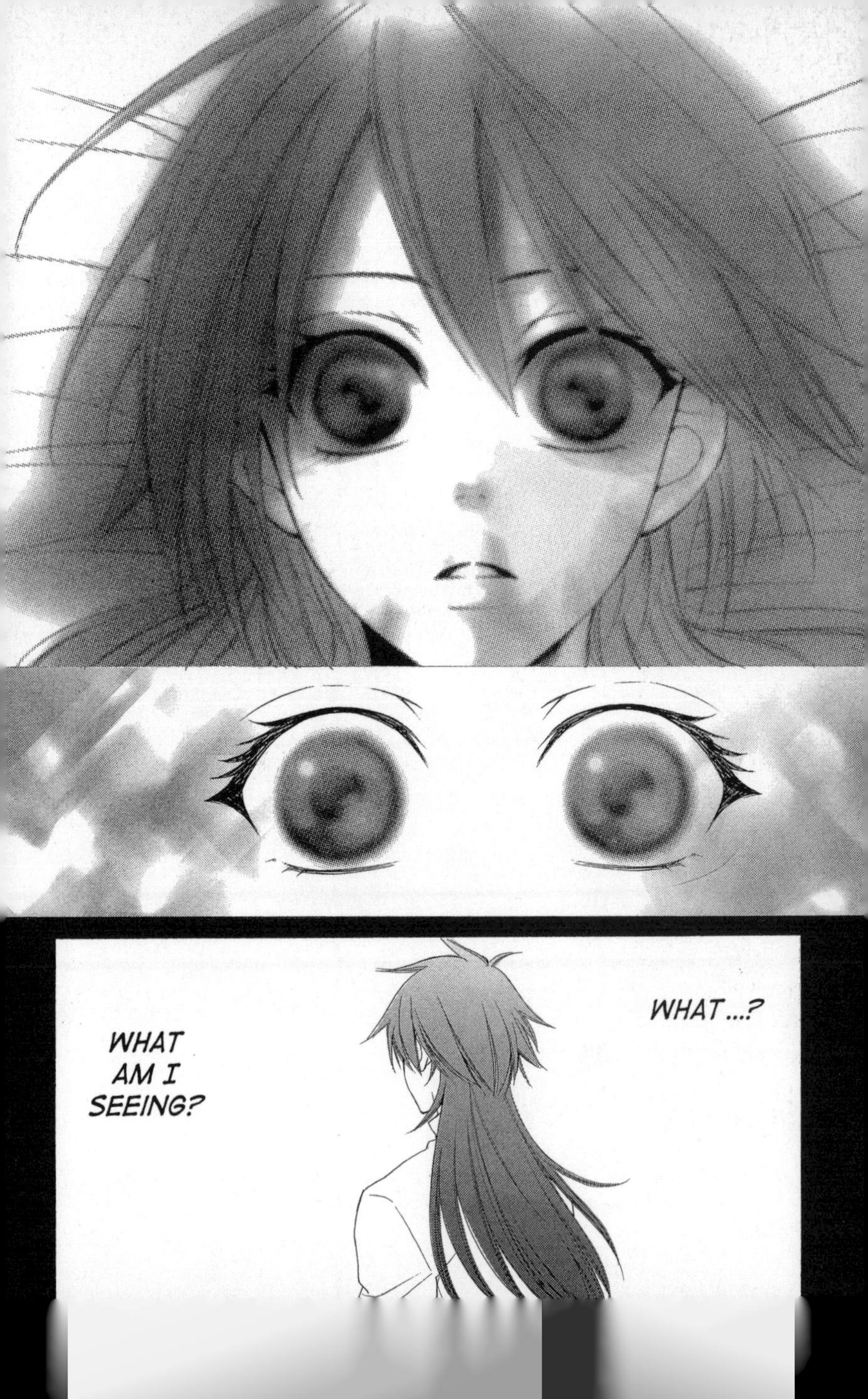
WHAT...?
WHAT AM I SEEING?

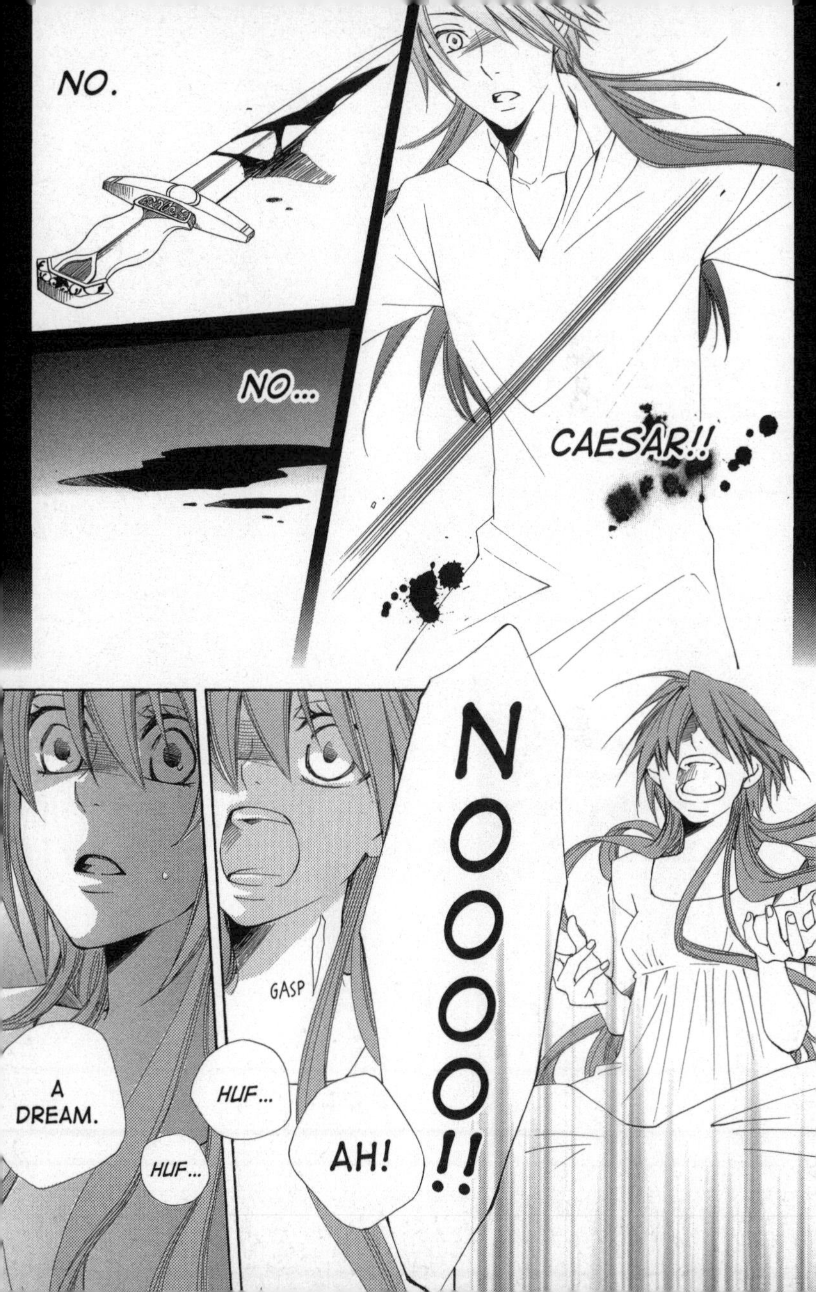
CAESAR!!
NO.
NO...
NOOOO!!
GASP
HUF...
AH!
HUF...
A DREAM.

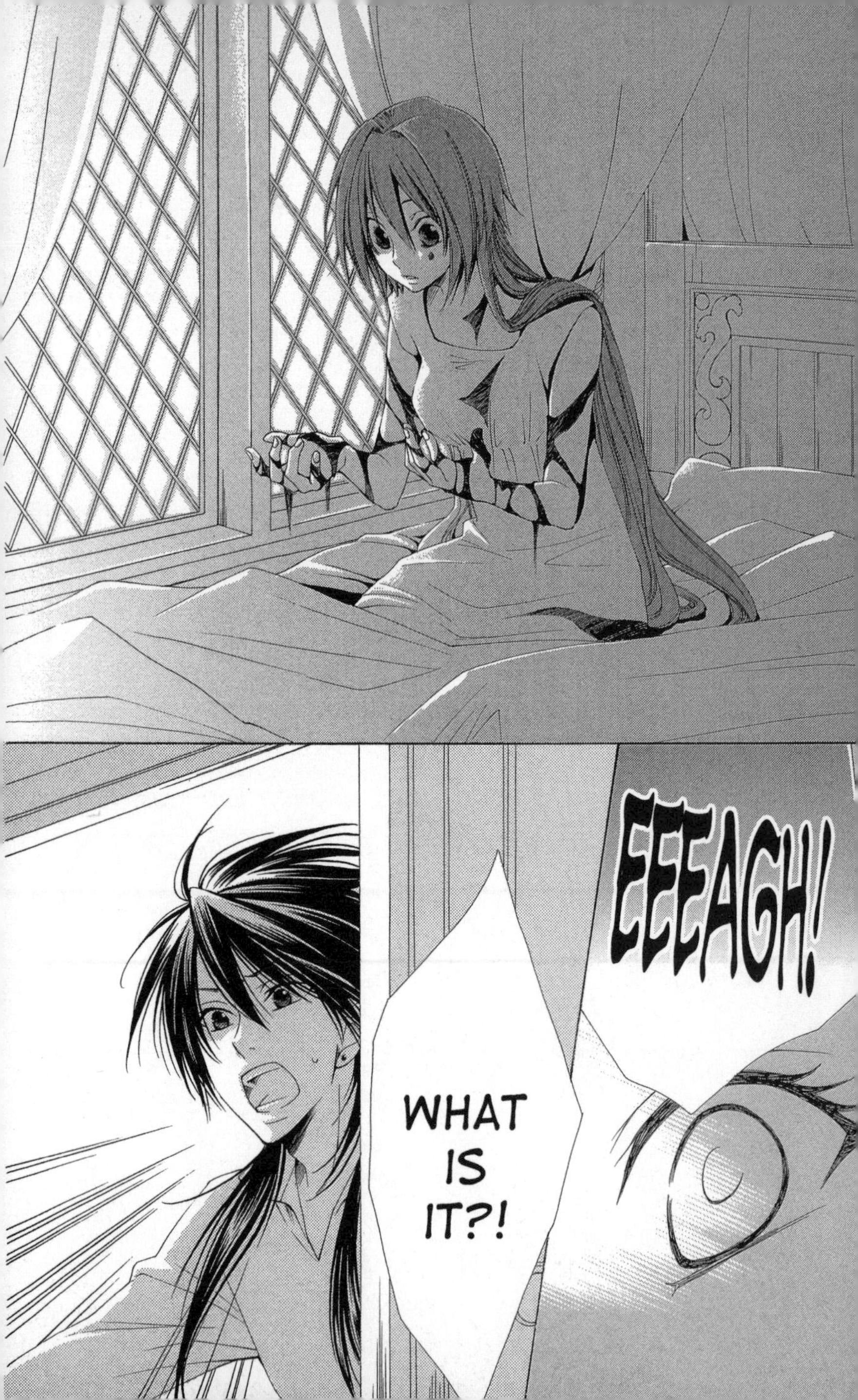
EEEAGH!
WHAT IS IT?!

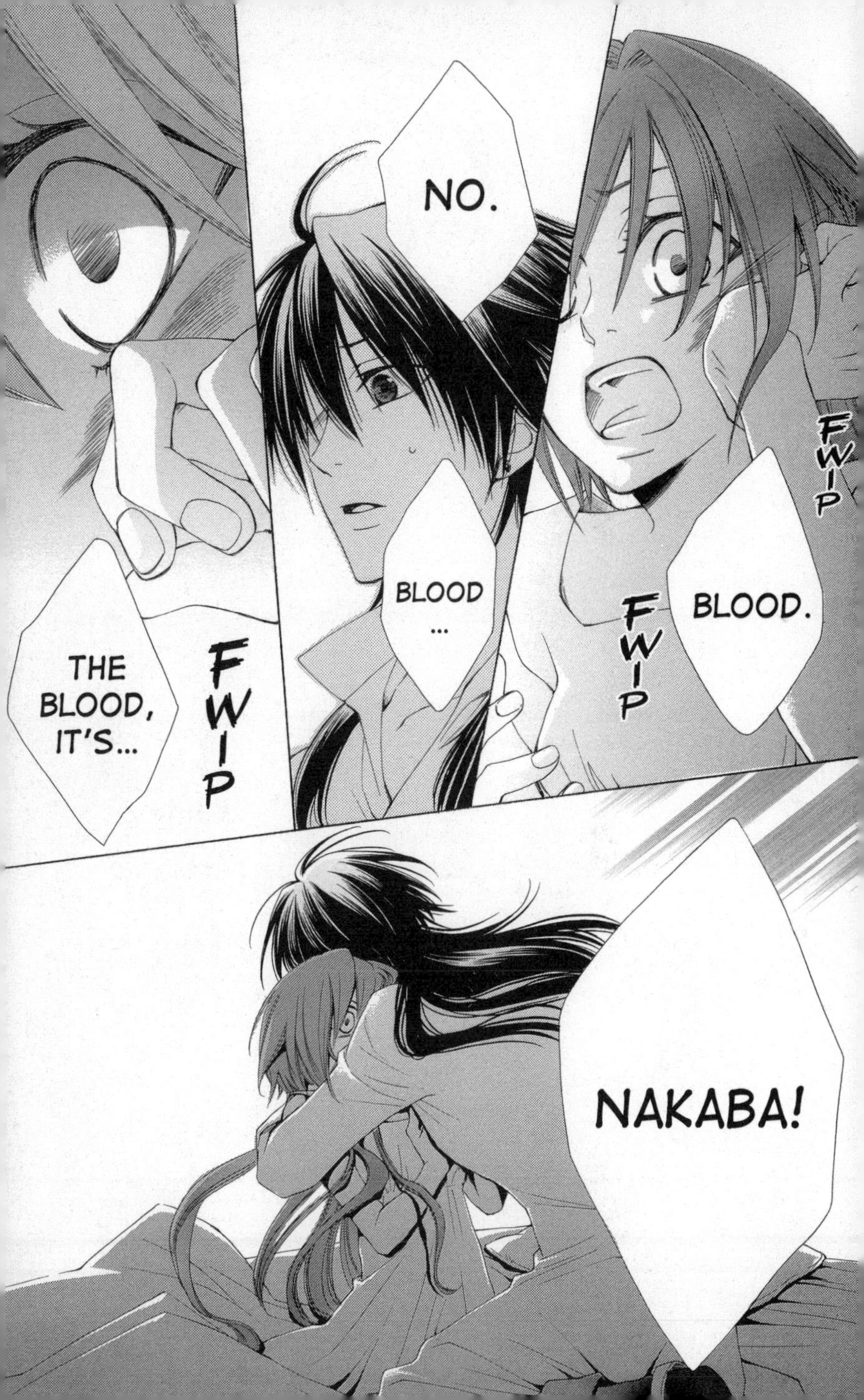
FWIP
BLOOD.
FWIP
NO.
BLOOD ...
THE BLOOD, IT'S...
FWIP
NAKABA!

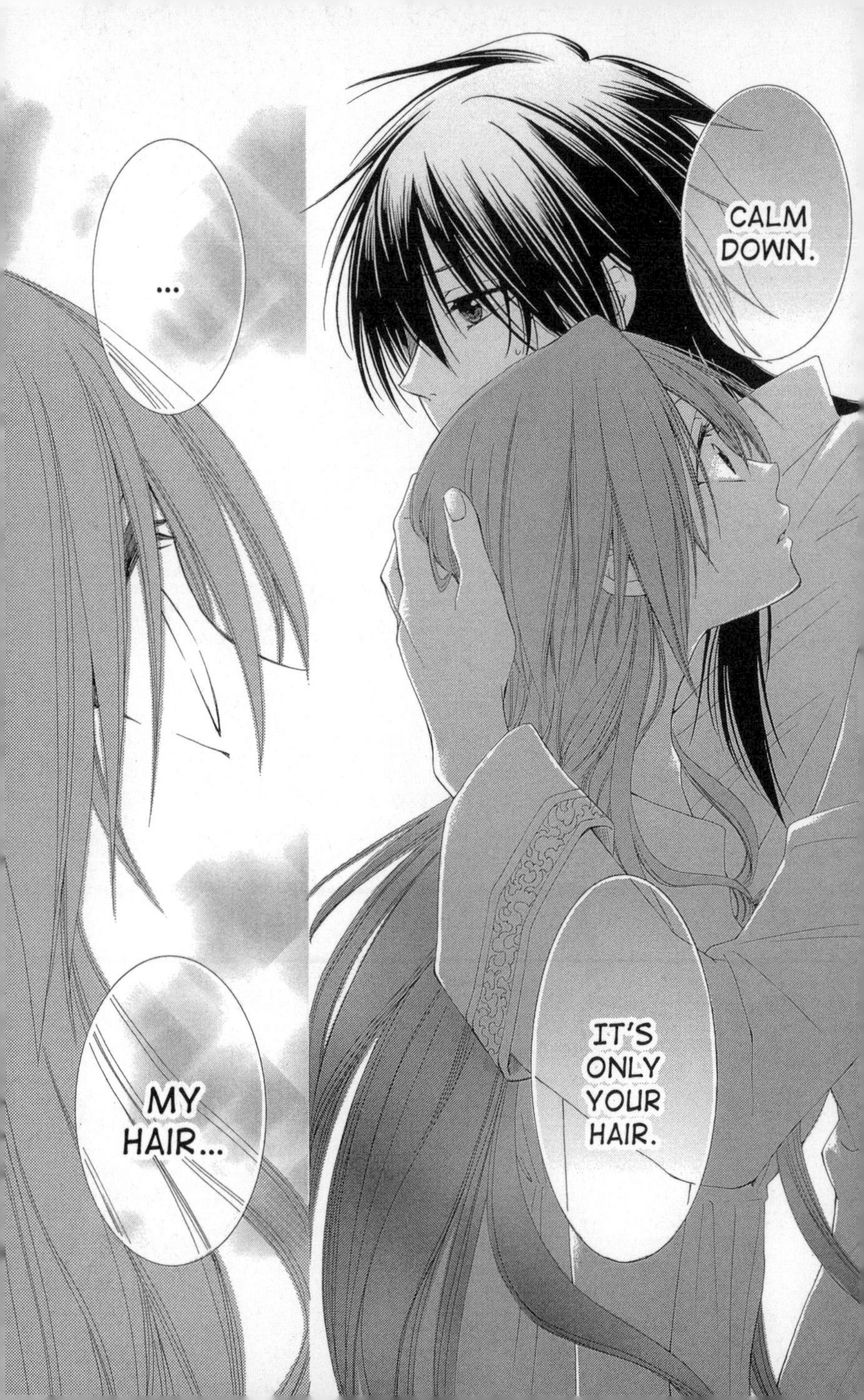
CALM DOWN.
IT'S ONLY YOUR HAIR.
...
MY HAIR...

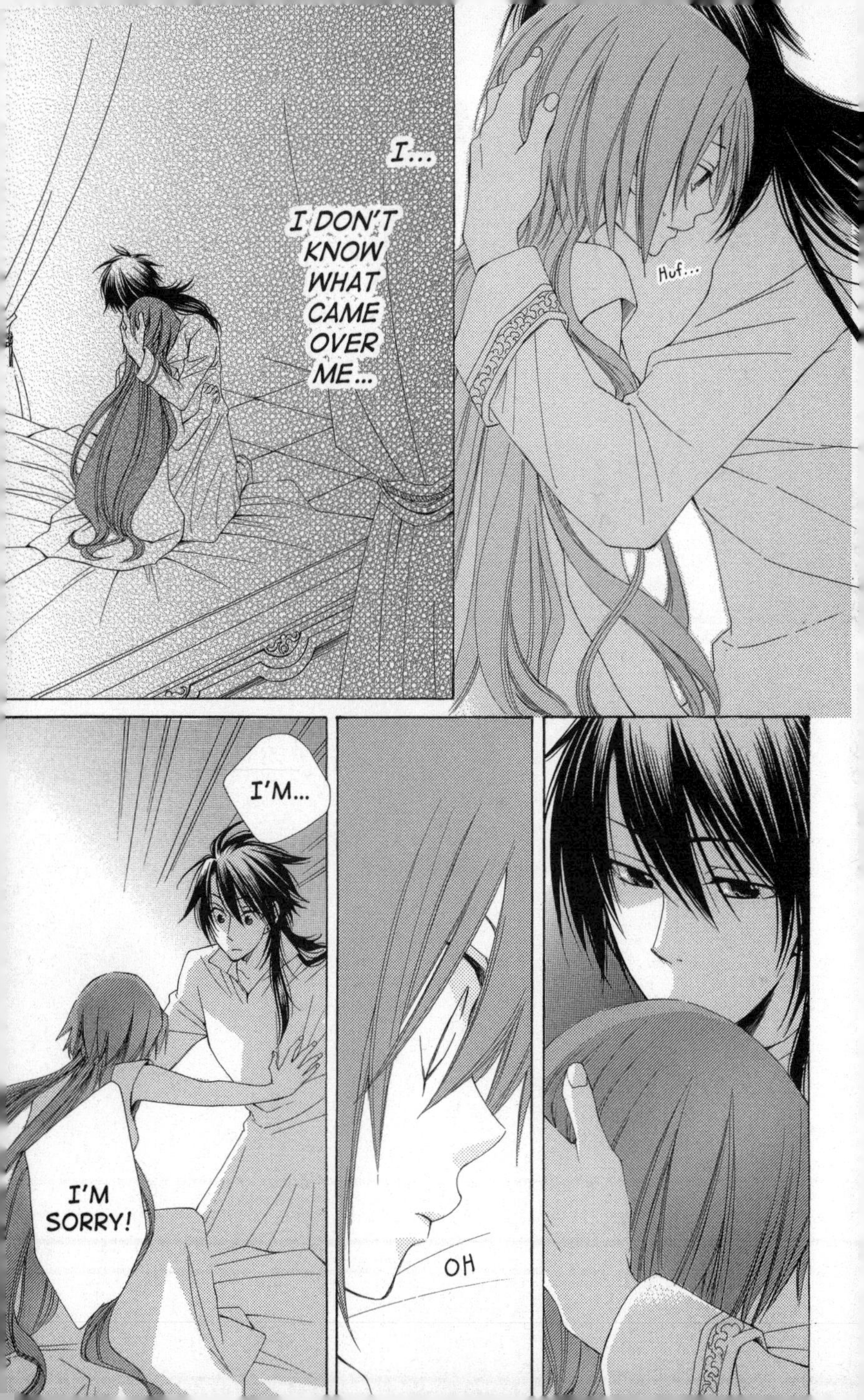
Huf...
I...
I DON'T KNOW WHAT CAME OVER ME...
OH
I'M...
I'M SORRY!

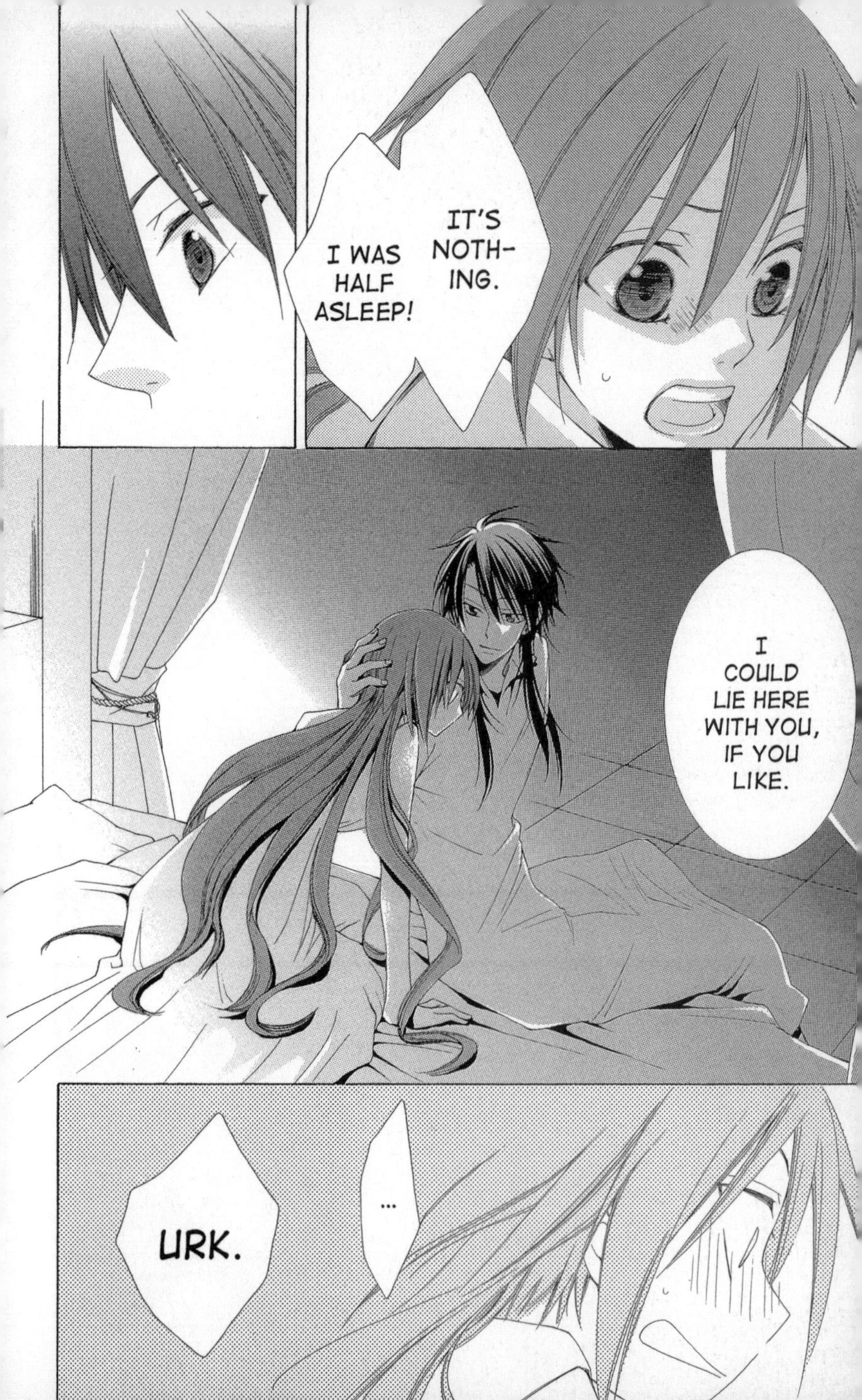
IT'S NOTH-ING.
I WAS HALF ASLEEP!
I COULD LIE HERE WITH YOU, IF YOU LIKE.
...
URK.

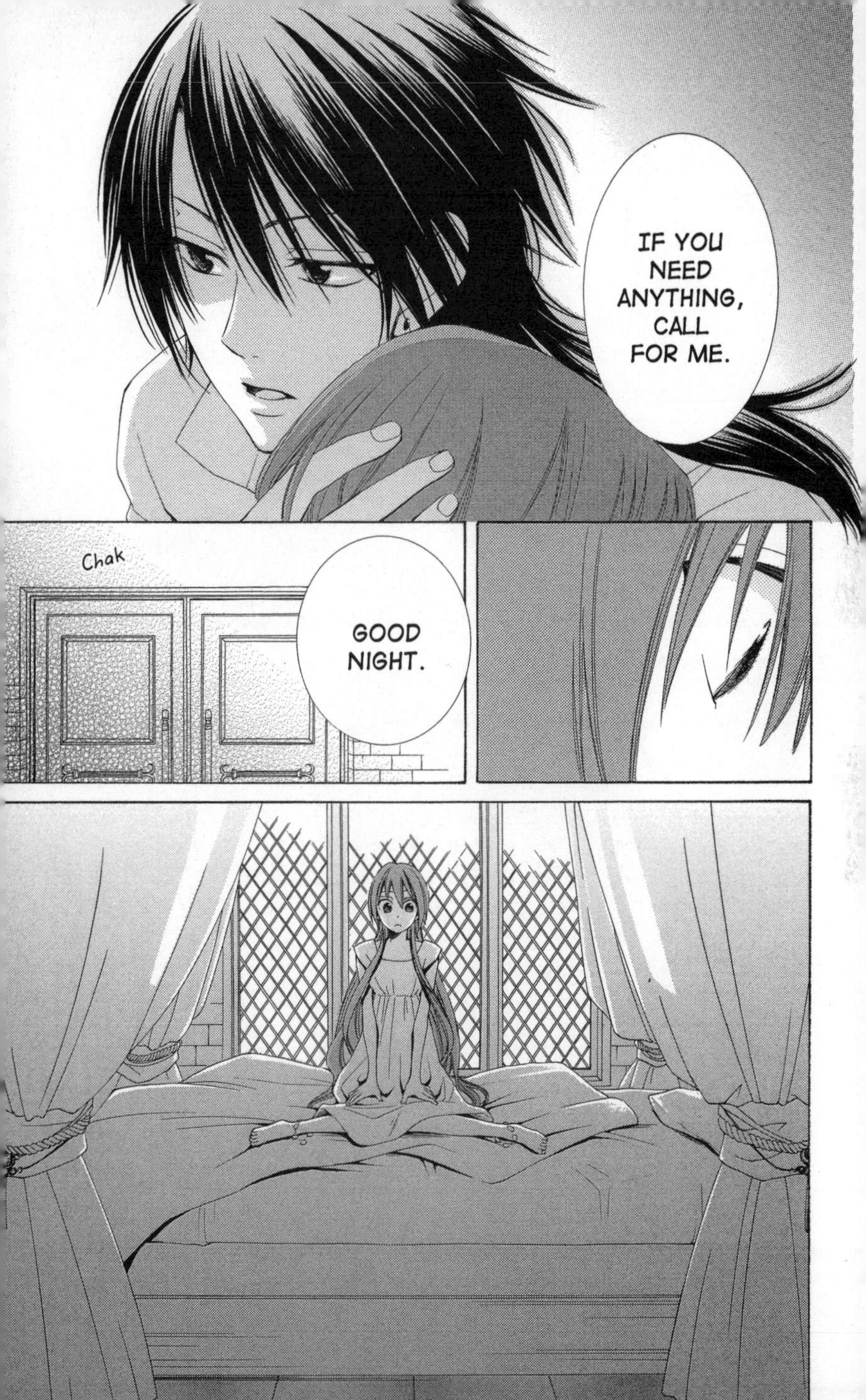
IF YOU NEED ANYTHING, CALL FOR ME.
GOOD NIGHT.
Chak

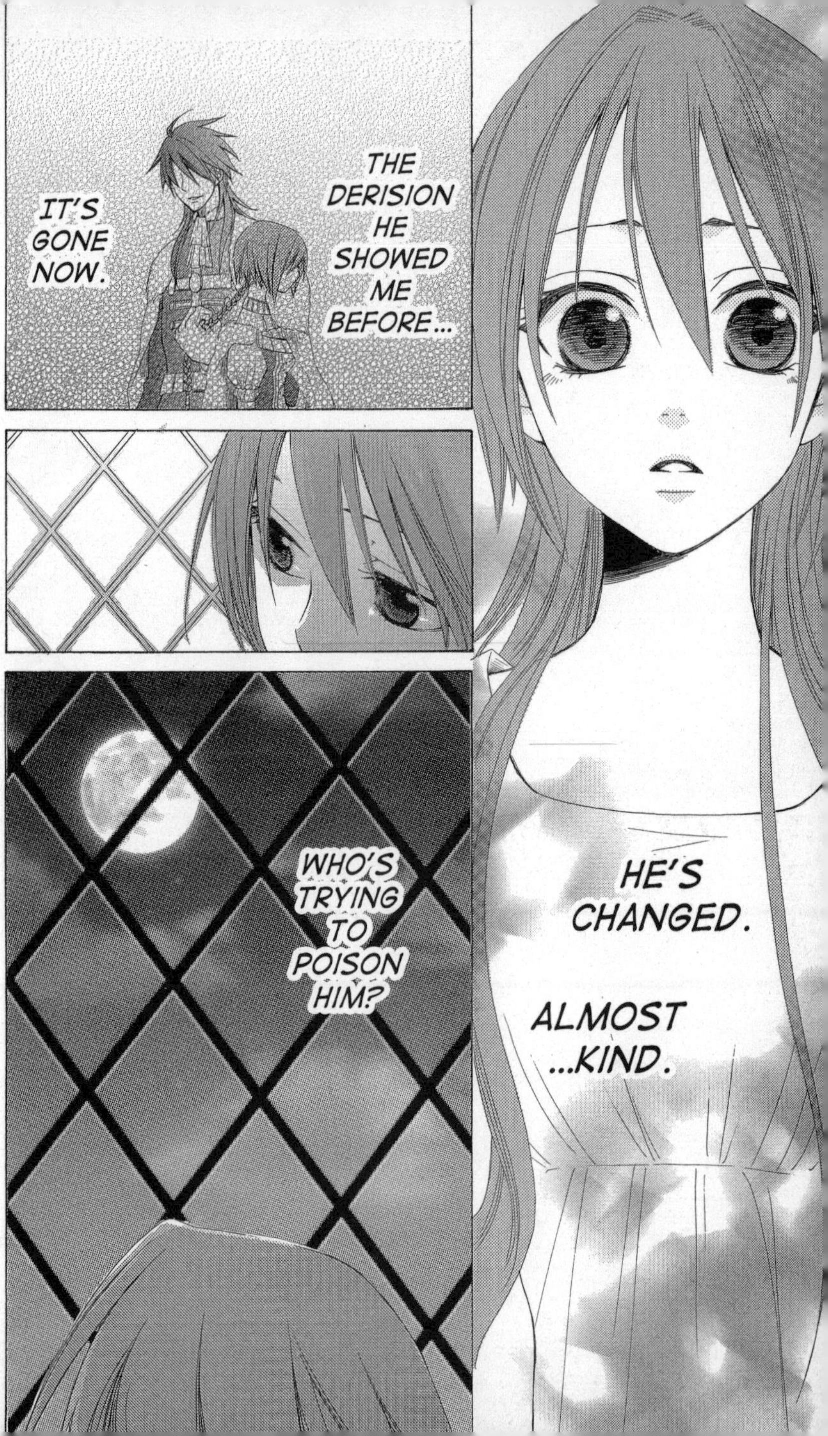
HE'S CHANGED.
ALMOST ...KIND.
THE DERISION HE SHOWED ME BEFORE...
IT'S GONE NOW.
WHO'S TRYING TO POISON HIM?

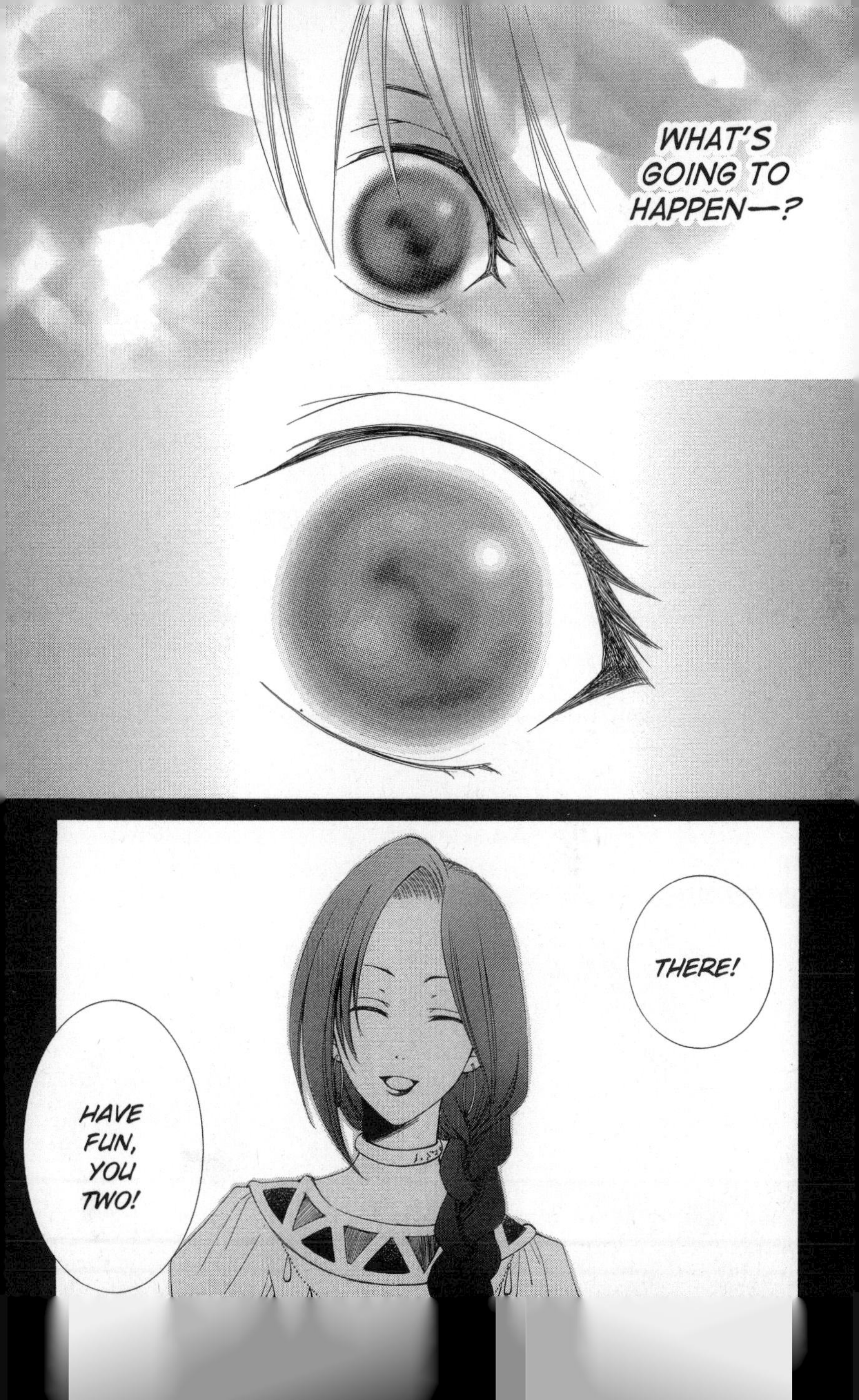
WHAT'S GOING TO HAPPEN—?
THERE!
HAVE FUN, YOU TWO!

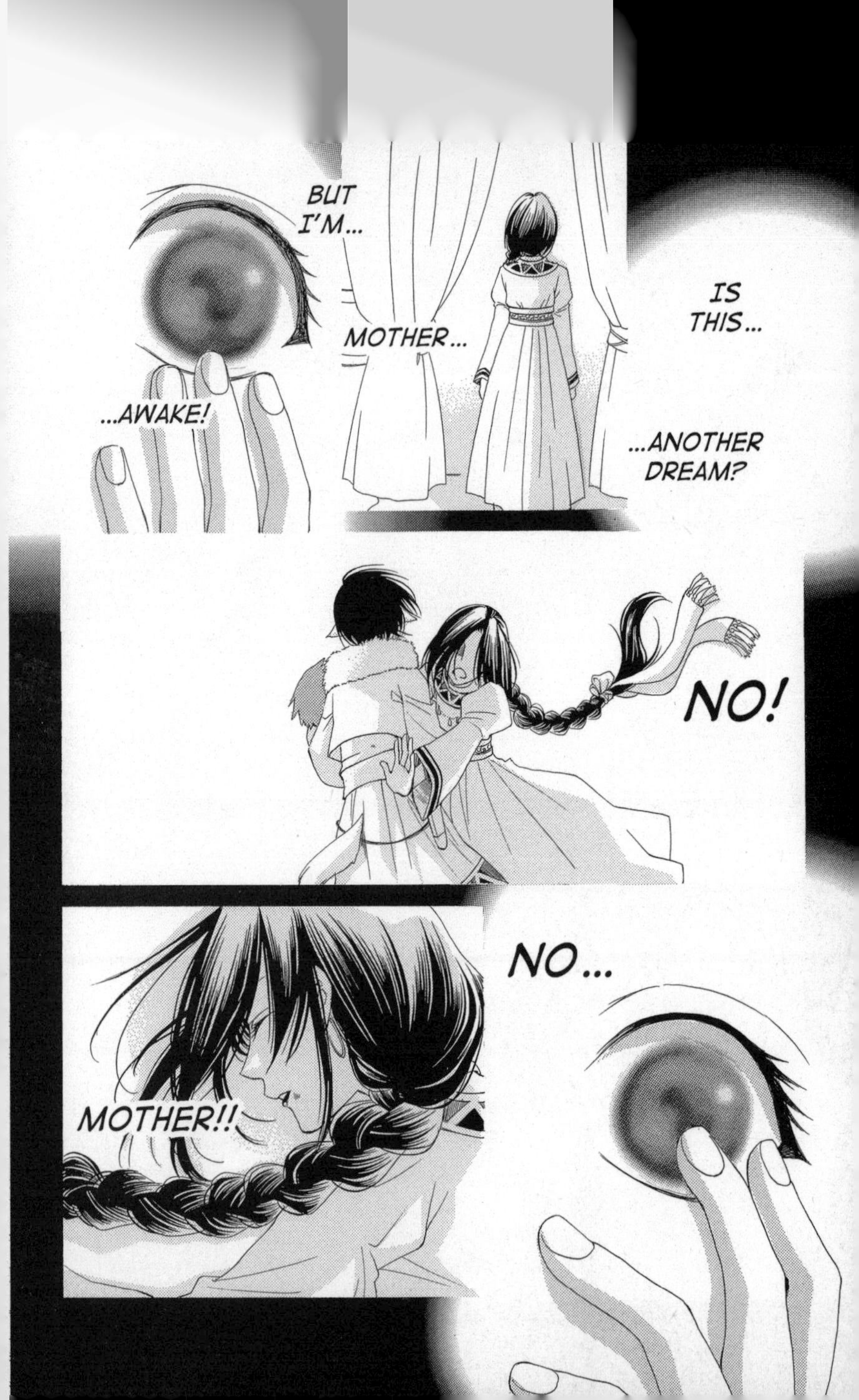
IS THIS...
...ANOTHER DREAM?
MOTHER...
BUT I'M...
...AWAKE!
NO!
NO...
MOTHER!!

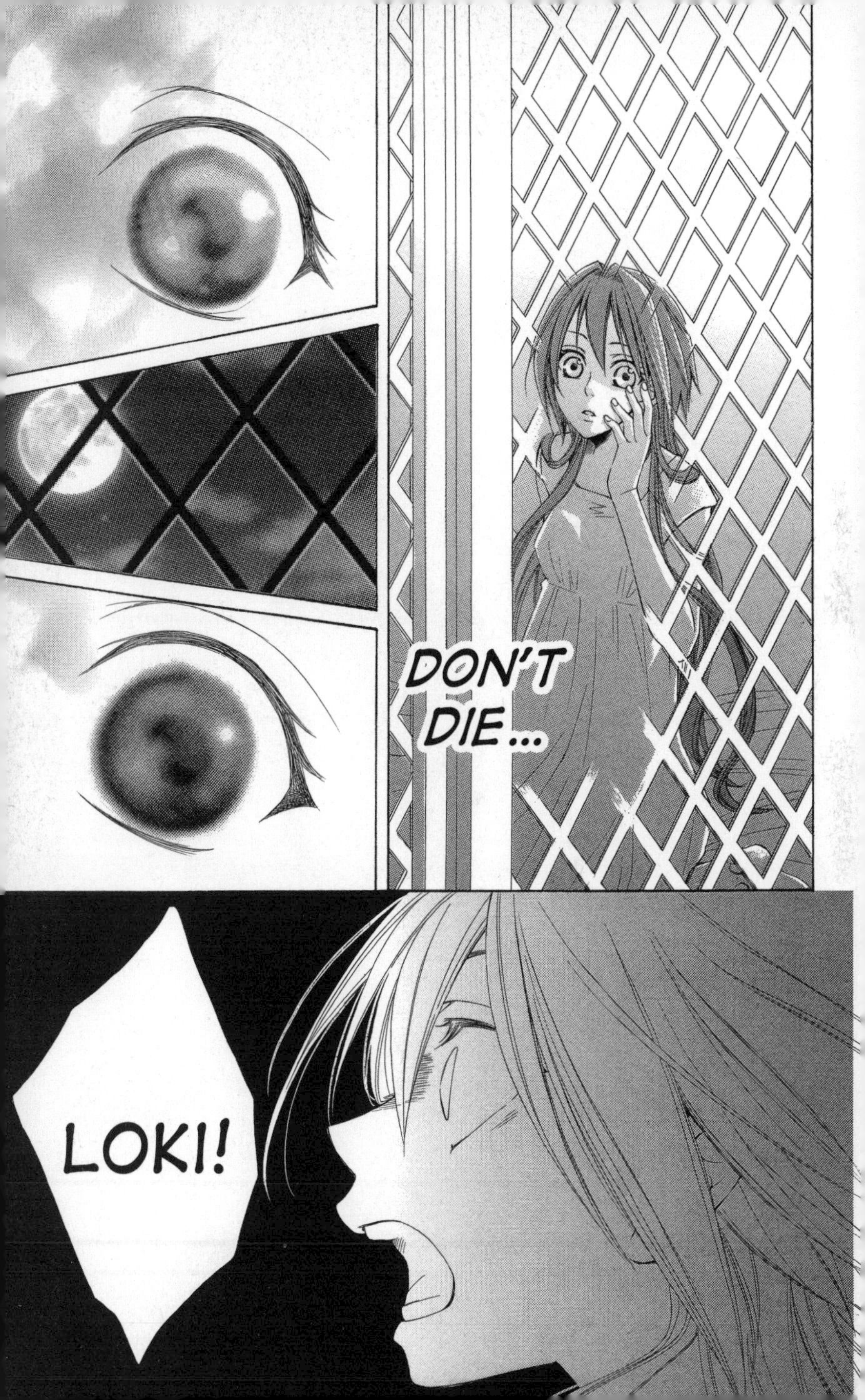
DON'T DIE...
LOKI!

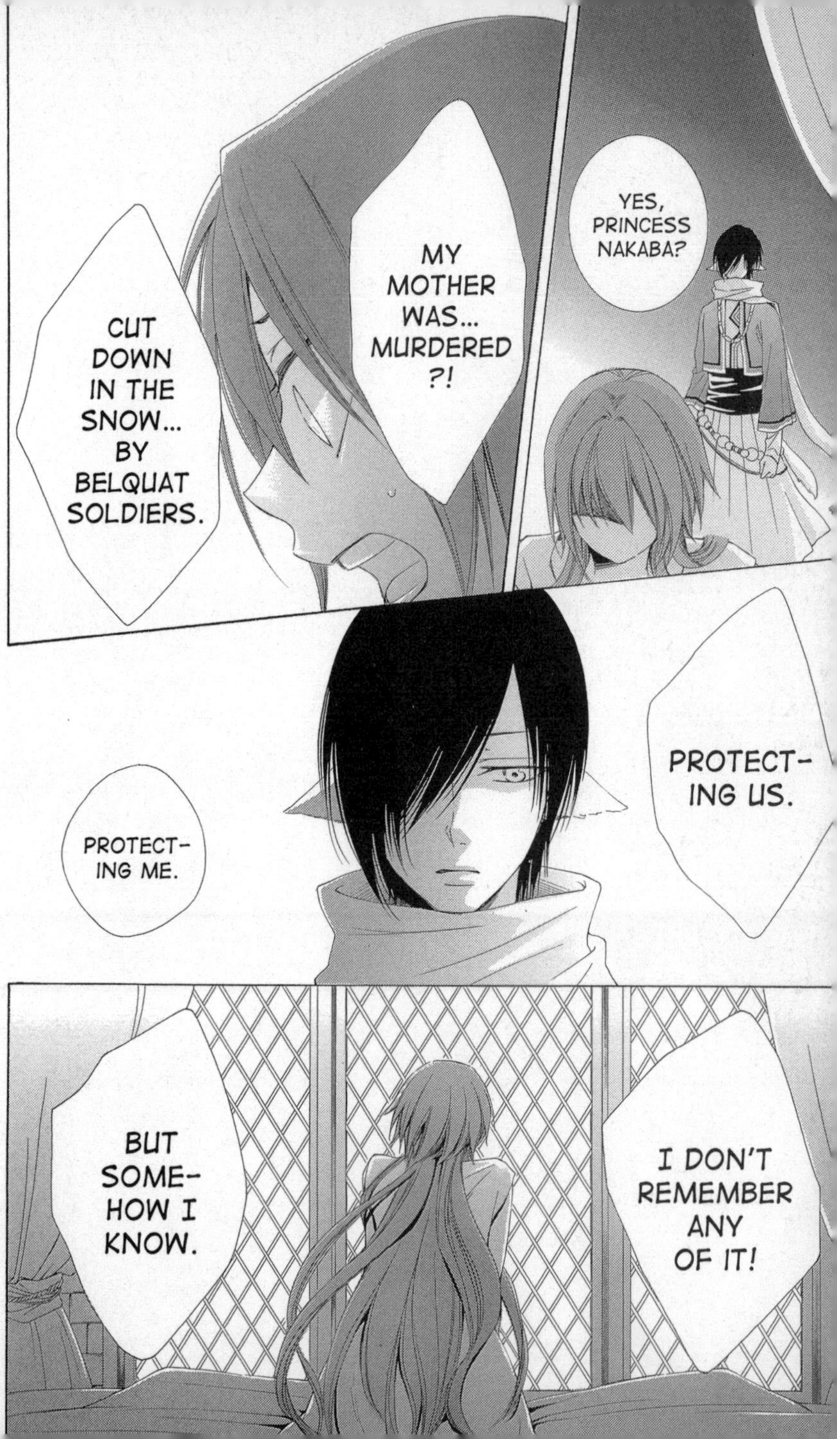
YES, PRINCESS NAKABA?
MY MOTHER WAS... MURDERED?!
CUT DOWN IN THE SNOW... BY BELQUAT SOLDIERS.
PROTECT-ING US.
PROTECT-ING ME.
I DON'T REMEMBER ANY OF IT!
BUT SOME-HOW I KNOW.

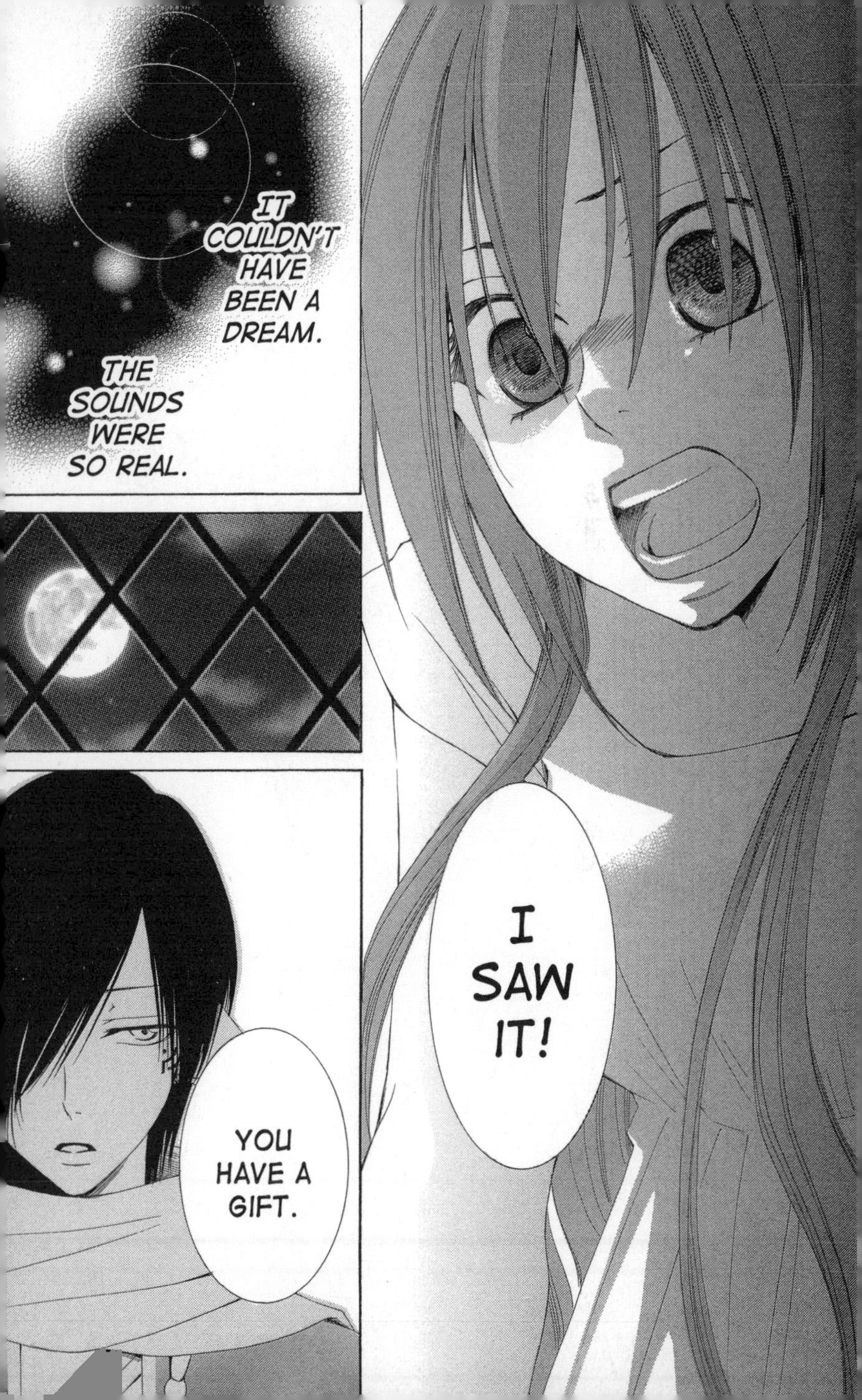
I SAW IT!
IT COULDN'T HAVE BEEN A DREAM.
THE SOUNDS WERE SO REAL.
YOU HAVE A GIFT.

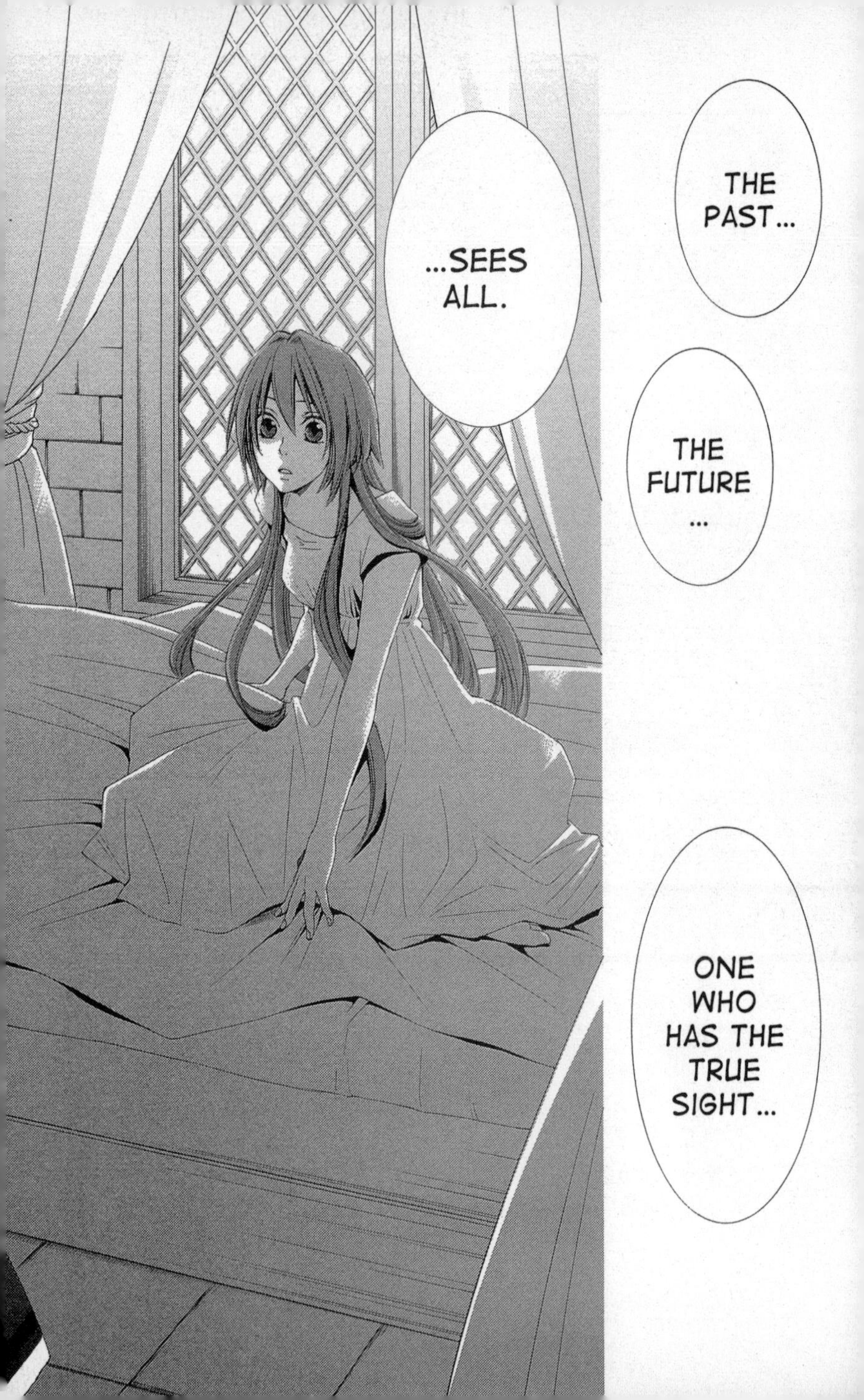
THE PAST...
THE FUTURE ...
ONE WHO HAS THE TRUE SIGHT...
...SEES ALL.

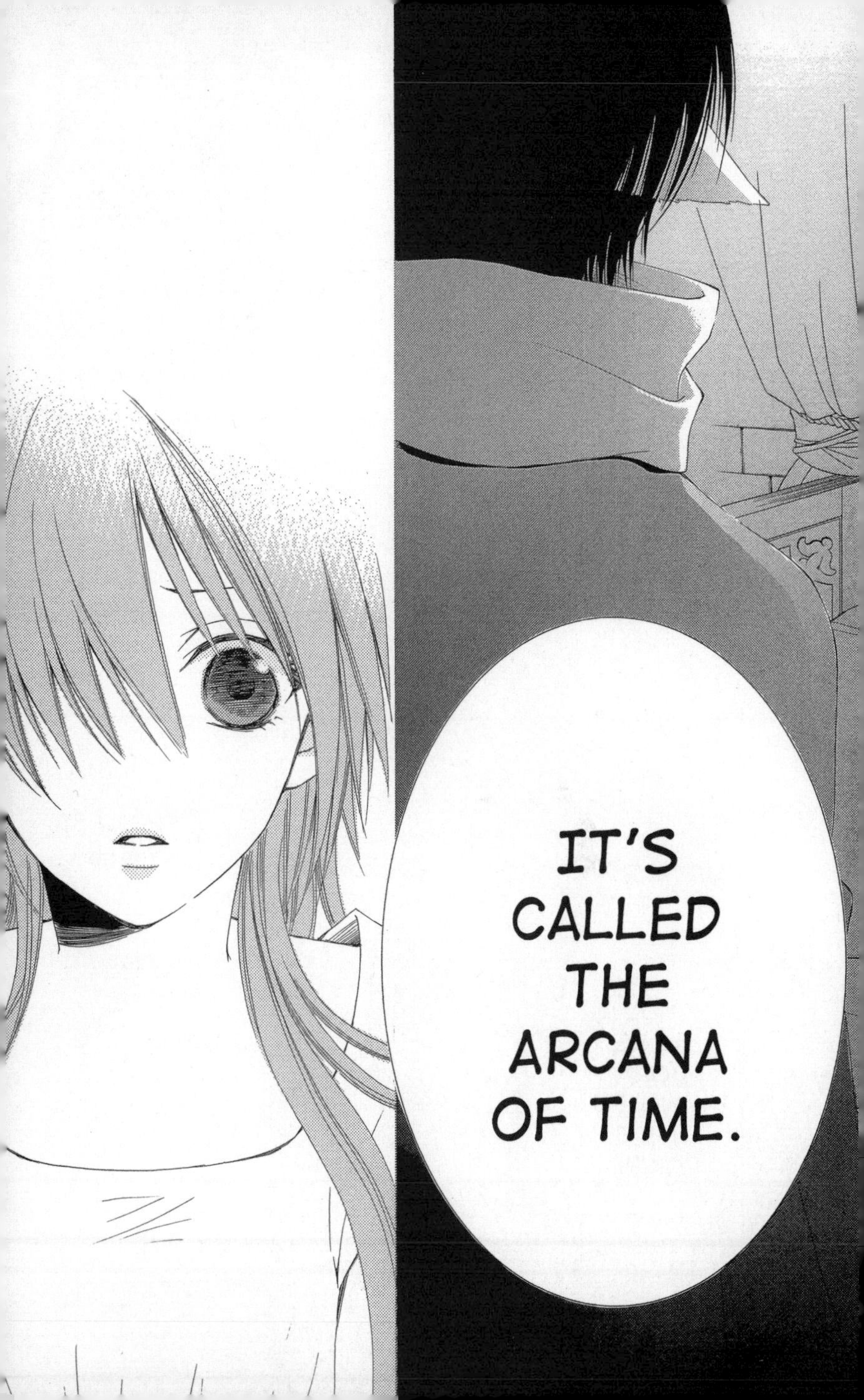
IT'S CALLED THE ARCANA OF TIME.

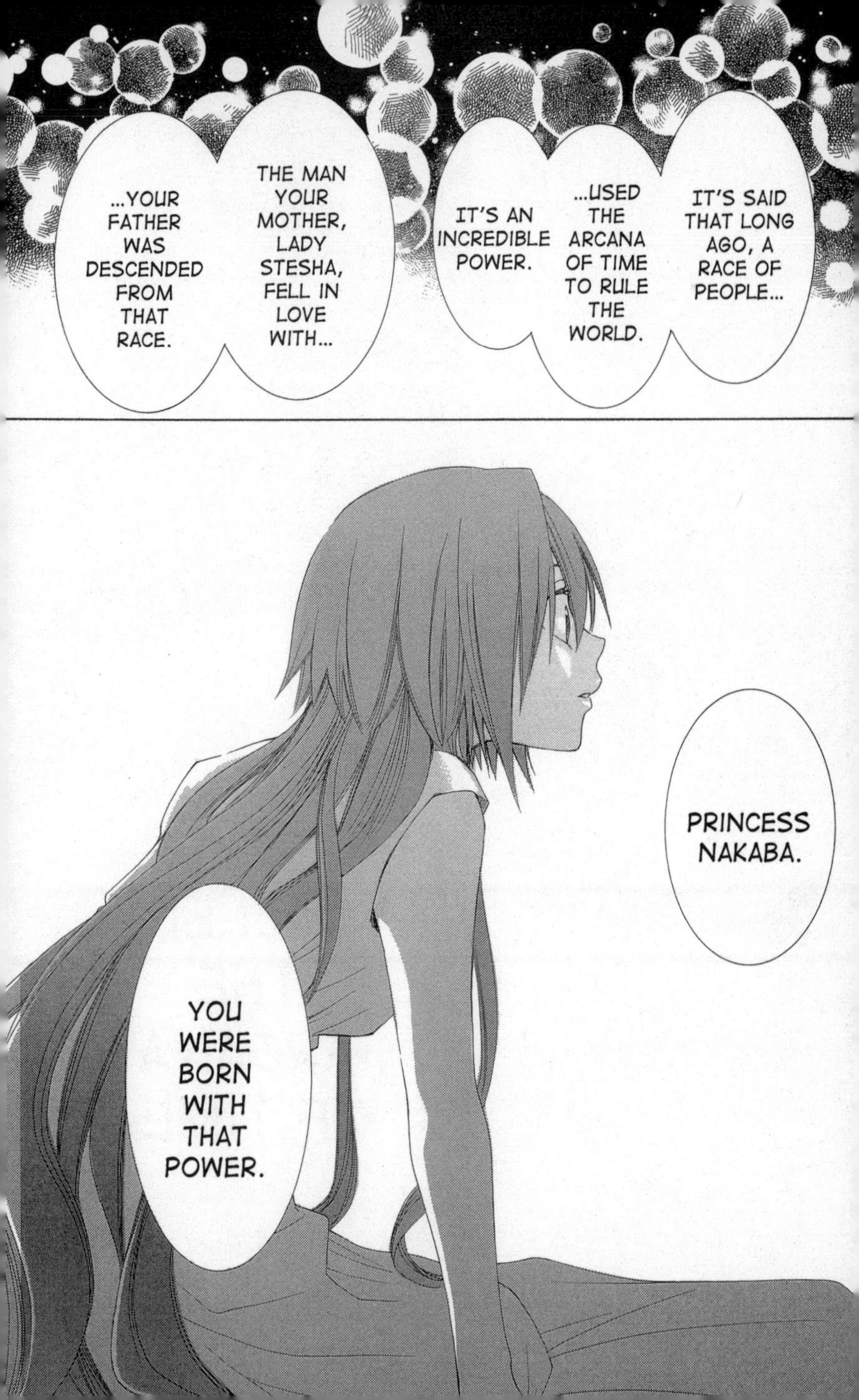
IT'S SAID THAT LONG AGO, A RACE OF PEOPLE...
...USED THE ARCANA OF TIME TO RULE THE WORLD.
IT'S AN INCREDIBLE POWER.
THE MAN YOUR MOTHER, LADY STESHA, FELL IN LOVE WITH...
...YOUR FATHER WAS DESCENDED FROM THAT RACE.
PRINCESS NAKABA.
YOU WERE BORN WITH THAT POWER.

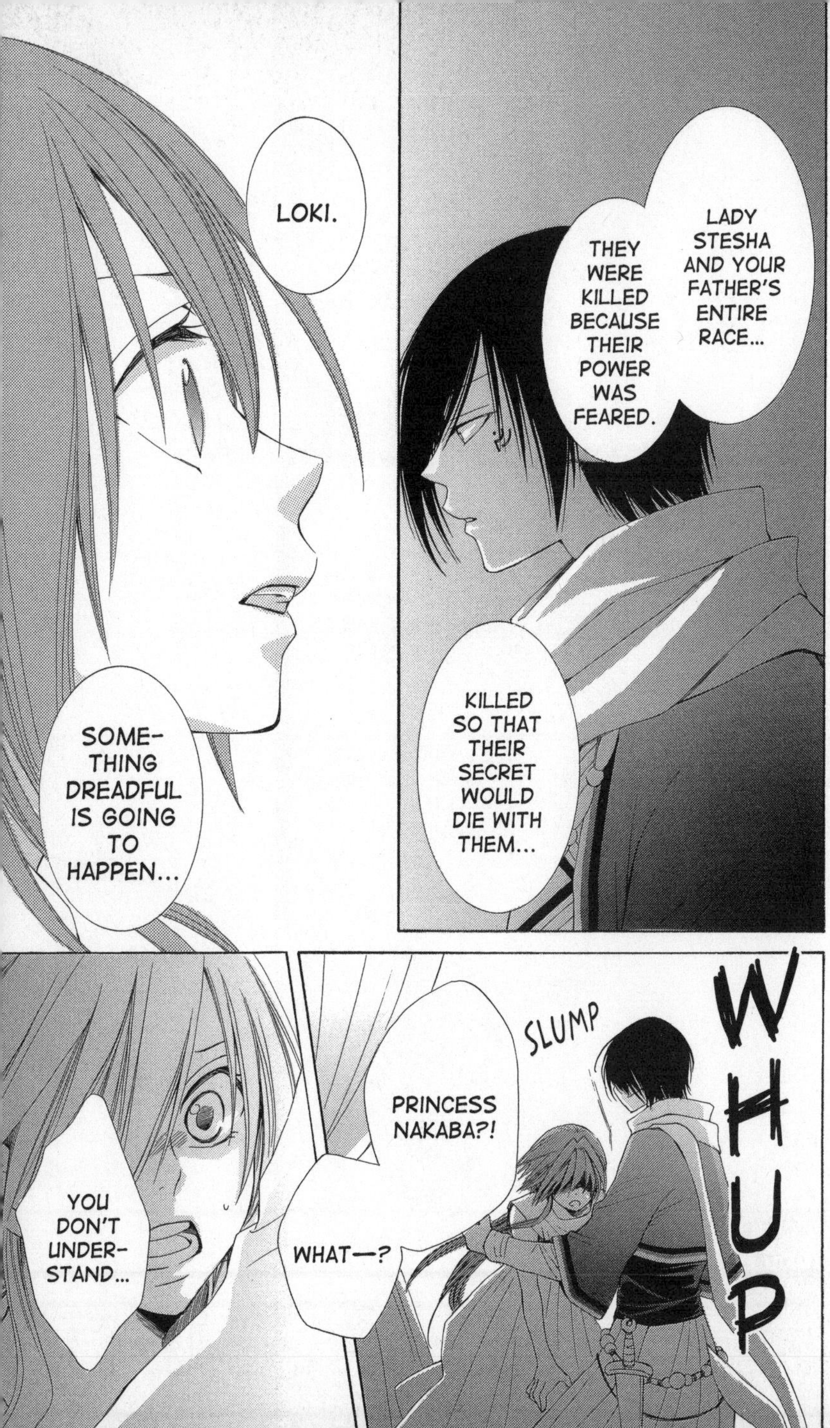
LADY STESHA AND YOUR FATHER'S ENTIRE RACE...
THEY WERE KILLED BECAUSE THEIR POWER WAS FEARED.
KILLED SO THAT THEIR SECRET WOULD DIE WITH THEM...
LOKI.
SOME-THING DREADFUL IS GOING TO HAPPEN...
WHUP
SLUMP
PRINCESS NAKABA?!
WHAT—?
YOU DON'T UNDER-STAND...

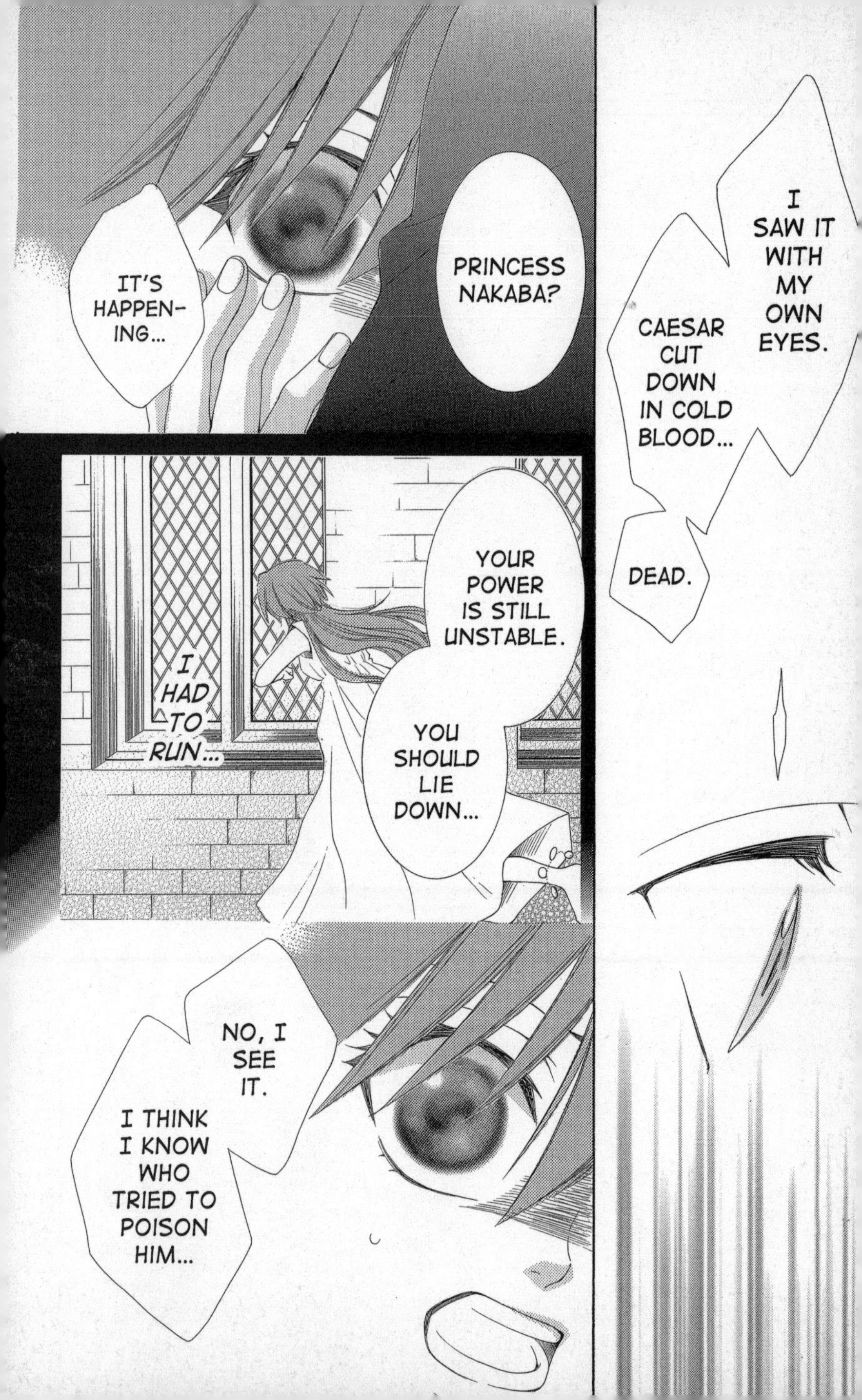
I SAW IT WITH MY OWN EYES.
CAESAR CUT DOWN IN COLD BLOOD...
DEAD.
PRINCESS NAKABA?
IT'S HAPPENING...
YOUR POWER IS STILL UNSTABLE.
YOU SHOULD LIE DOWN...
I HAD TO RUN...
NO, I SEE IT.
I THINK I KNOW WHO TRIED TO POISON HIM...

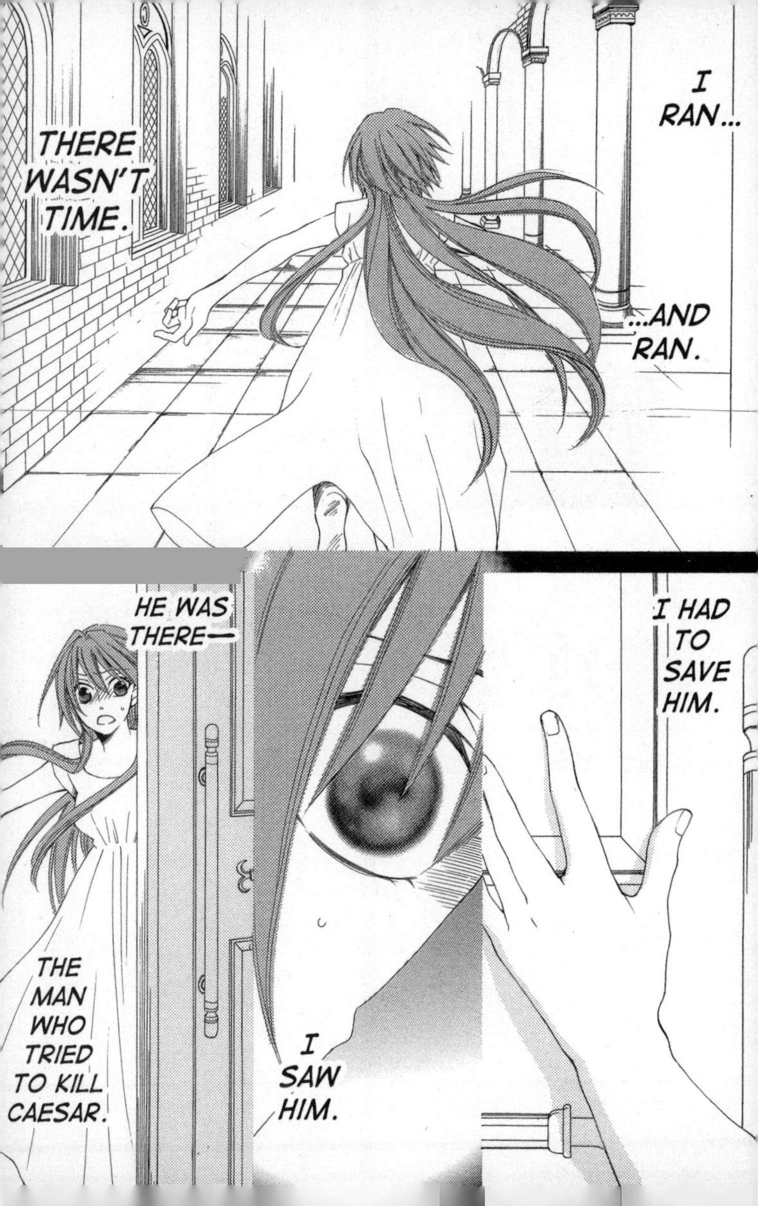
I RAN...
...AND RAN.
THERE WASN'T TIME.
I HAD TO SAVE HIM.
I SAW HIM.
HE WAS THERE—
THE MAN WHO TRIED TO KILL CAESAR.

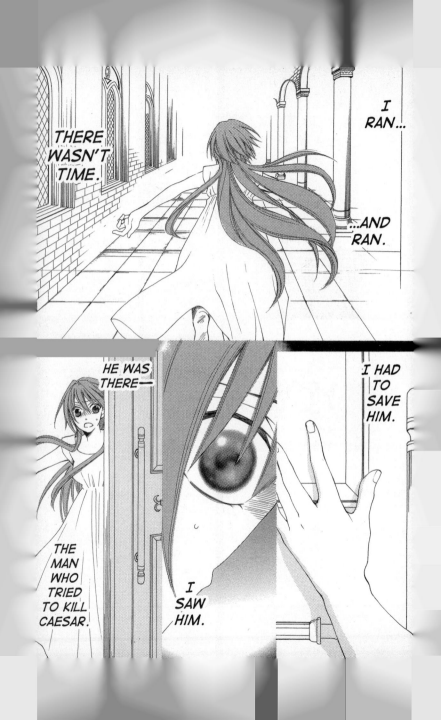

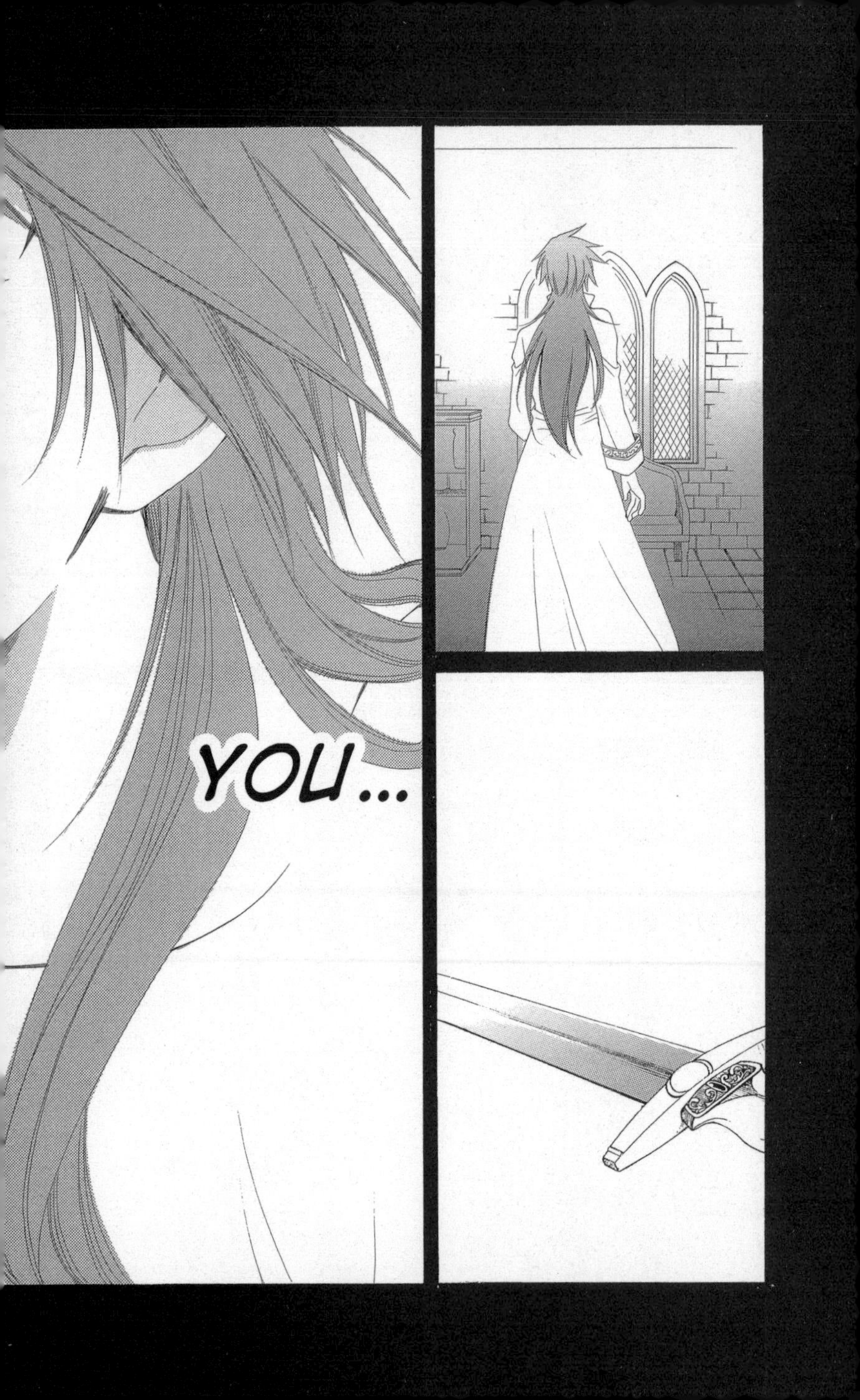
YOU...

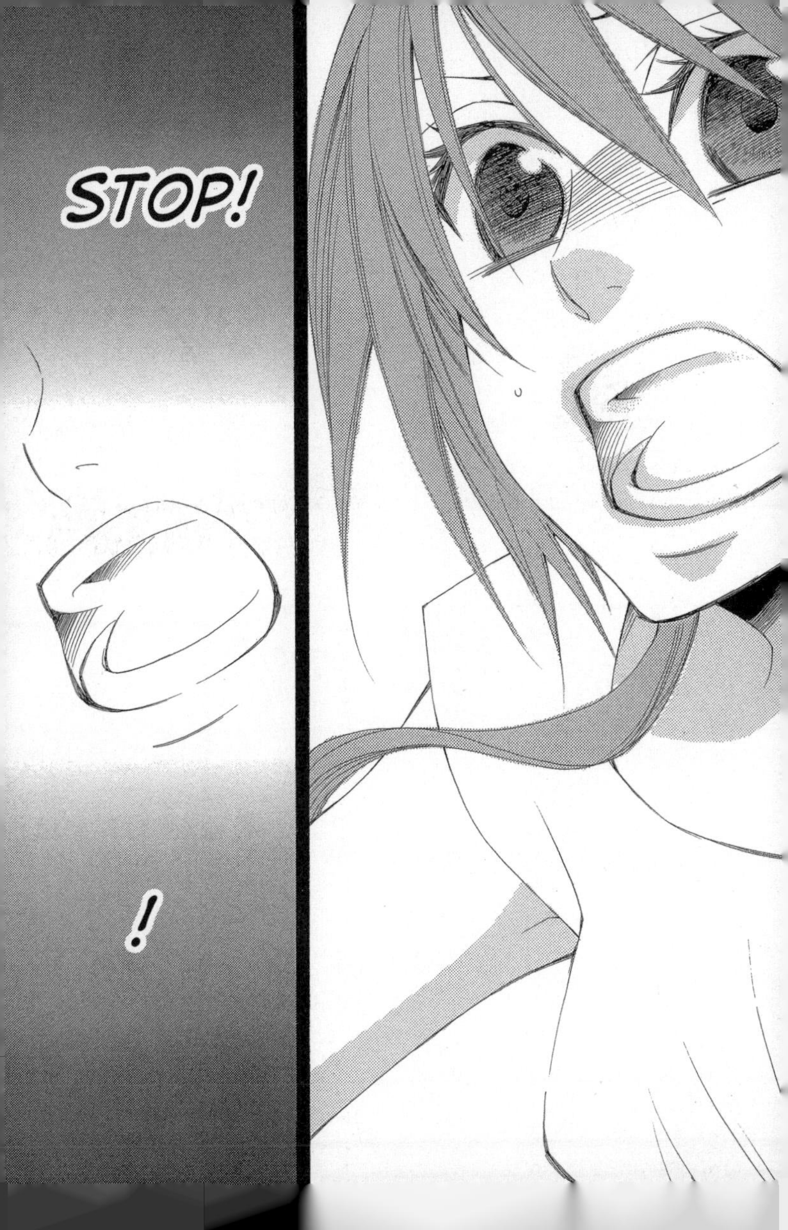
STOP!
!

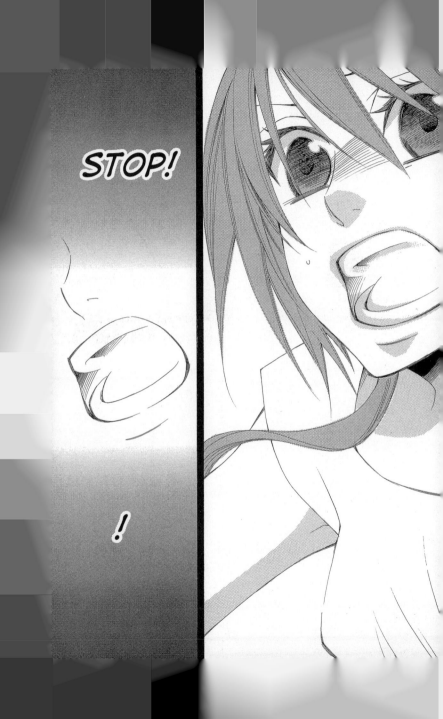

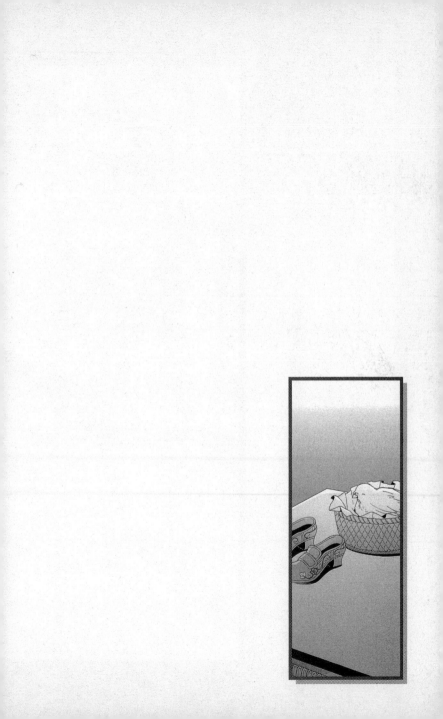

Chapter 6

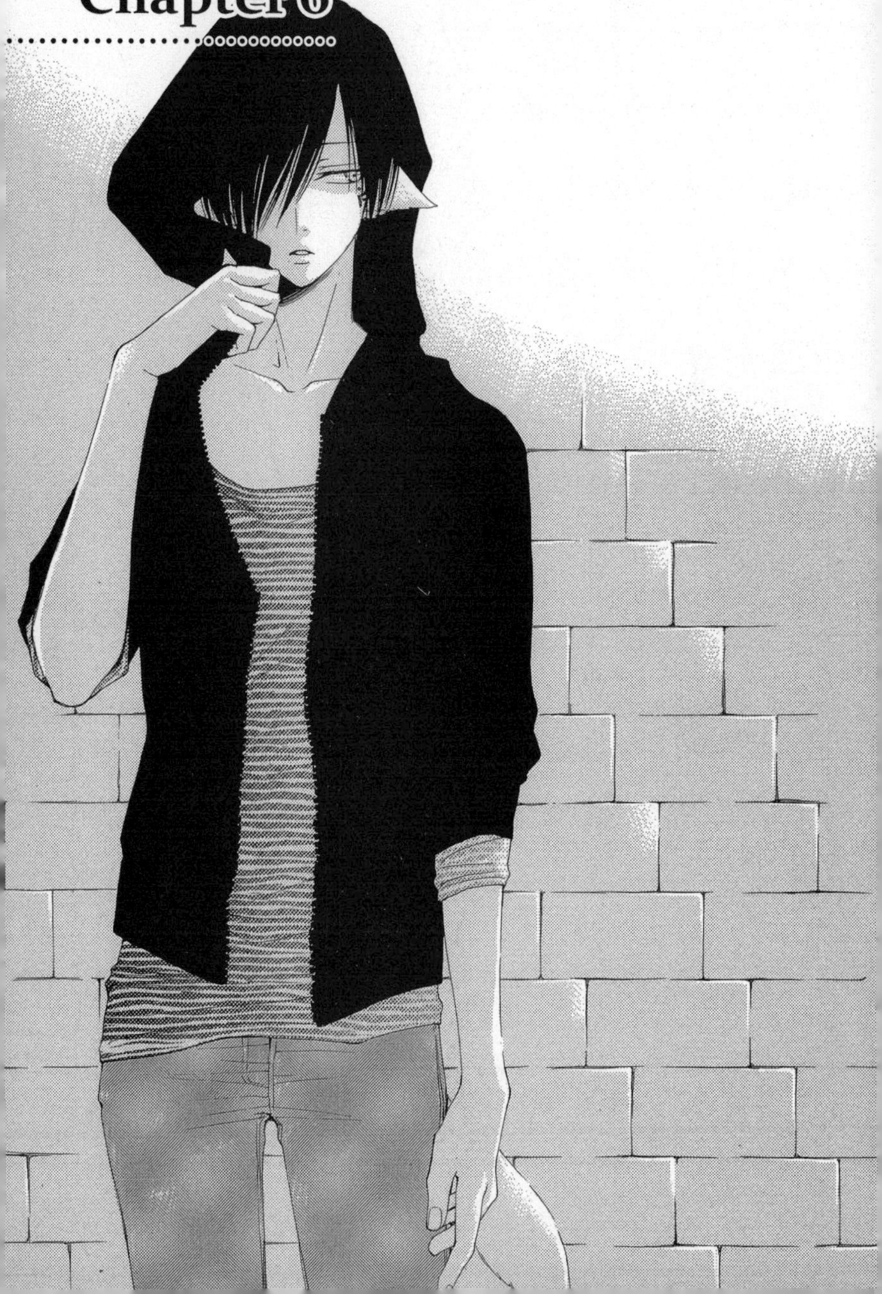

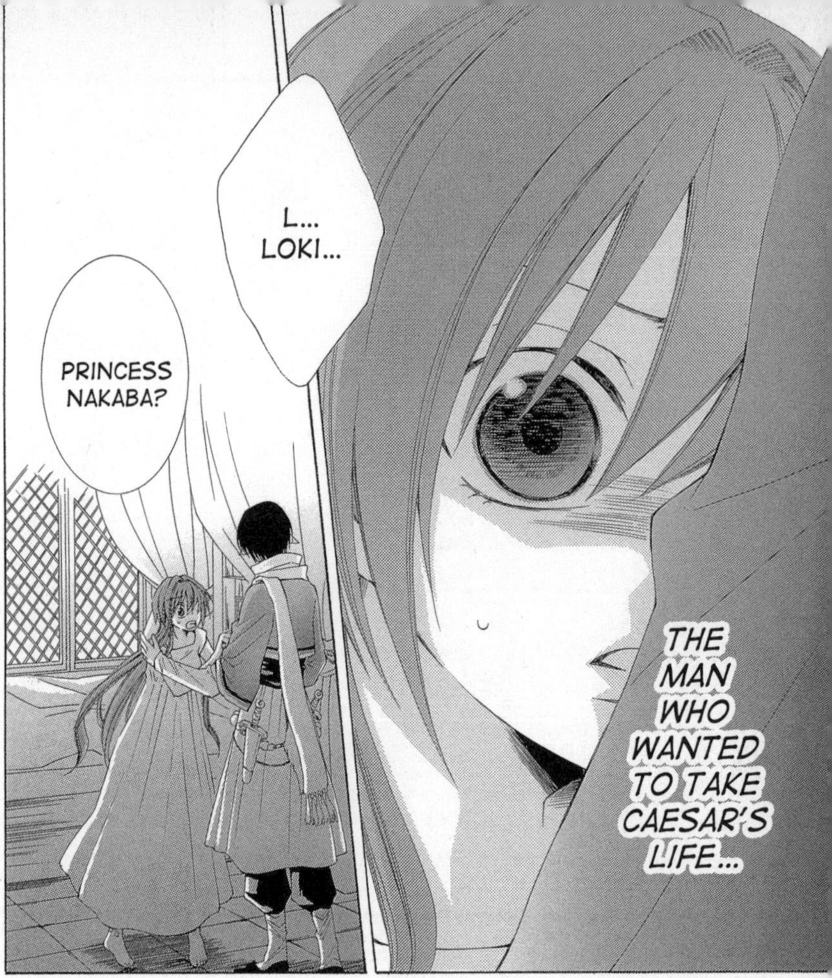
L... LOKI...
THE MAN WHO WANTED TO TAKE CAESAR'S LIFE...
PRINCESS NAKABA?

Dawn of the Arcana

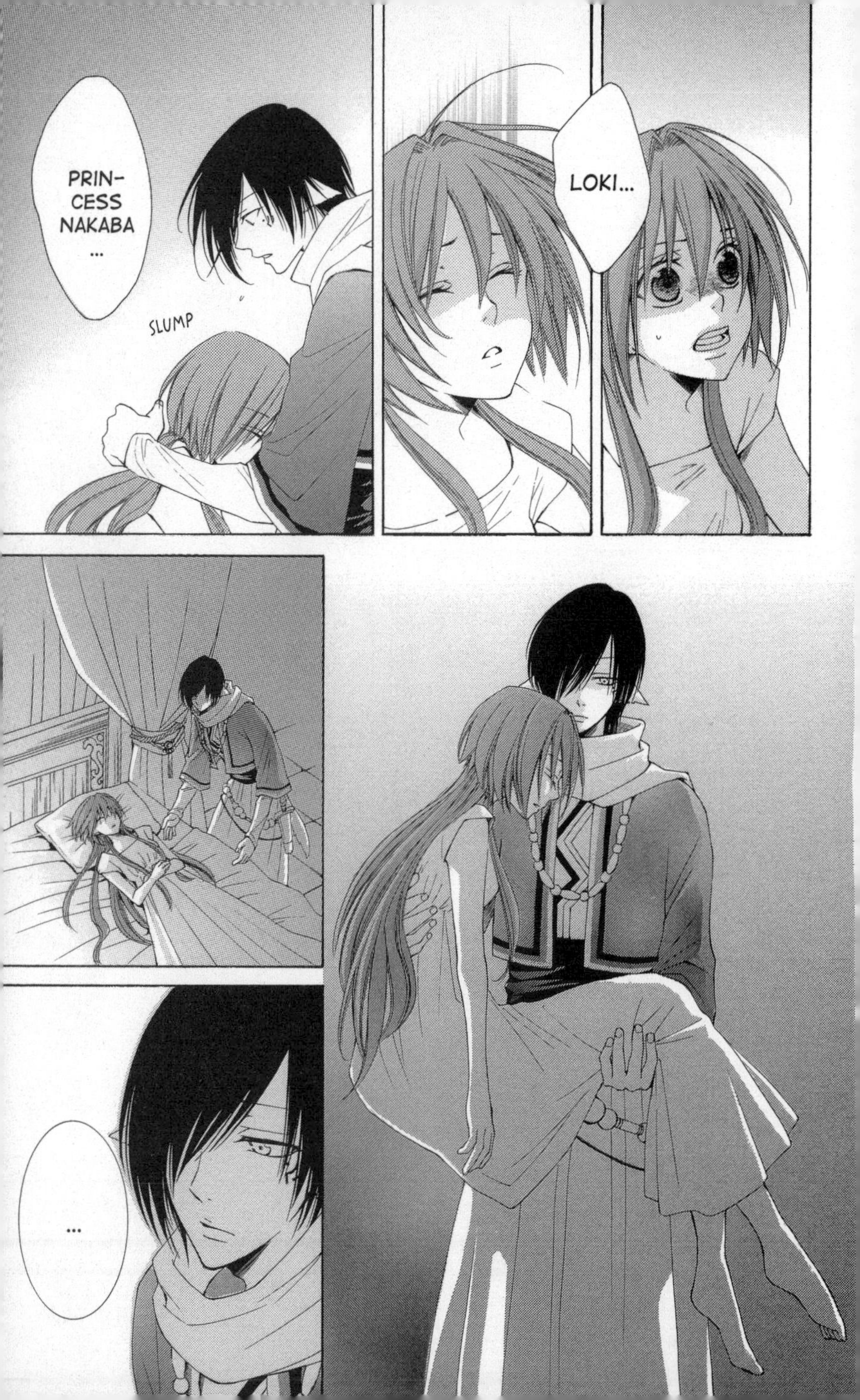
LOKI...
PRIN-CESS NAKABA...
SLUMP
...

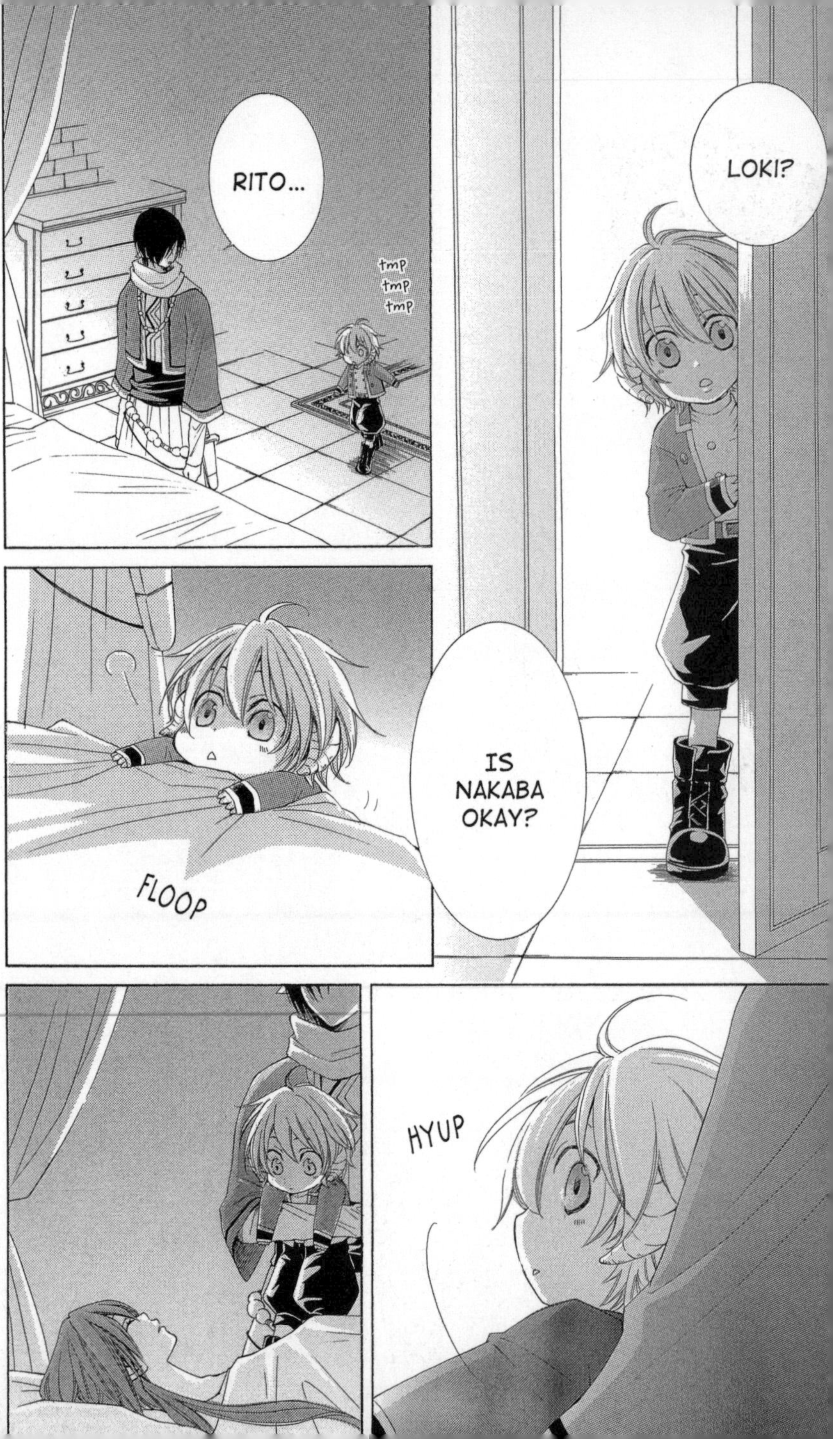
LOKI?
IS NAKABA OKAY?
RITO...
tmp tmp tmp
FLOOP
HYUP

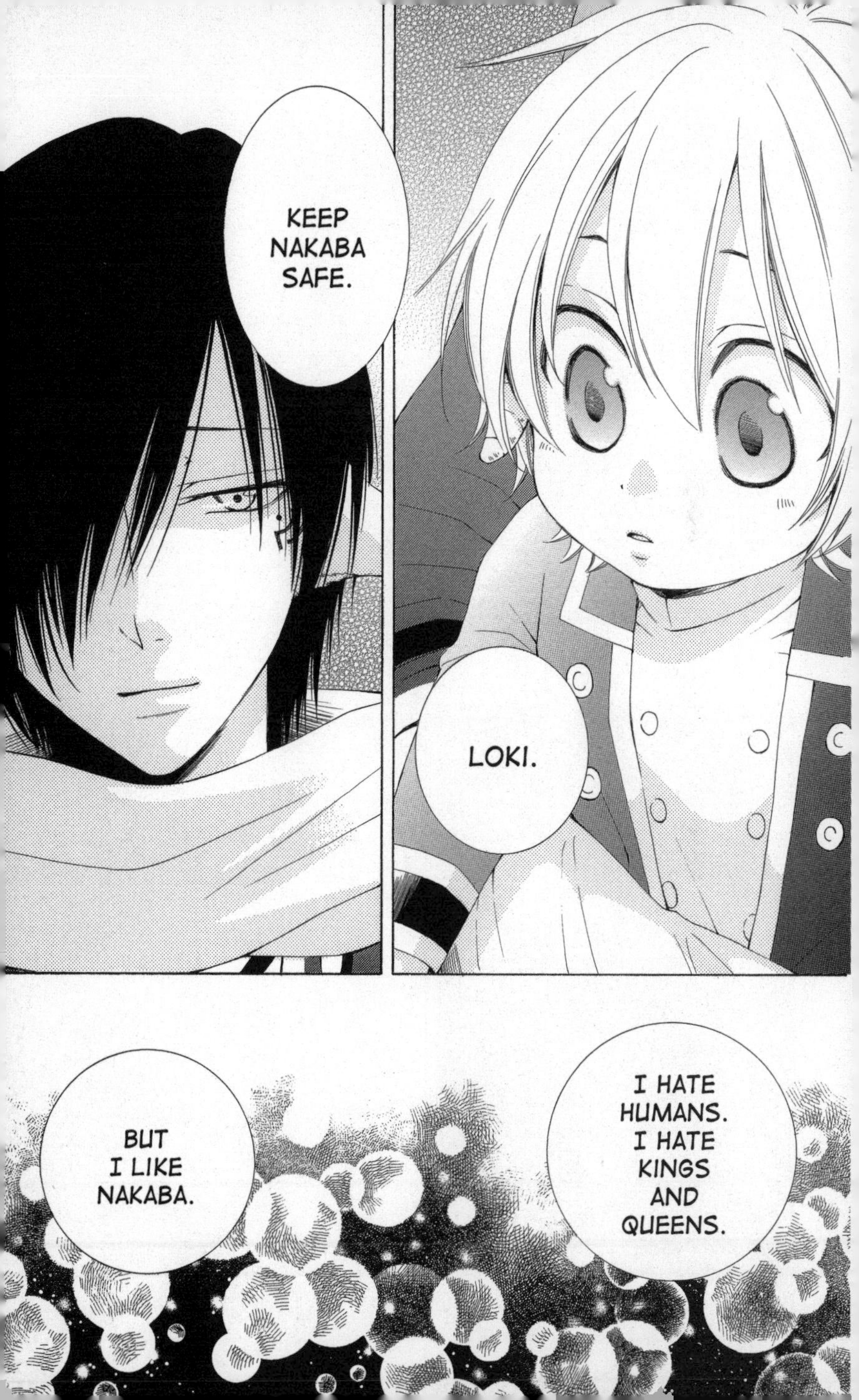
LOKI.
KEEP NAKABA SAFE.
I HATE HUMANS. I HATE KINGS AND QUEENS.
BUT I LIKE NAKABA.

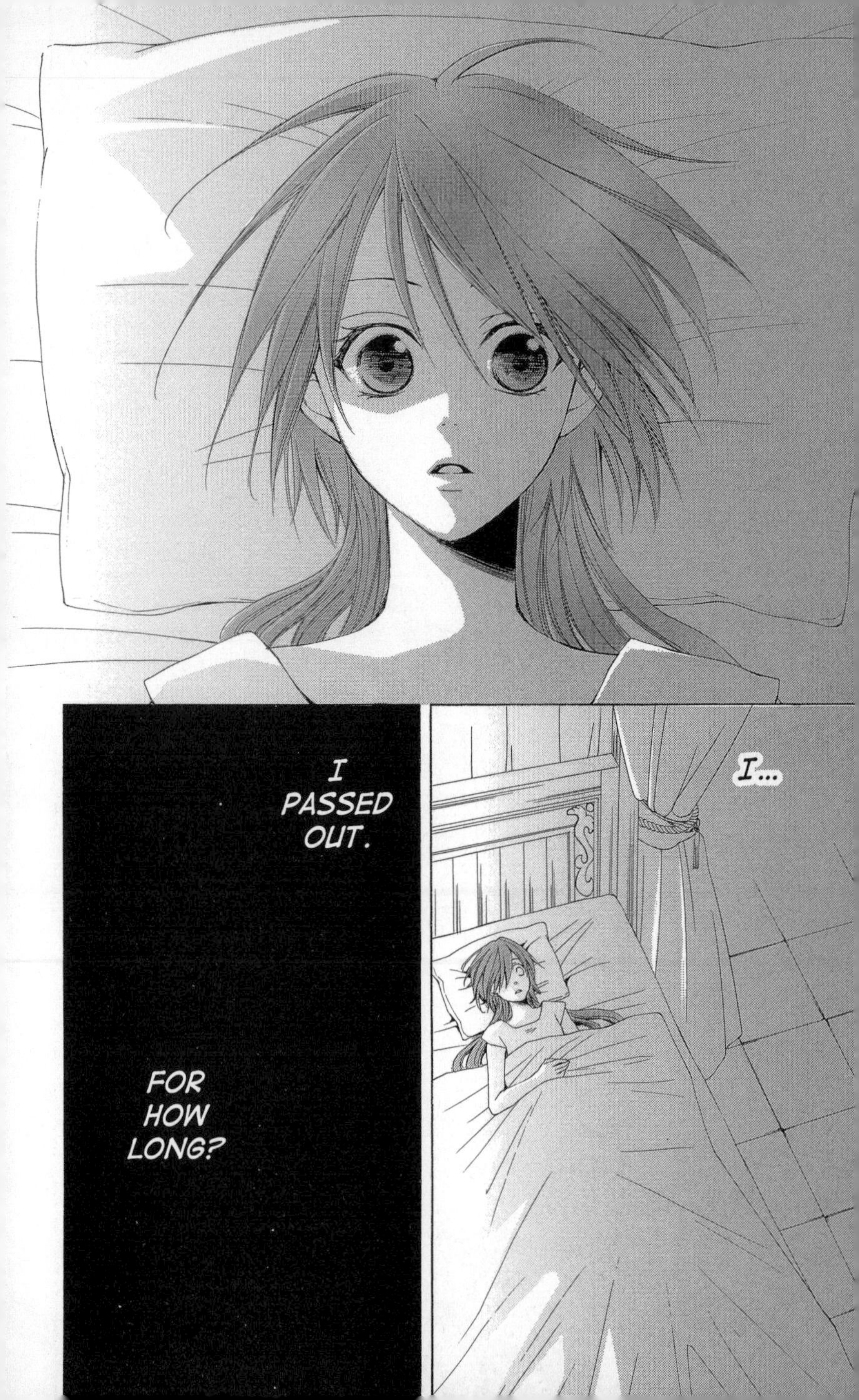
I...
I PASSED OUT.
FOR HOW LONG?

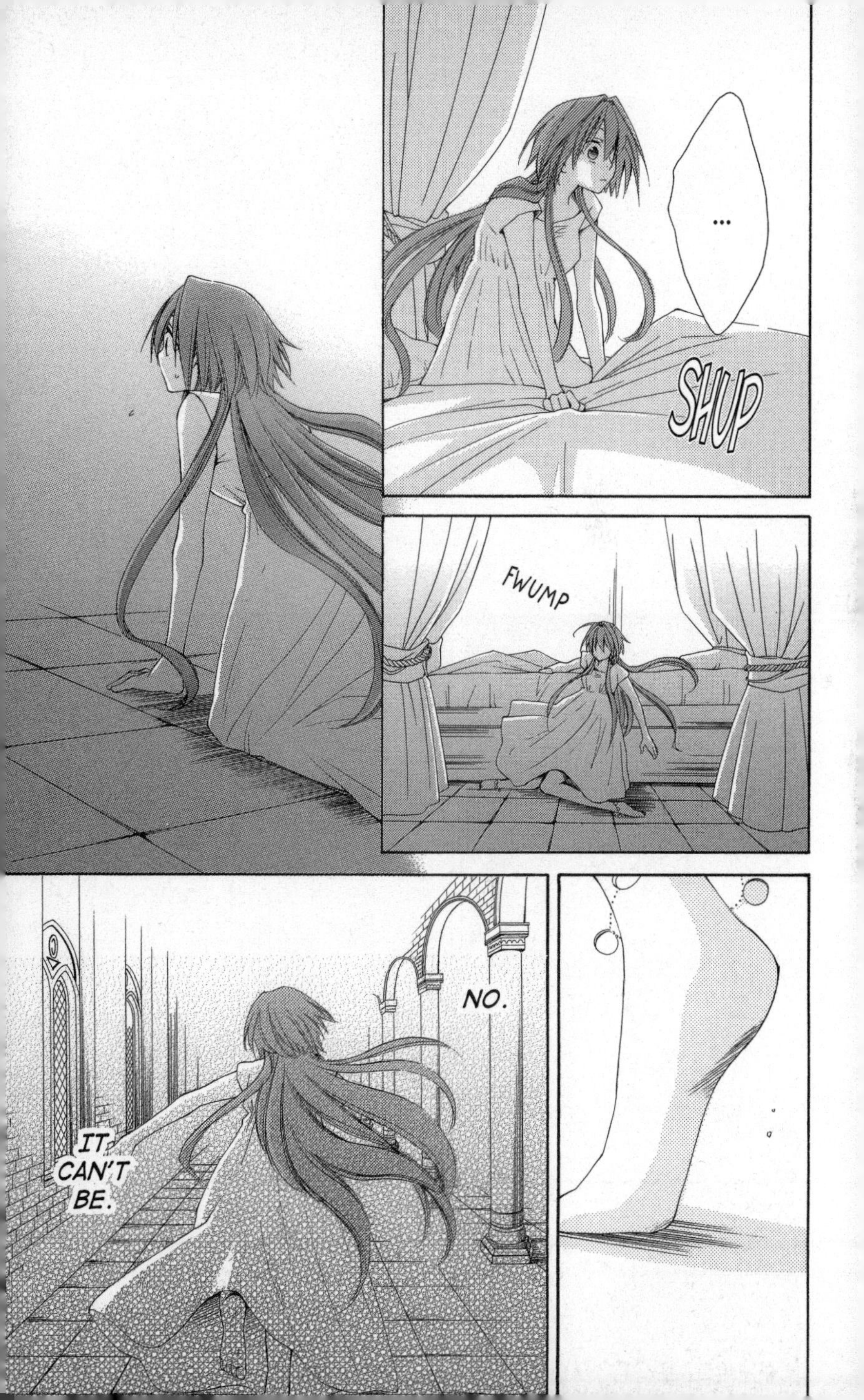
...
SHUP
FWUMP
NO.
IT CAN'T BE.

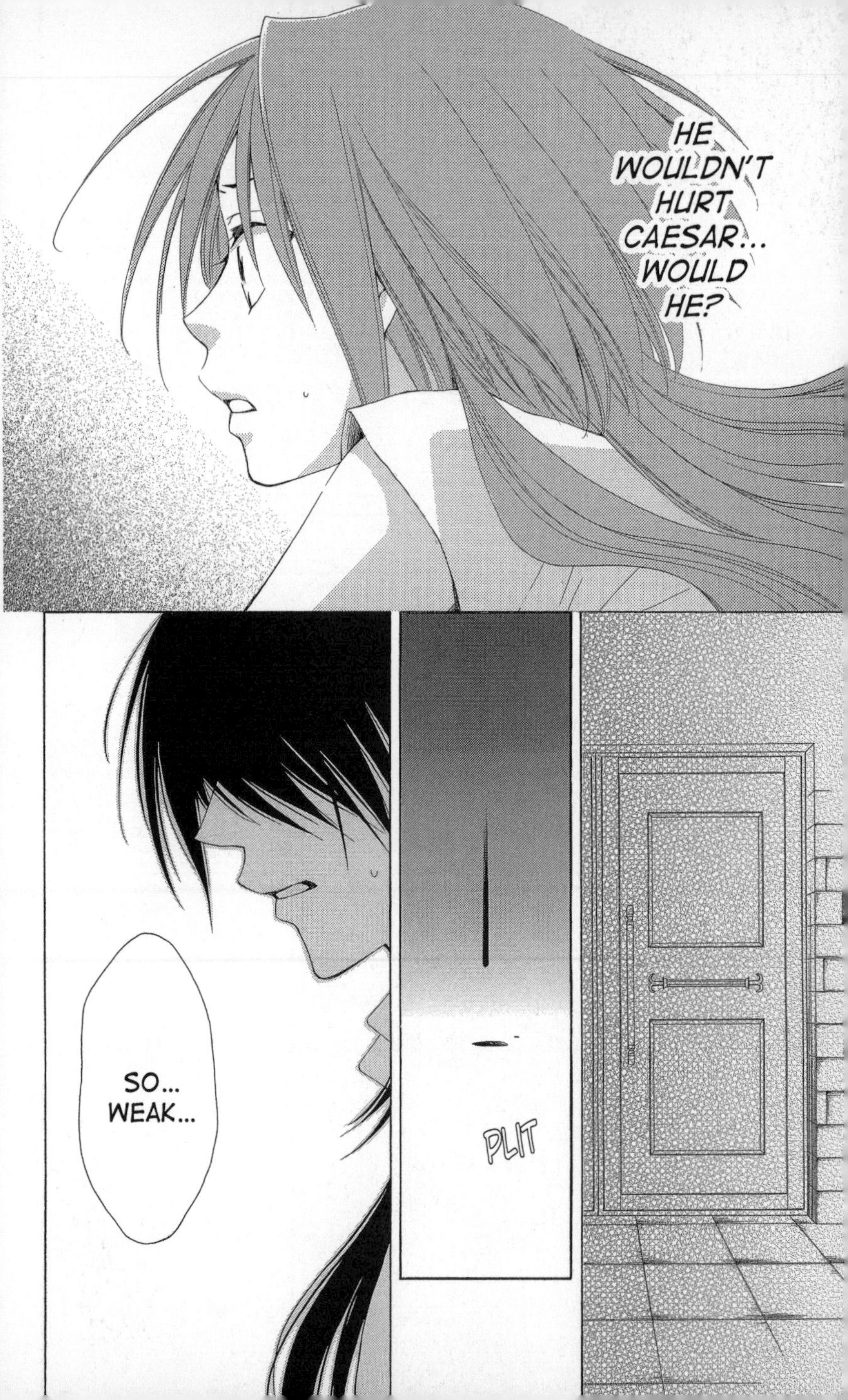
HE WOULDN'T HURT CAESAR... WOULD HE?
PLIT
SO... WEAK...

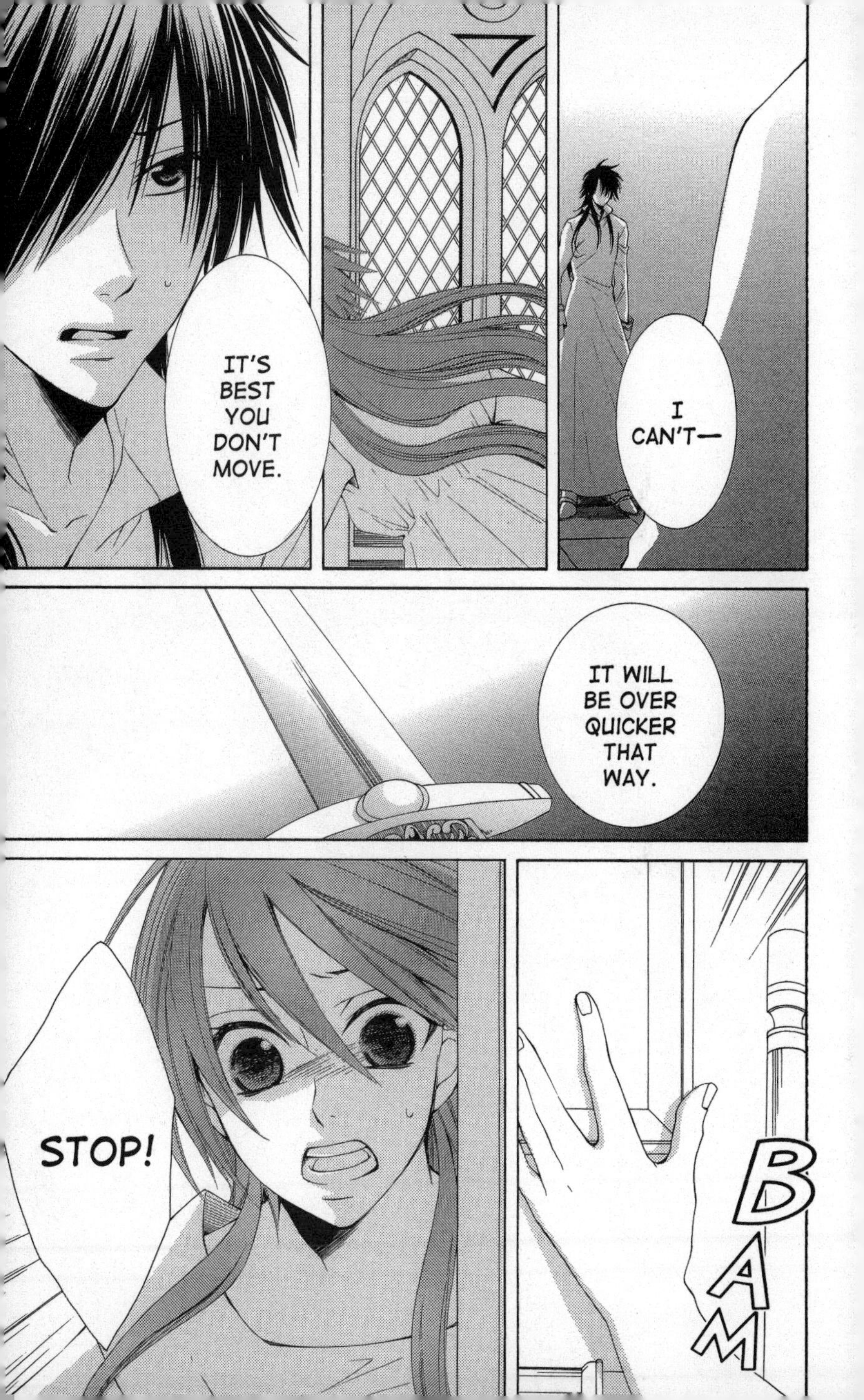
I CAN'T—
IT'S BEST YOU DON'T MOVE.
IT WILL BE OVER QUICKER THAT WAY.
BAM
STOP!

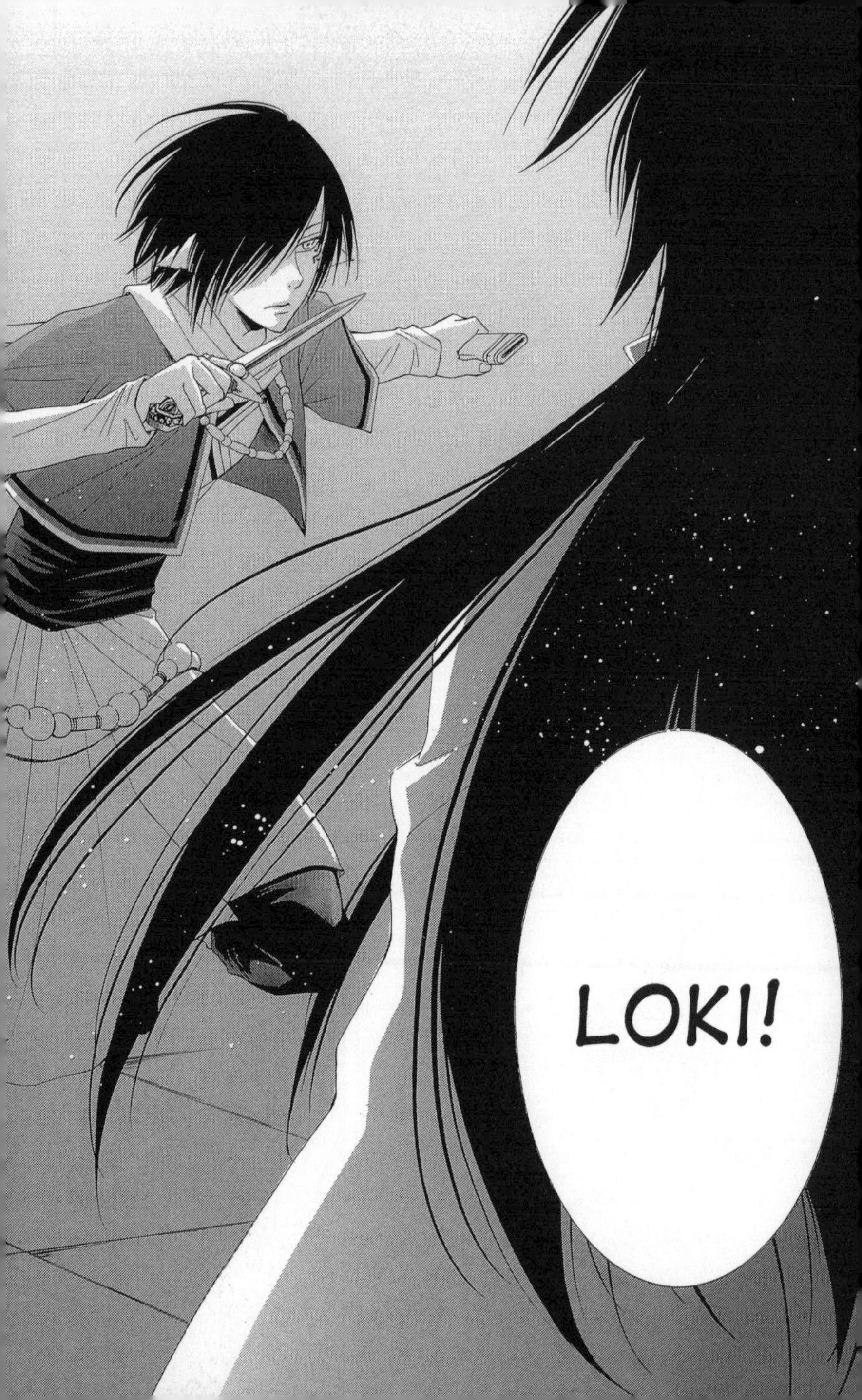
LOKI!

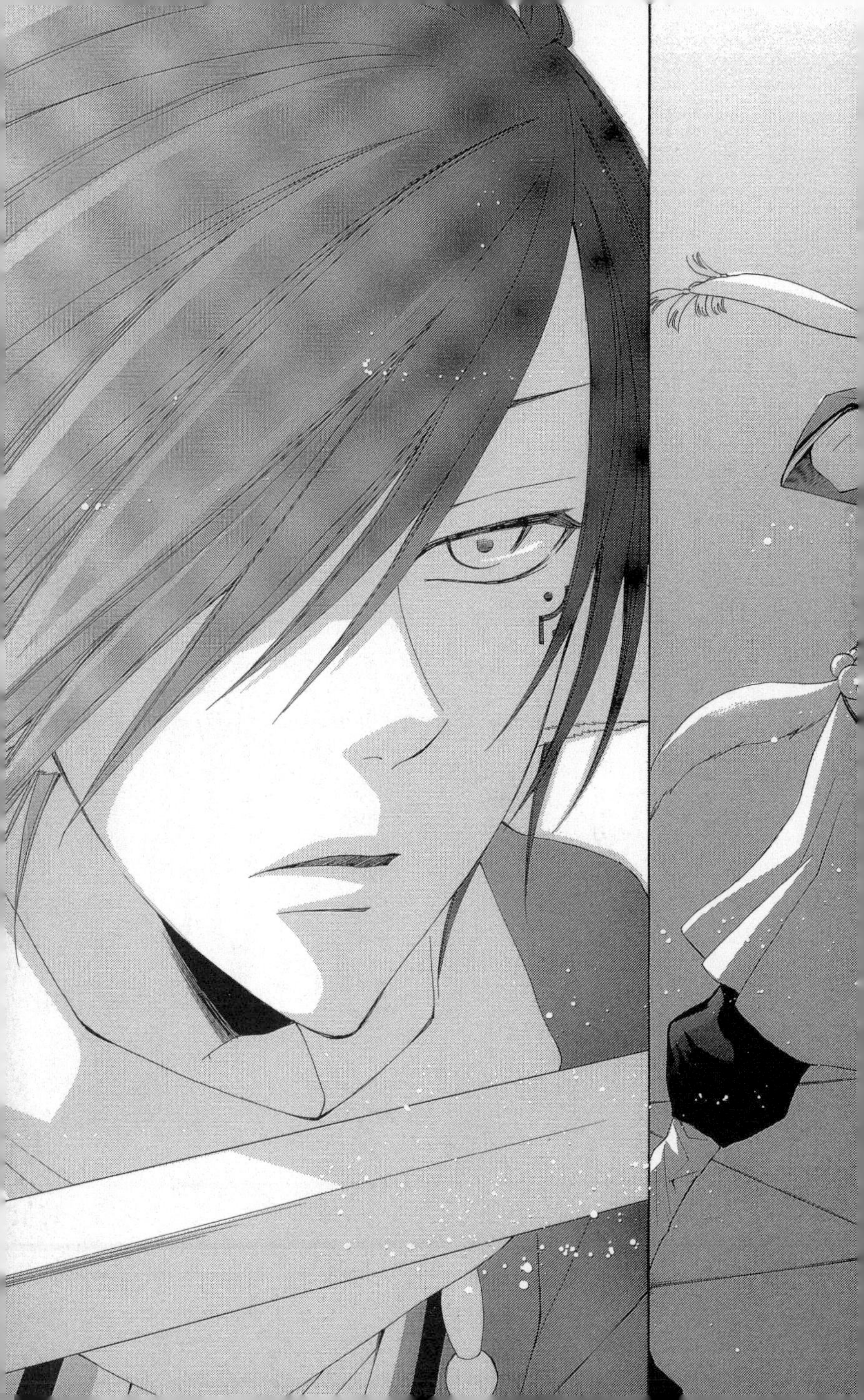

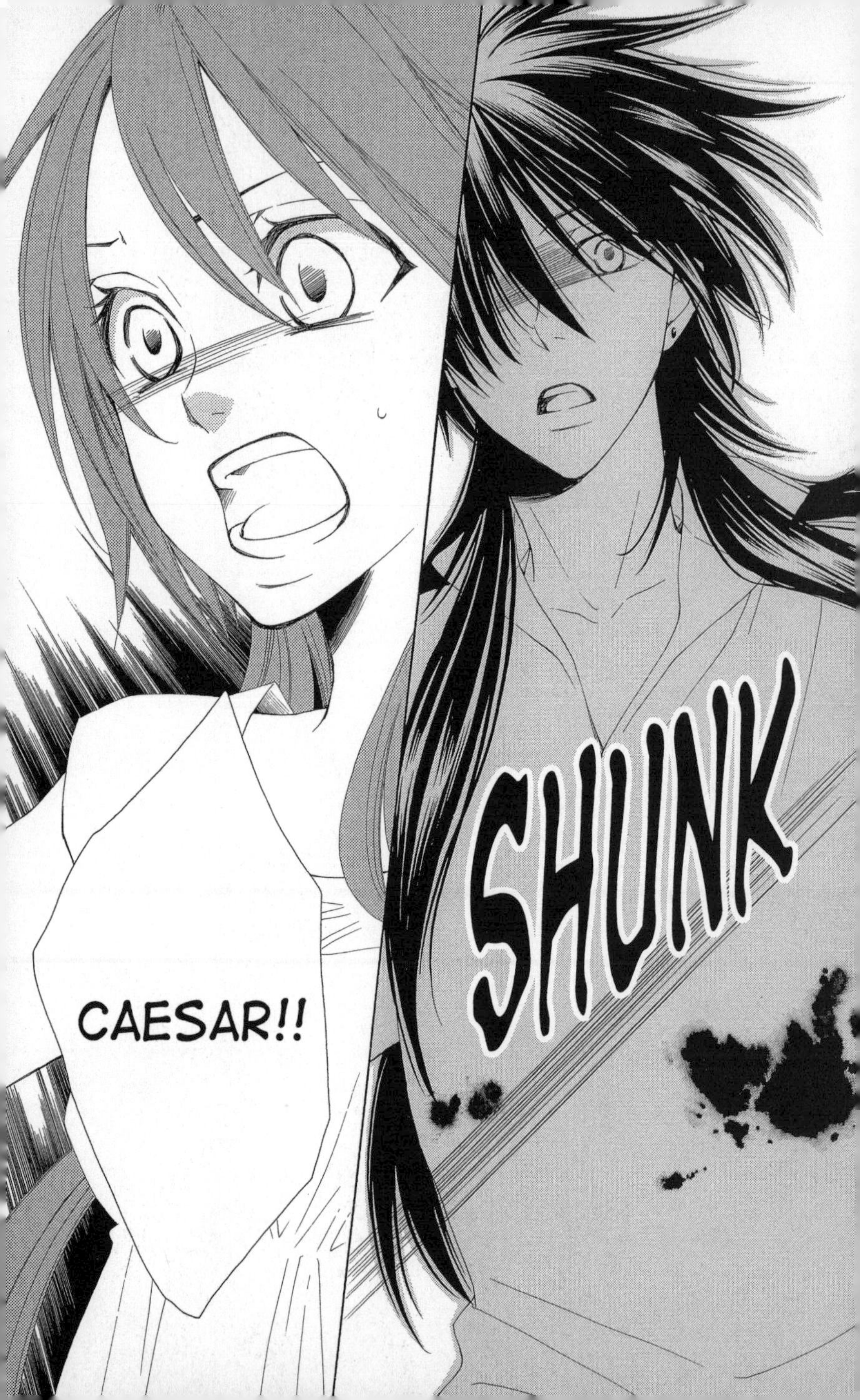
SHUNK
CAESAR!!

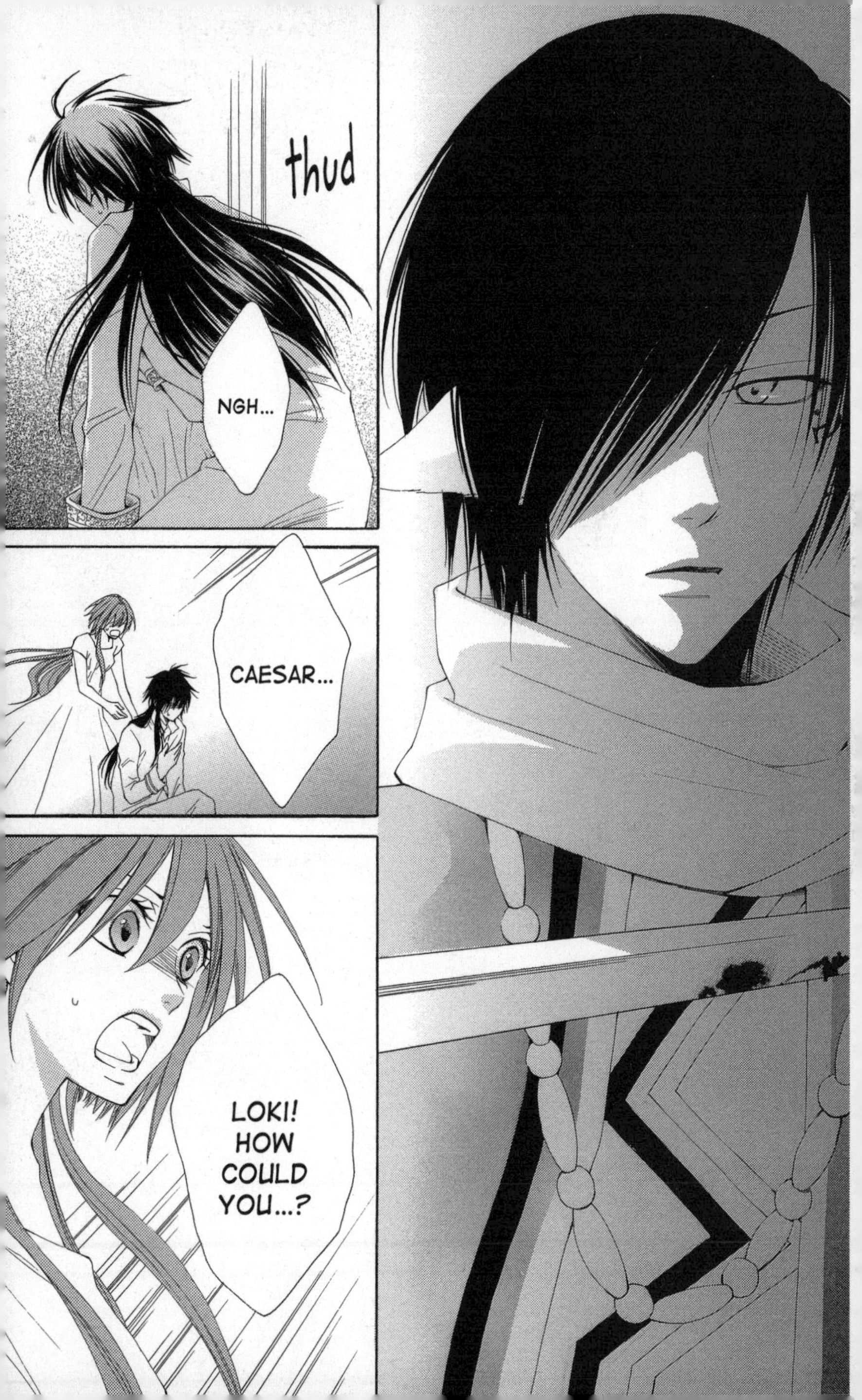
thud
NGH...
CAESAR...
LOKI! HOW COULD YOU...?

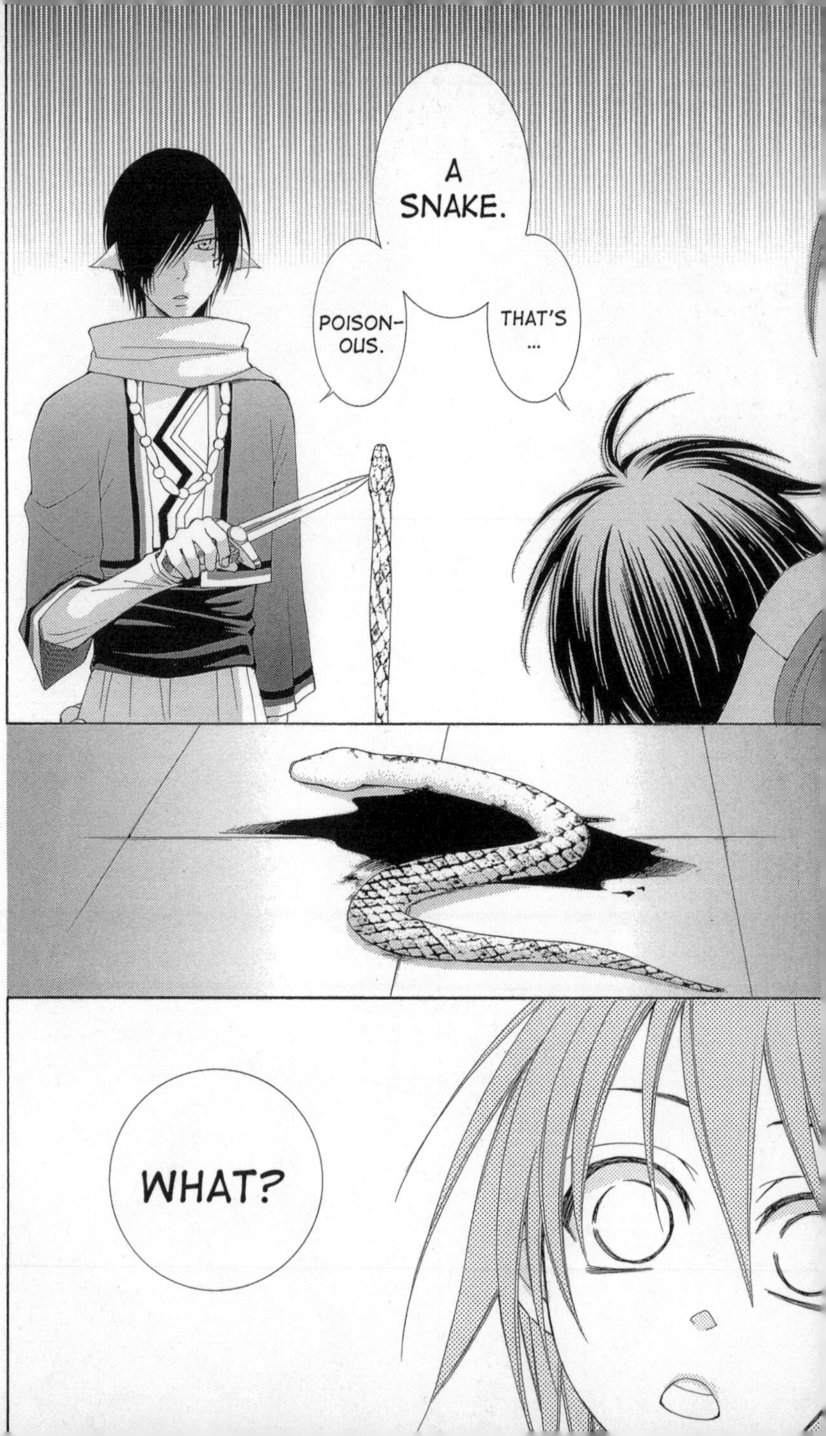
A SNAKE.
THAT'S ...
POISON-OUS.
WHAT?

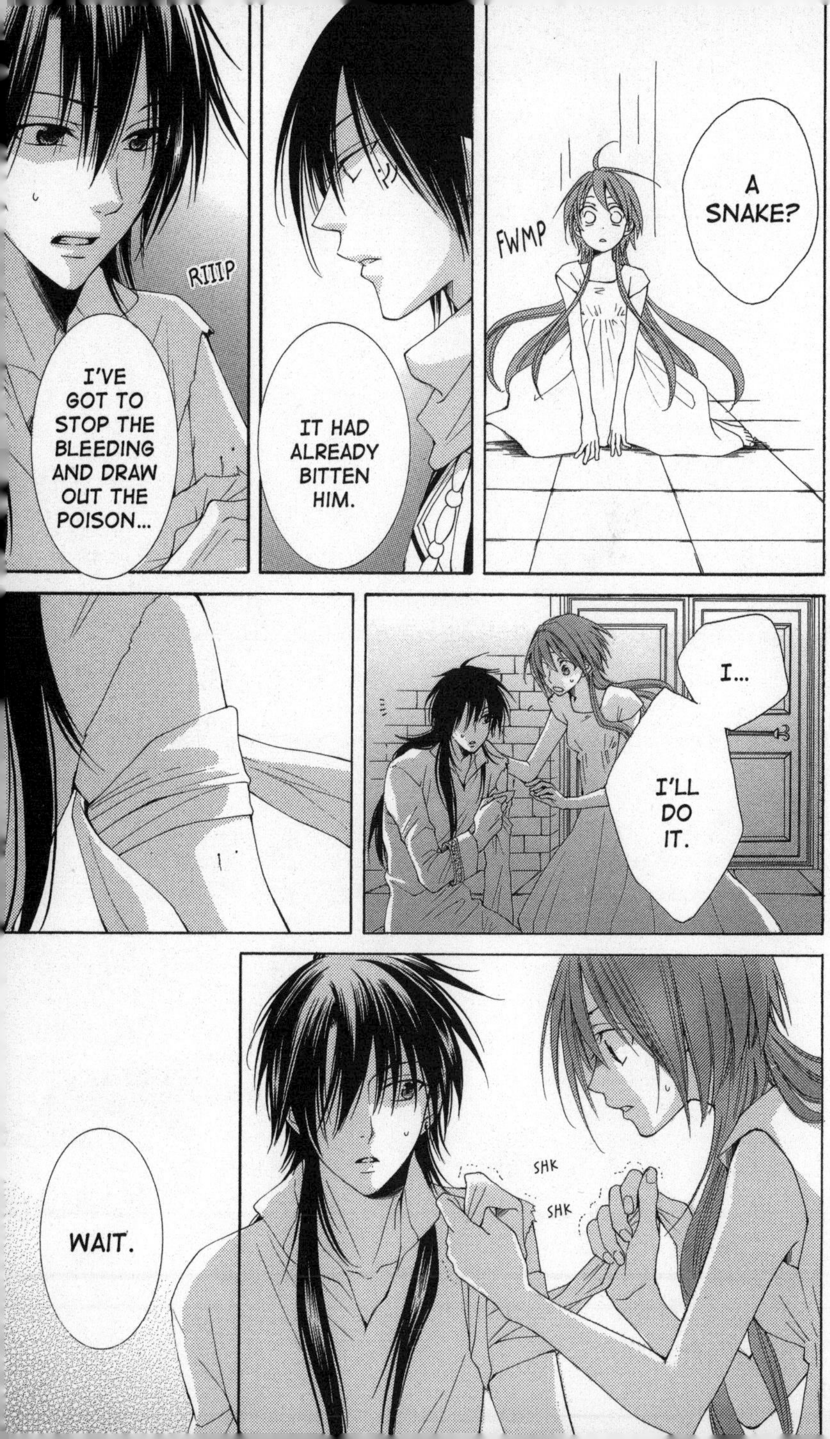

A SNAKE?
FWMP
IT HAD ALREADY BITTEN HIM.
RIIIP
I'VE GOT TO STOP THE BLEEDING AND DRAW OUT THE POISON...
I...
I'LL DO IT.
SHK
SHK
WAIT.

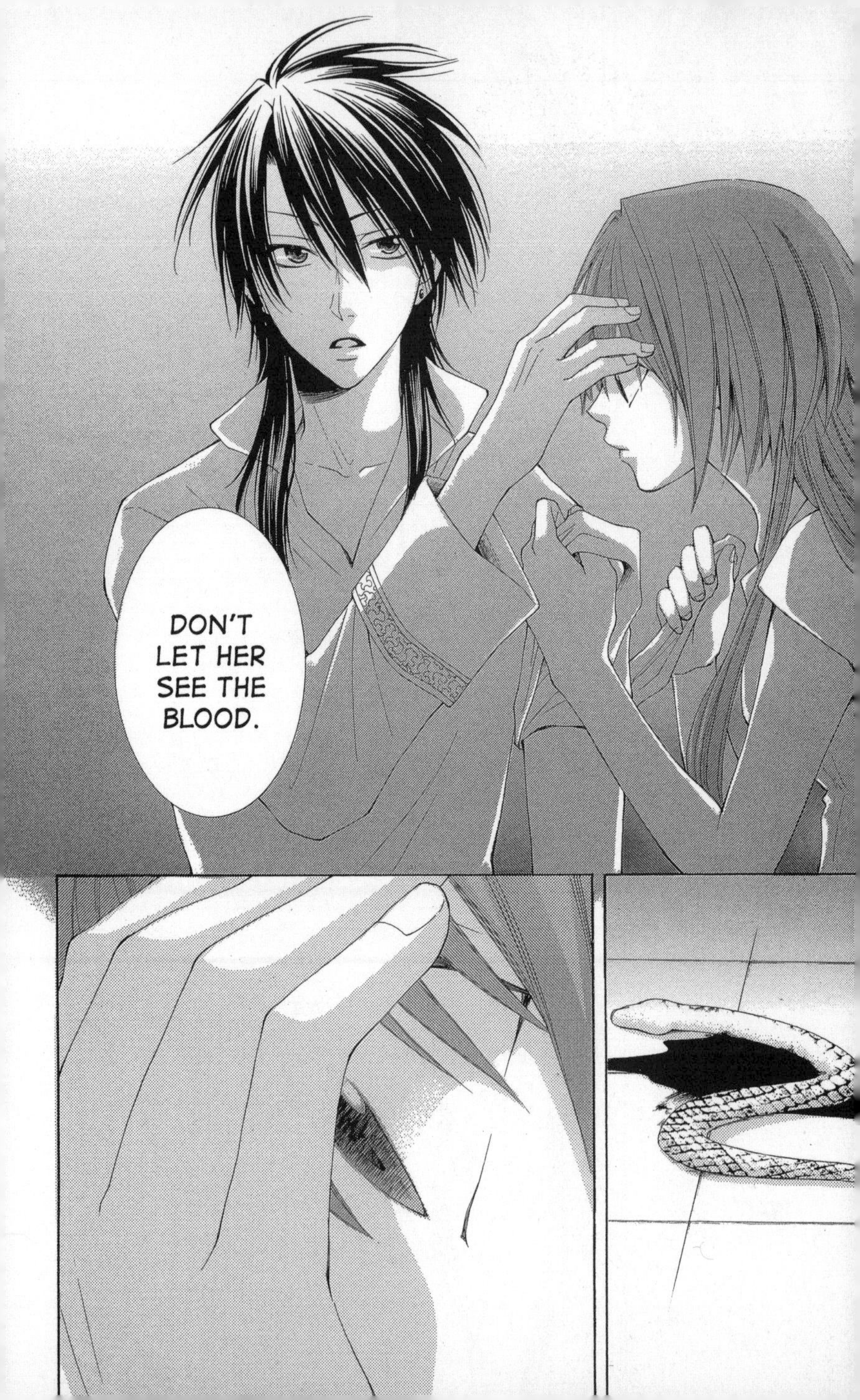
DON'T LET HER SEE THE BLOOD.

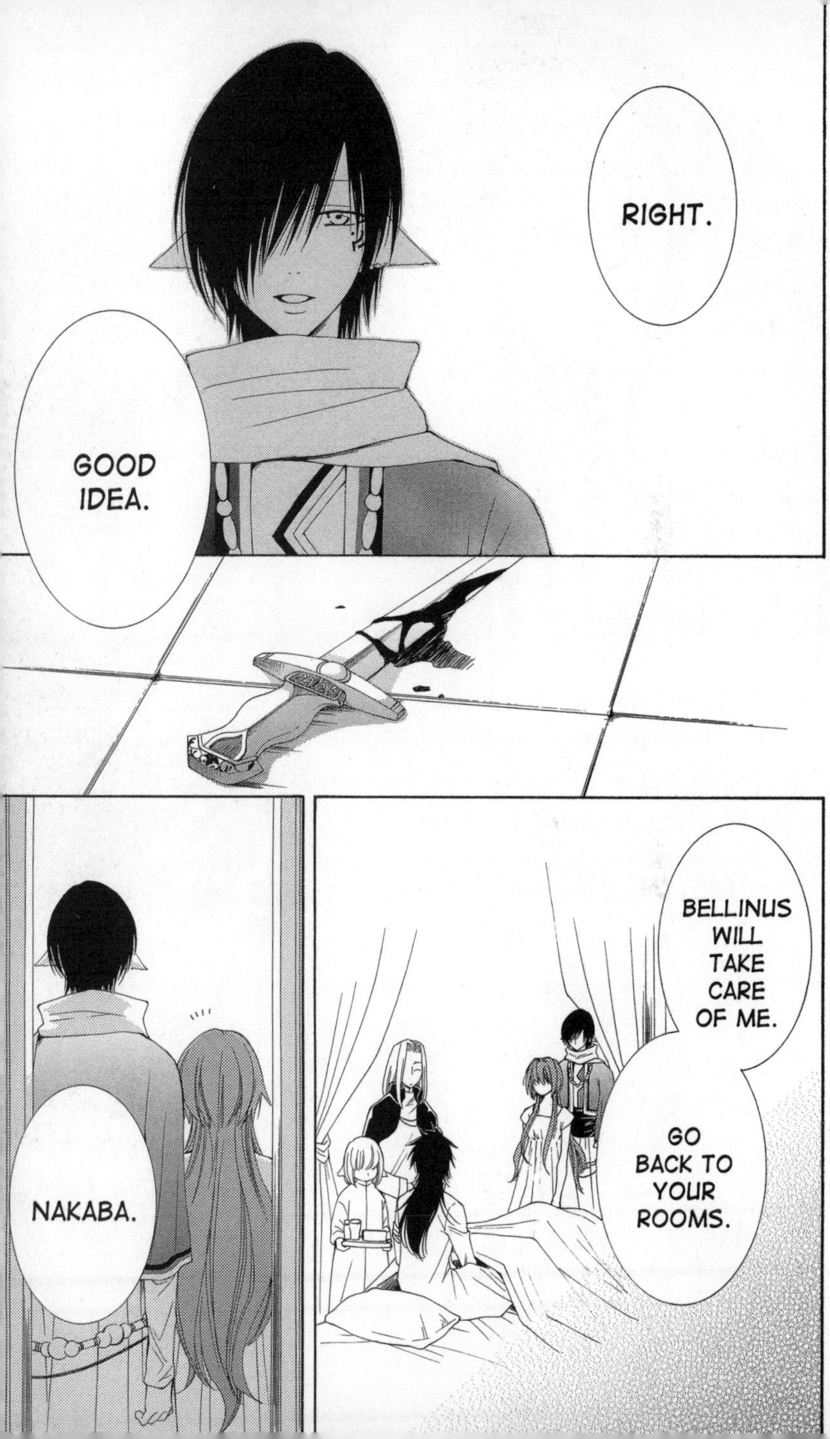
RIGHT.
GOOD IDEA.
BELLINUS WILL TAKE CARE OF ME.
GO BACK TO YOUR ROOMS.
NAKABA.

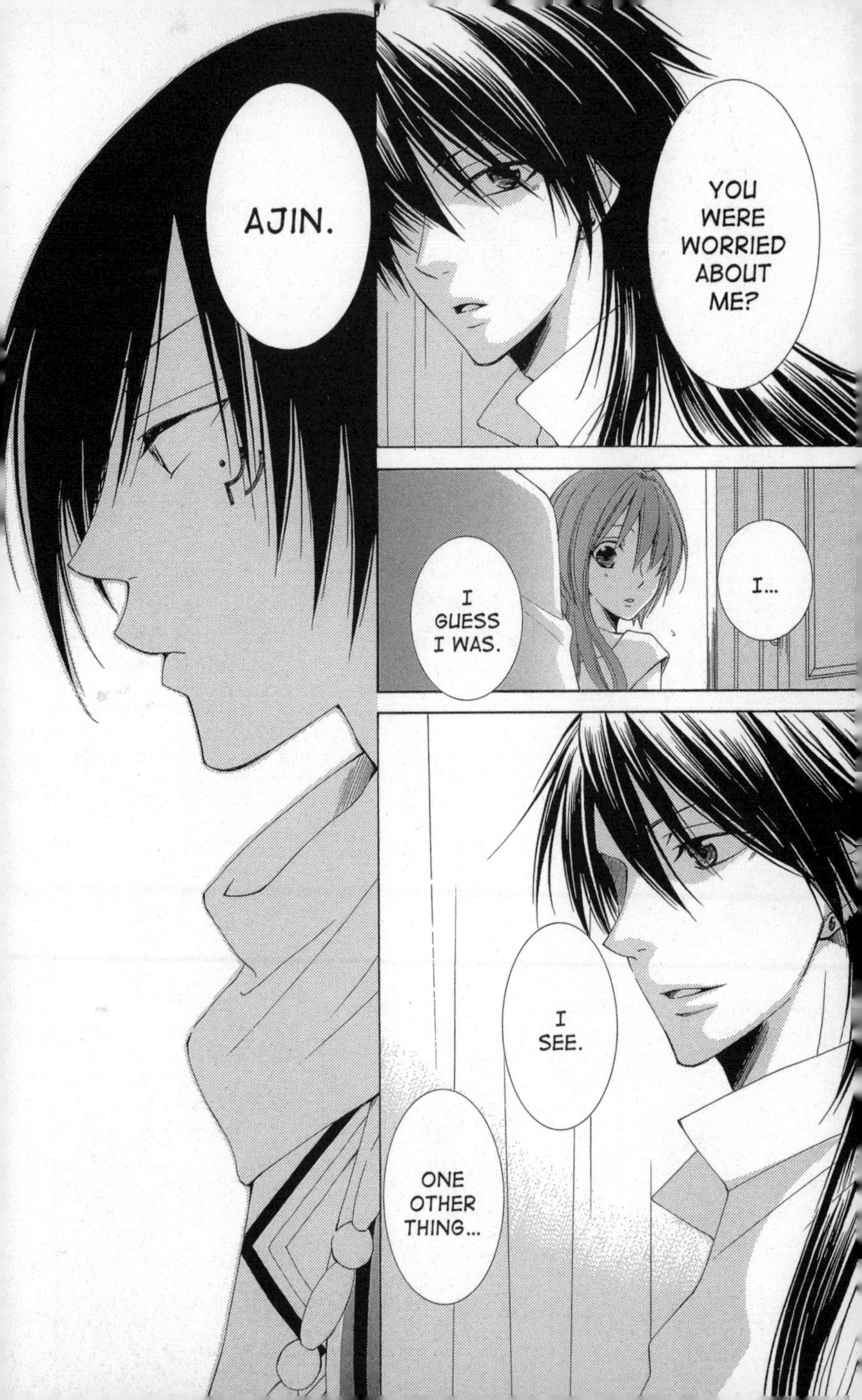
YOU WERE WORRIED ABOUT ME?
I...
I GUESS I WAS.
I SEE.
ONE OTHER THING...
AJIN.

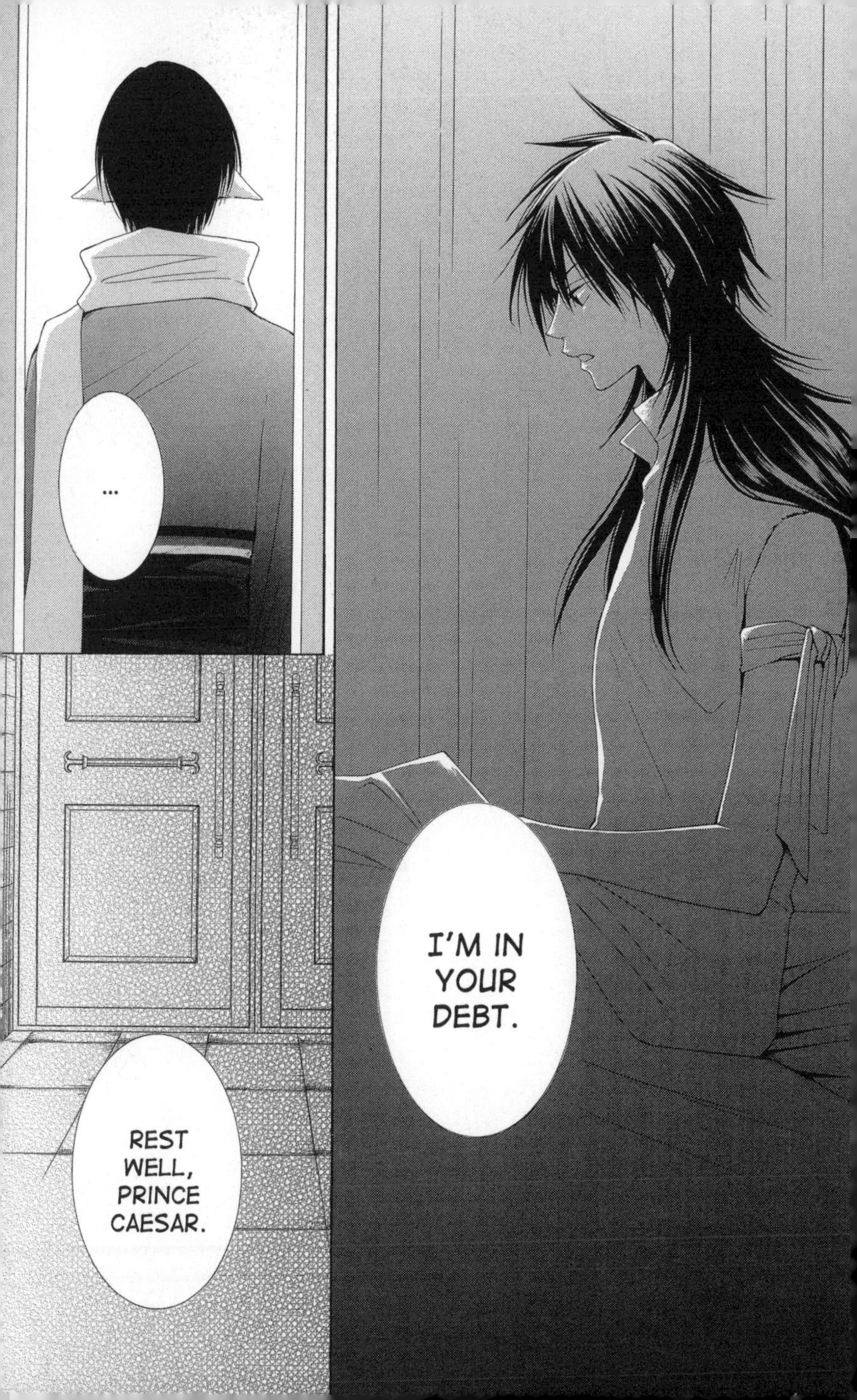
I'M IN YOUR DEBT.
...
REST WELL, PRINCE CAESAR.

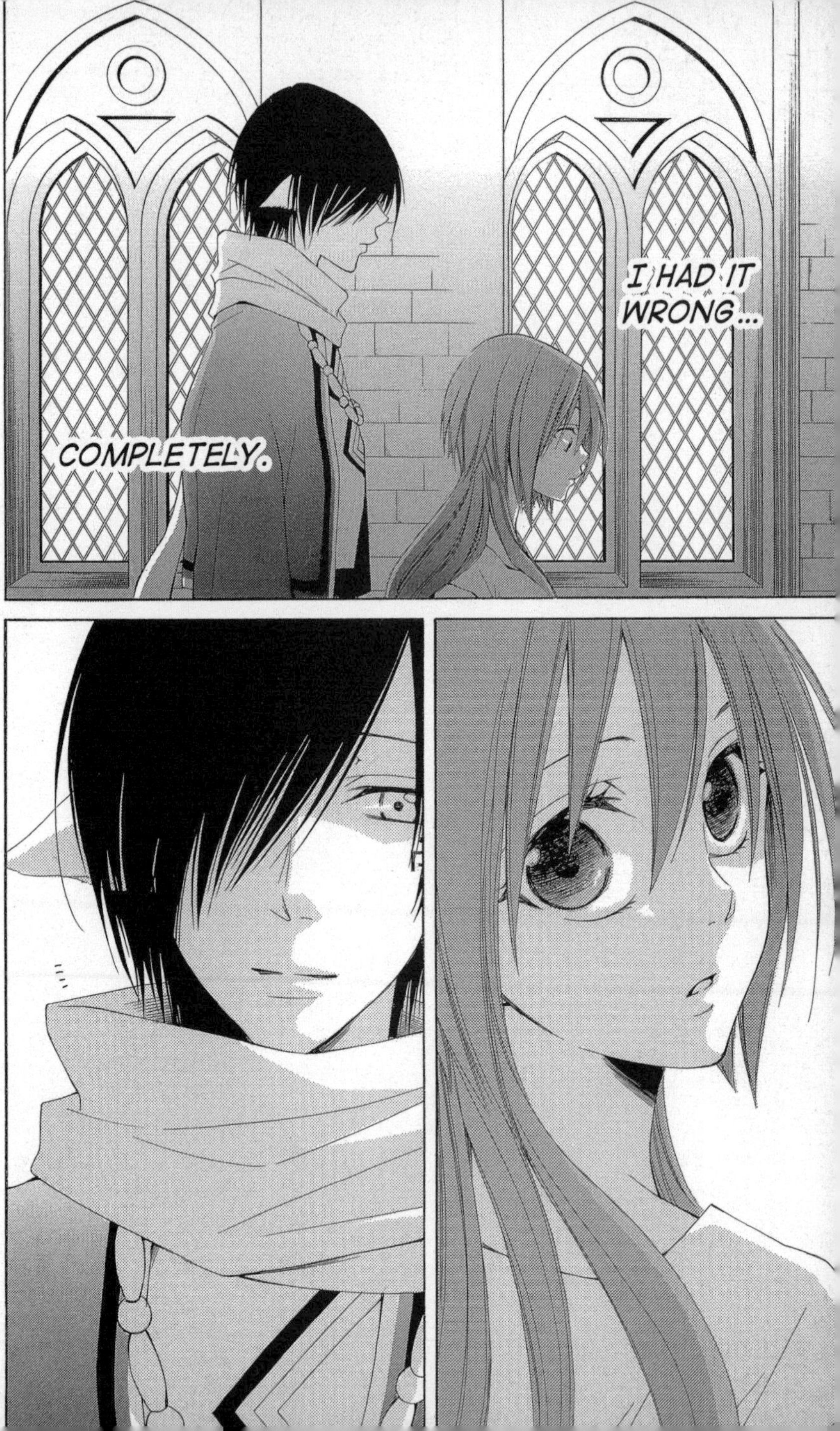
I HAD IT WRONG...
COMPLETELY.

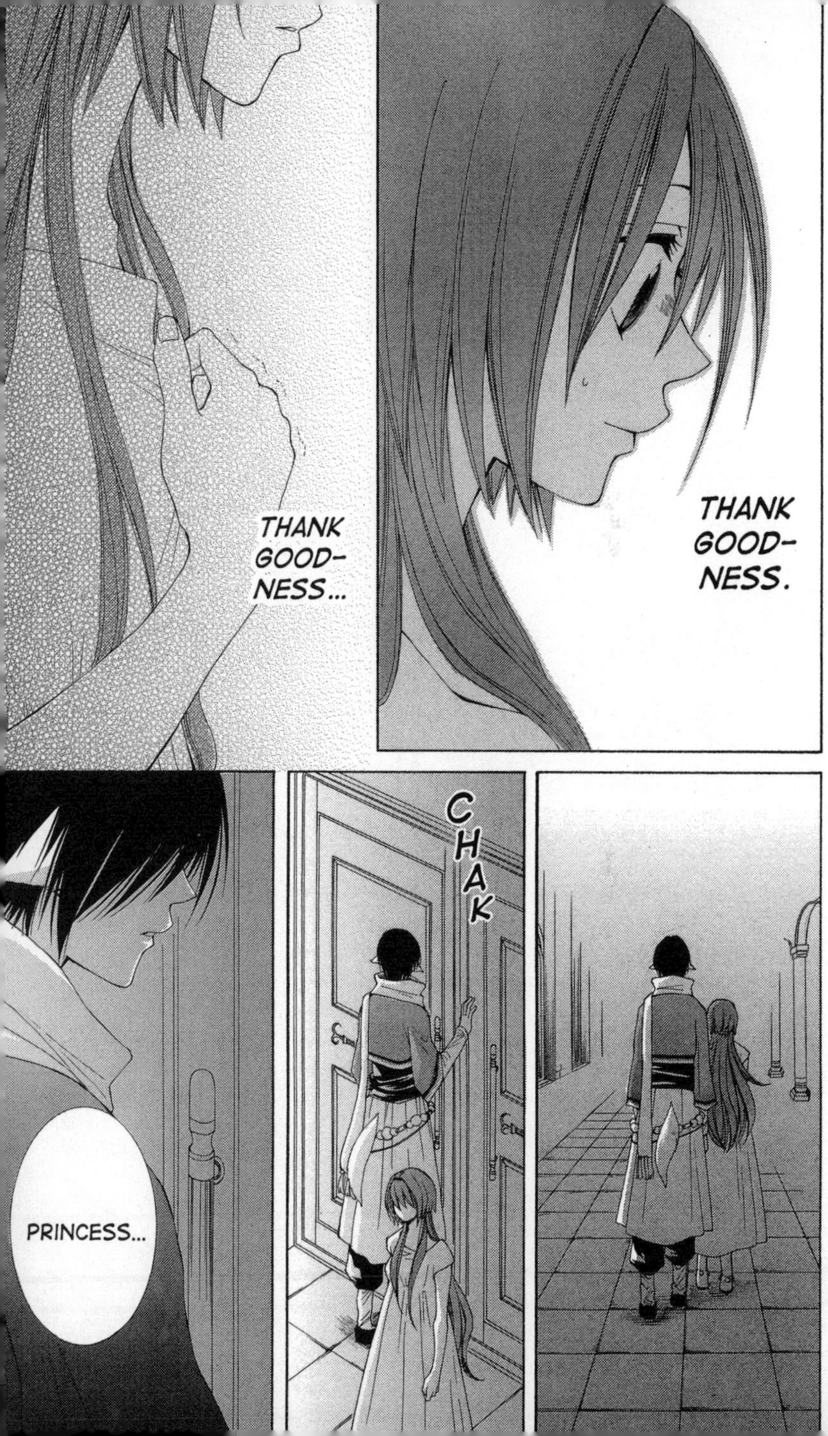
THANK GOOD-NESS.
THANK GOOD-NESS...
CHAK
PRINCESS...

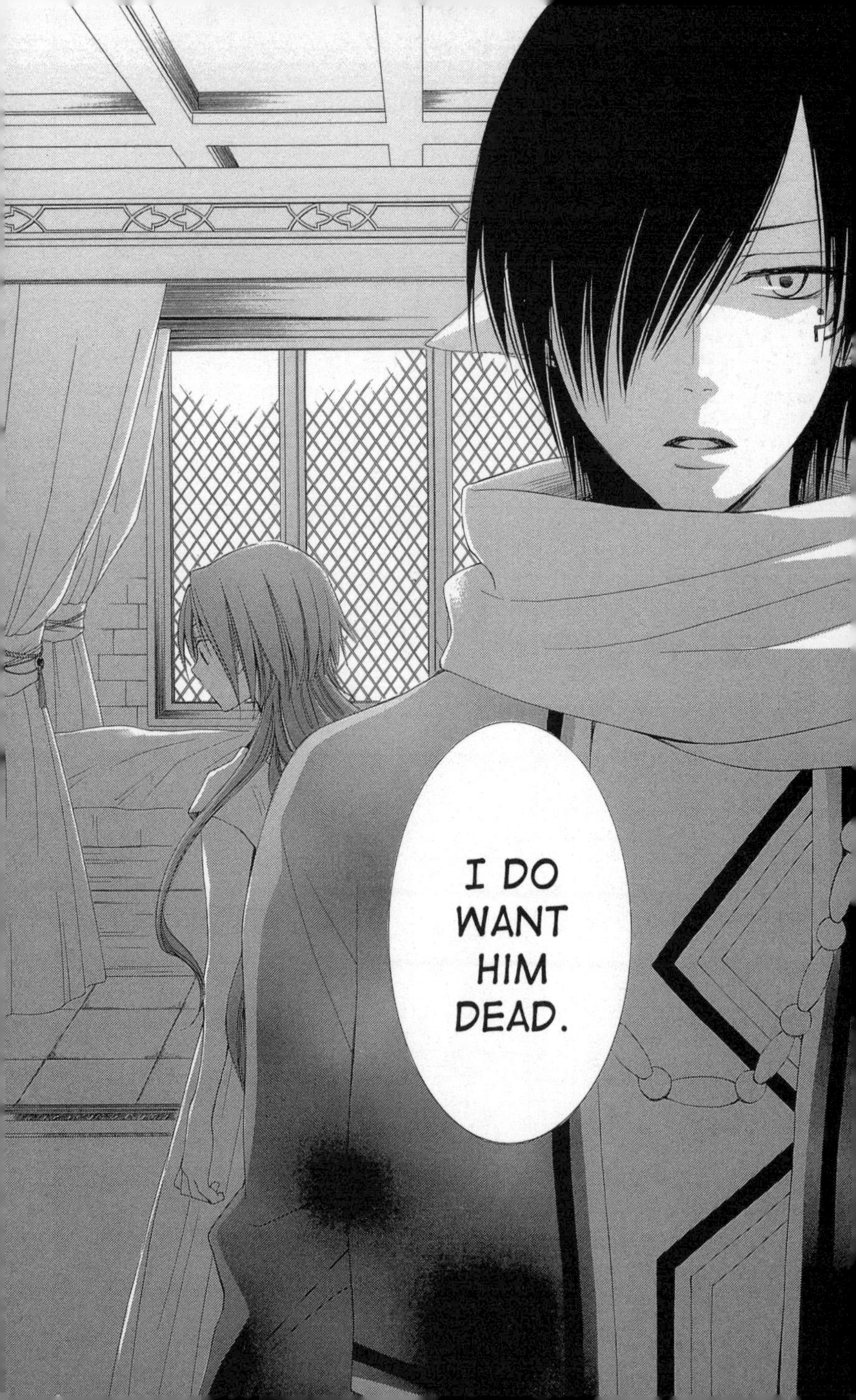
I DO WANT HIM DEAD.

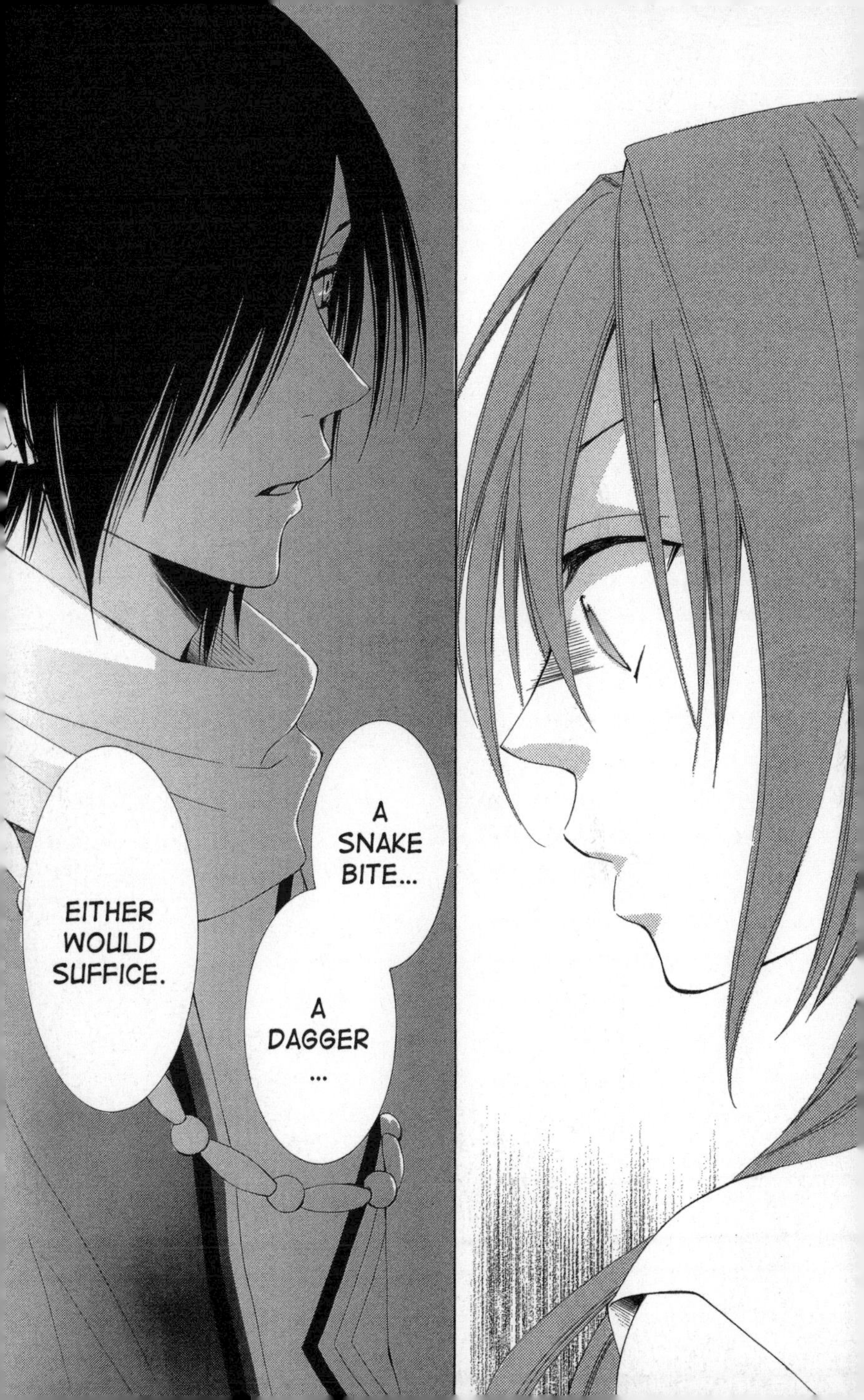
A SNAKE BITE...
A DAGGER ...
EITHER WOULD SUFFICE.

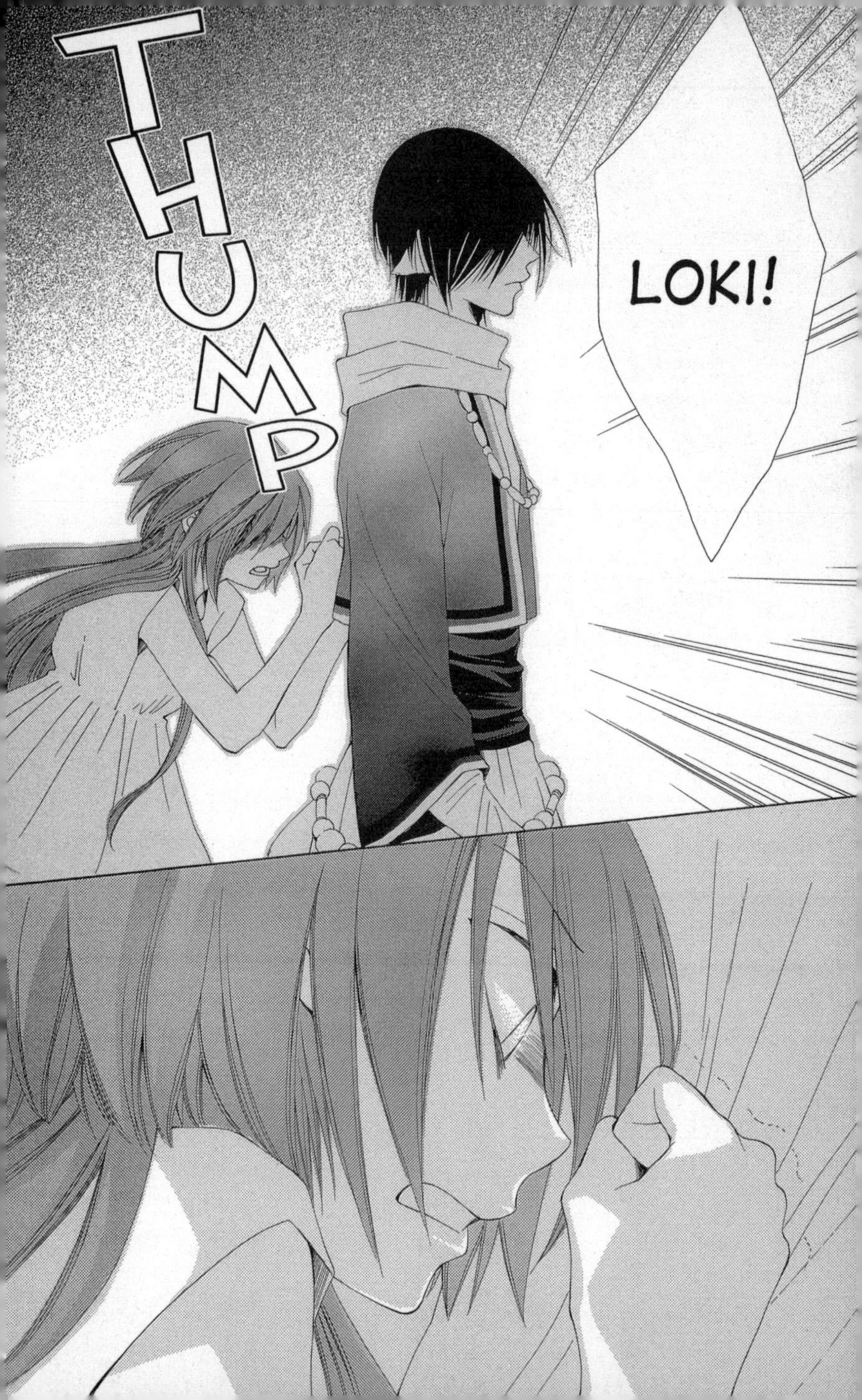
LOKI!
THUMP

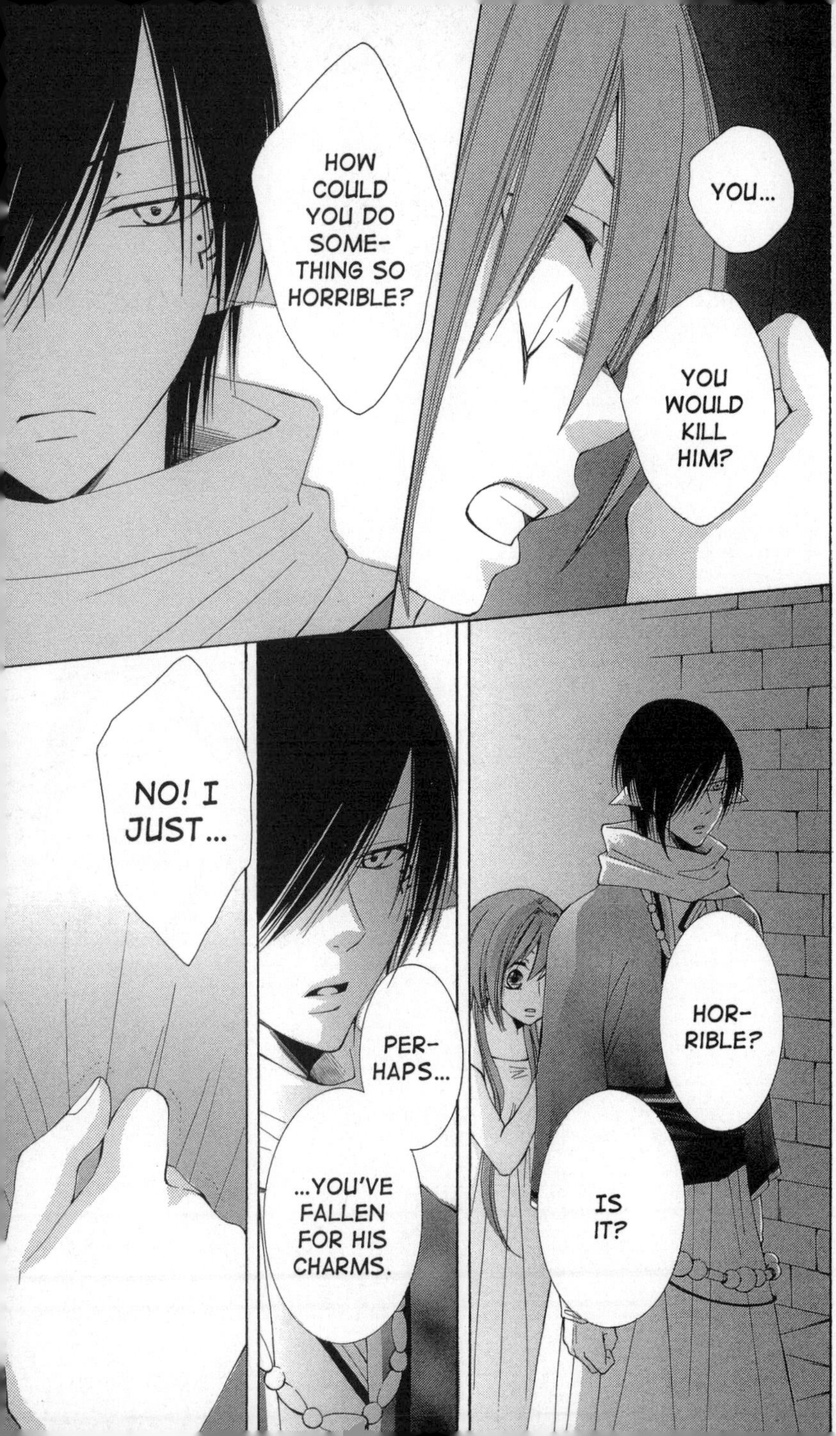
YOU...
YOU WOULD KILL HIM?
HOW COULD YOU DO SOME-THING SO HORRIBLE?
HOR-RIBLE?
IS IT?
PER-HAPS...
...YOU'VE FALLEN FOR HIS CHARMS.
NO! I JUST...

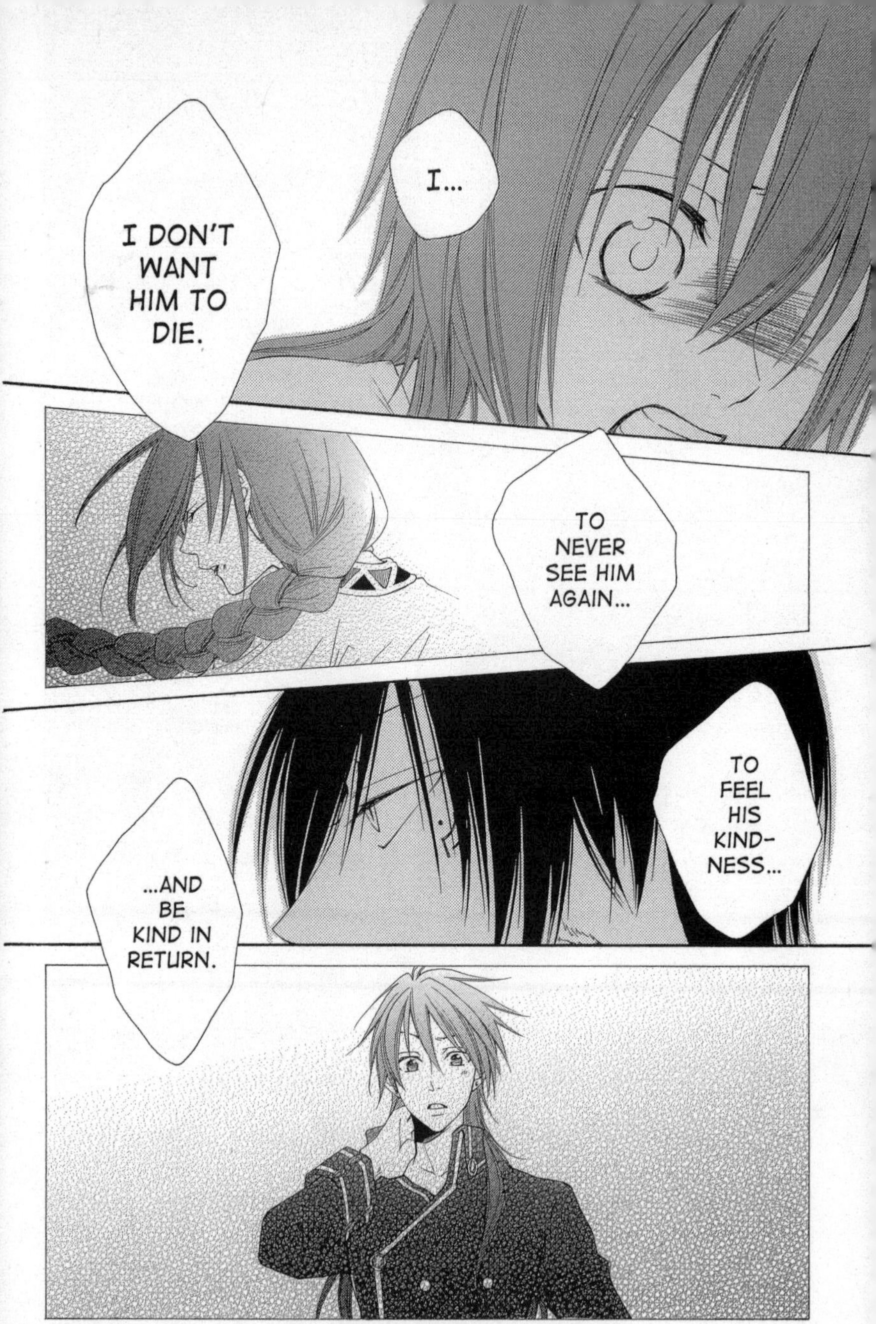
I...
I DON'T WANT HIM TO DIE.
TO NEVER SEE HIM AGAIN...
TO FEEL HIS KINDNESS...
...AND BE KIND IN RETURN.

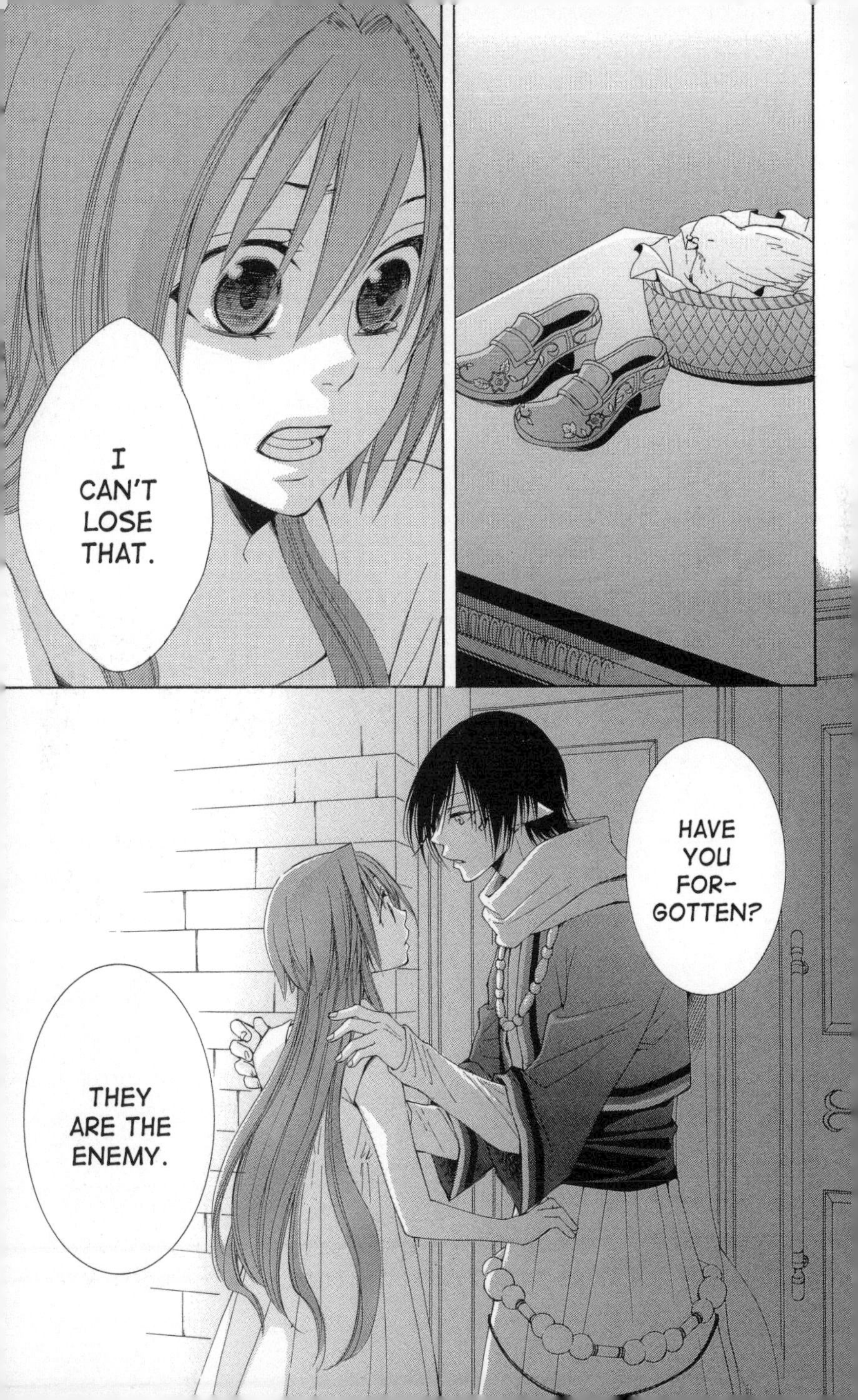
I CAN'T LOSE THAT.
HAVE YOU FOR-GOTTEN?
THEY ARE THE ENEMY.

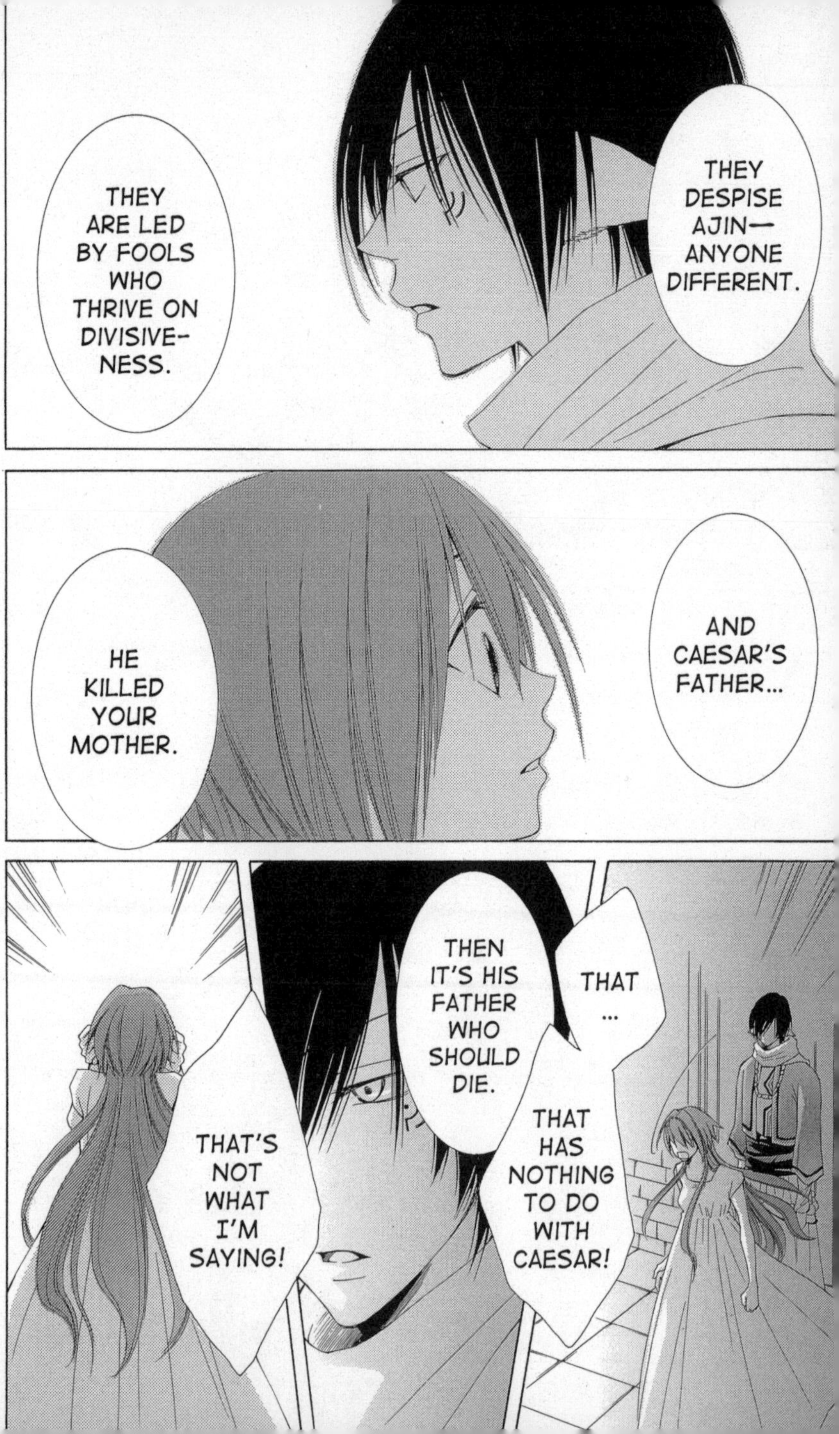
THEY DESPISE AJIN— ANYONE DIFFERENT.
THEY ARE LED BY FOOLS WHO THRIVE ON DIVISIVE-NESS.
AND CAESAR'S FATHER...
HE KILLED YOUR MOTHER.
THEN IT'S HIS FATHER WHO SHOULD DIE.
THAT ...
THAT HAS NOTHING TO DO WITH CAESAR!
THAT'S NOT WHAT I'M SAYING!

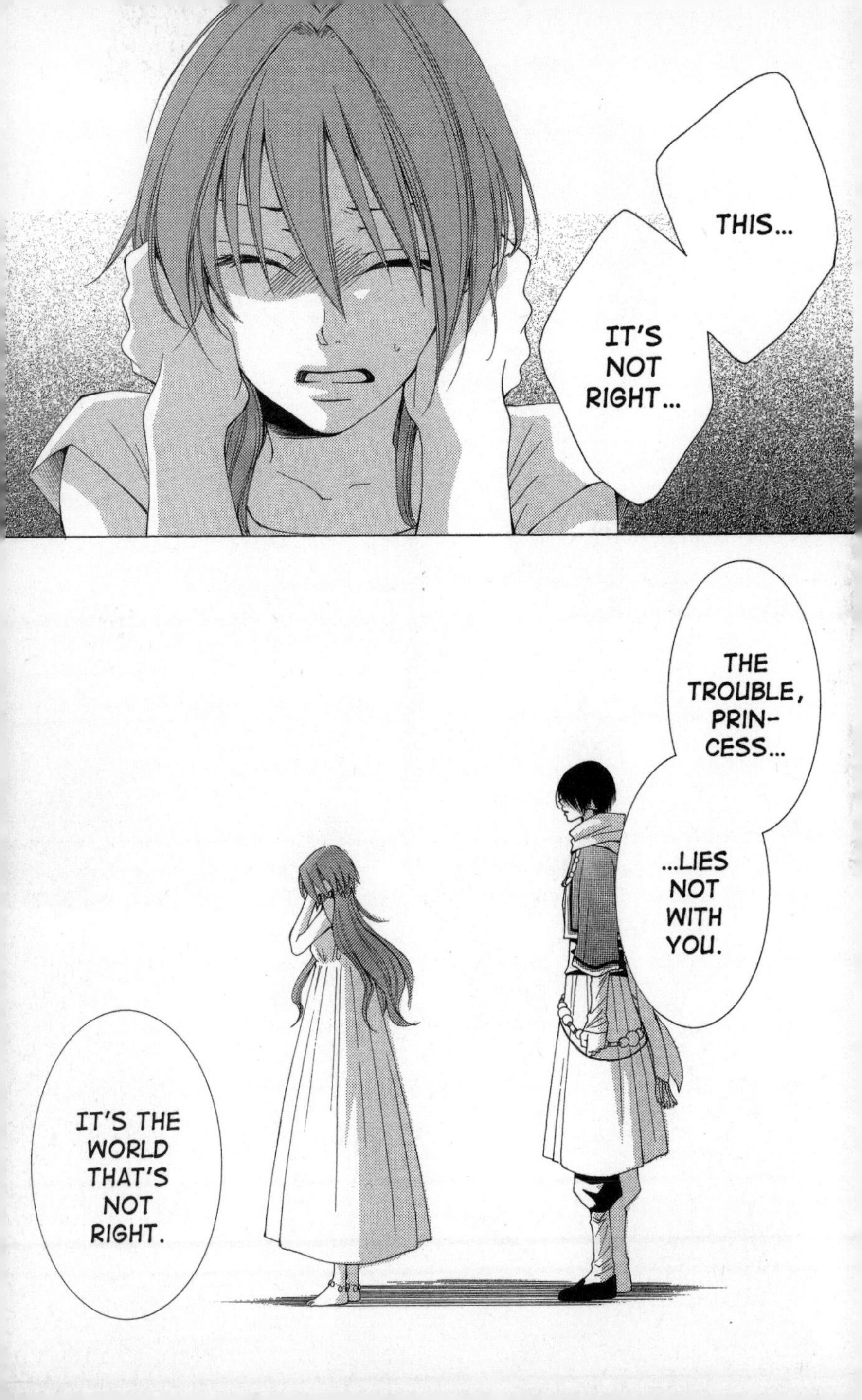
THIS...
IT'S NOT RIGHT...
THE TROUBLE, PRIN-CESS...
...LIES NOT WITH YOU.
IT'S THE WORLD THAT'S NOT RIGHT.

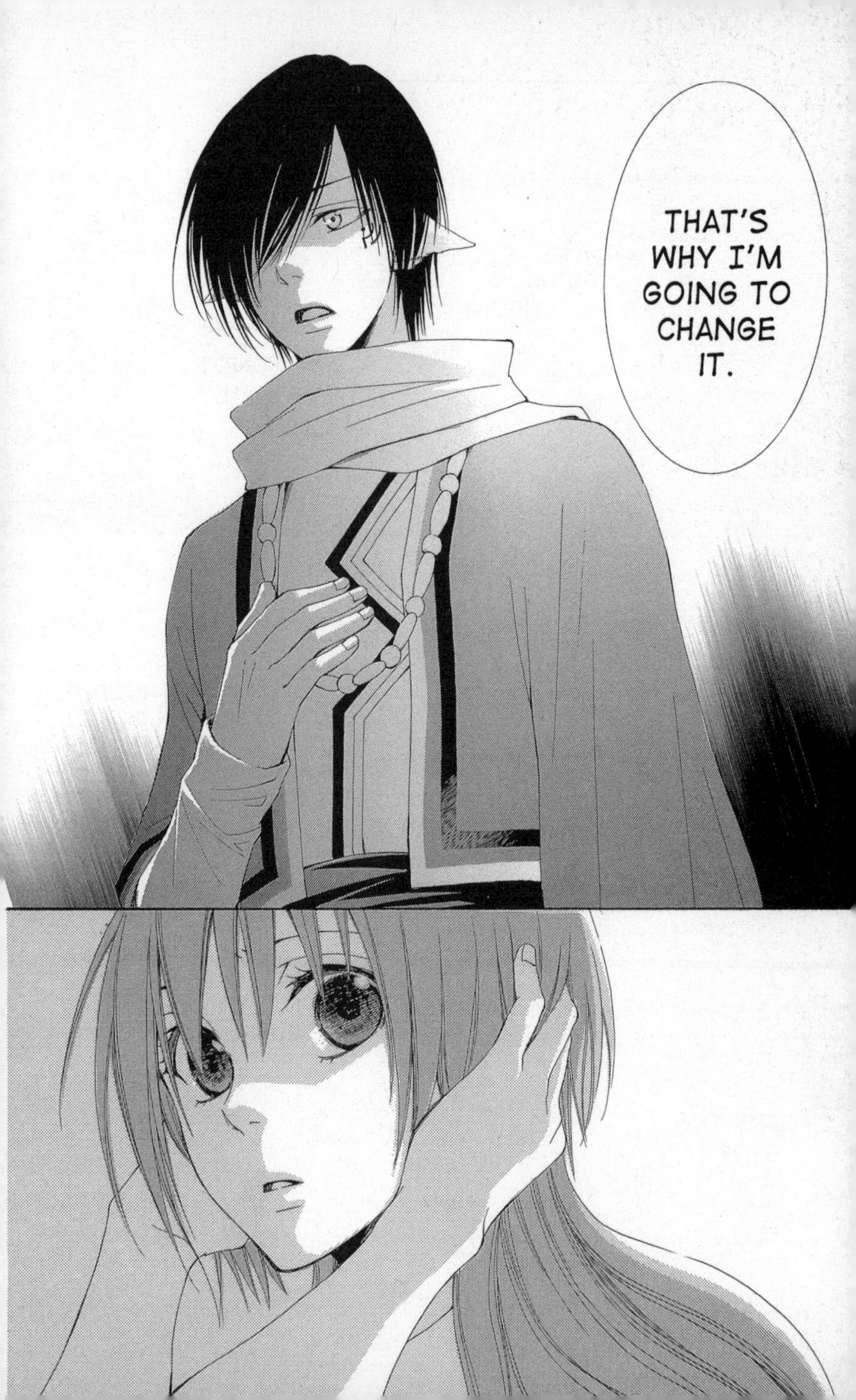
THAT'S WHY I'M GOING TO CHANGE IT.

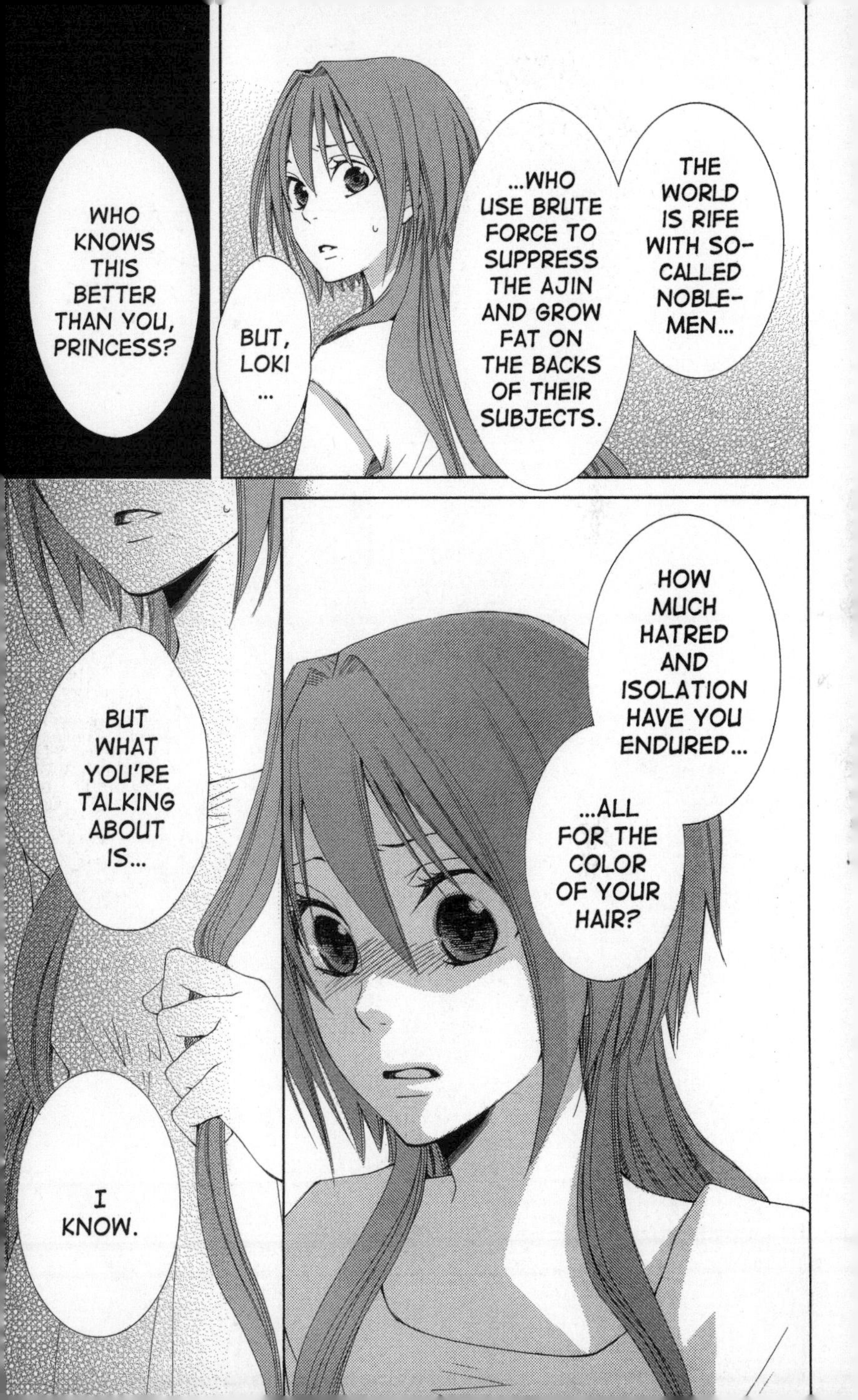
THE WORLD IS RIFE WITH SO-CALLED NOBLEMEN...
...WHO USE BRUTE FORCE TO SUPPRESS THE AJIN AND GROW FAT ON THE BACKS OF THEIR SUBJECTS.
BUT, LOKI ...
WHO KNOWS THIS BETTER THAN YOU, PRINCESS?
HOW MUCH HATRED AND ISOLATION HAVE YOU ENDURED...
...ALL FOR THE COLOR OF YOUR HAIR?
BUT WHAT YOU'RE TALKING ABOUT IS...
I KNOW.

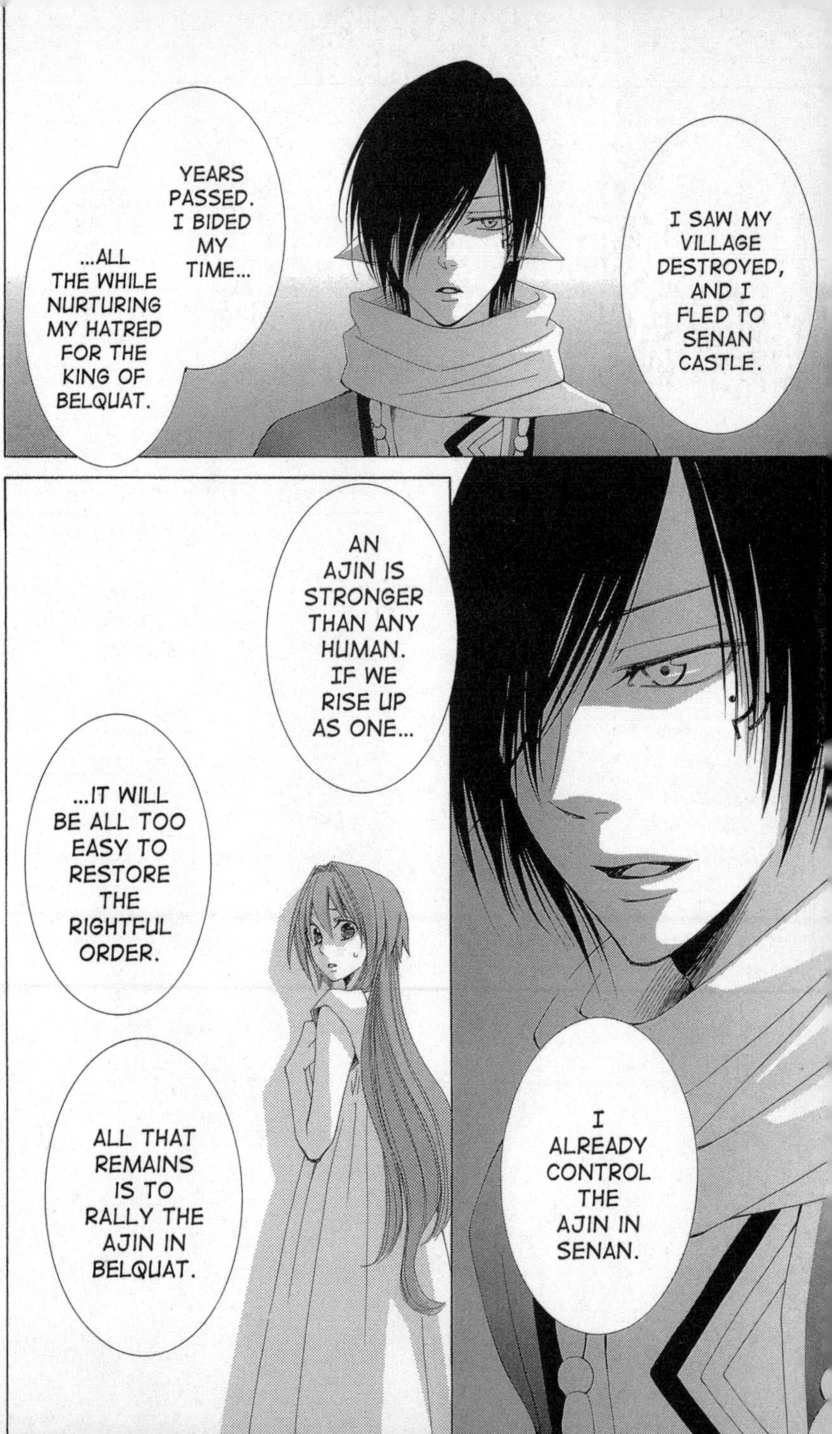
I SAW MY VILLAGE DESTROYED, AND I FLED TO SENAN CASTLE.
YEARS PASSED. I BIDED MY TIME...
...ALL THE WHILE NURTURING MY HATRED FOR THE KING OF BELQUAT.
AN AJIN IS STRONGER THAN ANY HUMAN. IF WE RISE UP AS ONE...
...IT WILL BE ALL TOO EASY TO RESTORE THE RIGHTFUL ORDER.
I ALREADY CONTROL THE AJIN IN SENAN.
ALL THAT REMAINS IS TO RALLY THE AJIN IN BELQUAT.

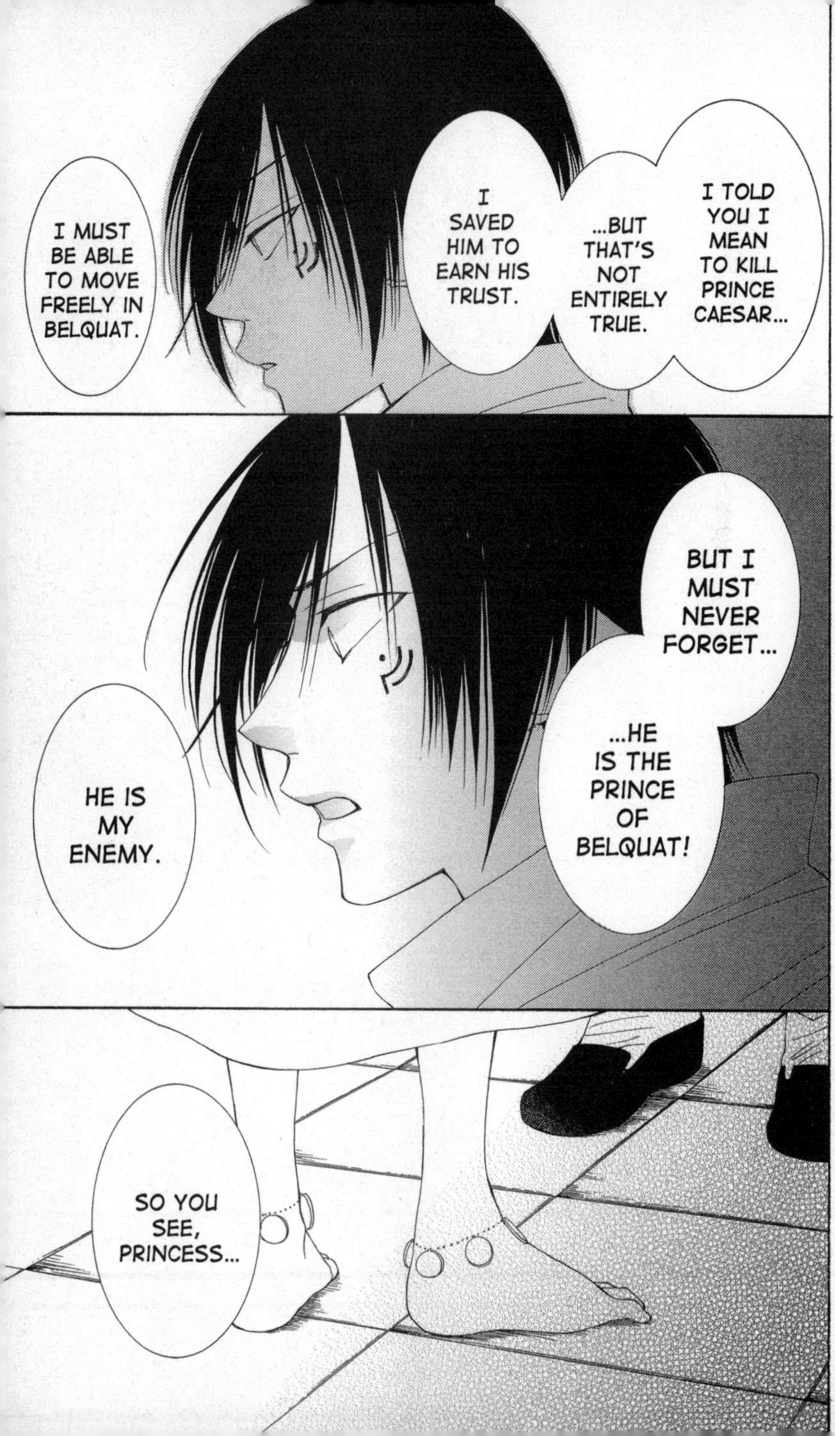
I TOLD YOU I MEAN TO KILL PRINCE CAESAR...
...BUT THAT'S NOT ENTIRELY TRUE.
I SAVED HIM TO EARN HIS TRUST.
I MUST BE ABLE TO MOVE FREELY IN BELQUAT.
BUT I MUST NEVER FORGET...
...HE IS THE PRINCE OF BELQUAT!
HE IS MY ENEMY.
SO YOU SEE, PRINCESS...

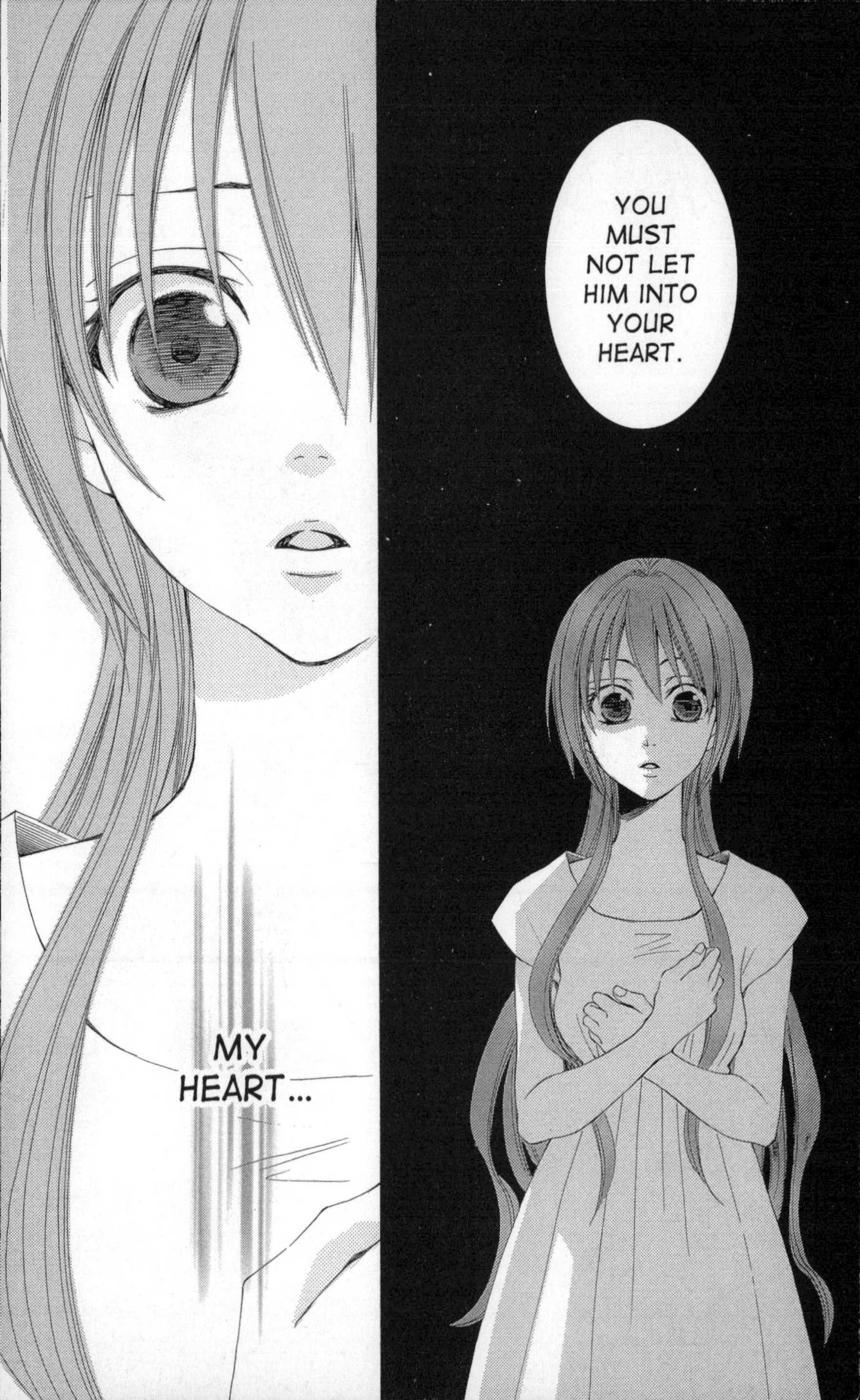
YOU MUST NOT LET HIM INTO YOUR HEART.
MY HEART...

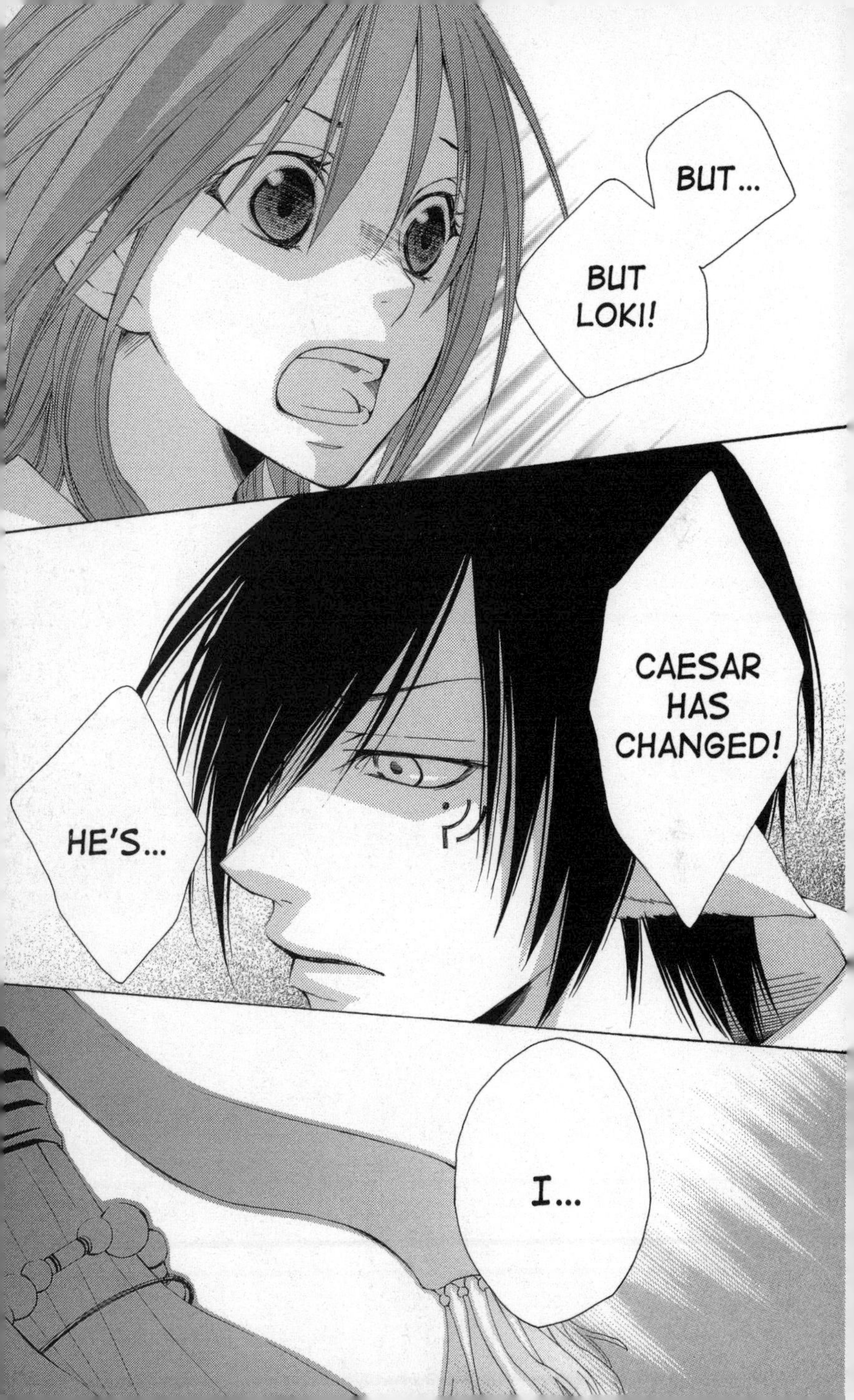
BUT...
BUT LOKI!
CAESAR HAS CHANGED!
HE'S...
I...

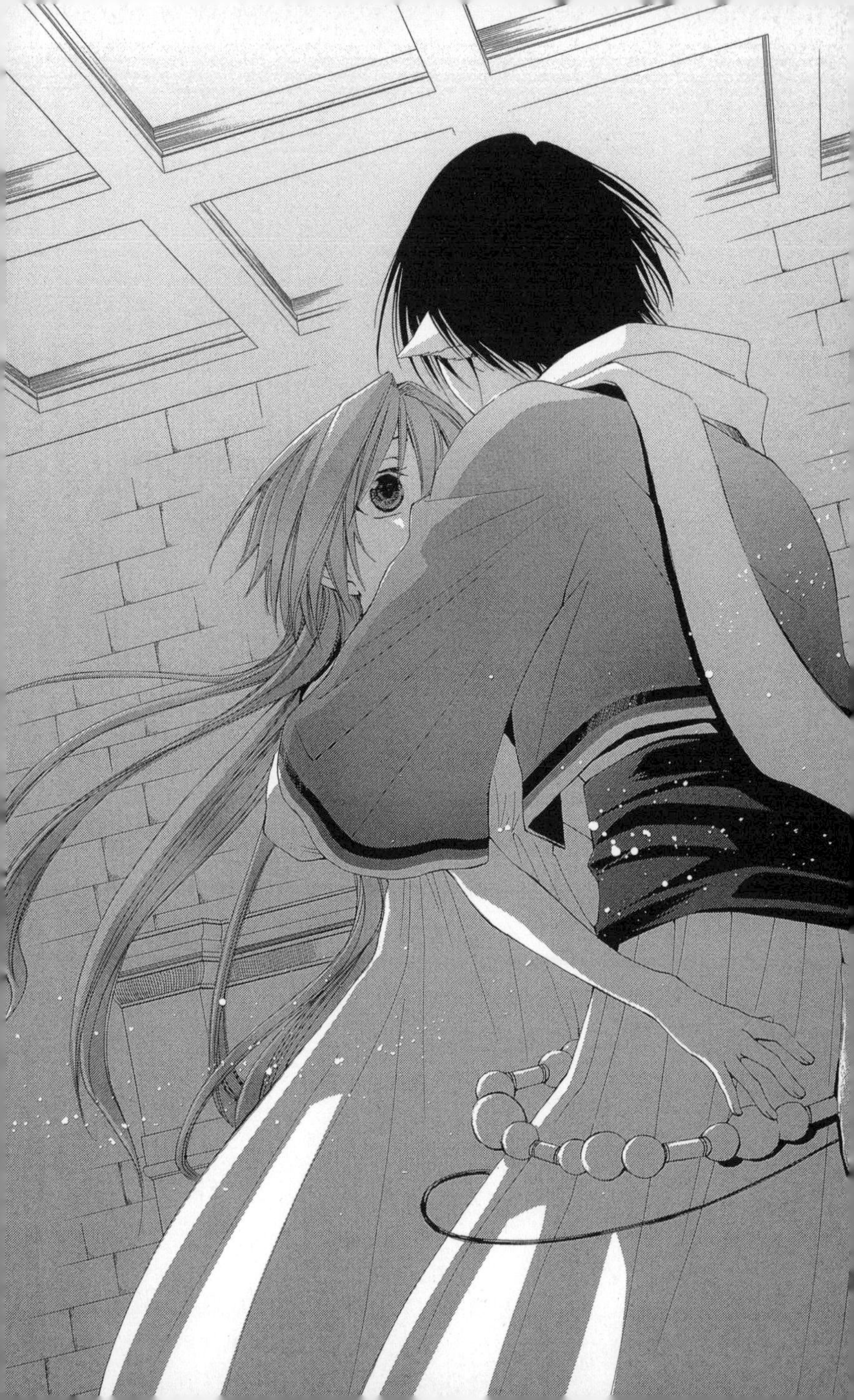

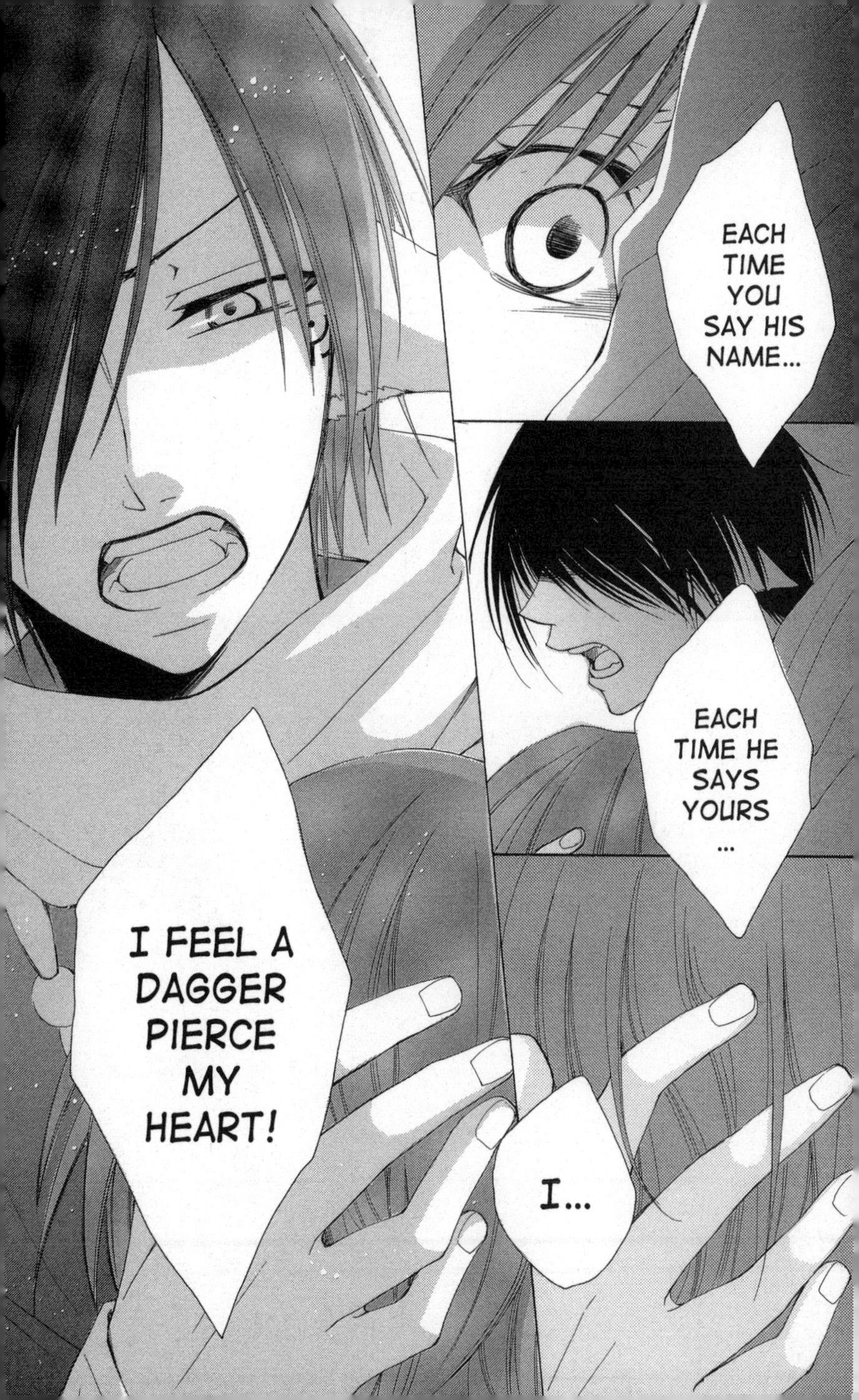
EACH TIME YOU SAY HIS NAME...
EACH TIME HE SAYS YOURS ...
I...
I FEEL A DAGGER PIERCE MY HEART!

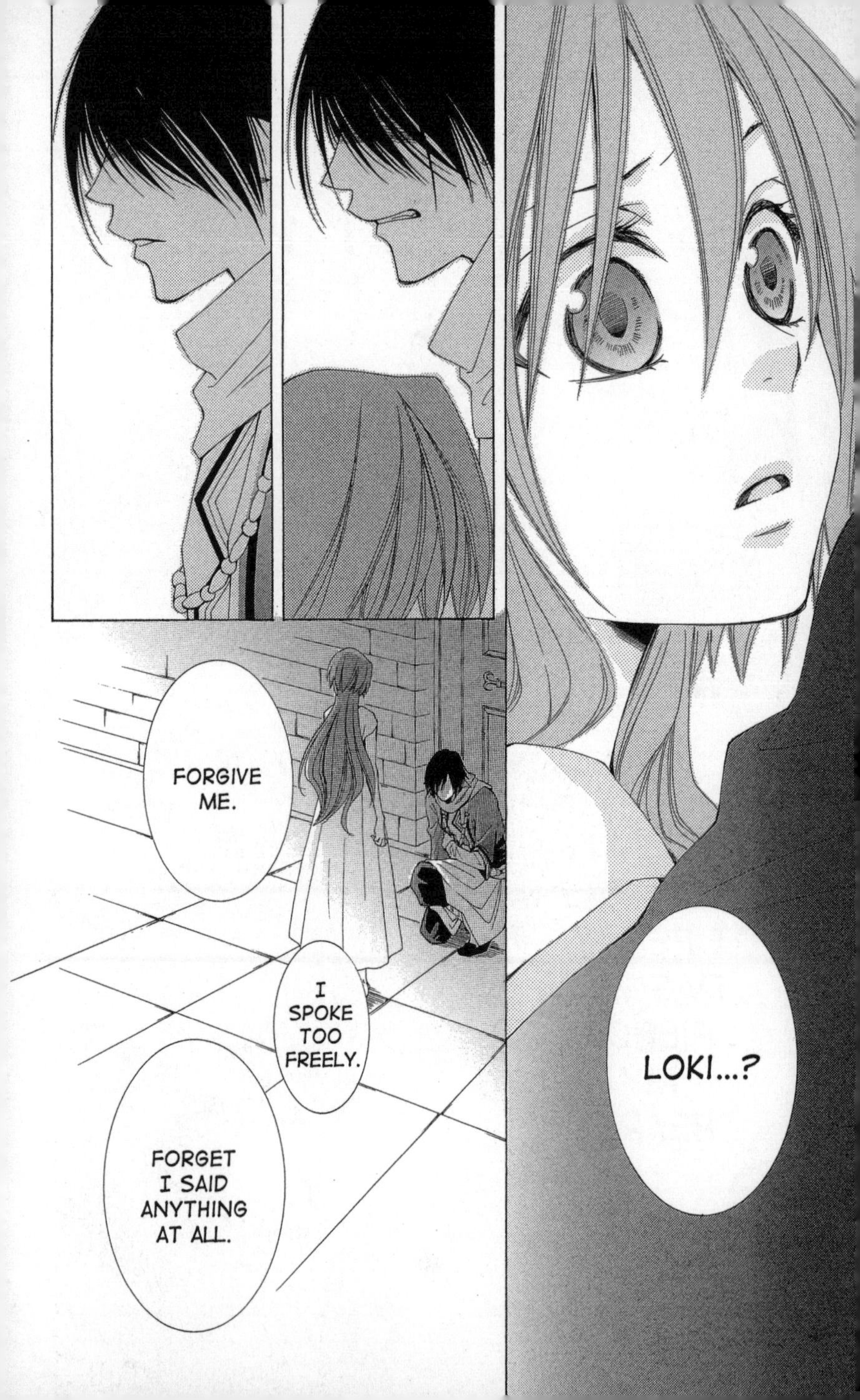
LOKI...?
FORGIVE ME.
I SPOKE TOO FREELY.
FORGET I SAID ANYTHING AT ALL.

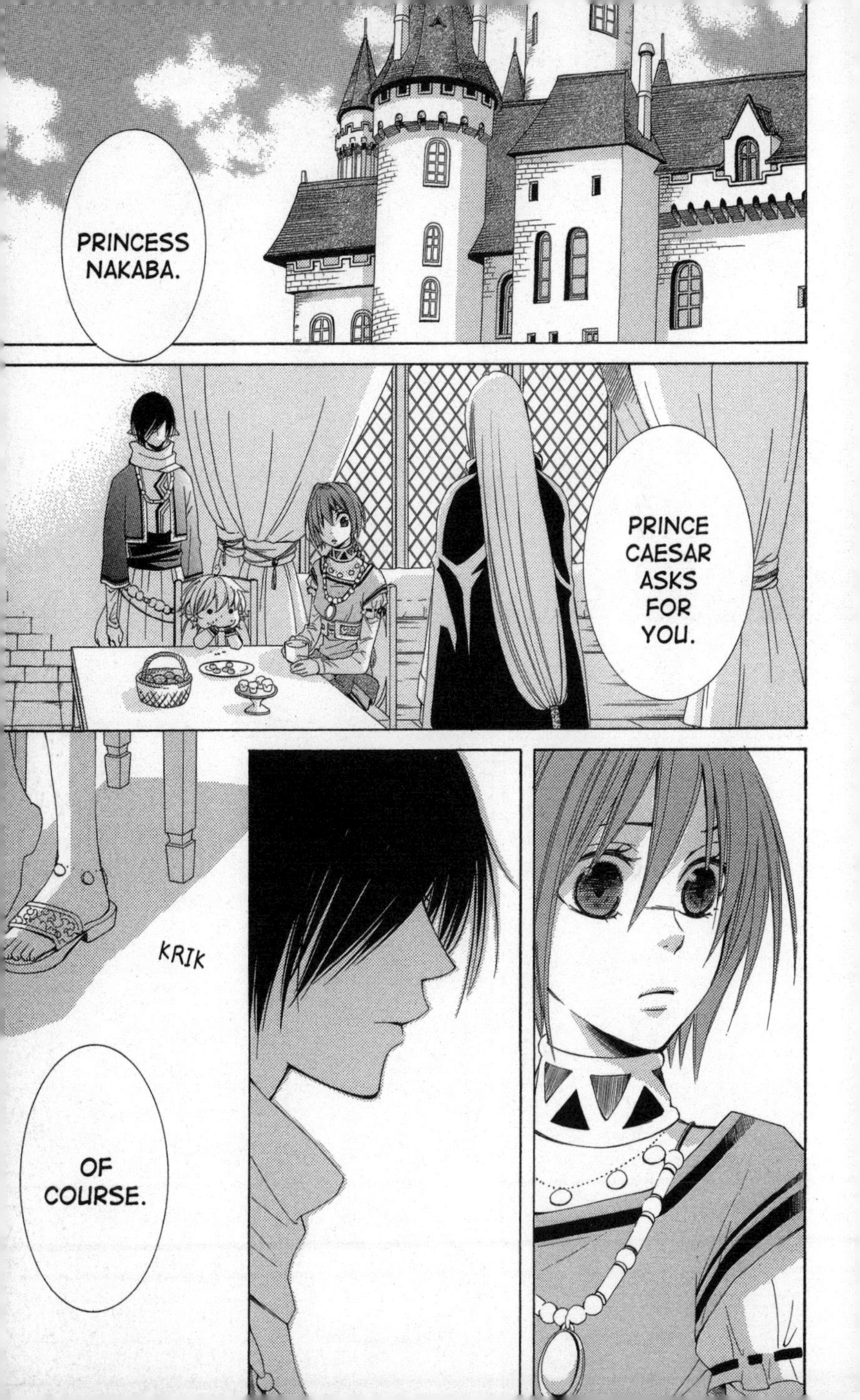
PRINCESS NAKABA.
PRINCE CAESAR ASKS FOR YOU.
KRIK
OF COURSE.

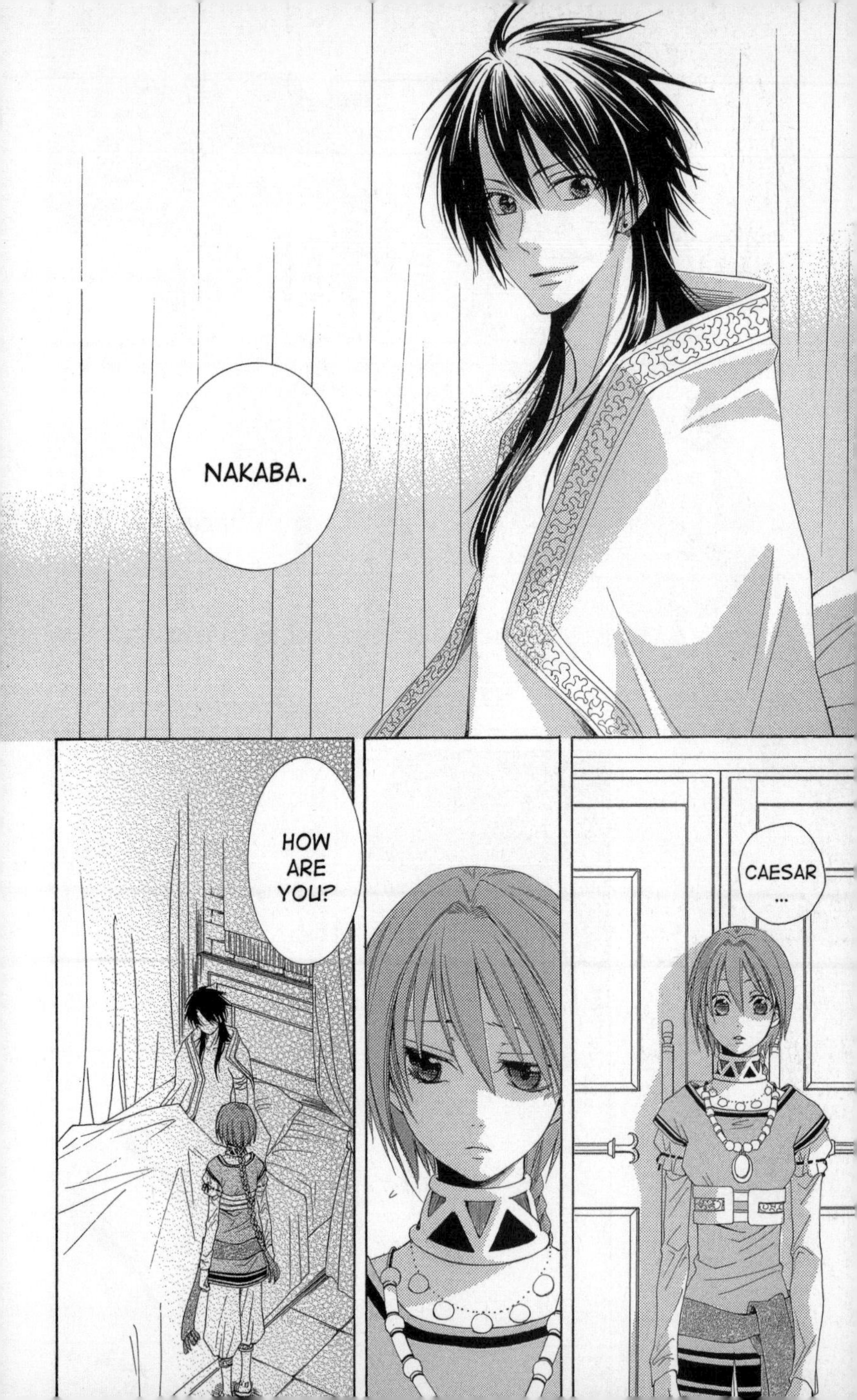
NAKABA.
CAESAR ...
HOW ARE YOU?

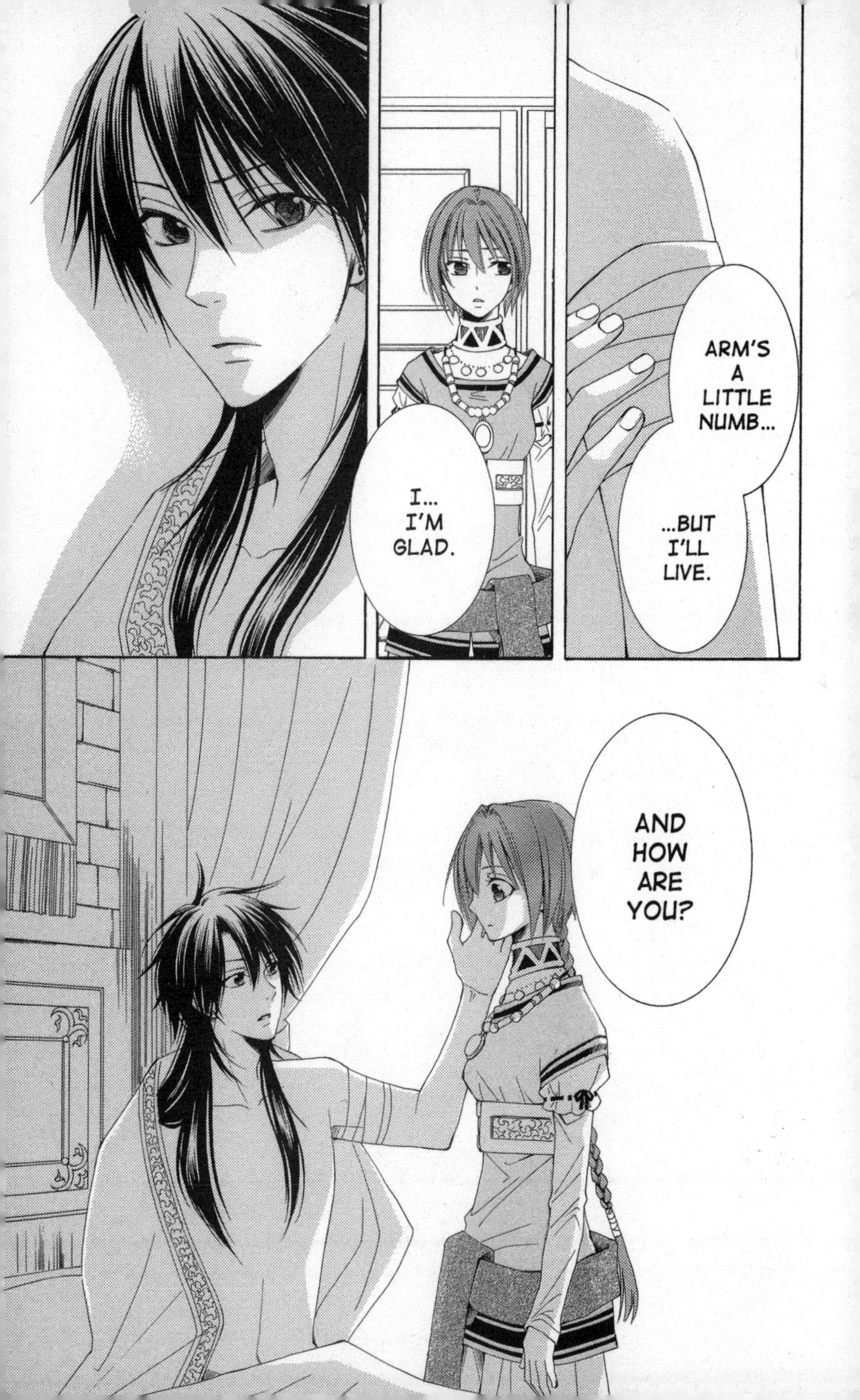
ARM'S A LITTLE NUMB...
...BUT I'LL LIVE.
I... I'M GLAD.
AND HOW ARE YOU?

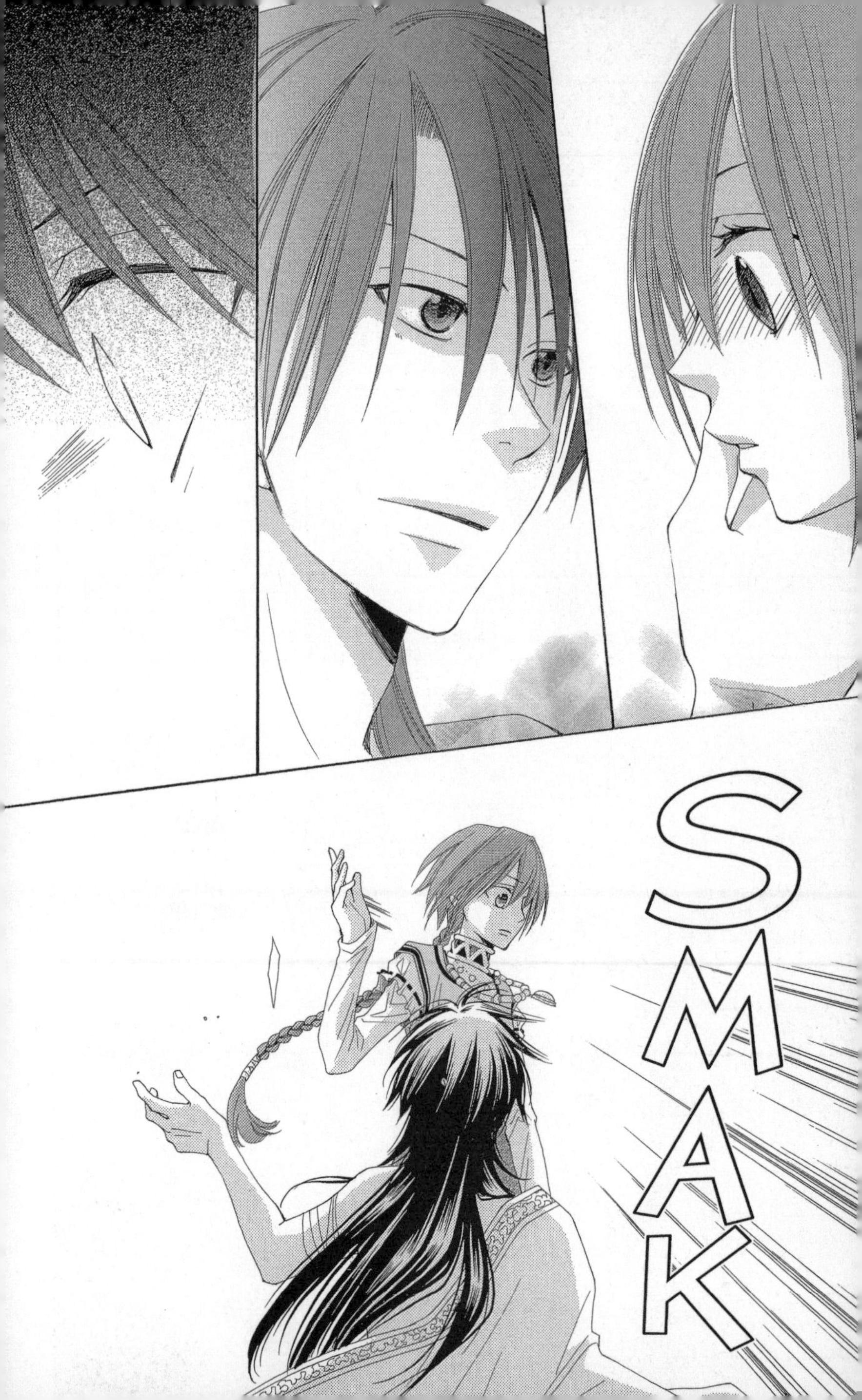
SMAK

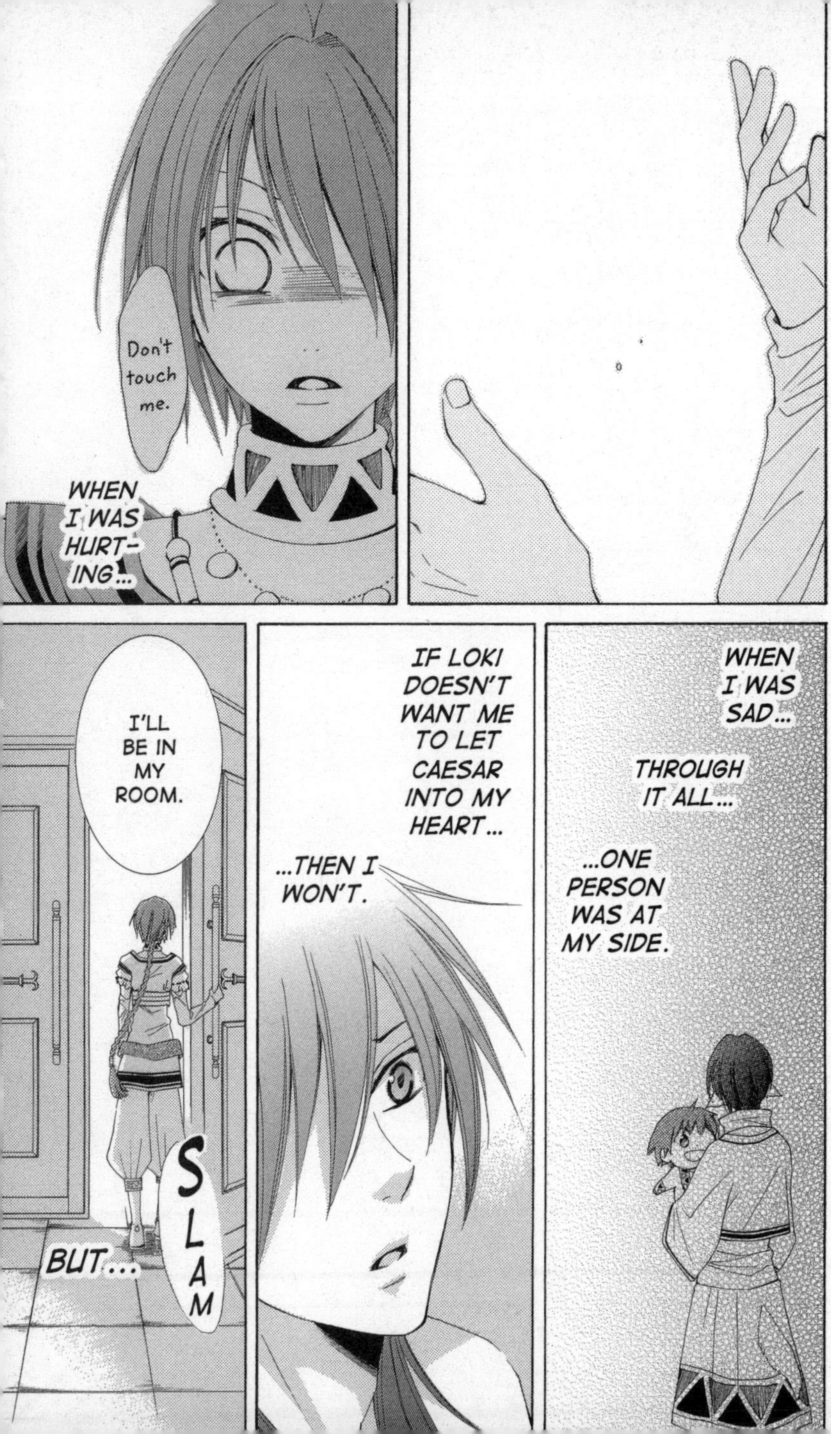
Don't touch me.
WHEN I WAS HURTING...
WHEN I WAS SAD...
THROUGH IT ALL...
...ONE PERSON WAS AT MY SIDE.
IF LOKI DOESN'T WANT ME TO LET CAESAR INTO MY HEART...
...THEN I WON'T.
I'LL BE IN MY ROOM.
SLAM
BUT...

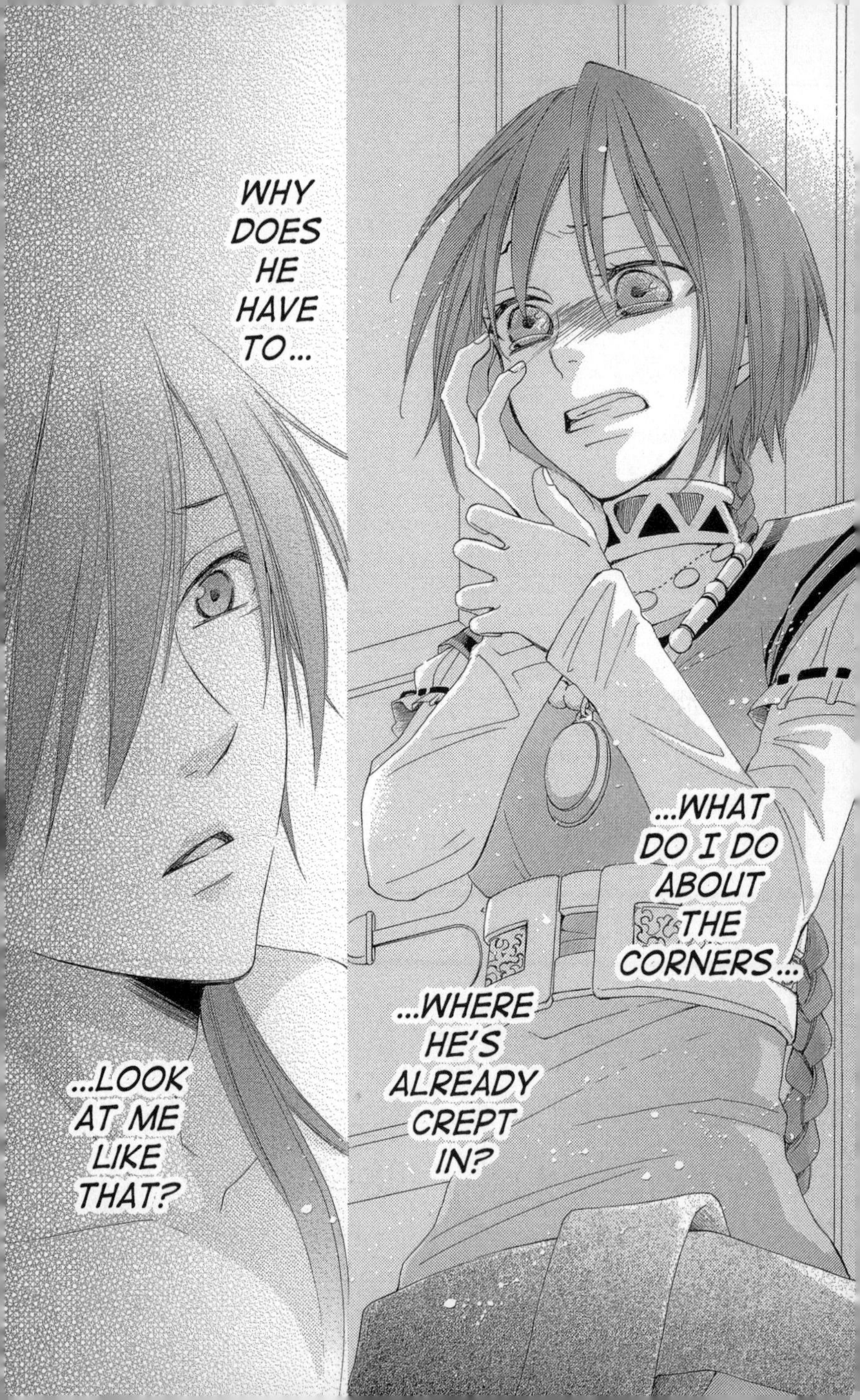
...WHAT DO I DO ABOUT THE CORNERS...
...WHERE HE'S ALREADY CREPT IN?
WHY DOES HE HAVE TO...
...LOOK AT ME LIKE THAT?

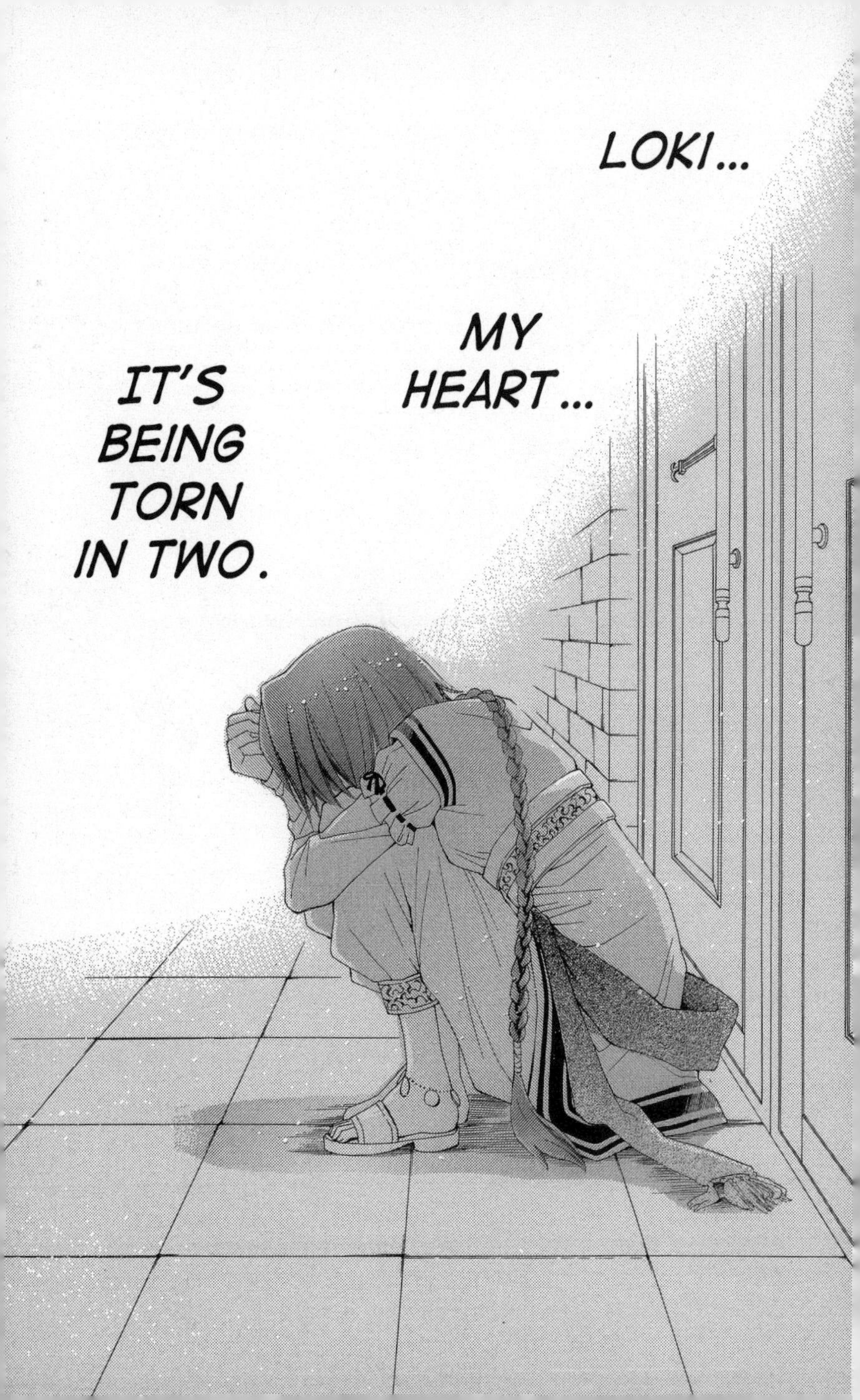
LOKI...
MY HEART...
IT'S BEING TORN IN TWO.

Left-Hand-Drawn Loki from Right-handed Me

Since I asked everyone else to flex their artistic abilities by drawing various Arcana characters from memory, I thought I would join in by drawing Louise from memory. But that seemed like setting the bar too low, so instead, I took a stab at drawing Loki with my left hand. I think this is how it would turn out if I tried drawing him with my right hand during a level 4-like earthquake on the Japanese seismic intensity scale. The lines are a little wobbly, but it's not too bad... I'm actually a little disappointed it didn't turn out more interesting...

Someone sent me a cute present in a recent letter—a Nakaba keychain like this (→)! The eyes are cute, the hair is cute, and now I have it proudly displayed hanging from a light stand. I can't tell you how happy I am that someone went to the trouble of making this and sending it to me! I've thought about trying my hand at making miniatures. I know it's not easy, but it sounds like fun. I get excited just looking through all the supplies and materials they have at the store. If I can find the time, maybe I'll study up and give it a try. (*Laugh*)

Send feedback to:
Rei Toma
c/o Dawn of the Arcana Editor
Viz Media
P.O. Box 77010
San Francisco, CA 94107

I enjoy each and every letter. They really keep me going! Thanks so much!!

Here's hoping I see you all again in the third volume!

Rei Toma

Chapter 7

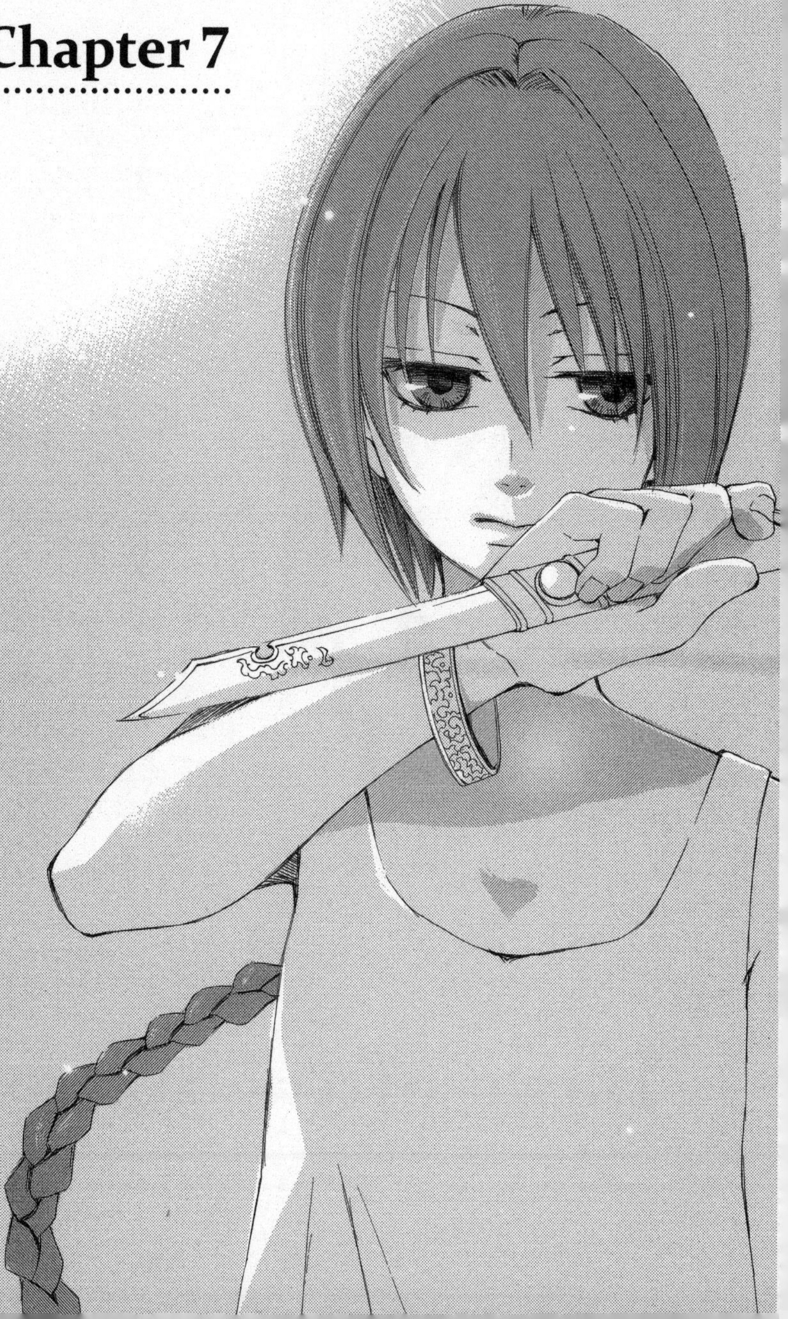

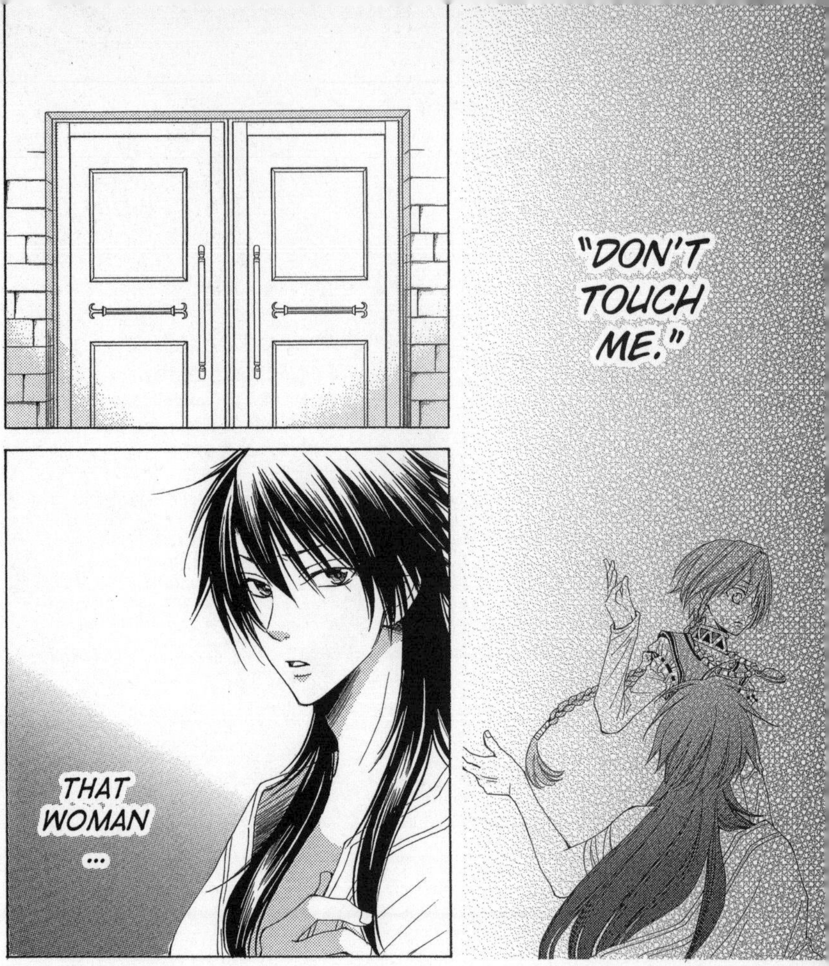
"DON'T TOUCH ME."
THAT WOMAN ...

Dawn of the Arcana

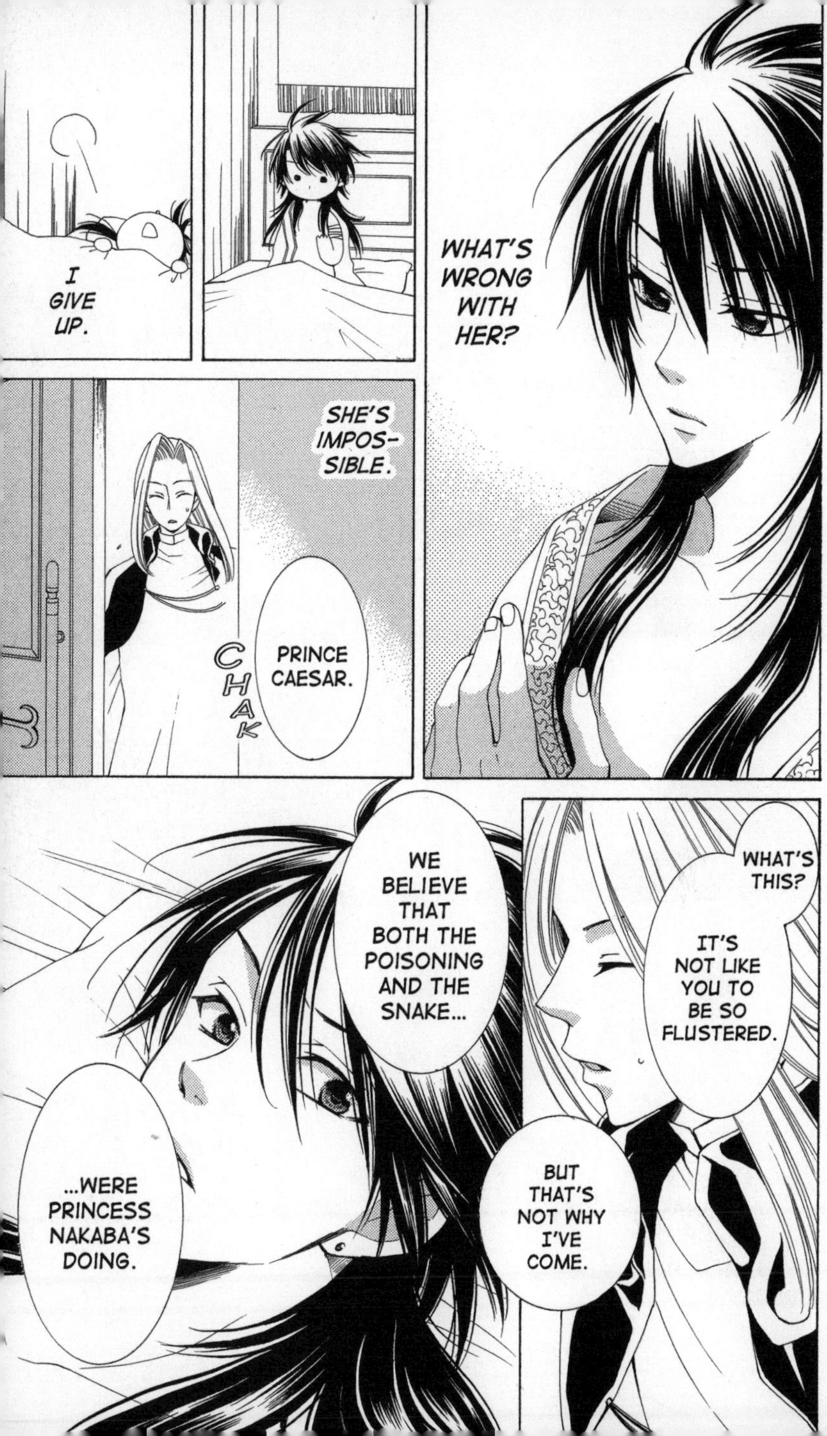
WHAT'S WRONG WITH HER?
I GIVE UP.
SHE'S IMPOSSIBLE.
CHAK
PRINCE CAESAR.
WHAT'S THIS?
IT'S NOT LIKE YOU TO BE SO FLUSTERED.
BUT THAT'S NOT WHY I'VE COME.
WE BELIEVE THAT BOTH THE POISONING AND THE SNAKE...
...WERE PRINCESS NAKABA'S DOING.

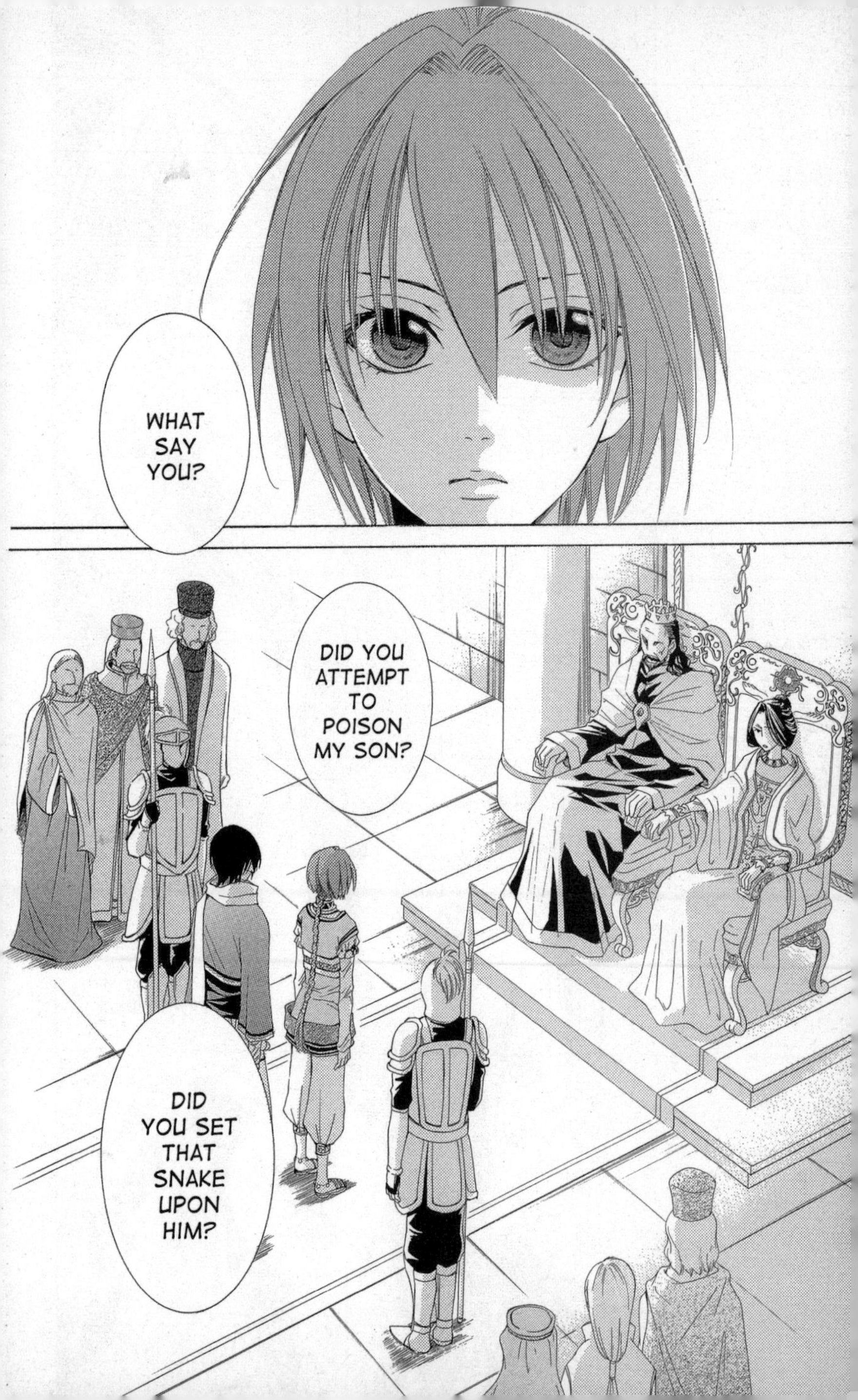
WHAT SAY YOU?
DID YOU ATTEMPT TO POISON MY SON?
DID YOU SET THAT SNAKE UPON HIM?

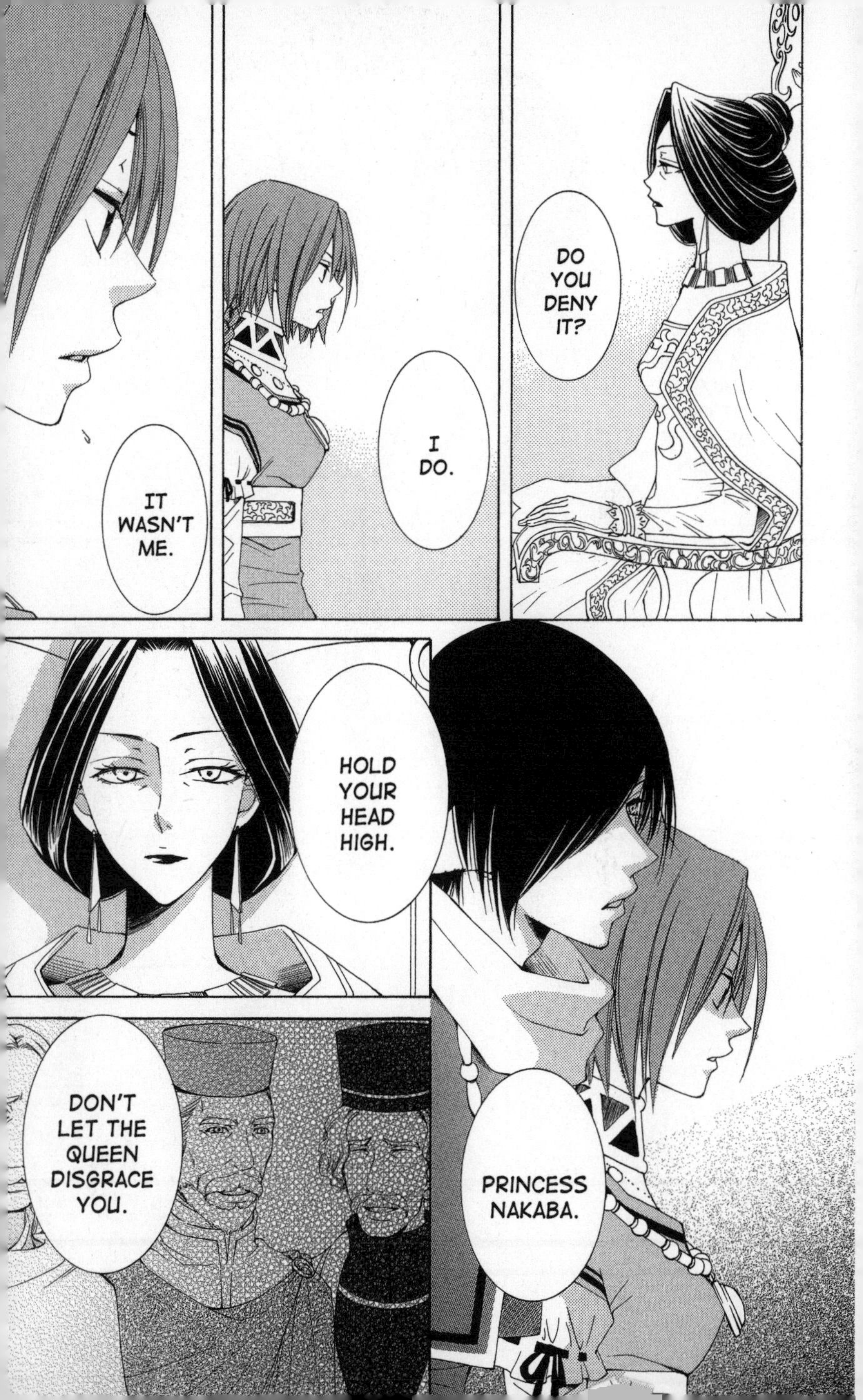
DO YOU DENY IT?
I DO.
IT WASN'T ME.
PRINCESS NAKABA.
HOLD YOUR HEAD HIGH.
DON'T LET THE QUEEN DISGRACE YOU.

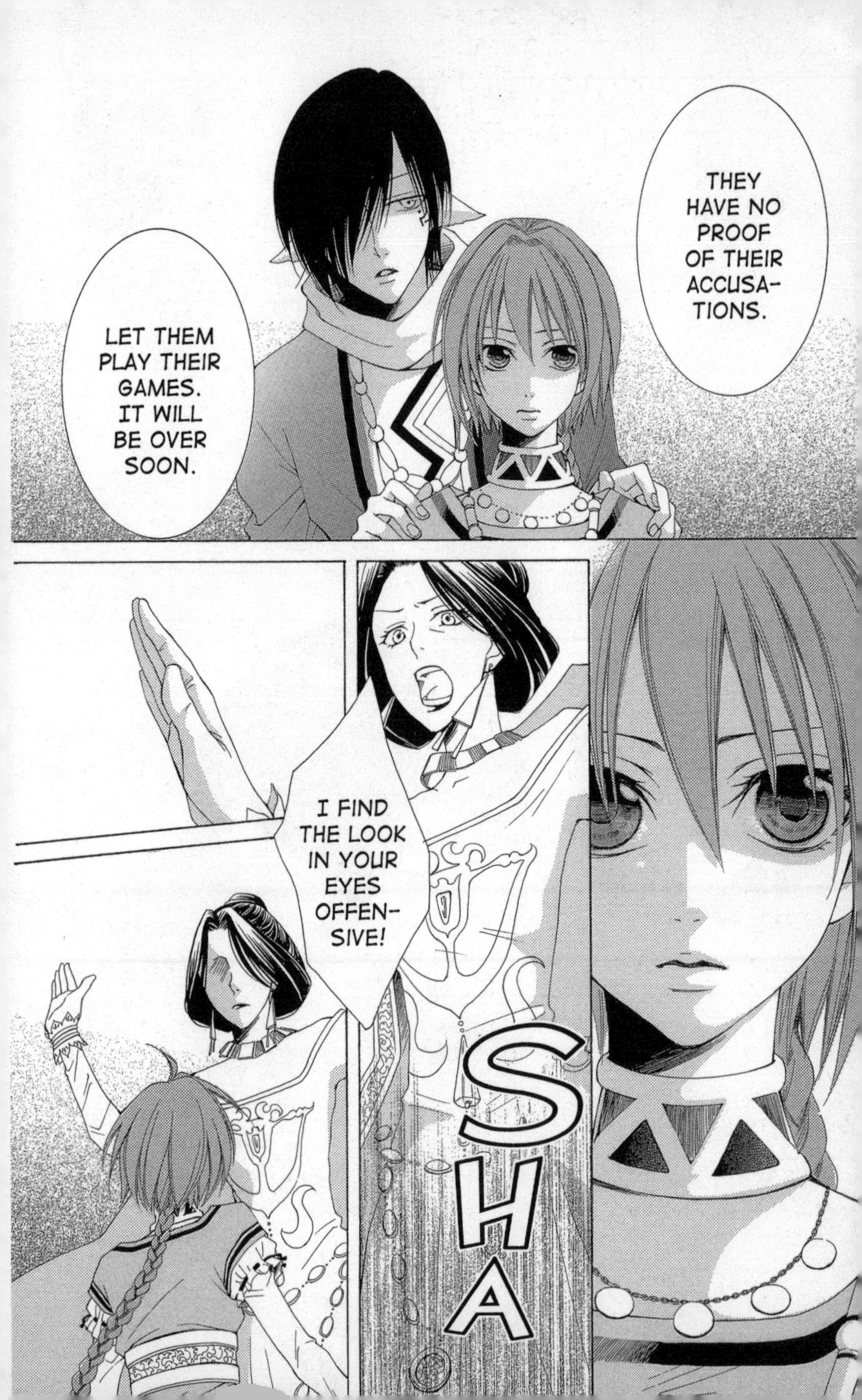
THEY HAVE NO PROOF OF THEIR ACCUSA-TIONS.
LET THEM PLAY THEIR GAMES. IT WILL BE OVER SOON.
I FIND THE LOOK IN YOUR EYES OFFEN-SIVE!
SHA

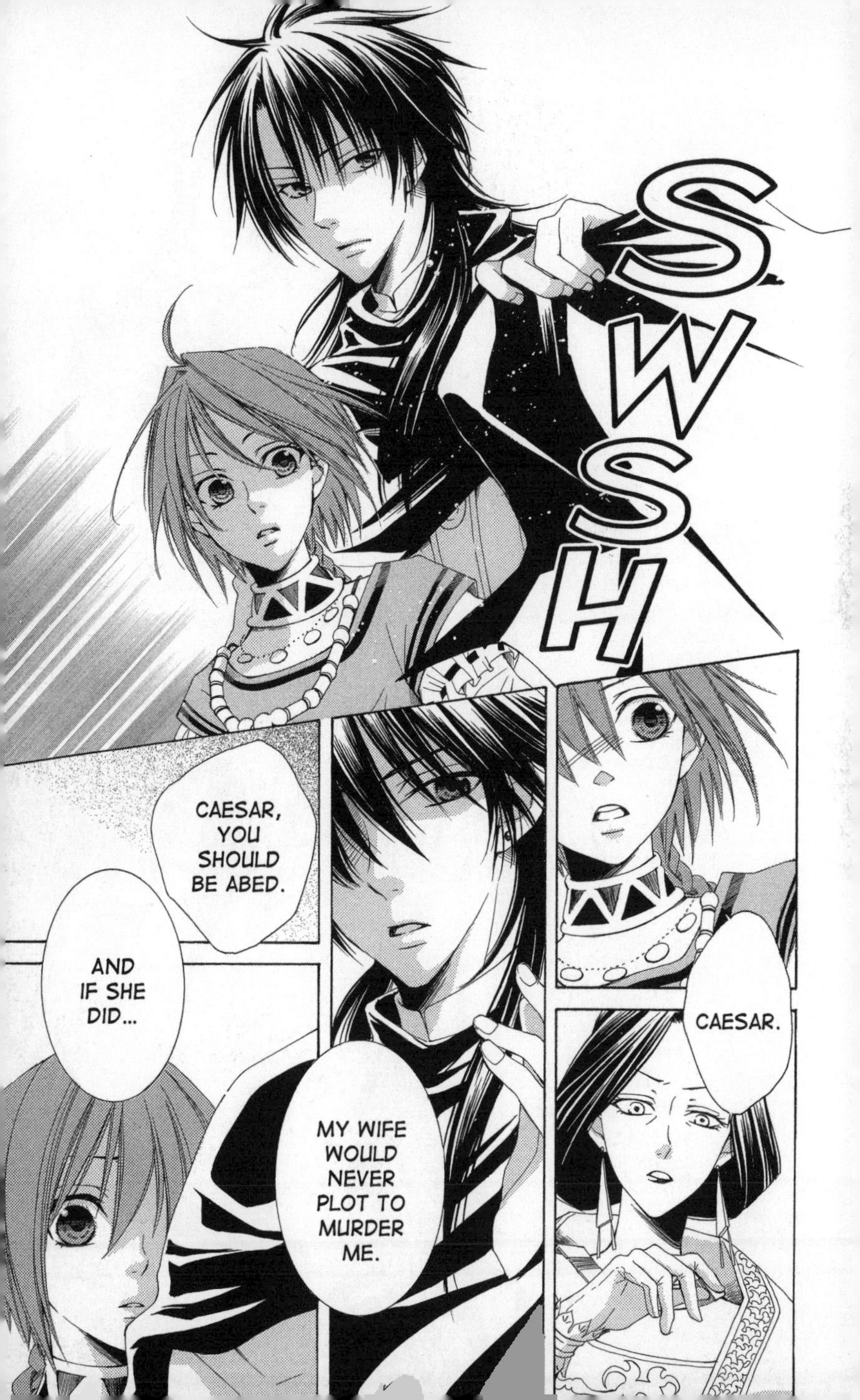
SWSSH
CAESAR.
CAESAR, YOU SHOULD BE ABED.
AND IF SHE DID...
MY WIFE WOULD NEVER PLOT TO MURDER ME.

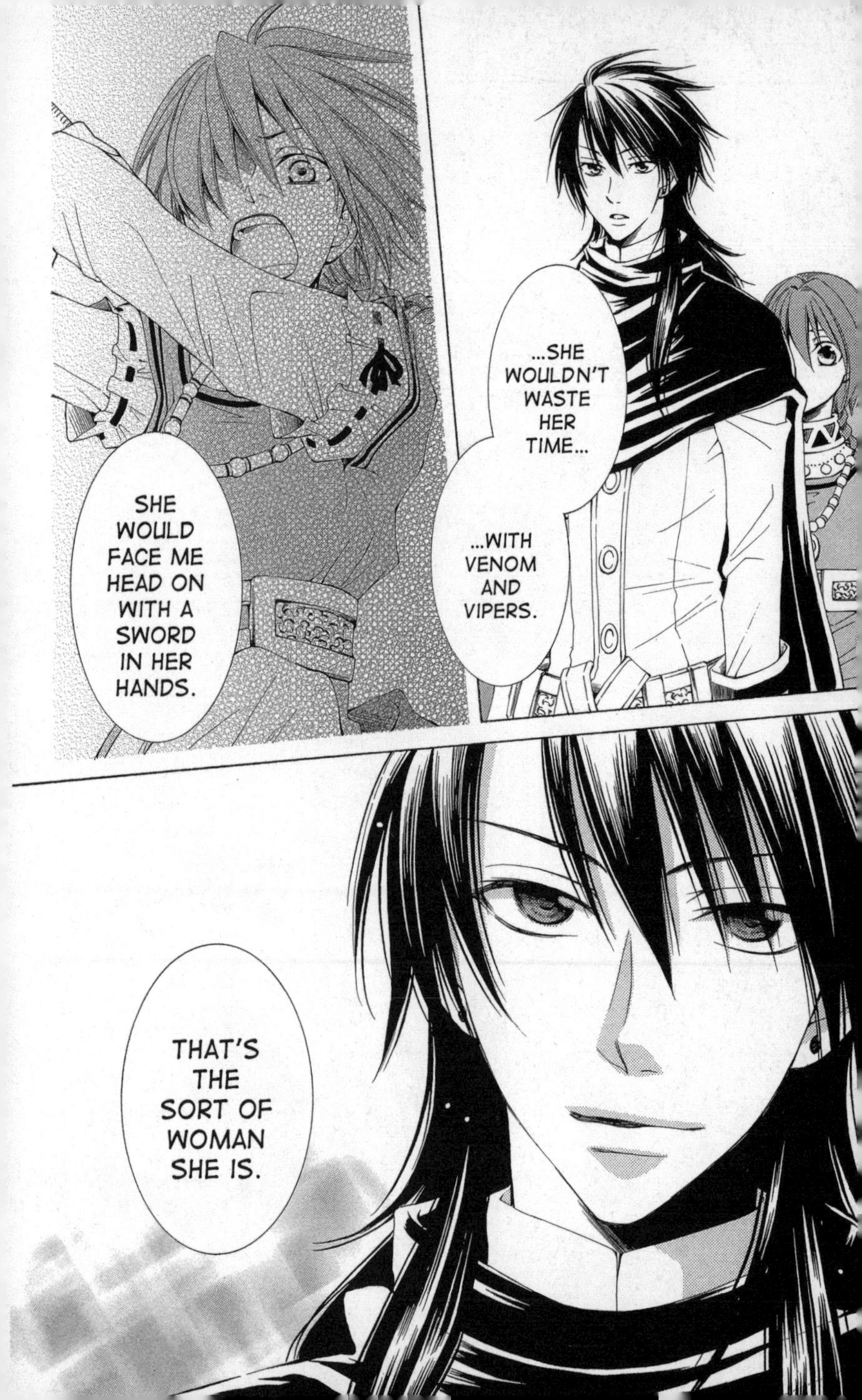
...SHE WOULDN'T WASTE HER TIME...
...WITH VENOM AND VIPERS.
SHE WOULD FACE ME HEAD ON WITH A SWORD IN HER HANDS.
THAT'S THE SORT OF WOMAN SHE IS.

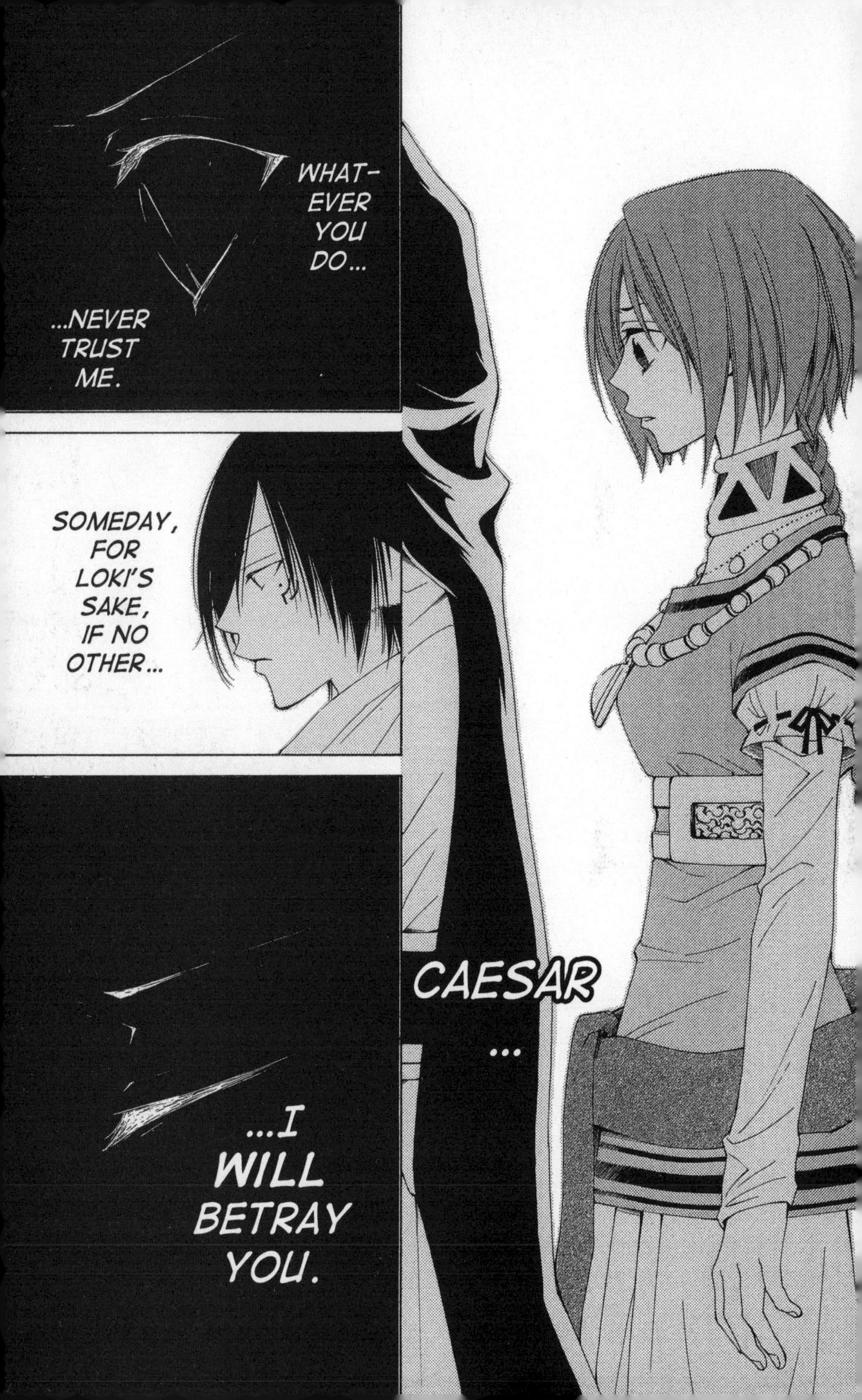
CAESAR ...
WHAT-EVER YOU DO...
...NEVER TRUST ME.
SOMEDAY, FOR LOKI'S SAKE, IF NO OTHER...
...I WILL BETRAY YOU.

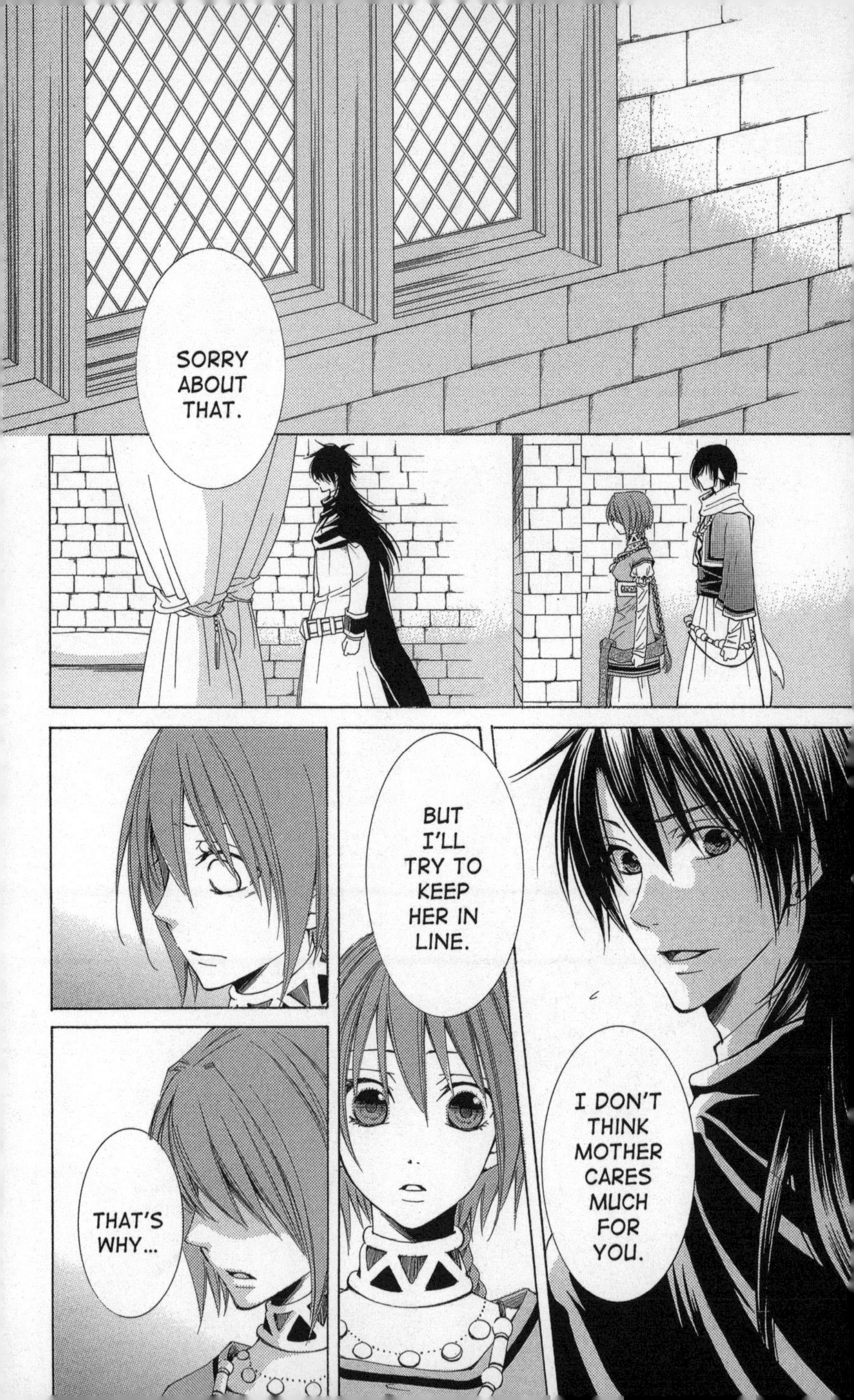
SORRY ABOUT THAT.
I DON'T THINK MOTHER CARES MUCH FOR YOU.
BUT I'LL TRY TO KEEP HER IN LINE.
THAT'S WHY...

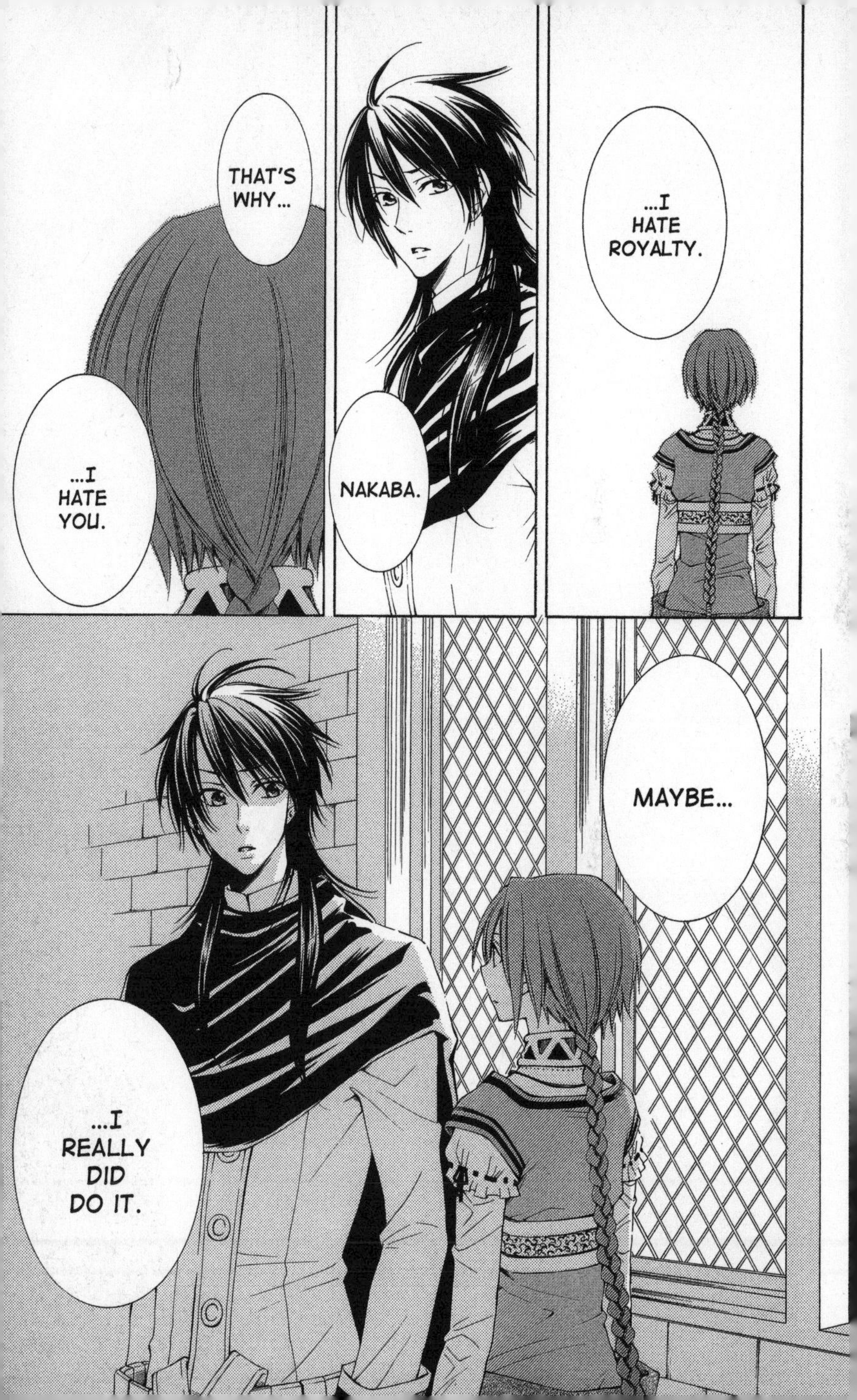
...I HATE ROYALTY.
NAKABA.
THAT'S WHY...
...I HATE YOU.
MAYBE...
...I REALLY DID DO IT.

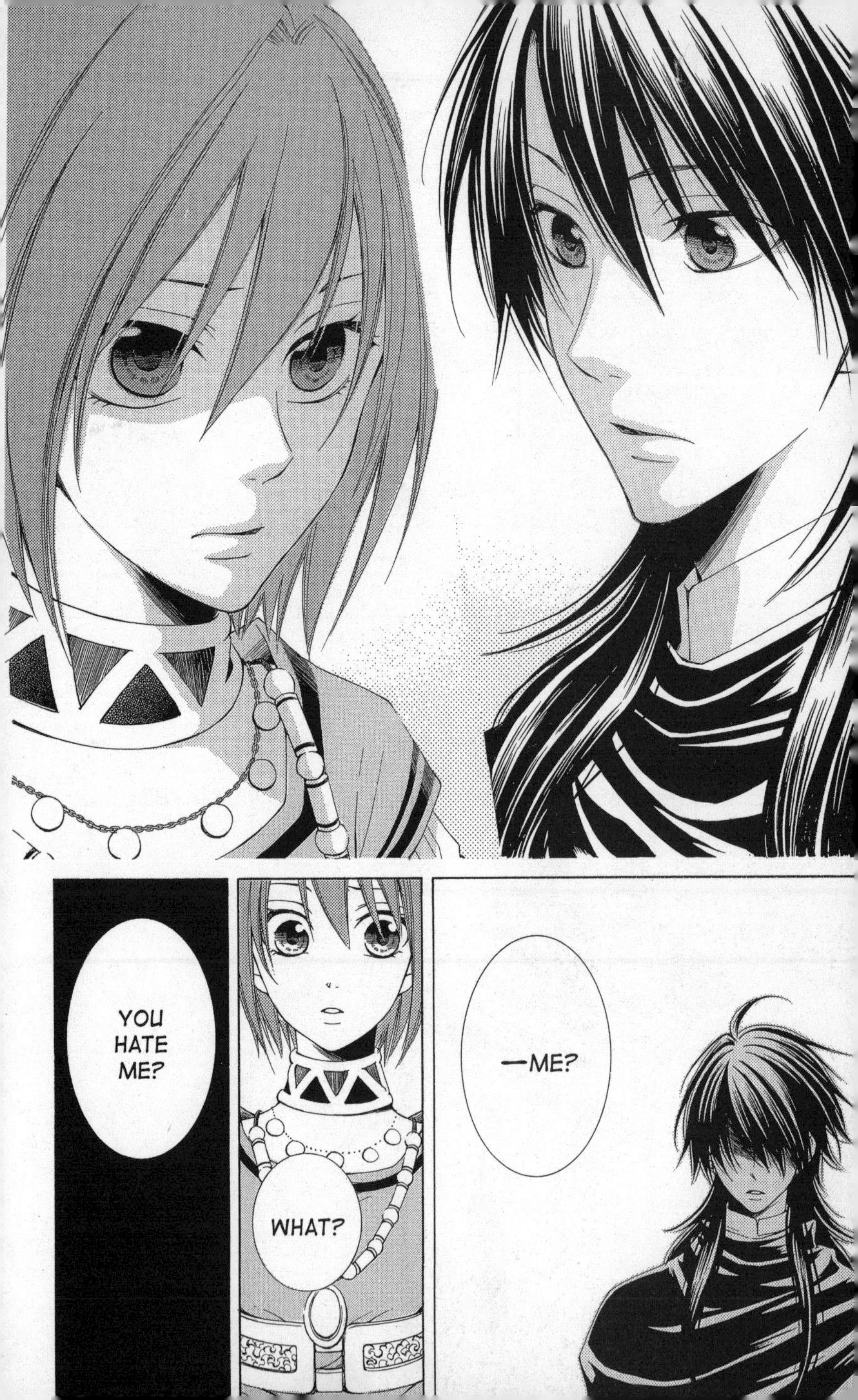
—ME?
WHAT?
YOU HATE ME?

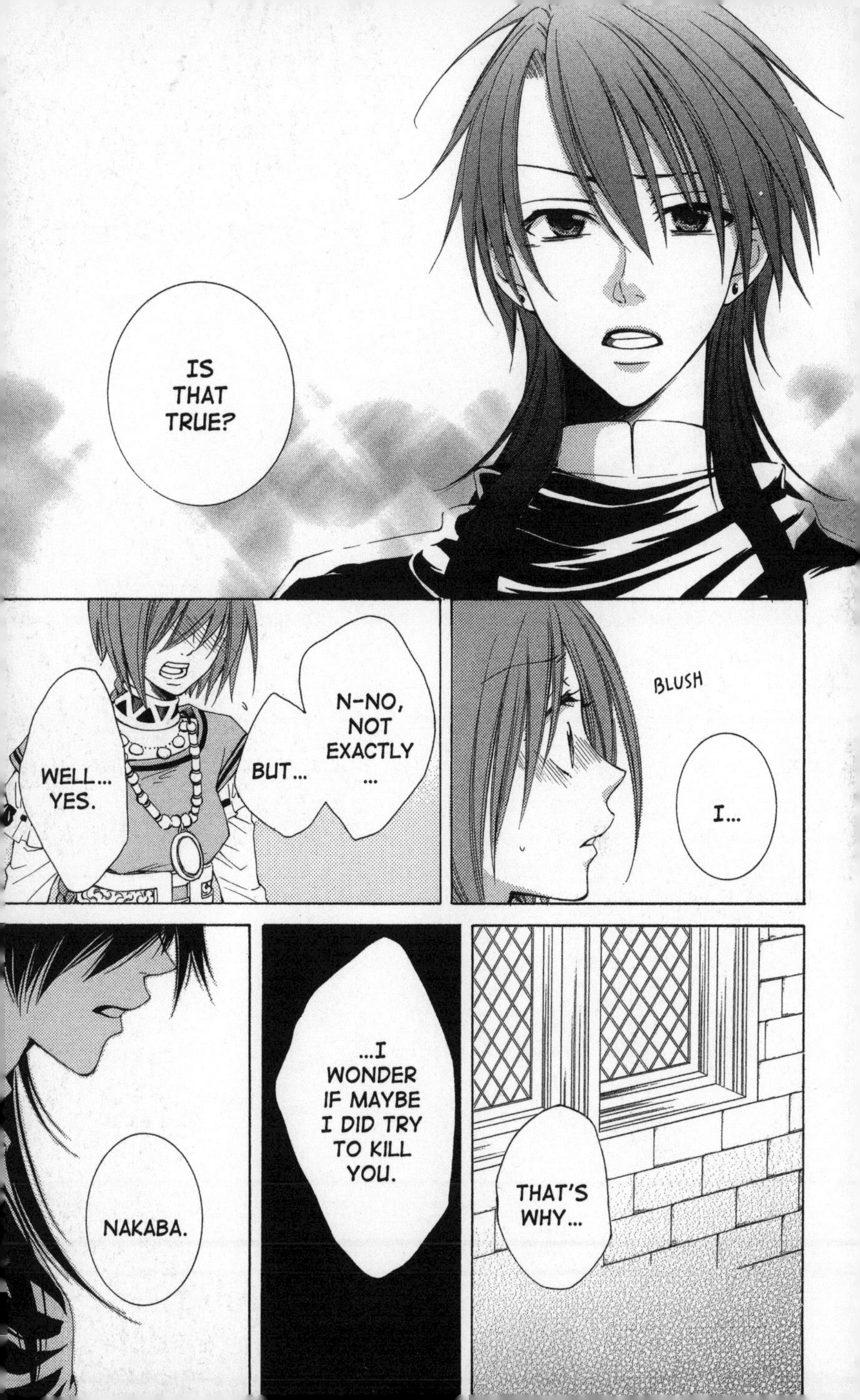
IS THAT TRUE?
BLUSH
I...
N-NO, NOT EXACTLY...
BUT...
WELL... YES.
THAT'S WHY...
...I WONDER IF MAYBE I DID TRY TO KILL YOU.
NAKABA.

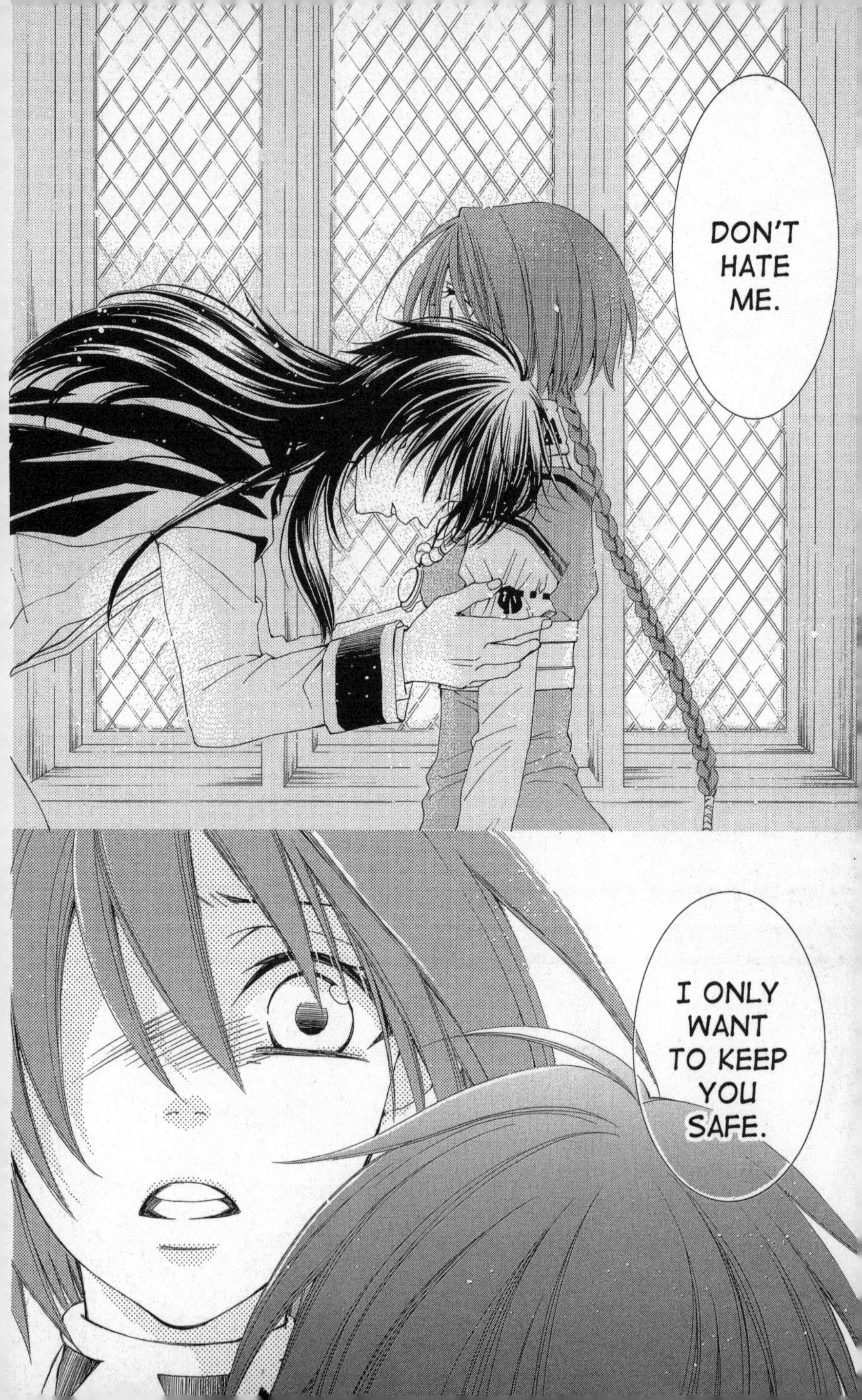
DON'T HATE ME.
I ONLY WANT TO KEEP YOU SAFE.

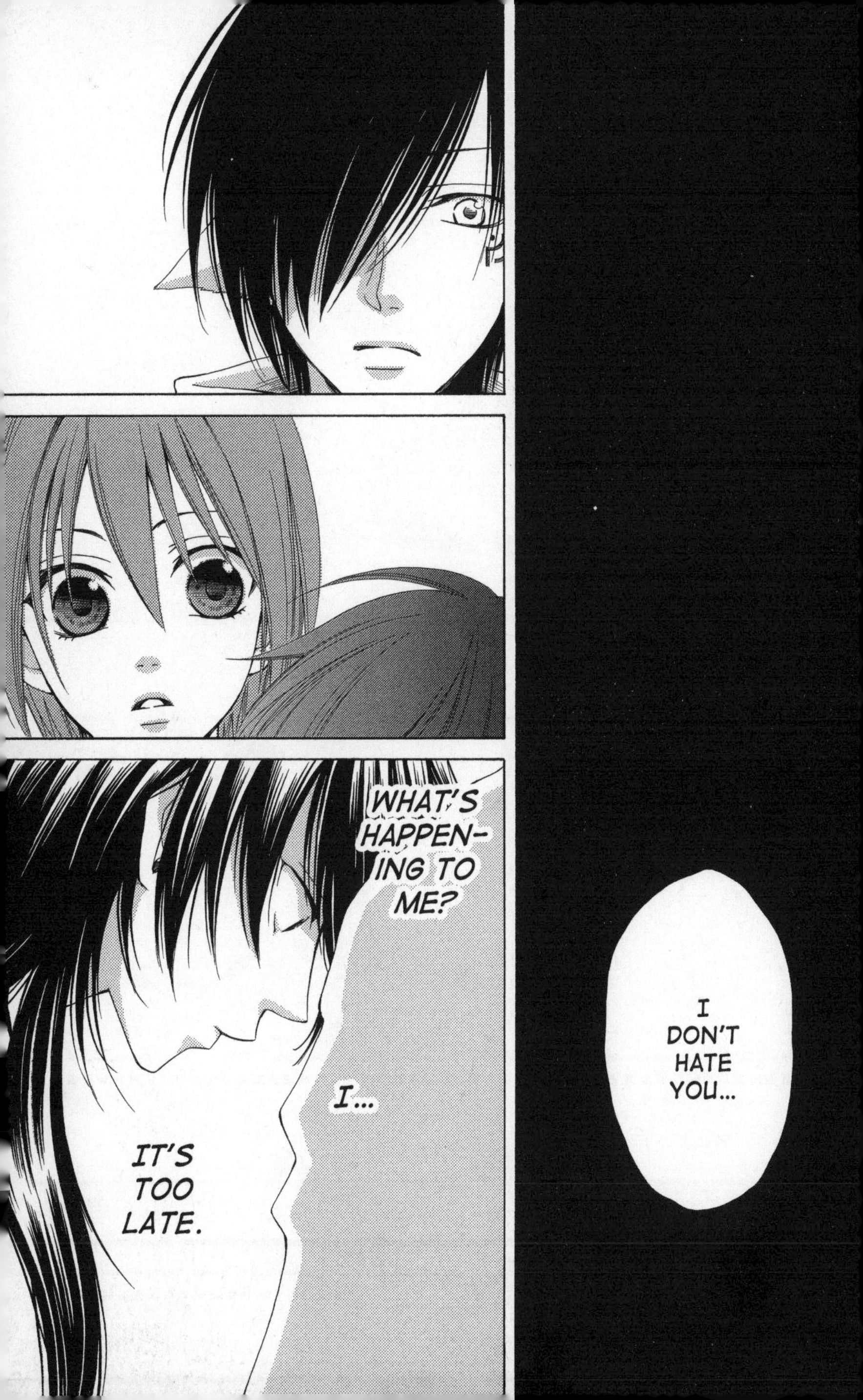
I DON'T HATE YOU...
WHAT'S HAPPEN-ING TO ME?
I...
IT'S TOO LATE.

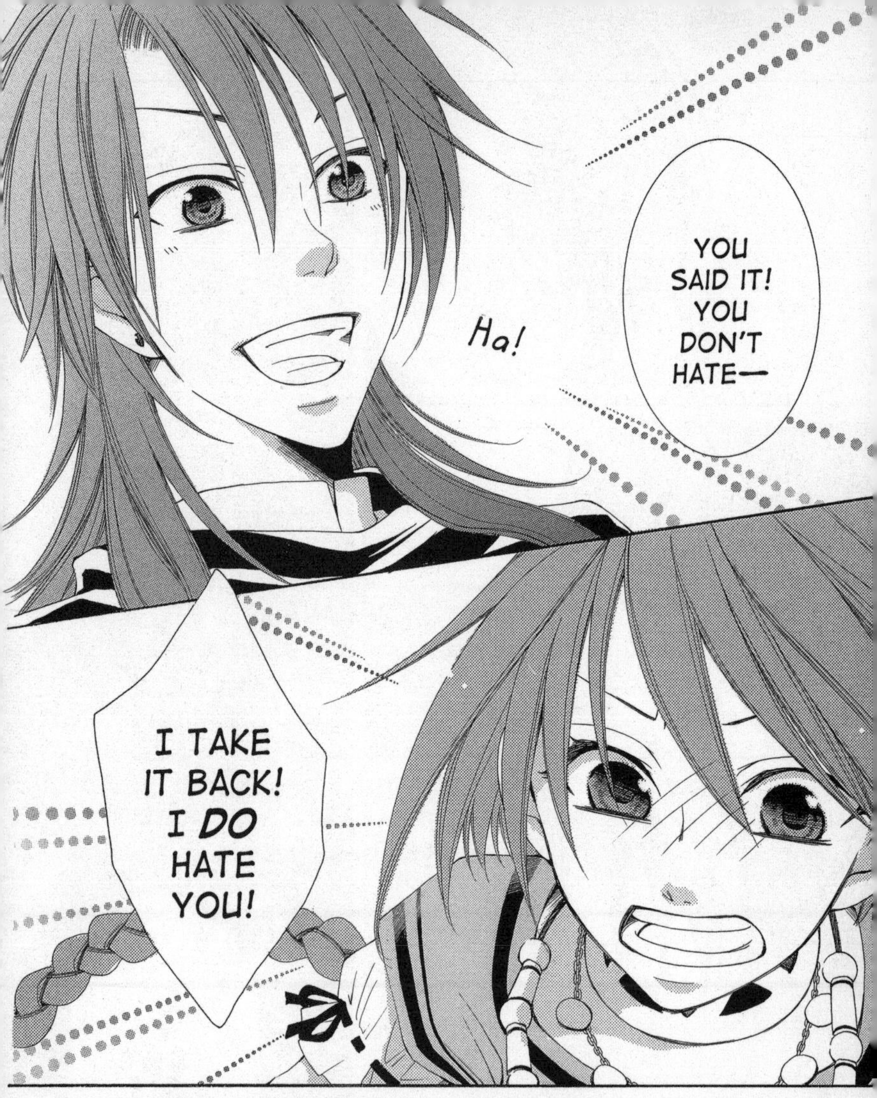
YOU SAID IT! YOU DON'T HATE—
Ha!
I TAKE IT BACK! I *DO* HATE YOU!

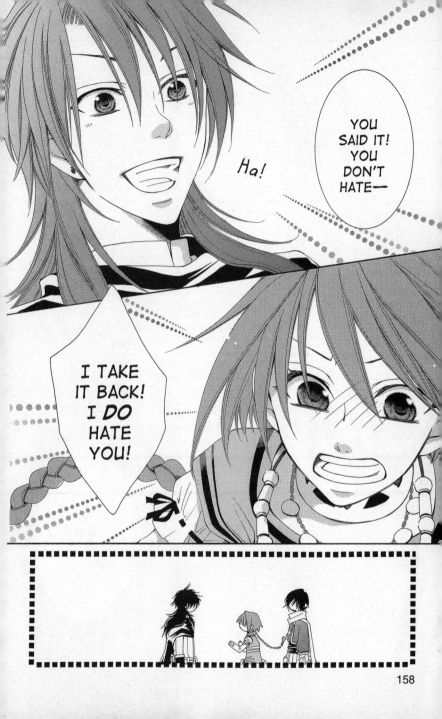

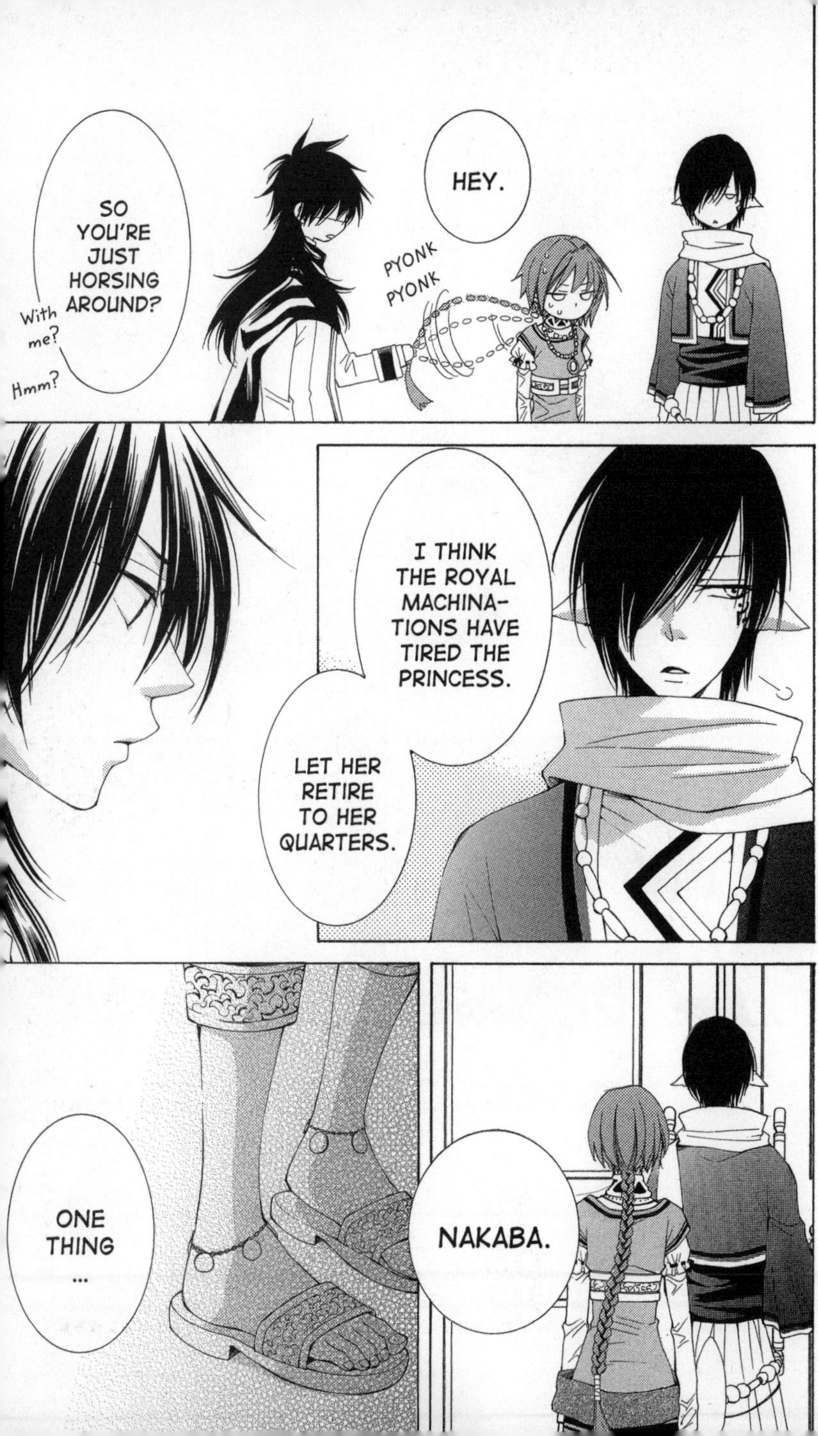
HEY.
PYONK PYONK
SO YOU'RE JUST HORSING AROUND?
With me?
Hmm?
I THINK THE ROYAL MACHINA-TIONS HAVE TIRED THE PRINCESS.
LET HER RETIRE TO HER QUARTERS.
NAKABA.
ONE THING ...

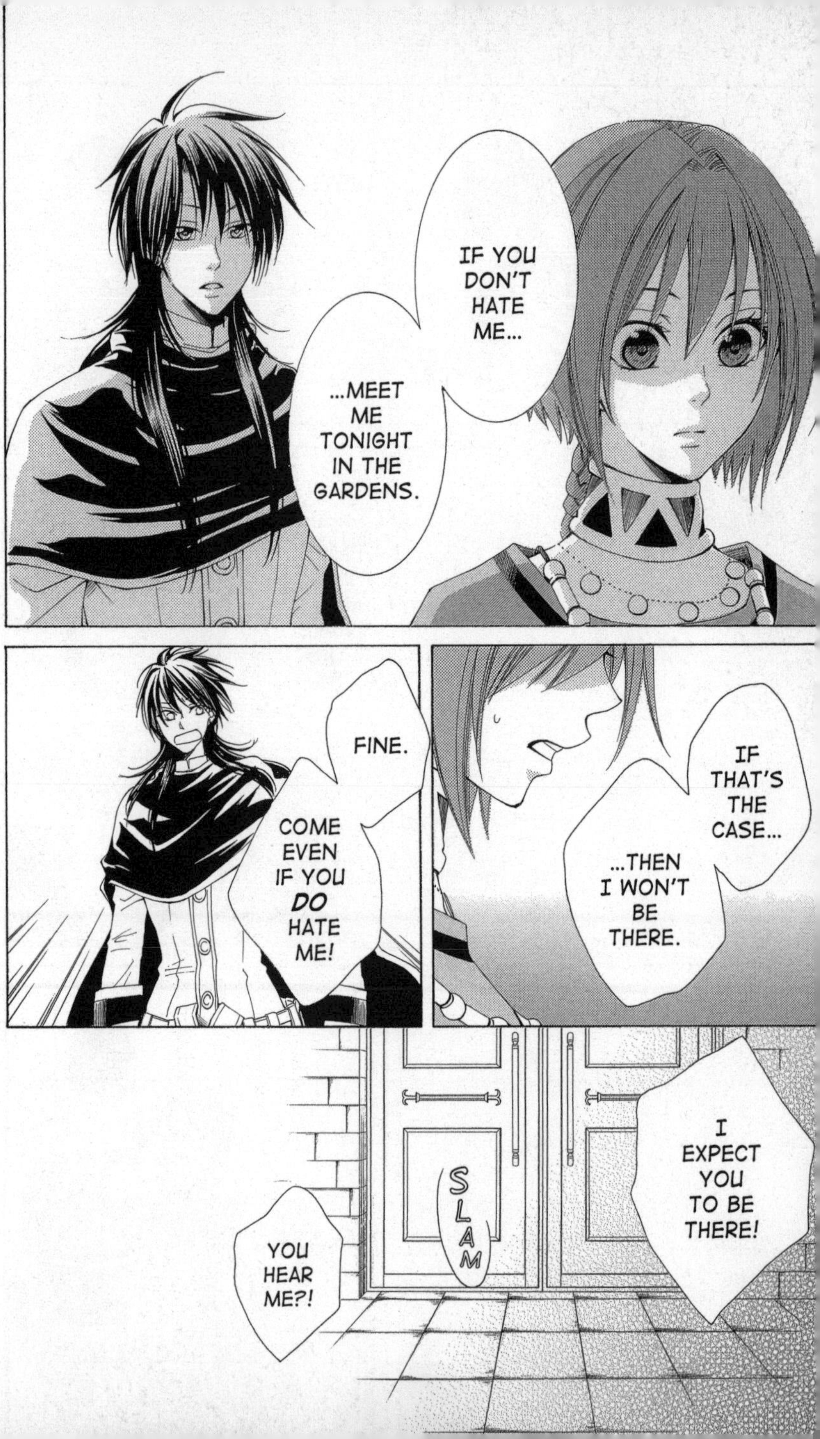
IF YOU DON'T HATE ME...
...MEET ME TONIGHT IN THE GARDENS.
IF THAT'S THE CASE...
...THEN I WON'T BE THERE.
FINE.
COME EVEN IF YOU *DO* HATE ME!
I EXPECT YOU TO BE THERE!
SLAM
YOU HEAR ME?!

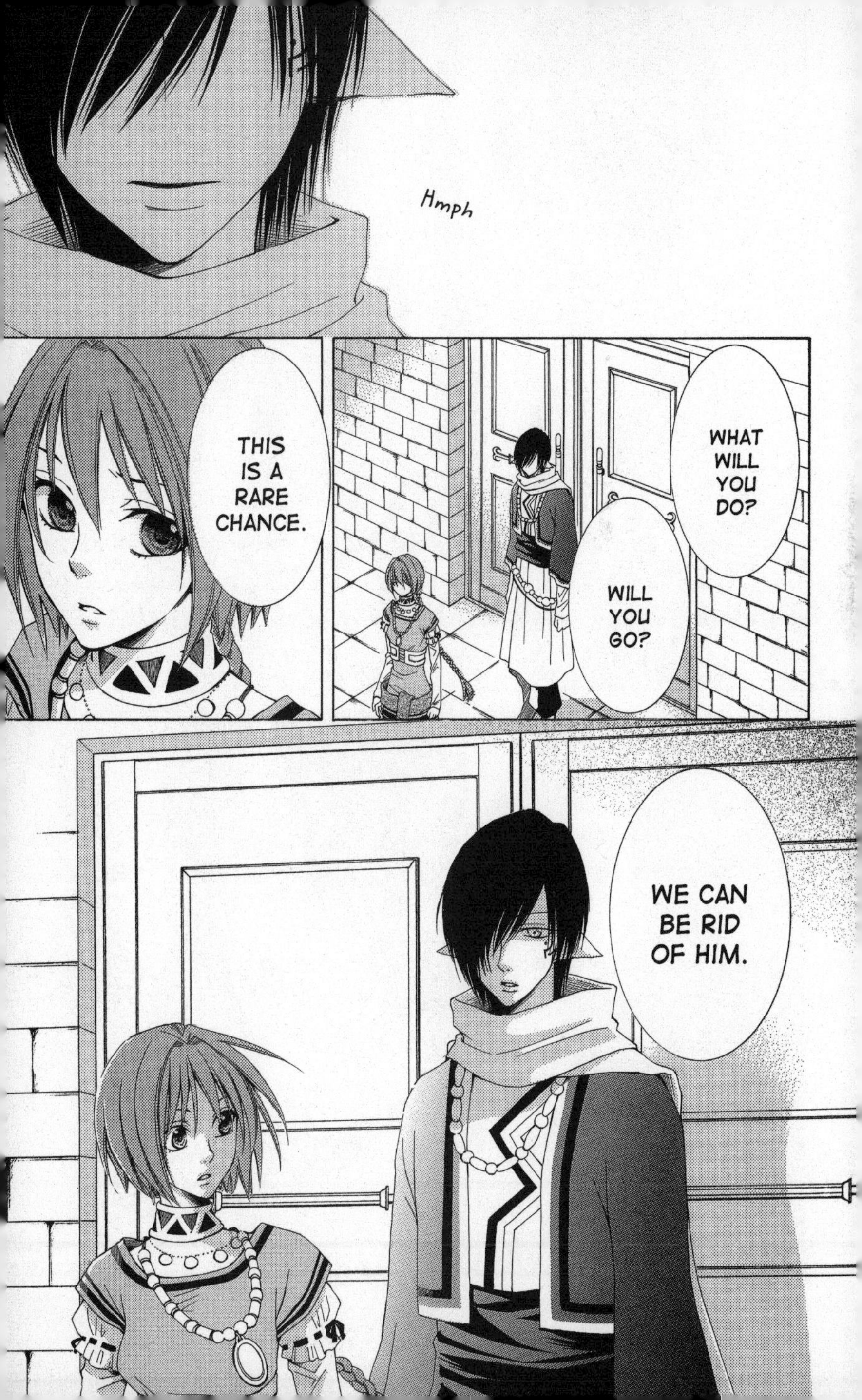
Hmph
WHAT WILL YOU DO?
WILL YOU GO?
THIS IS A RARE CHANCE.
WE CAN BE RID OF HIM.

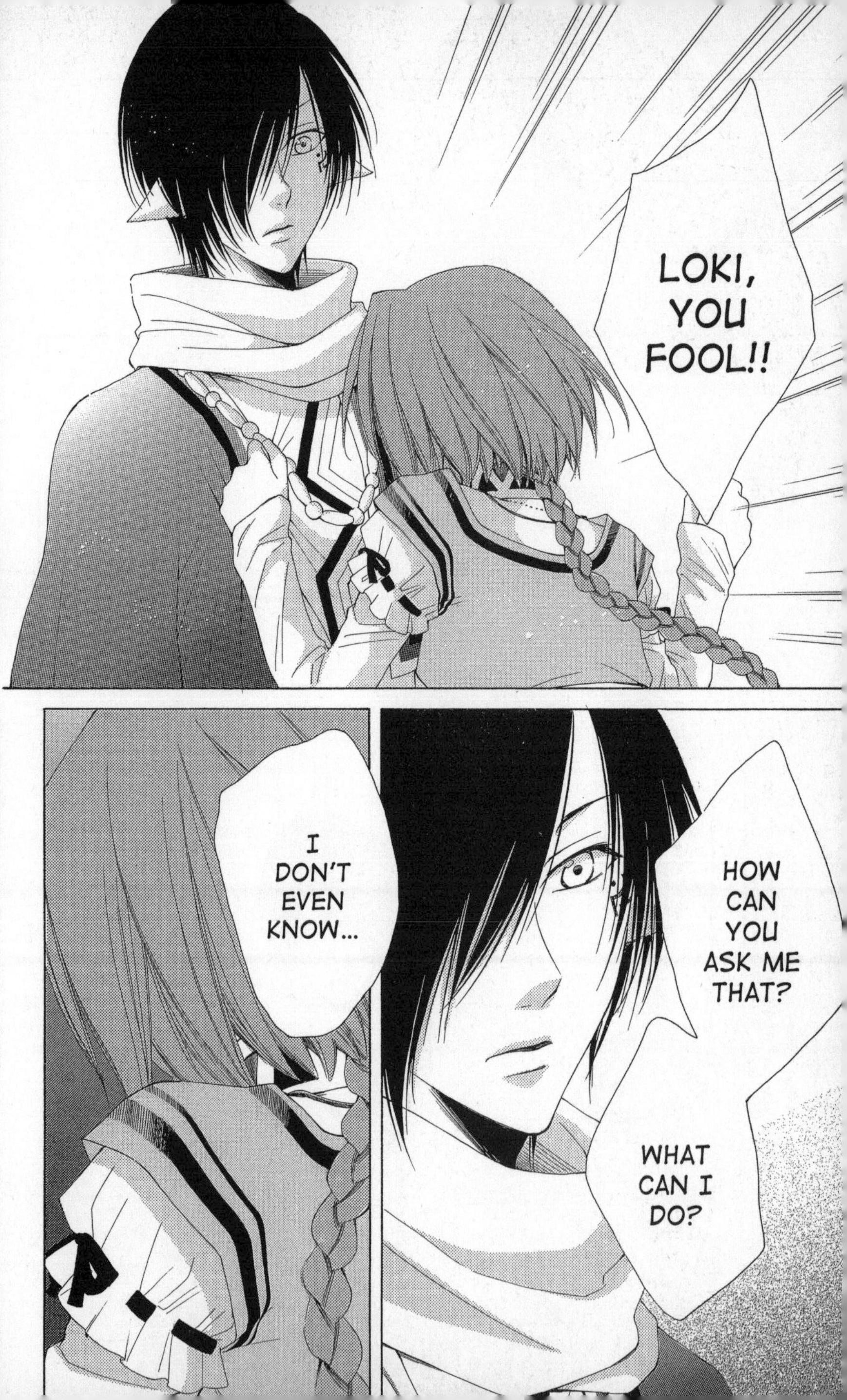
LOKI, YOU FOOL!!
HOW CAN YOU ASK ME THAT?
WHAT CAN I DO?
I DON'T EVEN KNOW...

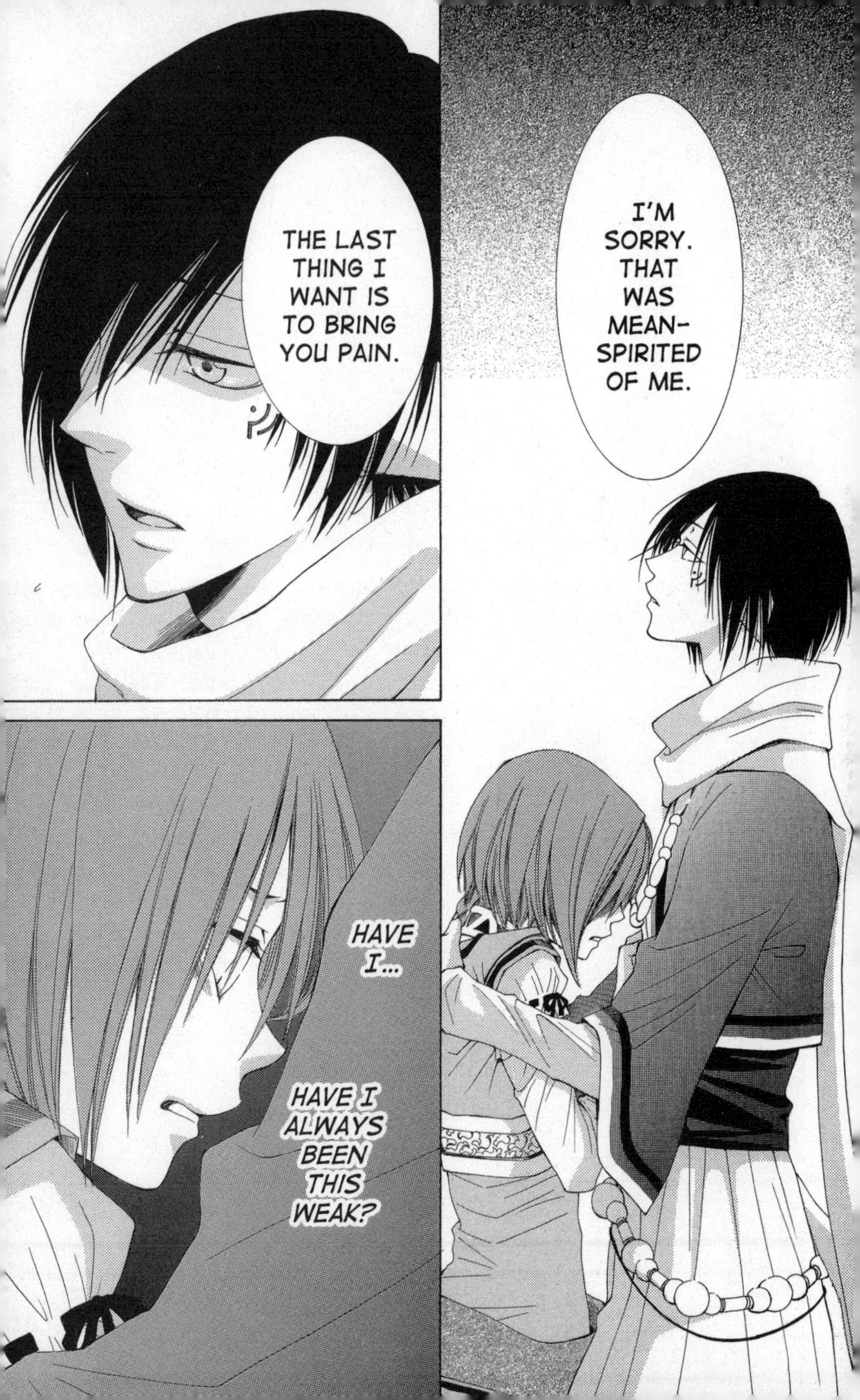
I'M SORRY. THAT WAS MEAN-SPIRITED OF ME.
THE LAST THING I WANT IS TO BRING YOU PAIN.
HAVE I...
HAVE I ALWAYS BEEN THIS WEAK?

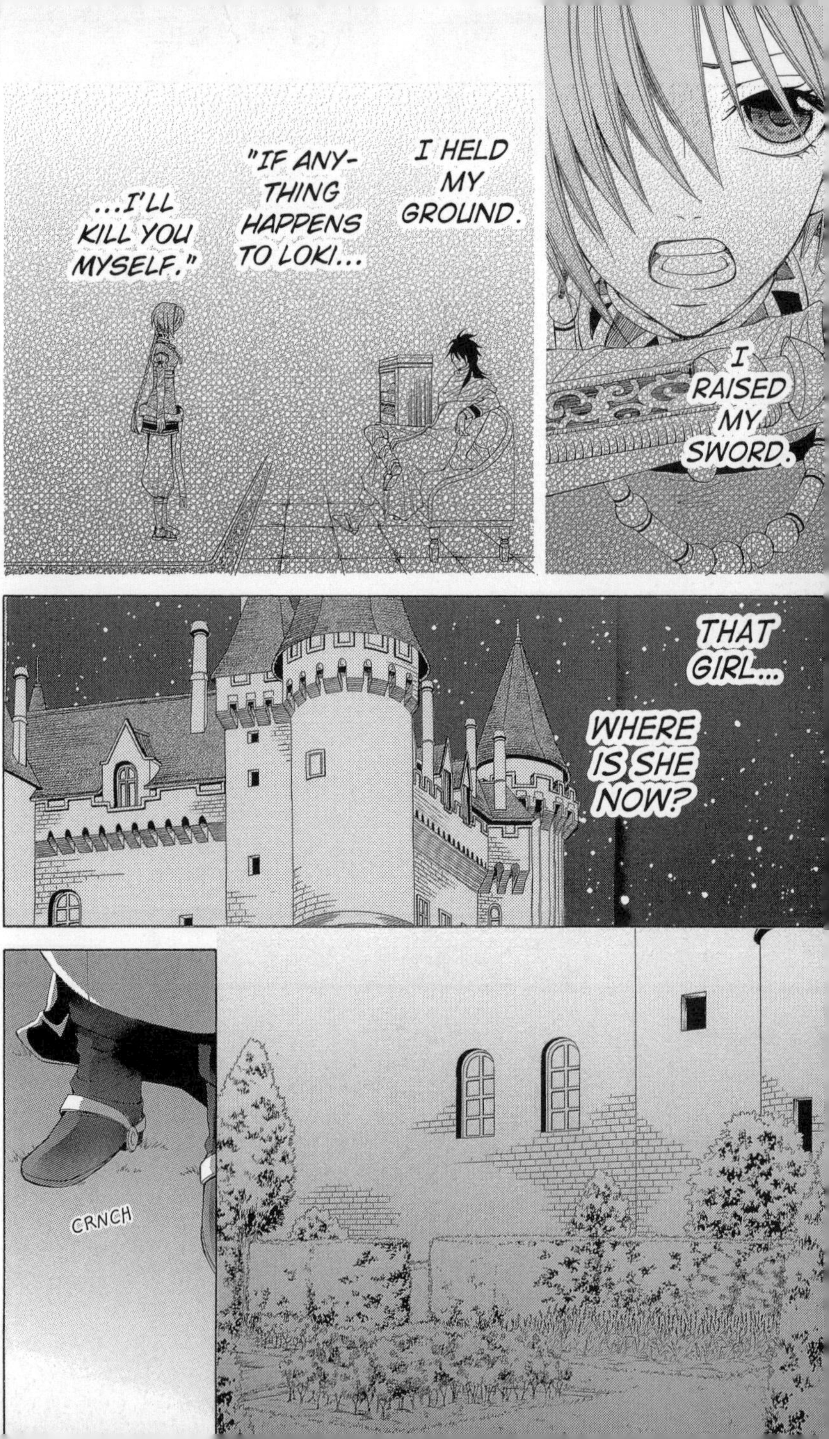
I RAISED MY SWORD.
I HELD MY GROUND.
"IF ANY-THING HAPPENS TO LOKI...
...I'LL KILL YOU MYSELF."
THAT GIRL...
WHERE IS SHE NOW?
CRNCH

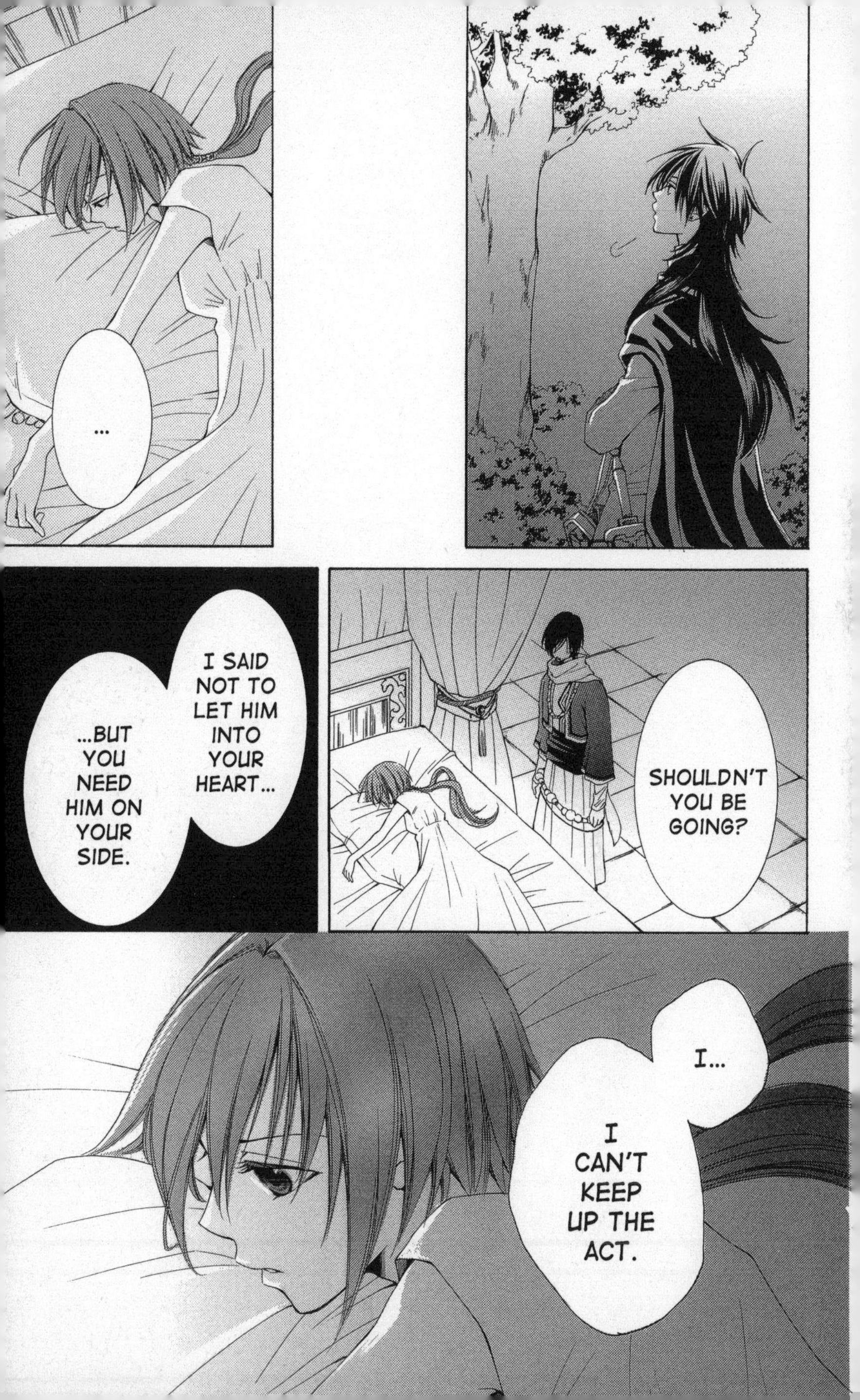
...
SHOULDN'T YOU BE GOING?
I SAID NOT TO LET HIM INTO YOUR HEART...
...BUT YOU NEED HIM ON YOUR SIDE.
I...
I CAN'T KEEP UP THE ACT.

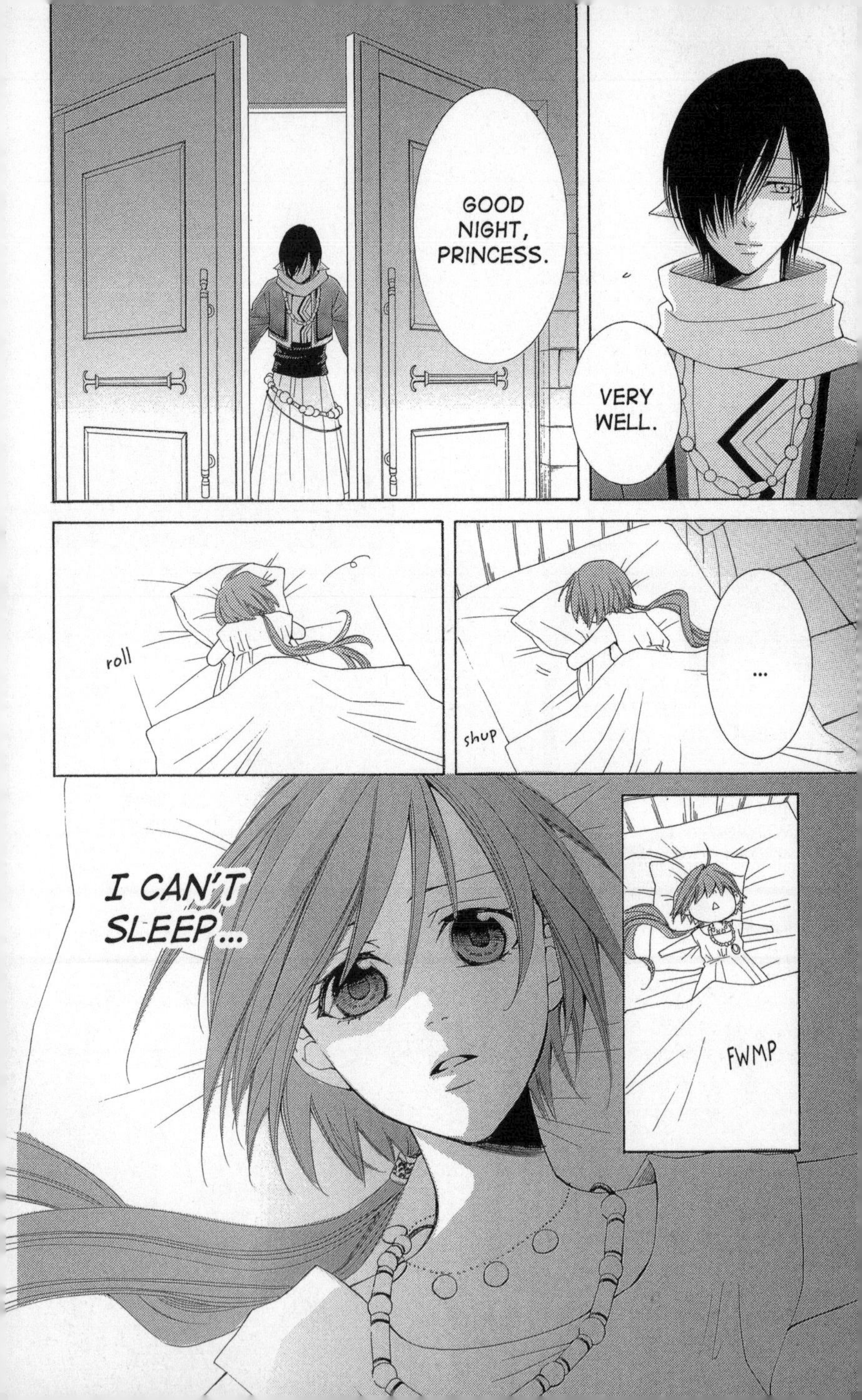
VERY WELL.
GOOD NIGHT, PRINCESS.
...
shup
roll
FWMP
I CAN'T SLEEP...

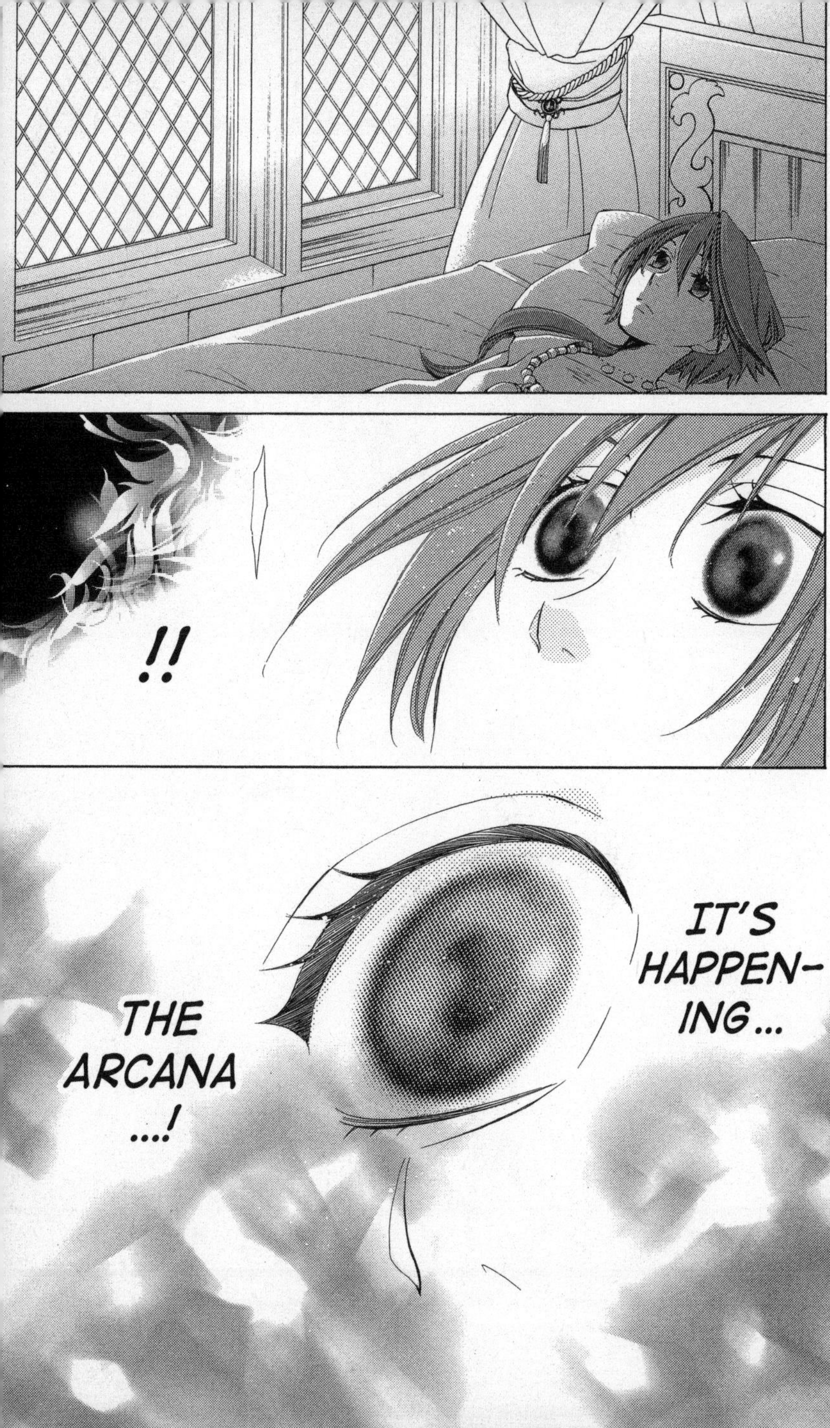
!!
IT'S HAPPEN-ING...
THE ARCANA ...!

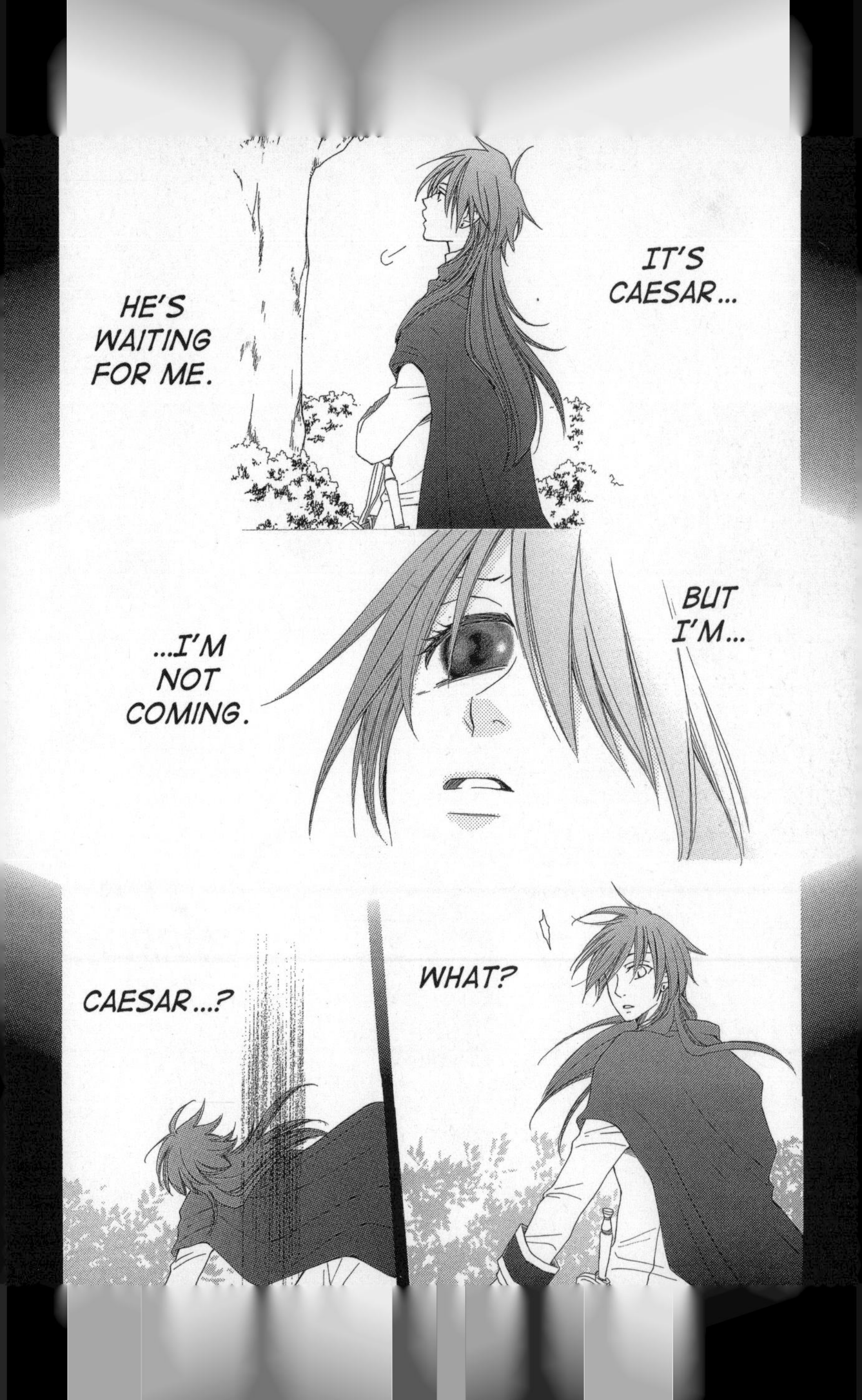
IT'S CAESAR...
HE'S WAITING FOR ME.
BUT I'M...
...I'M NOT COMING.
WHAT?
CAESAR...?

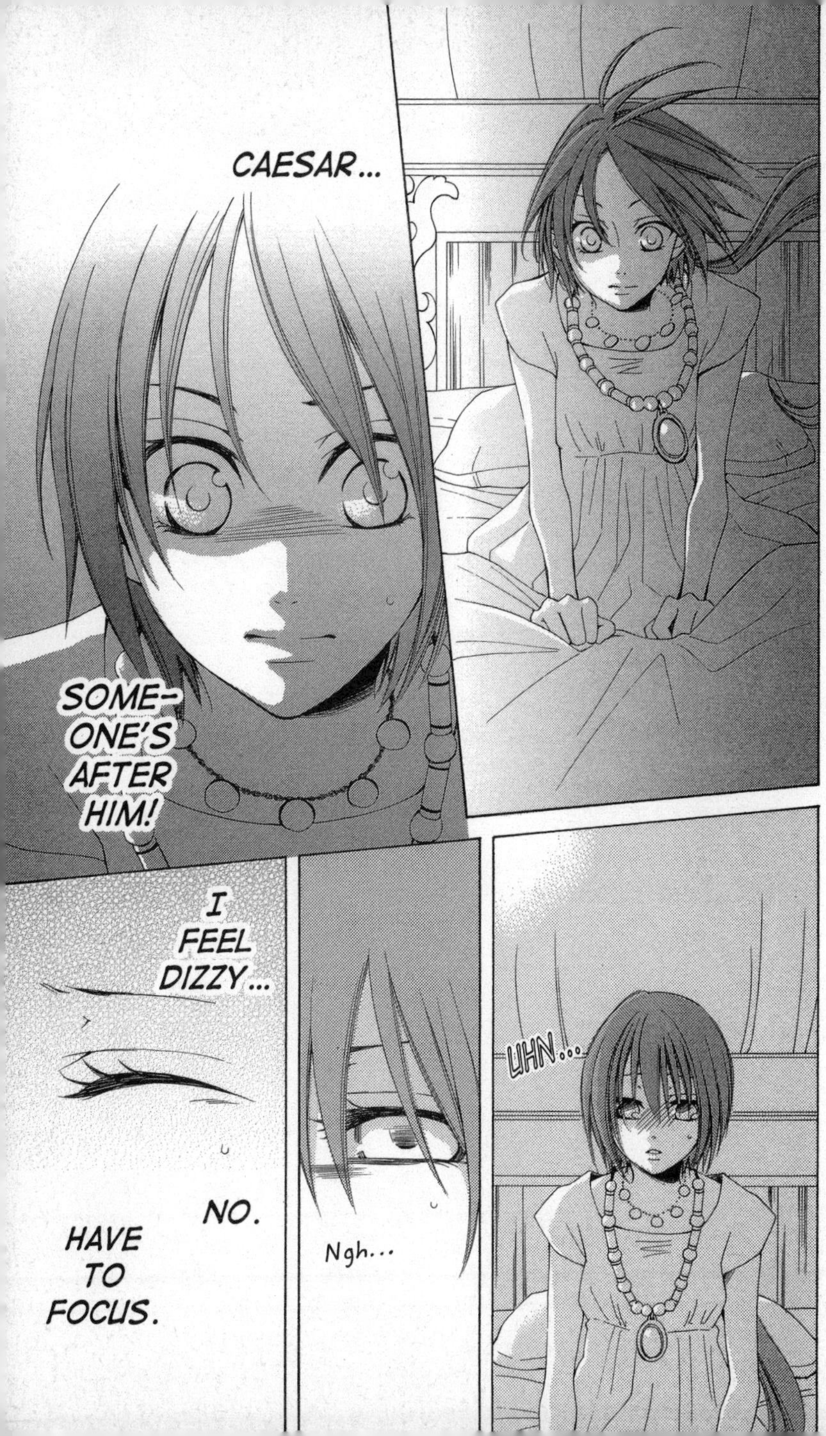
CAESAR...
SOME-ONE'S AFTER HIM!
UHN...
Ngh...
I FEEL DIZZY...
NO.
HAVE TO FOCUS.

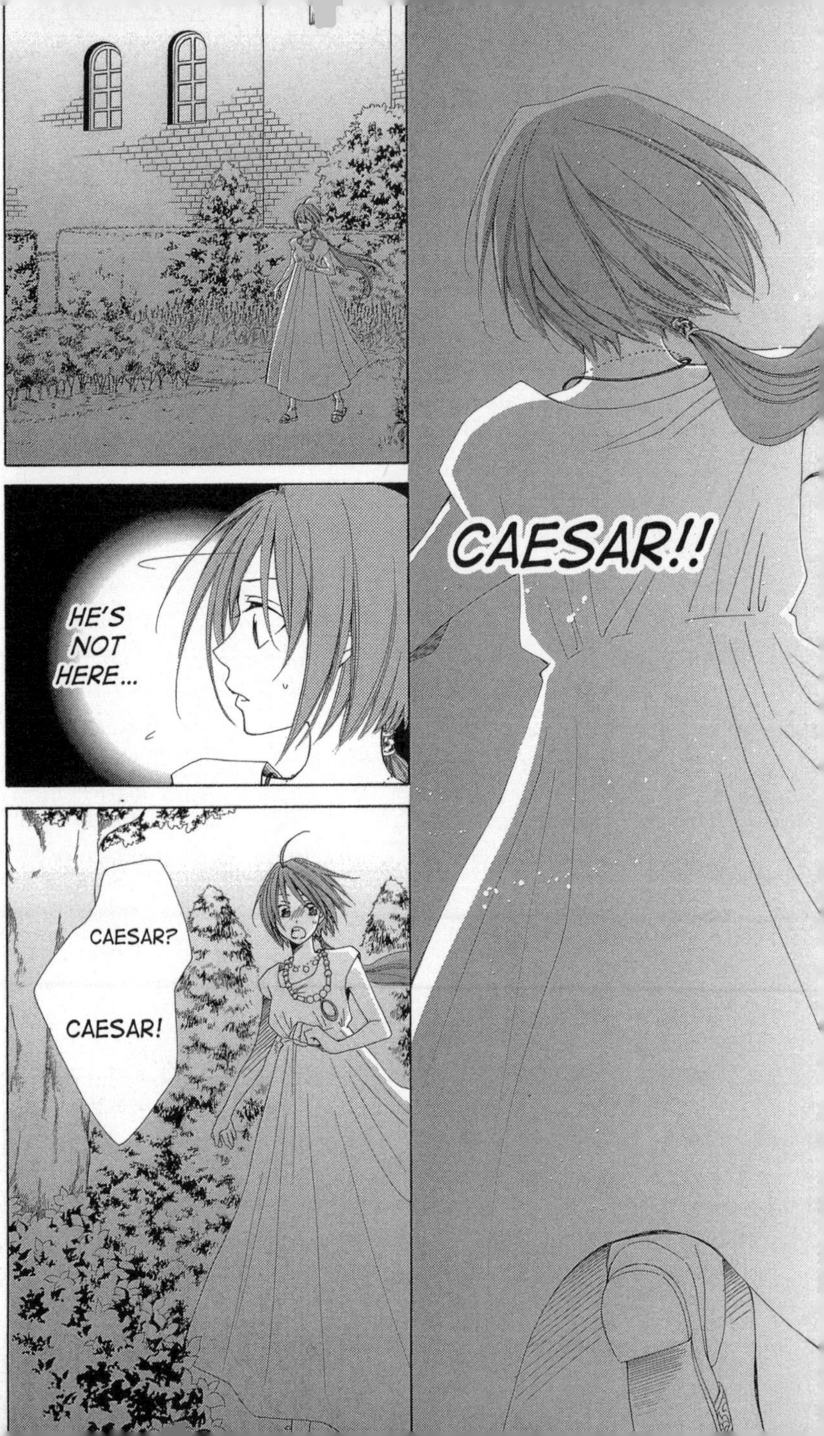
CAESAR!!
HE'S NOT HERE...
CAESAR?
CAESAR!

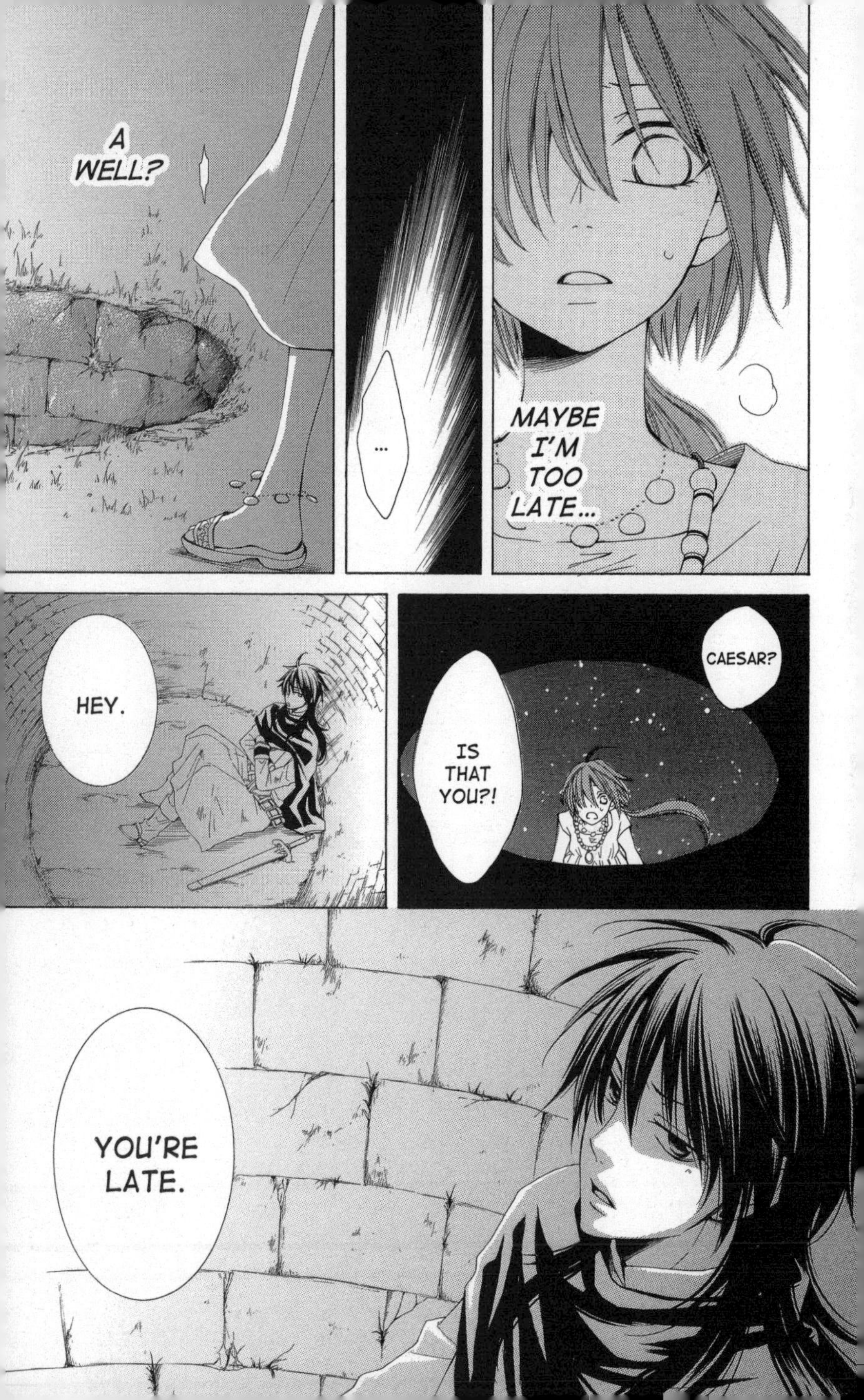
MAYBE I'M TOO LATE...
...
A WELL?
CAESAR?
IS THAT YOU?!
HEY.
YOU'RE LATE.

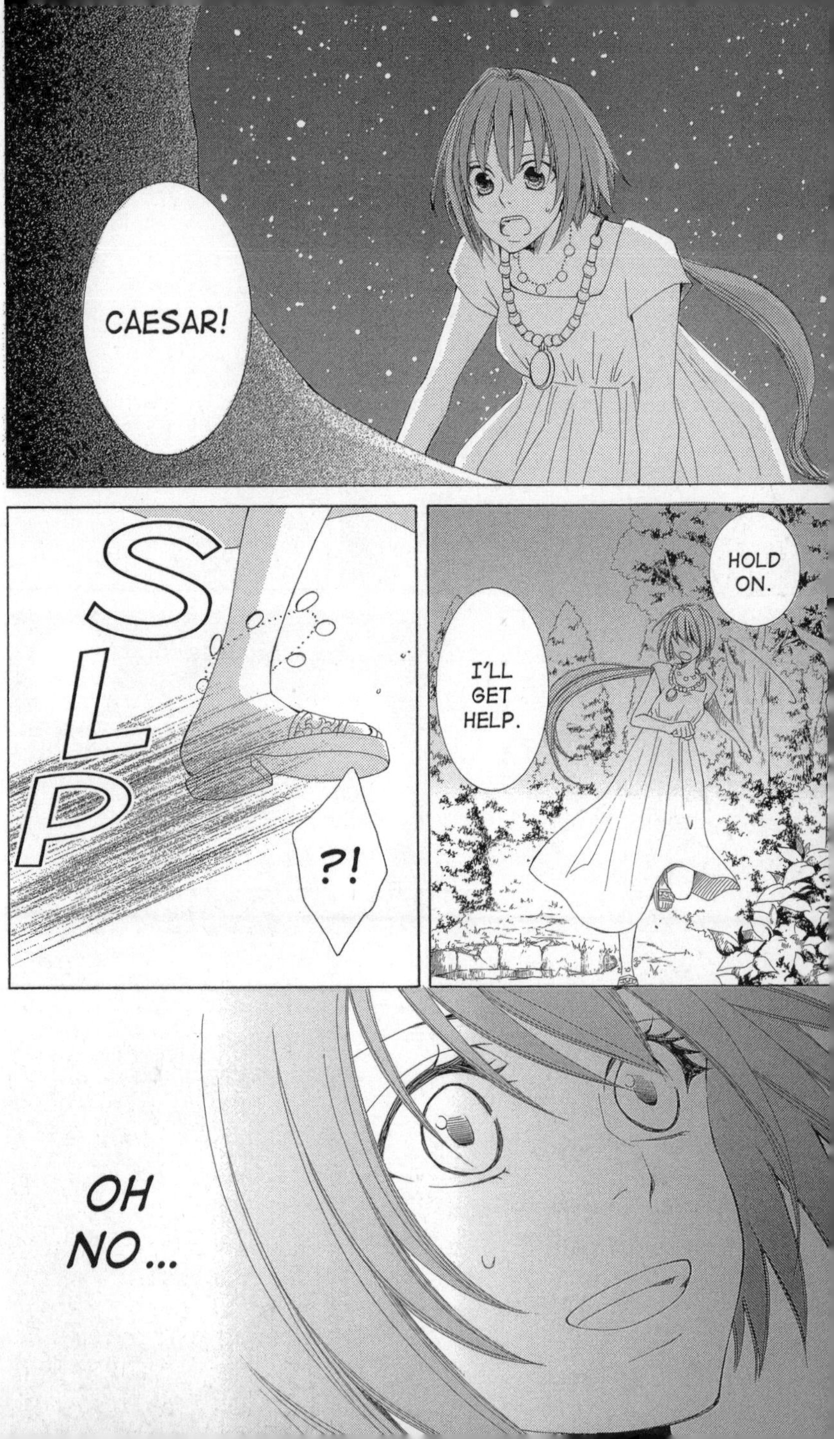
CAESAR!
HOLD ON.
I'LL GET HELP.
SLP
?!
OH NO...

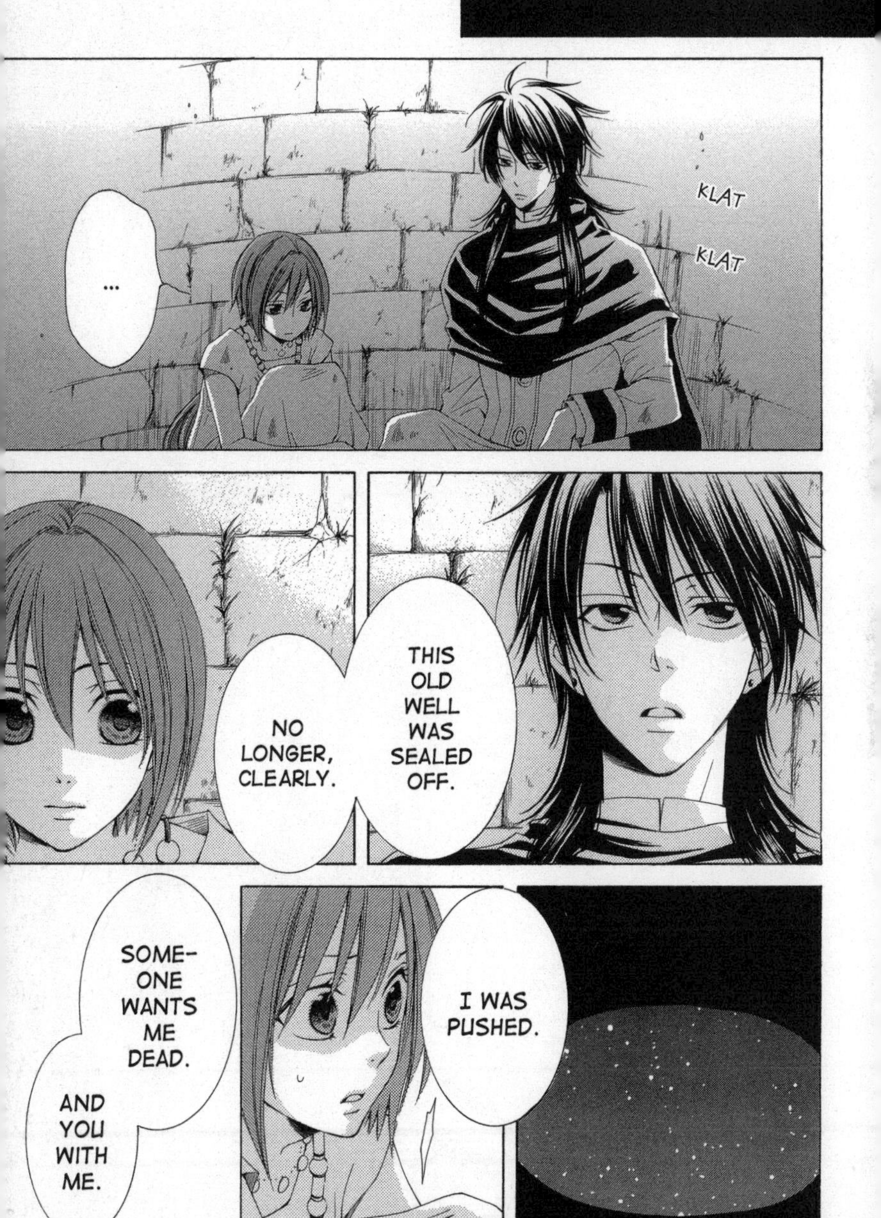
KLAT
KLAT
...
THIS OLD WELL WAS SEALED OFF.
NO LONGER, CLEARLY.
I WAS PUSHED.
SOME-ONE WANTS ME DEAD.
AND YOU WITH ME.

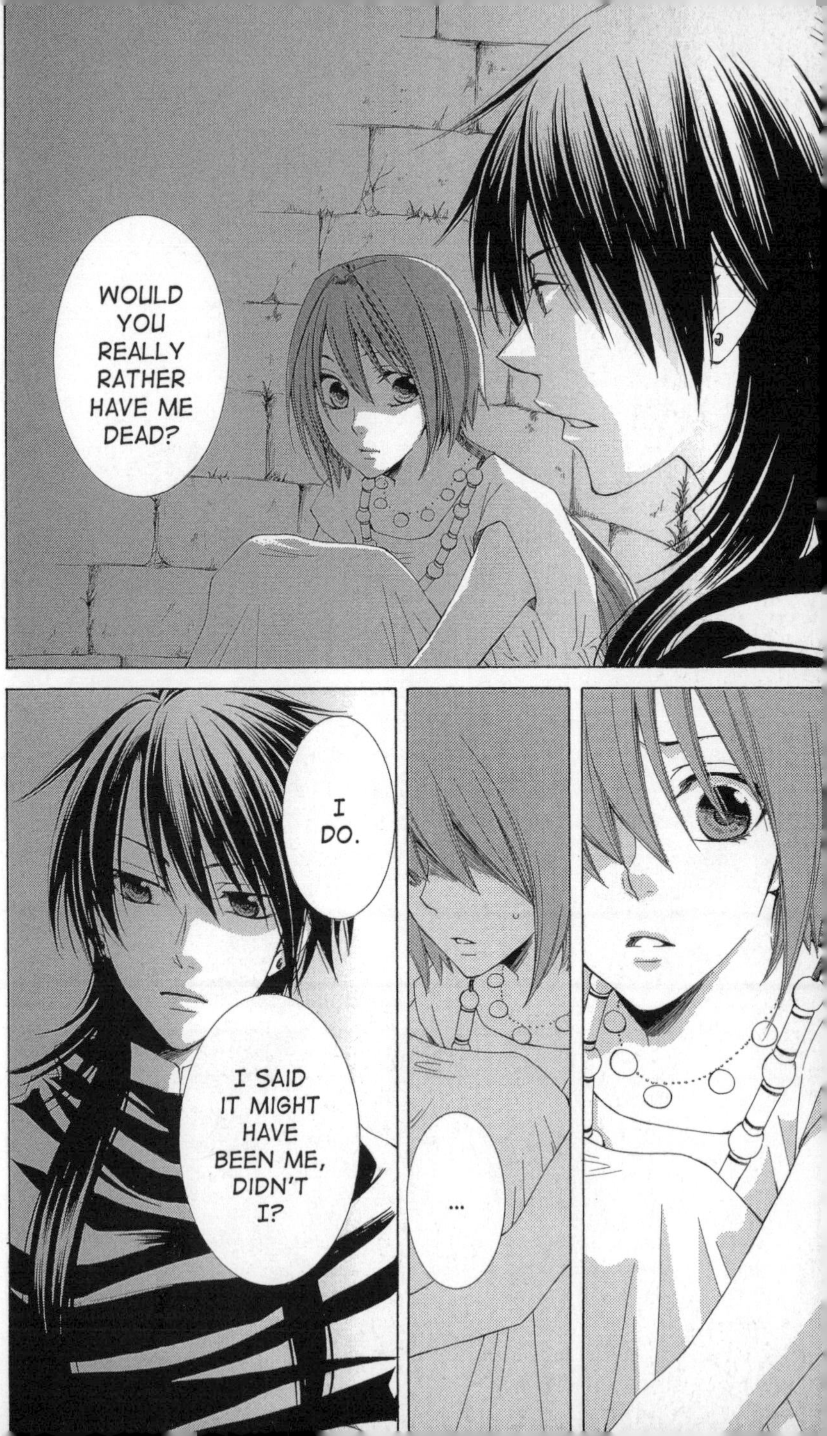
WOULD YOU REALLY RATHER HAVE ME DEAD?
...
I DO.
I SAID IT MIGHT HAVE BEEN ME, DIDN'T I?

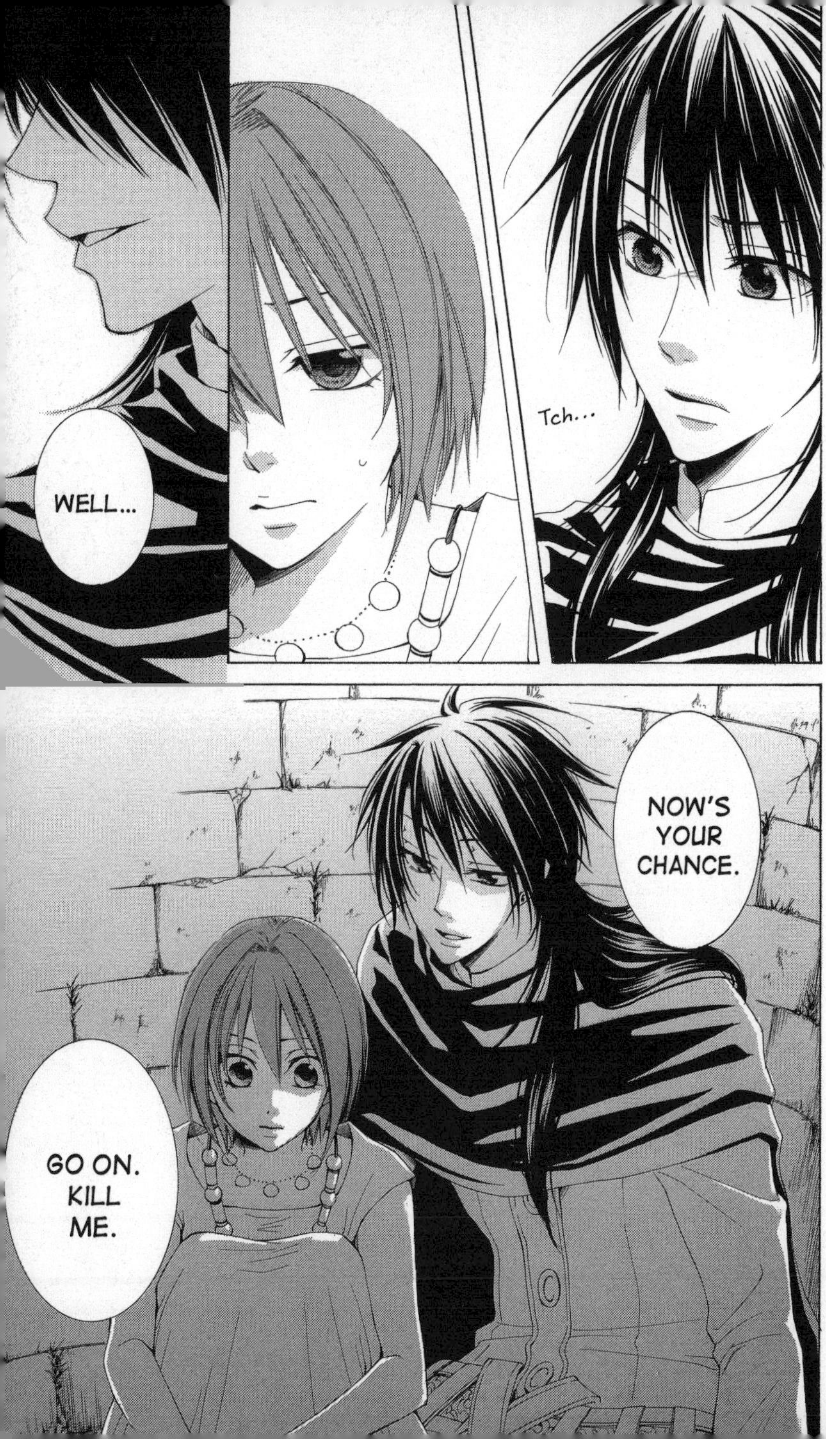
Tch...
WELL...
NOW'S YOUR CHANCE.
GO ON. KILL ME.

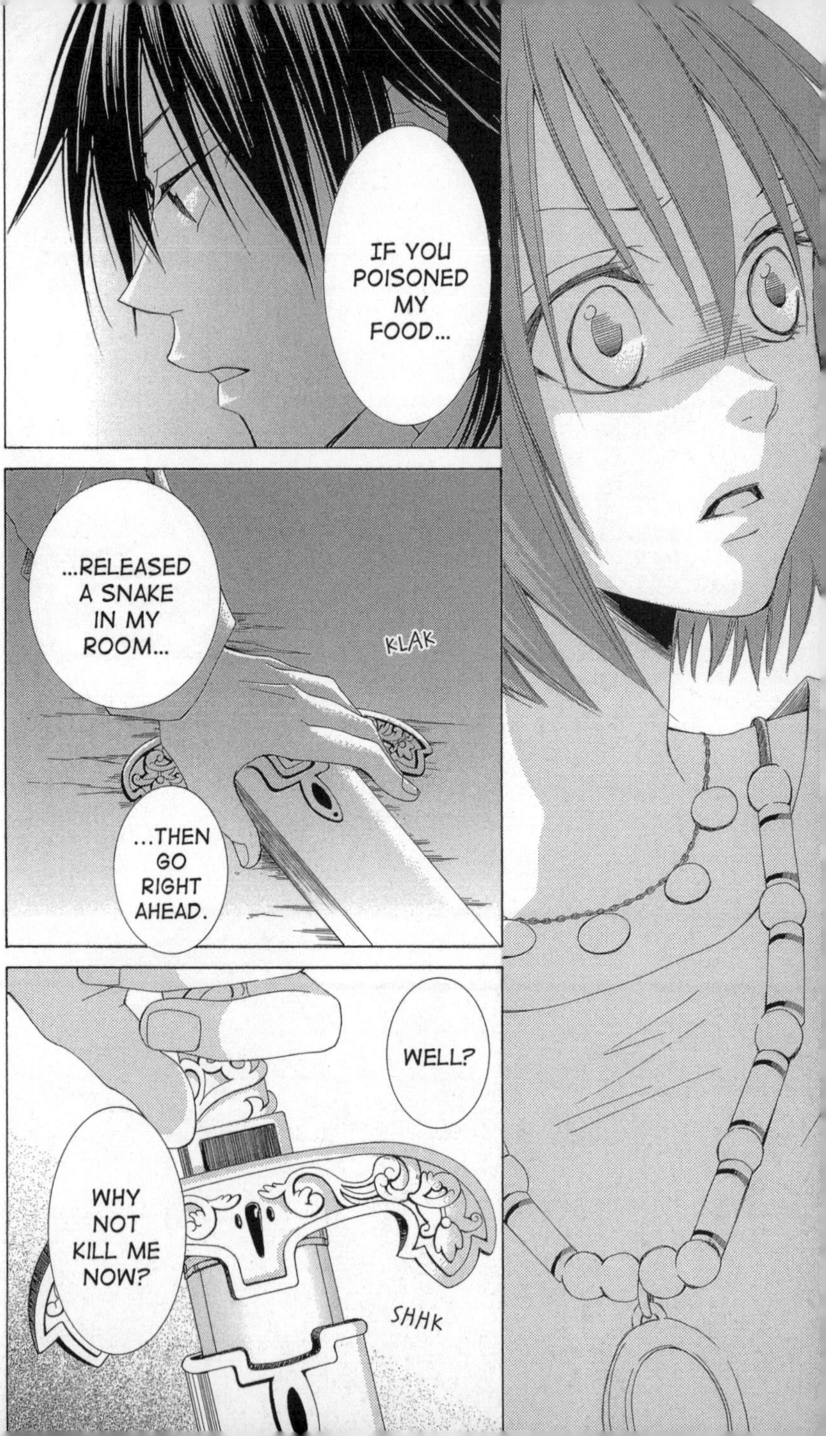
IF YOU POISONED MY FOOD...
...RELEASED A SNAKE IN MY ROOM...
KLAK
...THEN GO RIGHT AHEAD.
WELL?
WHY NOT KILL ME NOW?
SHHK

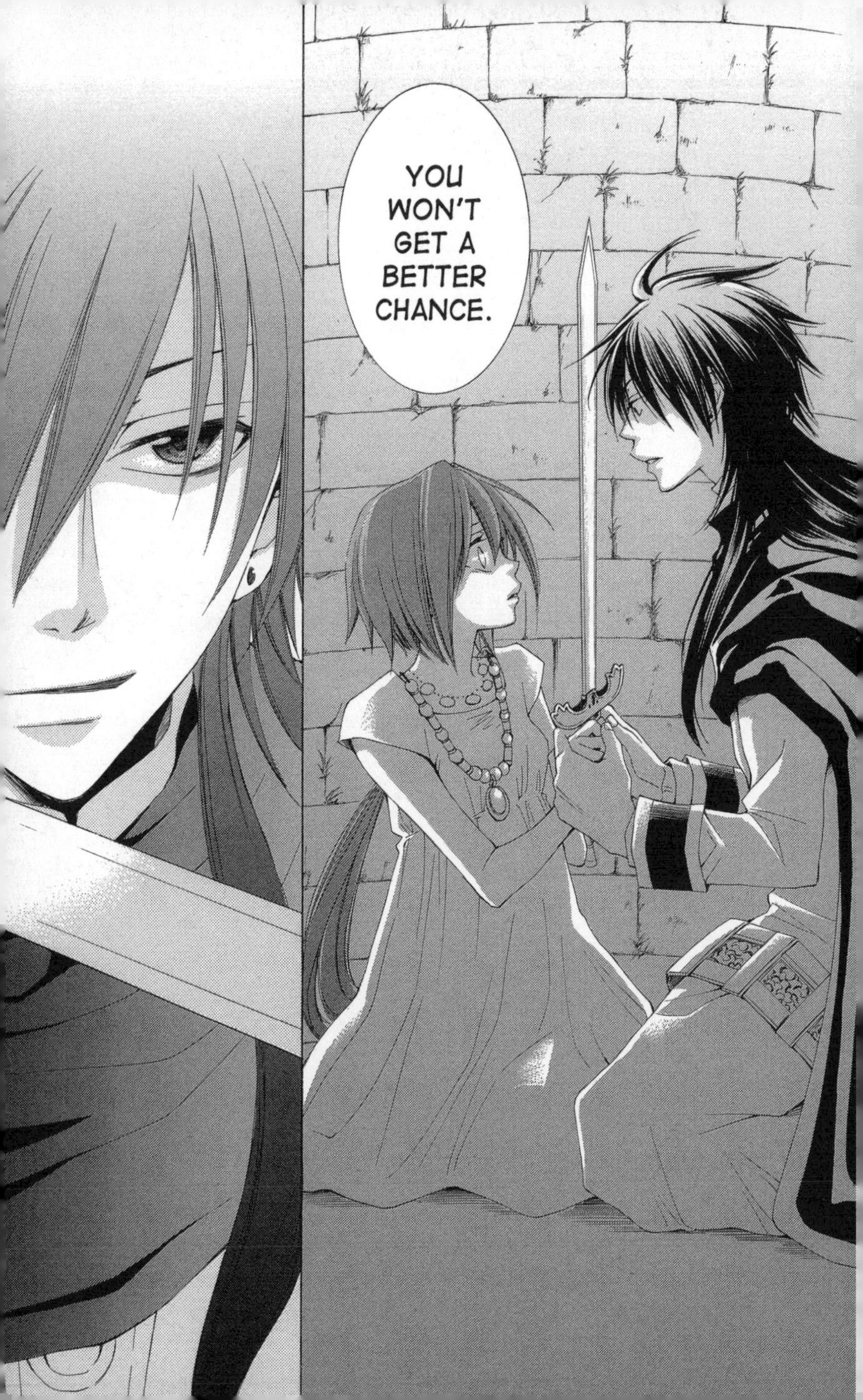
YOU WON'T GET A BETTER CHANCE.

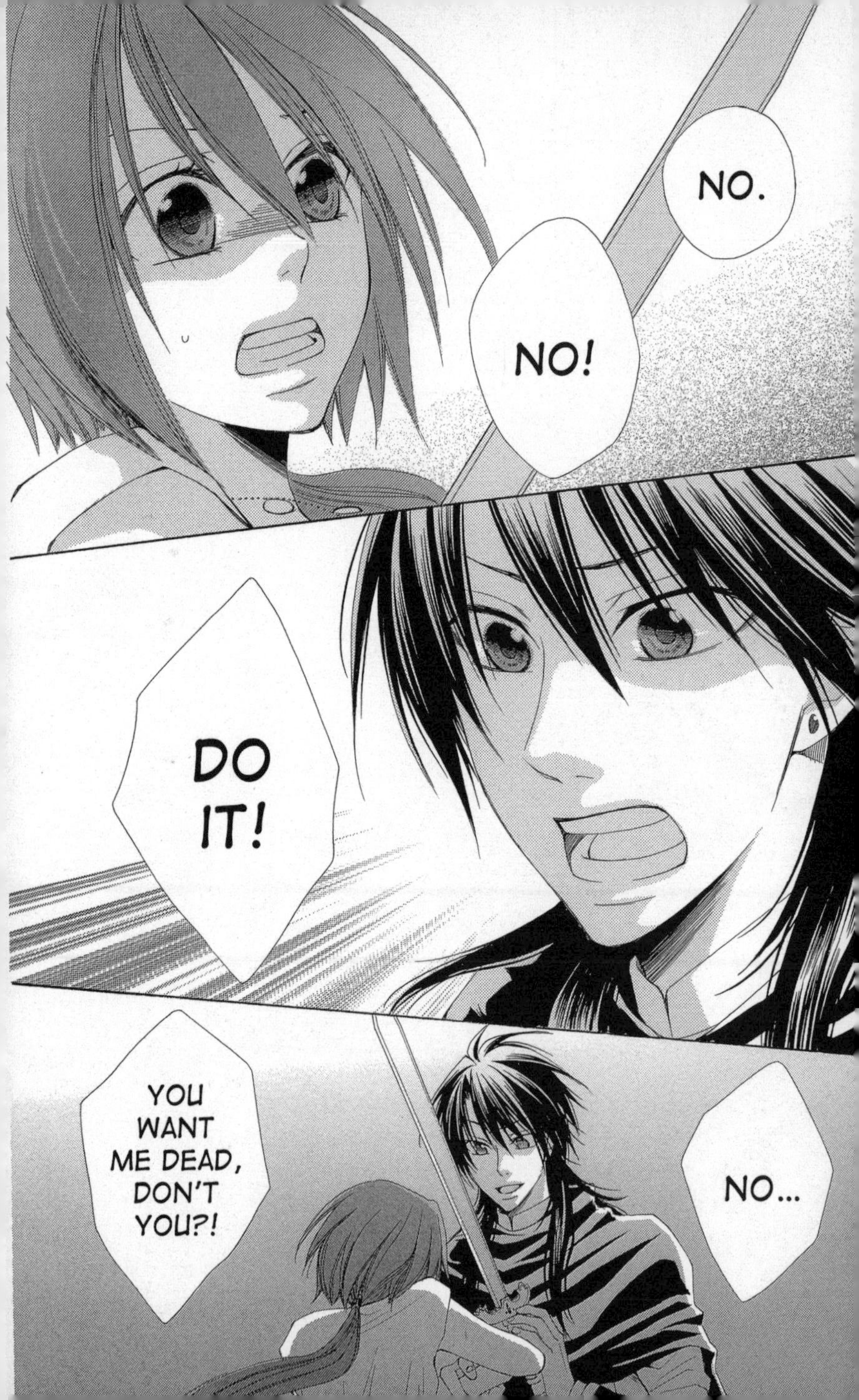
NO.
NO!
DO IT!
YOU WANT ME DEAD, DON'T YOU?!
NO...

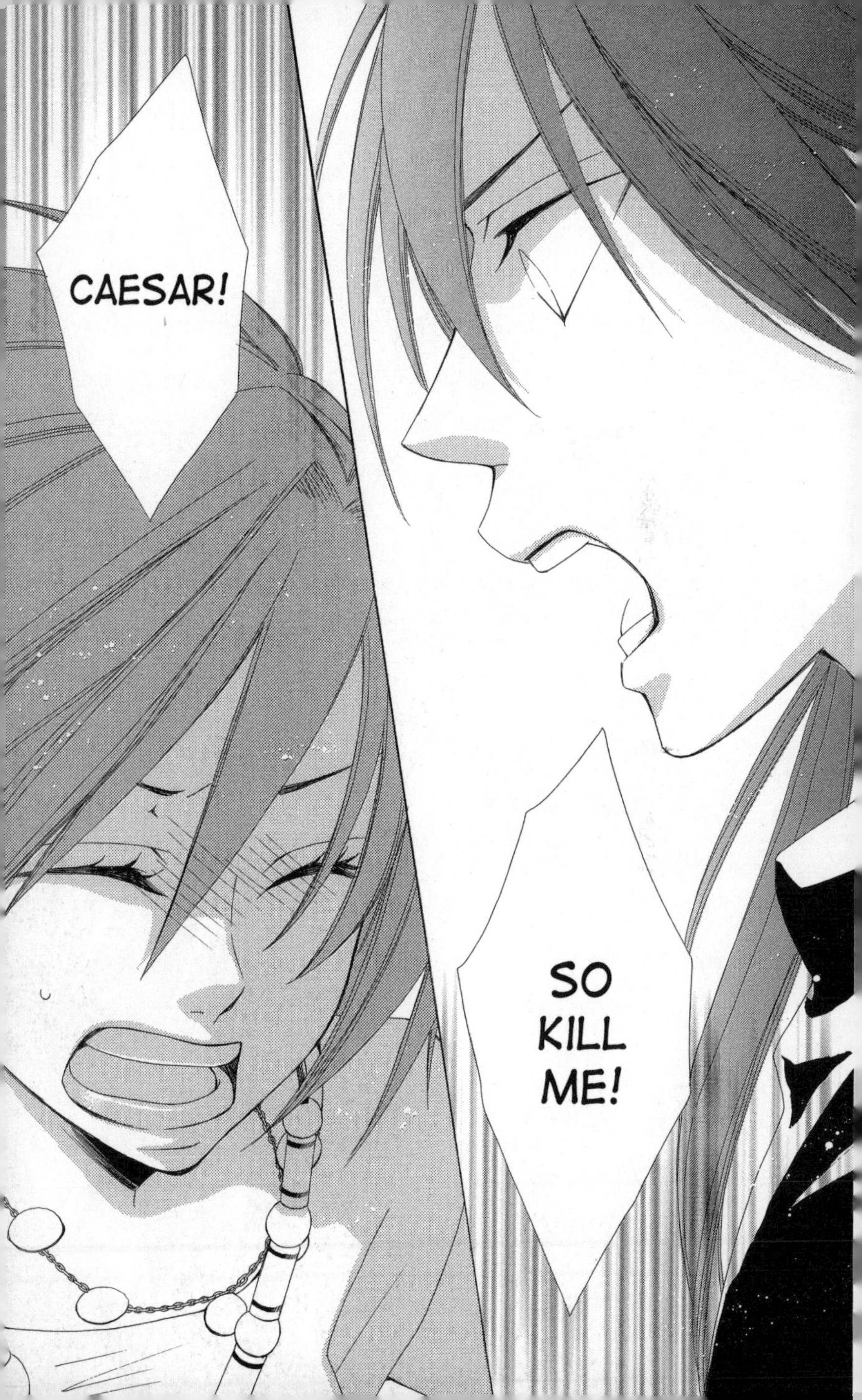
CAESAR!
SO KILL ME!

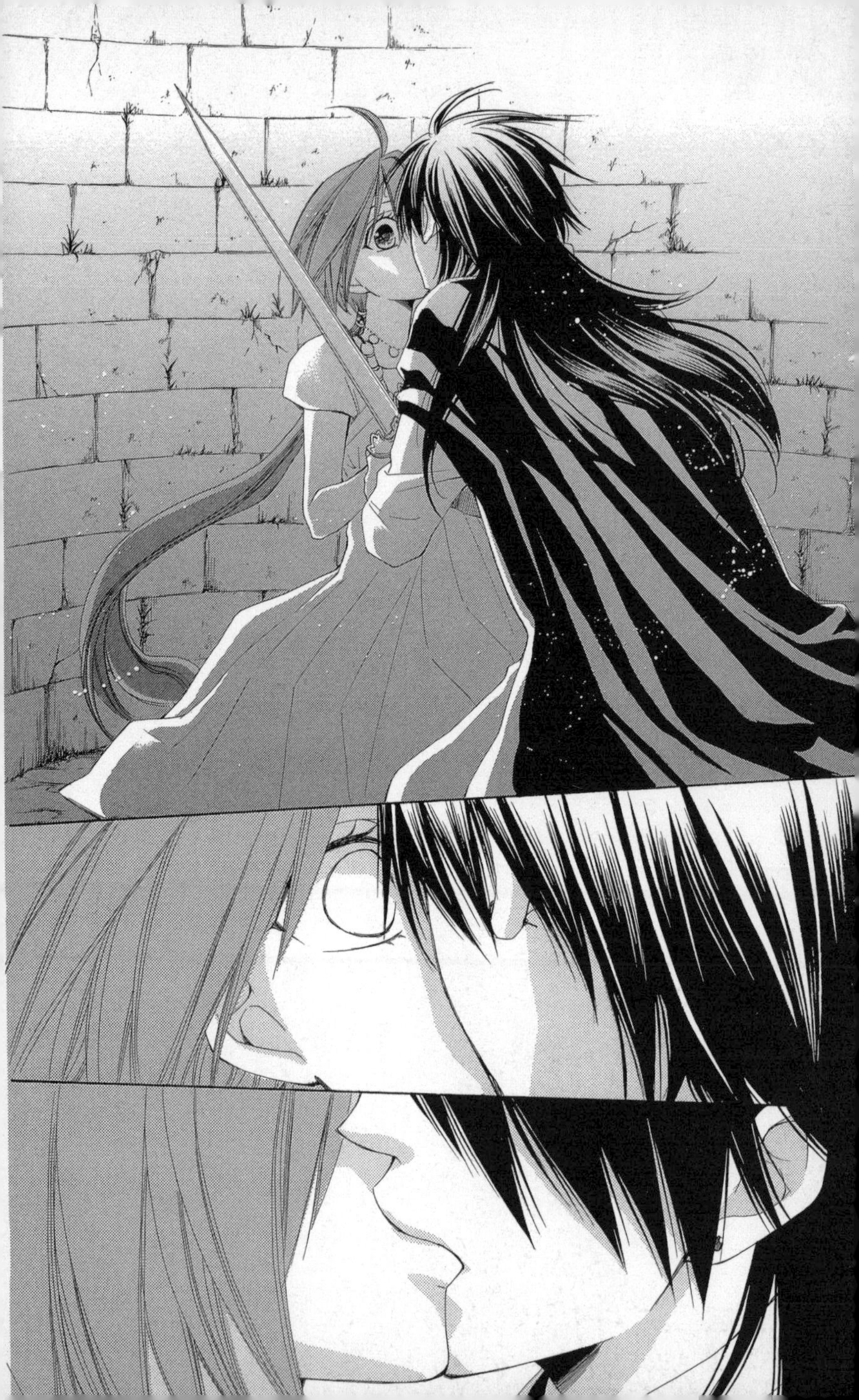

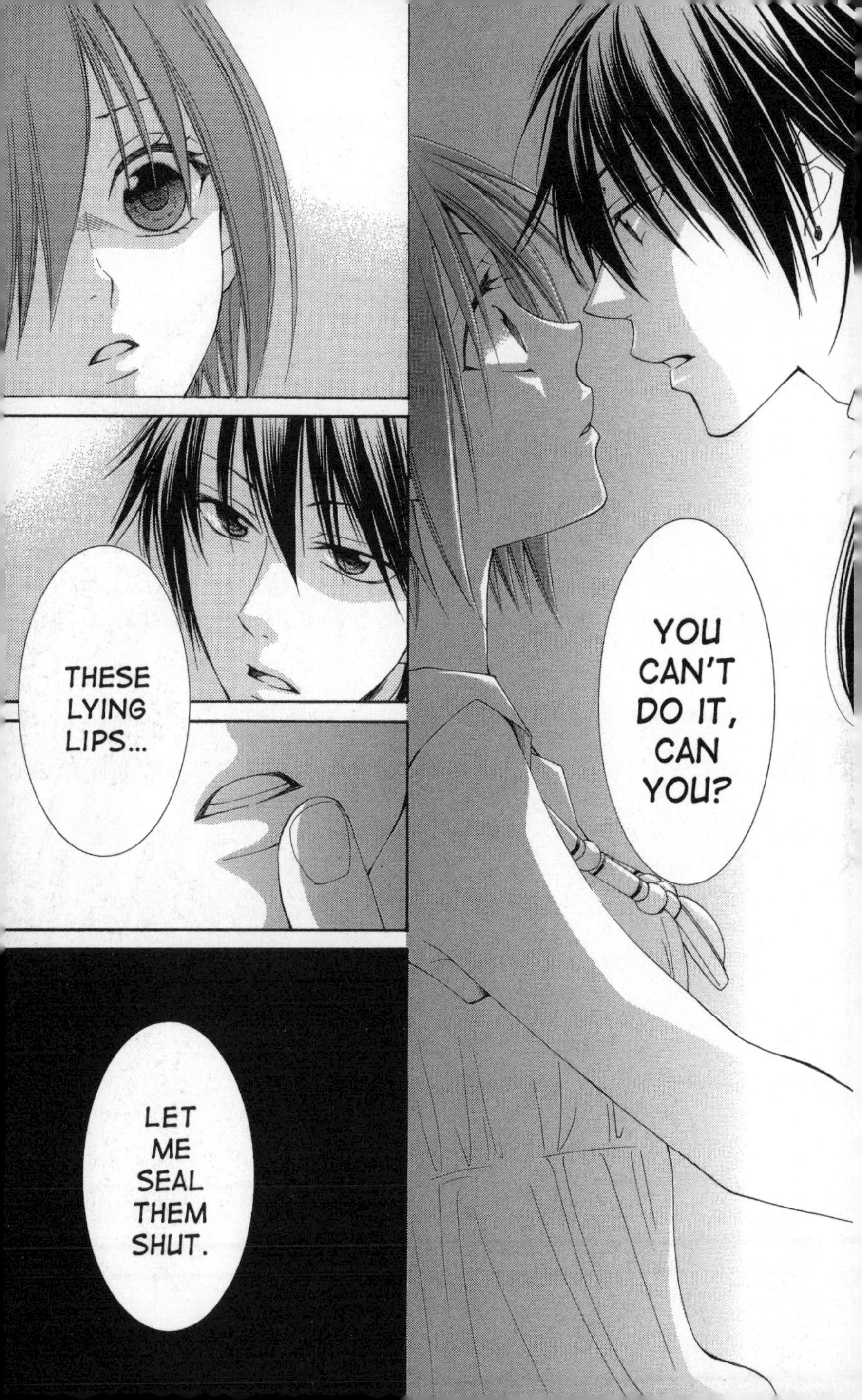
YOU CAN'T DO IT, CAN YOU?
THESE LYING LIPS...
LET ME SEAL THEM SHUT.

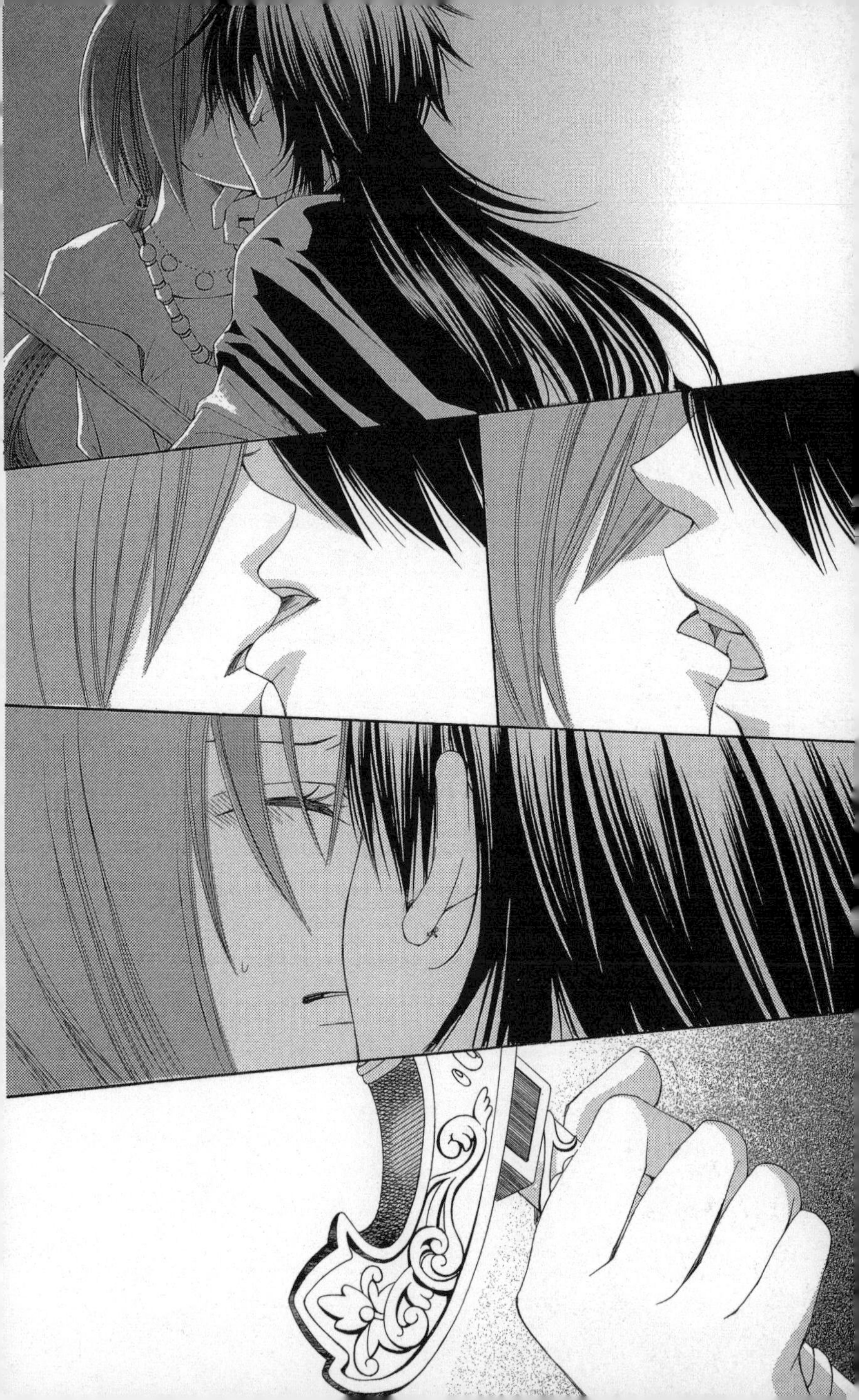

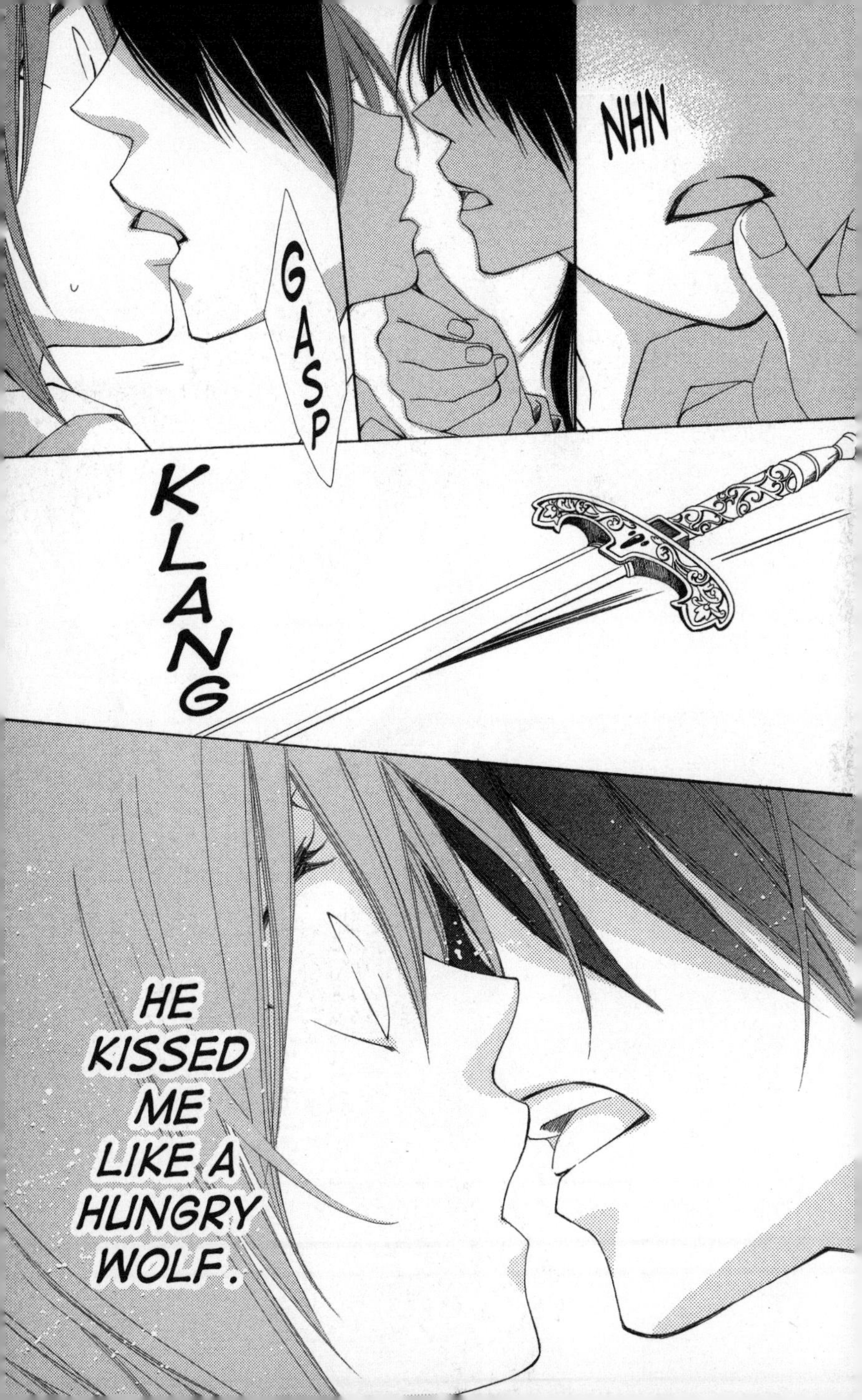
NHN
GASP
KLANG
HE KISSED ME LIKE A HUNGRY WOLF.

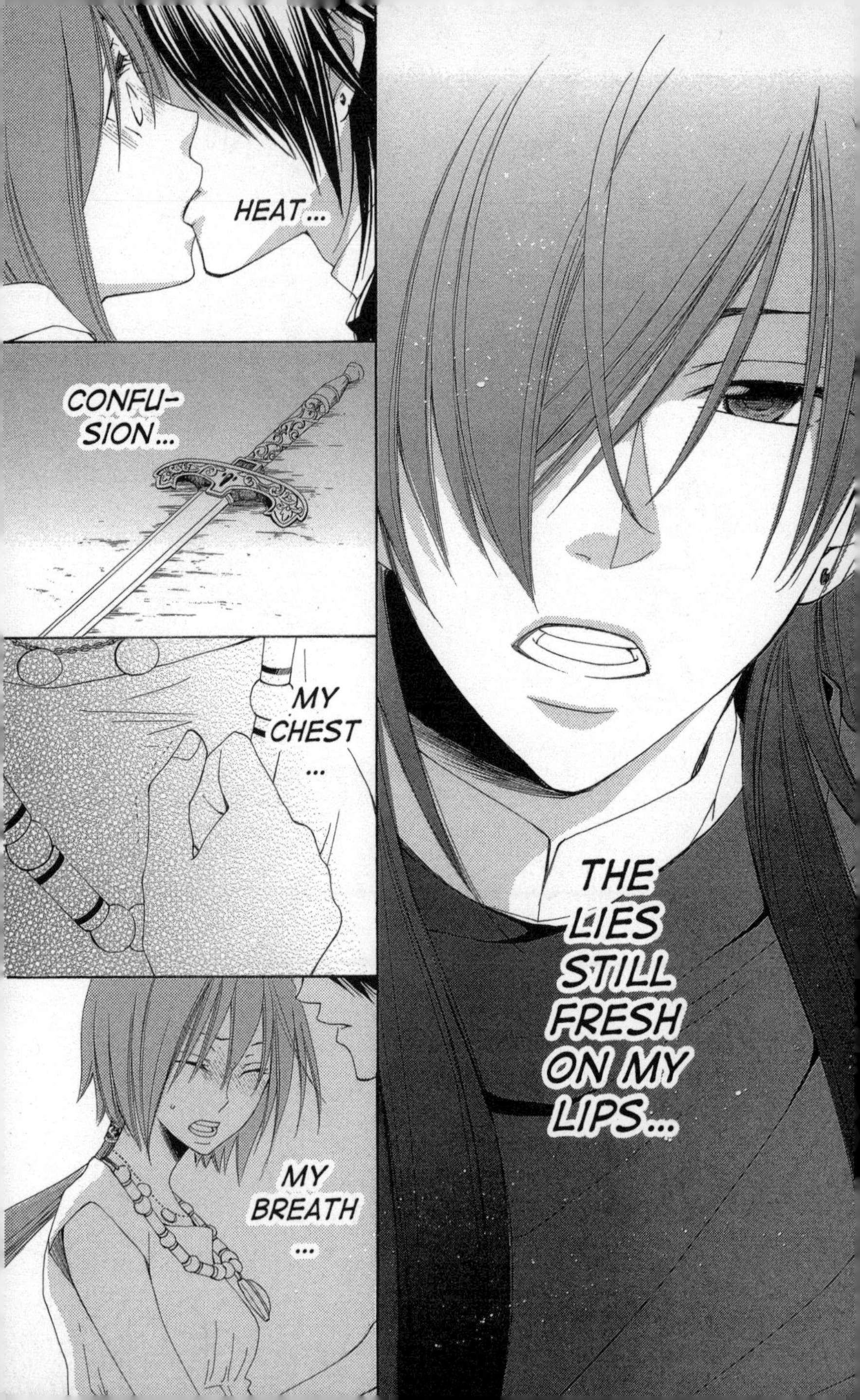
THE LIES STILL FRESH ON MY LIPS...
HEAT...
CONFU-SION...
MY CHEST ...
MY BREATH ...

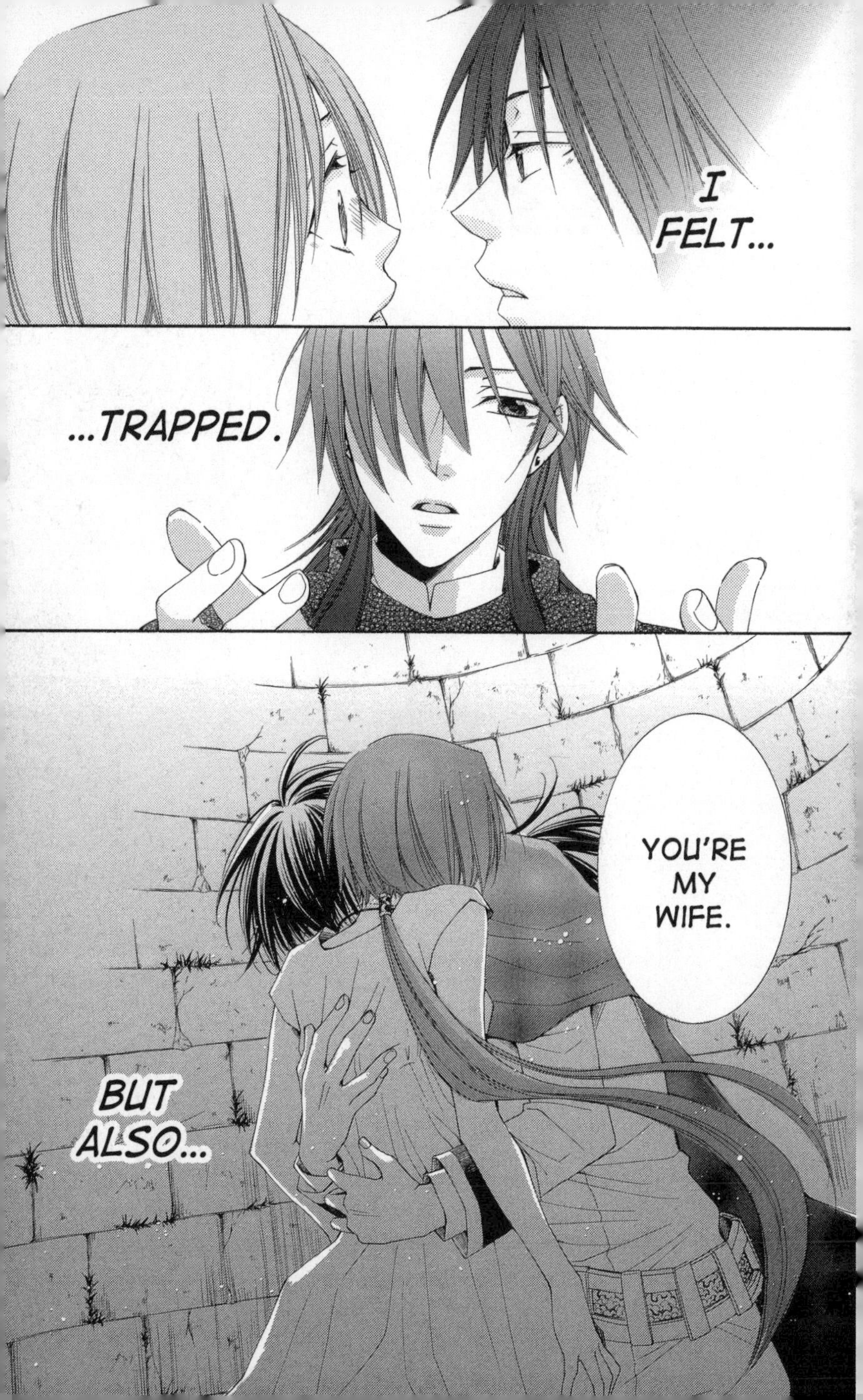
I FELT...
...TRAPPED.
YOU'RE MY WIFE.
BUT ALSO...

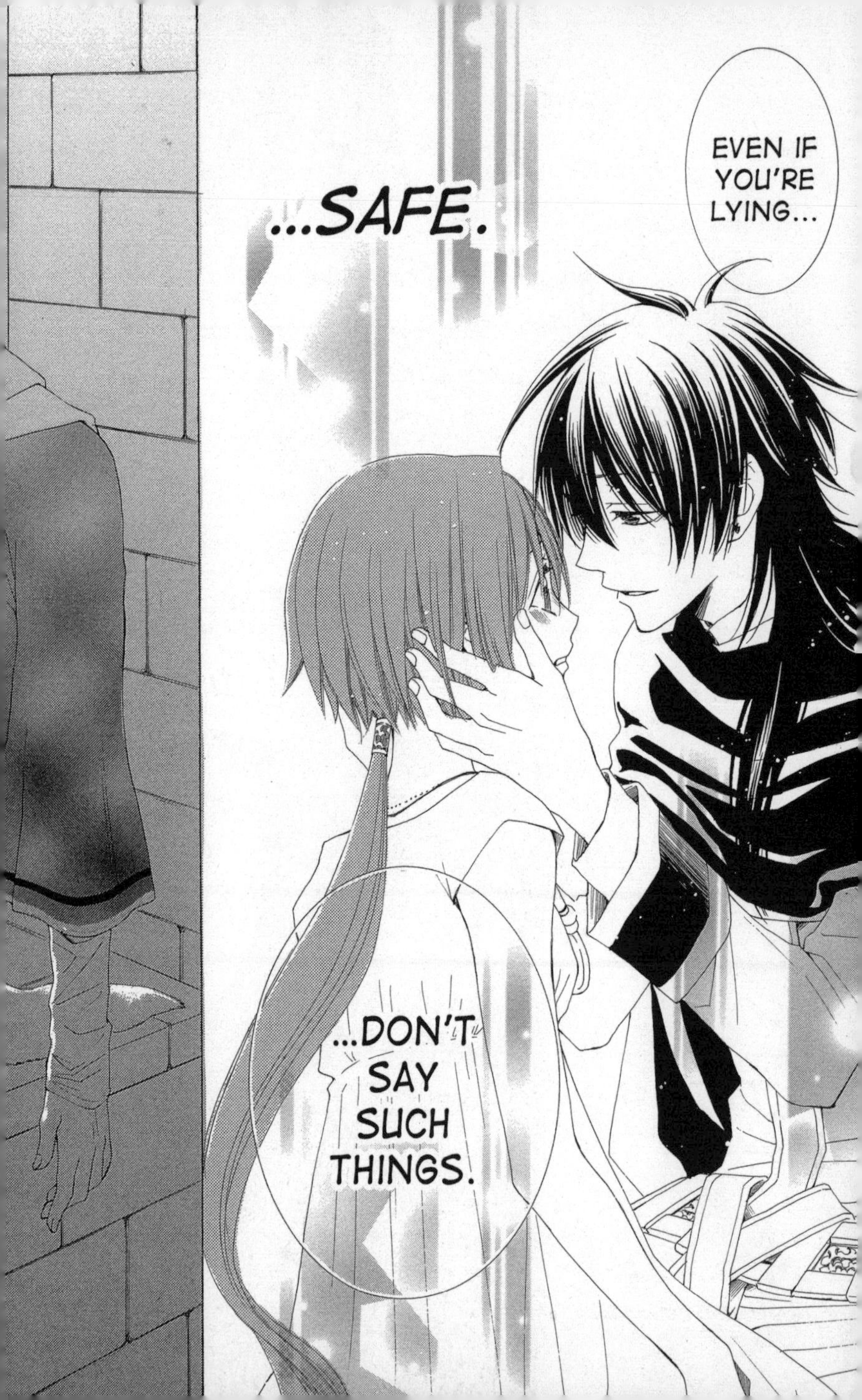
EVEN IF YOU'RE LYING...
...SAFE.
...DON'T SAY SUCH THINGS.

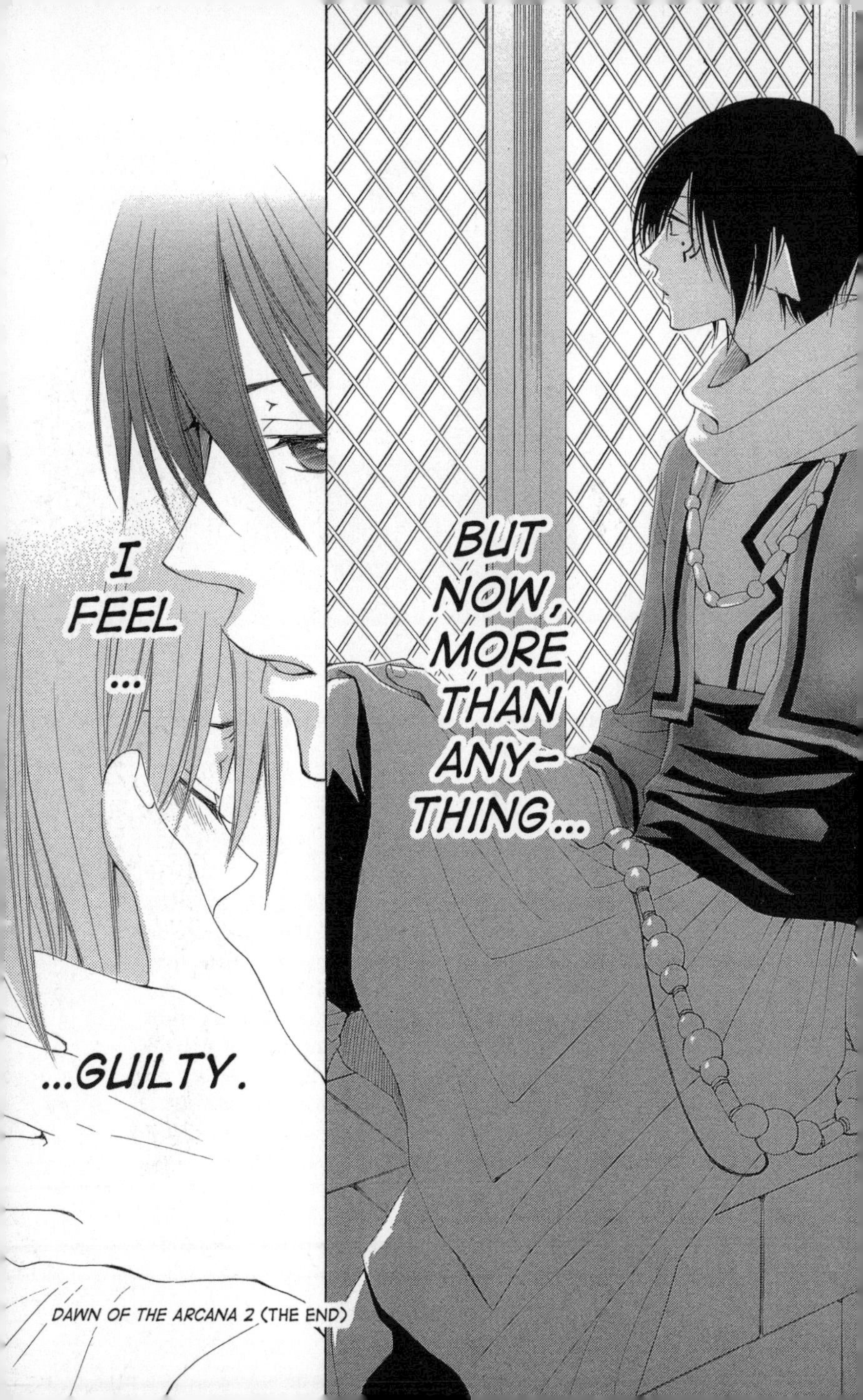
BUT NOW, MORE THAN ANY-THING...
I FEEL...
...GUILTY.
DAWN OF THE ARCANA 2 (THE END)

Here's volume 2! There are still a few places and people not in the story yet... Can't wait! (*laugh*)

–Rei Toma

Rei Toma has been drawing since childhood, but she only began drawing manga because of her graduation project in design school. When she drew a short-story manga, *Help Me, Dentist,* for the first time, it attracted a publisher's attention and she made her debut right away. Her magnificent art style became popular, and after she debuted as a manga artist, she became known as an illustrator for novels and video game character designs. Her current manga series, *Dawn of the Arcana,* is her first long-running manga series, and it has been a hit in Japan, selling over a million copies.

DAWN OF THE ARCANA
VOLUME 2
Shojo Beat Edition

STORY AND ART BY
REI TOMA

© 2009 Rei TOMA/Shogakukan
All rights reserved.
Original Japanese edition "REIMEI NO ARCANA"
published by SHOGAKUKAN Inc.

Translation & Adaptation/Alexander O. Smith
Touch-up Art & Lettering/Freeman Wong
Design/Yukiko Whitley
Editor/Amy Yu

Printed in the U.S.A.

Published by VIZ Media, LLC
P.O. Box 77010
San Francisco, CA 94107

10 9 8 7 6 5 4
First printing, February 2012
Fourth printing, June 2015

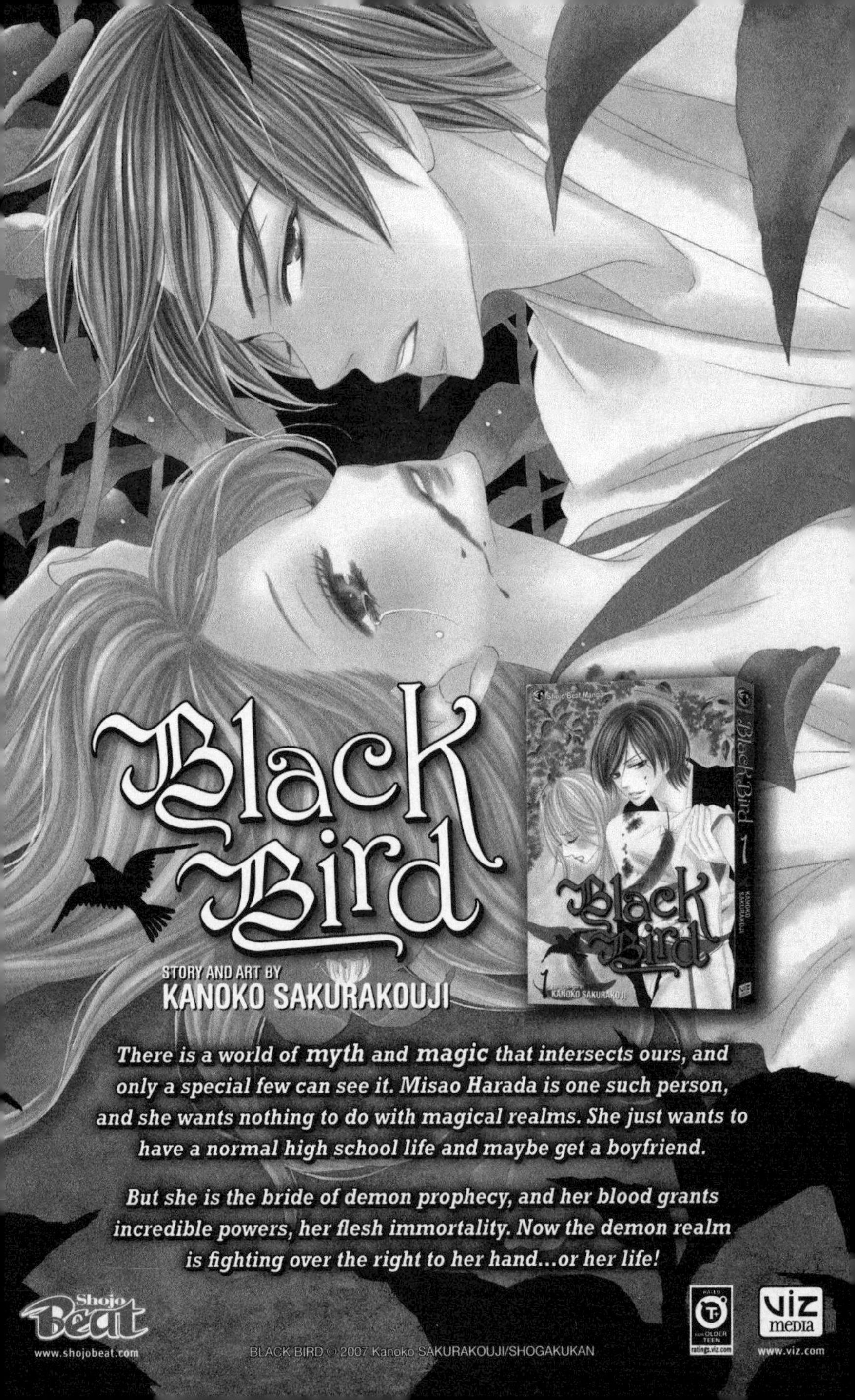
Black Bird
STORY AND ART BY
KANOKO SAKURAKOUJI
Shojo Beat Manga
Black Bird
1
KANOKO SAKURAKOUJI
There is a world of myth and magic that intersects ours, and only a special few can see it. Misao Harada is one such person, and she wants nothing to do with magical realms. She just wants to have a normal high school life and maybe get a boyfriend.
But she is the bride of demon prophecy, and her blood grants incredible powers, her flesh immortality. Now the demon realm is fighting over the right to her hand...or her life!
Shojo Beat
www.shojobeat.com
BLACK BIRD © 2007 Kanoko SAKURAKOUJI/SHOGAKUKAN
RATED T+ FOR OLDER TEEN
ratings.viz.com
viz media
www.viz.com

Honey Blood

Story & Art by Miko Mitsuki

Hinata can't help but be drawn to Junya, but could it be that he's actually a vampire?

When a girl at her school is attacked by what seems to be a vampire, high school student Hinata Sorazono refuses to believe that vampires even exist. But then she meets her new neighbor, Junya Tokinaga, the author of an incredibly popular vampire romance novel… Could it be that Junya's actually a vampire—and worse yet, the culprit?!

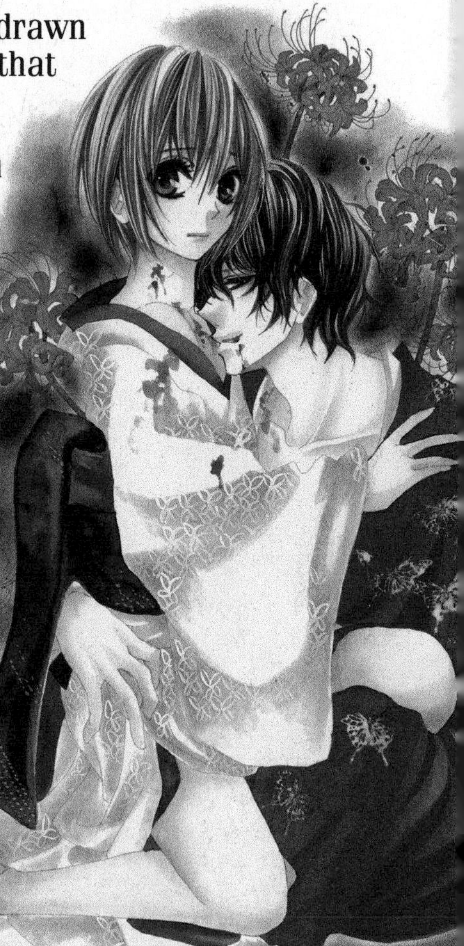

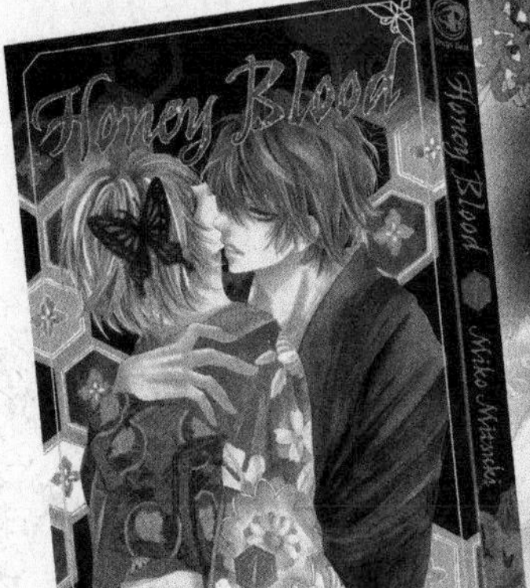
Honey Blood
Honey Blood
Miko Mitsuki
Story & Art by Miko Mitsuki

This is the last page.

In keeping with the original Japanese comic format, this book reads from right to left—so action, sound effects, and word balloons are completely reversed. This preserves the orientation of the original artwork—plus, it's fun! Check out the diagram shown here to get the hang of things, and then turn to the other side of the book to get started!

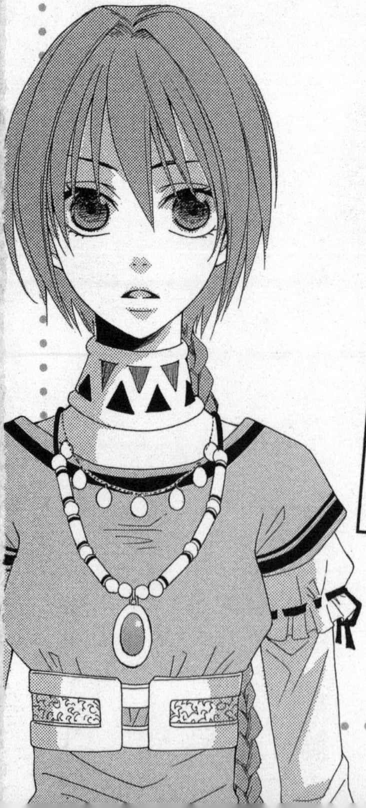

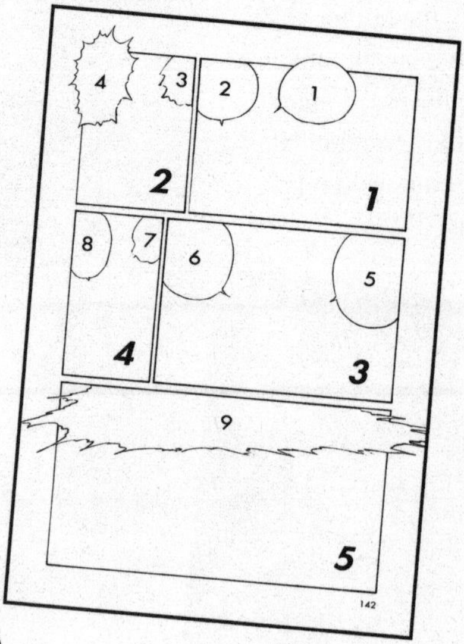
1
1
2
2
3
4
2
5
6
3
7
8
4
9
5
142